Managing Microsoft's Remote Installation Services

Managing Microsoft's Remote Installation Services

A Practical Guide

Søren Rasmussen
Michael Iversen

ELSEVIER
DIGITAL
PRESS

Amsterdam • Boston • Heidelberg • London • New York • Oxford
Paris • San Diego • San Francisco • Singapore • Sydney • Tokyo

Elsevier Digital Press
30 Corporate Drive, Suite 400, Burlington, MA 01803, USA
Linacre House, Jordan Hill, Oxford OX2 8DP, UK

Library of Congress Cataloging-in-Publication Data

Application submitted.

British Library Cataloguing-in-Publication Data

A catalogue record for this book is available from the British Library.

ISBN: 1-55558-337-7

For information on all Elsevier Digital Press publications visit our Web site at www.books.elsevier.com

Printed in the United States of America

Transferred to Digital Printing 2008

Contents

Foreword

I remember one fateful afternoon when I asked my colleague Michael Iversen whether he'd be interested in writing a book with me. When he had finished laughing, his initial response was that he actually liked the idea. Neither of us had ever written a book before, but for us the idea seemed thrilling.

Agreeing on the subject was easy. Naturally, we chose to write about a topic for which we found ourselves professionally fit to move forward in the writing process. We are both IT Specialists working for IBM Global Services, and because we had both been working together on a variety of Remote Installation Services installations at different types of organizations, we found ourselves highly qualified to share our knowledge about this deployment technology with other people.

When writing a book, we think it is essential to keep the purpose for doing so clear at all times. For us, the purpose has been to try to do something different, to share our knowledge with the IT community, and to learn how to express this knowledge in writing. Now that this book is finished, we have learned a tremendous amount about writing. We have exerted a lot of effort and spent a lot of time, and there have been times when our motivation seemed forgotten. At the end of the day, it has been hard work, but it has certainly been worth the effort. We hope you will enjoy reading this book as much as we have enjoyed writing it.

Why this book?

The idea of writing this book about Remote Installation Services came up because of necessity. Necessity being the fact that there is no specialized literature in the marketplace covering in-depth knowledge about Remote Installation Services in either Windows 2000 or Windows 2003. Anyone who has worked with Remote Installation Services will know how to install Remote Installation Services and get the fundamental technology working. Similarly, those who have worked with Remote Installation Services will also have learned that issues relating to client installation problems or advanced issues are not really documented very well in any book.

Specific information can be sparse and dotted among various sources of information. Finding information on certain advanced issues could often take several visits to various Web sites, sometimes only to find that described solutions to your issue did not work. Being IBM specialists and working with Remote Installation Services in real-life installations every day, we soon found this to be a major source of irritation. For that reason, this book is now available.

We want to show you how this beautiful, wonderful technology can help you perform powerful computer deployments at your fingertips. We have used all of our theoretical knowledge about Remote Installation Services and merged it together with all of our real-life experiences, written it down, and this is the result. This book is intended to be a single point of entry to all you need to know about Remote Installation Services—from understanding what Remote Installation Services is, how to implement it, how to install it, how to tune it, how to perform advanced tasks of deploying software, and how to make deployment be beneficial and easy for you and your business. Use it as a practical guide, use it as an information source to understand the theoretical application of RIS, use it as a source of inspiration, or use it as a reference guide. Use it in any way you wish.

In this book, we have also written several sections about the concept of "One Image Fits All." Understanding this concept is easy: by using simple techniques you can heavily minimize the amount of client operating system images used in any organization. Carrying the concept out into real life will end up saving you time, hassle, administrative overhead, disk space, maintenance windows, and money. We suggest you look into it. In the real world we have implemented this concept in many organizations—small and large businesses—and it really does work.

Note: This book was written to reflect Remote Installation Services in Windows Server 2003, but 95% of the information is also relevant to Remote Installation Services in Windows 2000 Server. Throughout the book, it is clearly mentioned whenever information applies only to Windows 2000 Server.

Intended audience

The intended audience for this book is anyone looking for new methods to deploy new computer operating system platforms to any amount of computers, be it 15 or 15,000. This may be IT administrators, IT consultants, or IT supporters. The reader should have fundamental knowledge about the Windows Server operating system platform. Having knowledge about your organization and its business operations and requirements will also be beneficial to you. Other than this background, this book will walk you through the concepts, technical details, and logistics of Remote Installation Services.

Acknowledgments

We would like to thank everyone who assisted in making the creation of this book possible. Also, warm thanks to our families, who have given us time and support during the writing of this book. Thanks to IBM Global Services Denmark for providing us the legal liberty to release this book. Finally, thank you to Digital Press/Elsevier and Theron Shreeve for believing in us.

Feedback about this book can be sent to:

Web site: www.it4experts.net
Michael Iversen: mi@it4experts.net
Søren Rasmussen: sr@it4experts.net.

1

Concepts of Deployment

This chapter introduces you to the basics of different deployment technologies. It will also discuss benefits and drawbacks of different deployment methods.

Highlights:

- Understand the fundamentals of computer deployment
- Understand which considerations to make before your deployment
- Explore different deployment methods
- Understand the beauty of Remote Installation Services
- Understand how to benefit from Remote Installation Services

1.1 Computer deployment

Deploying computer operating systems and software to multiple computers is a task that every single IT administrator, IT supporter, or IT manager is faced with at least once during his or her career. A release of a new operating system, for either client computers or server computers, will often initiate this process.

New operating systems such as Windows XP or Windows Server 2003 have more and better functionality than, for example, Windows NT Workstation or Windows 2000 Server. They don't have the drawbacks of older operating systems, they are easier to manage, they offer more possibilities, and they are more scalable, more stable, and more economic. You name it. Based on these facts, it is common to evaluate and explore new possibilities, to examine how the organization can benefit, and, based on the results of this evaluation, to decide whether to deploy or not. A significant amount of time will often be used exploring different deployment products, methods, and technologies. Then often more time will be used testing your choices.

Your business might consist of 15, 160, 475, or 12,000 computers. No matter the size of your organization, the deployment issues remain the same. Some considerations that affect your deployment process are as follows:

- Do you wish to upgrade to a new operating system or to deploy fresh installations?
- What are the people/business logistics involved?
- What is the time frame?
- How many physical sites are involved?
- How are the WAN connections between those sites?
- How is your LAN doing?
- Which applications will you deploy?
- Are those applications compliant with the operating system deployed?
- What other configuration issues exist (e.g., network services, browser services, application setup)?
- Will you be moving to a new Windows domain? Perhaps from Windows NT 4.0 to Windows Server 2003 and Active Directory?
- Would you like to leave it to the hands of every single user to do the job? If so, how would that affect the amount of calls placed to the support desk? And what would the error rate then be? How many installation faults would you have to correct?

In every single organization we've ever worked with, the scenario of having the end user install and configure operating systems as well as applications and network services is considered a really bad idea. Although we have come across it a few times, the end result has been anarchy, chaos, a damaged IT infrastructure, and a hard lesson learned with all the bells and whistles imaginable.

Although some organizations employ super-users to perform different types of assistance to end users, most super-users are often end users themselves, not IT professionals. Don't expect super-users to be skilled to handle complex deployment operations.

Planning is essential. To perform a successful deployment of a new client computer platform, you need tools to help you deploy correctly and to help minimize the time it will take to deploy a new client computer platform. The tools must also help you make the deployment as hassle-free as possible for the end user. Having the chance to deploy software along with the operating system, using the same deployment tool, will inarguably be beneficial to you as well.

Another fact worth taking into consideration is that in any organization there might have been different IT managers over time, each having his or her individual idea of which software to run and which hardware to use. It is not uncommon for a business to see a mixture of different computers (e.g., several brands such as Dell, IBM, Compaq, HP) with different hardware configurations. Some users might be using the Lotus Office Suite, some might use Microsoft Office, and others might be using Star Office.

There are really no limits to how complex an IT infrastructure can be or become over time. All of these considerations can make a computer deployment process become anything from logistically simple to logistically complex. For all these reasons (and many others), when deploying computers to match your hardware platforms and to include a fully configured operating system with applications, careful planning must be used.

Deploying a new client computer platform in an entire organization is, to any extent, a great chance to make a fresh beginning for the IT infrastructure in any organization. Different logistical approaches can be used. Some organizations might maintain several software platforms matching different hardware platforms, whereas some might not. Deploying several software platforms matching different hardware platforms to hundreds or even thousands of different computers is a logistical nightmare given the amount of software platforms that must be created and maintained. Maintaining as few software platforms as possible and matching as much hardware as possible in a simple, efficient manner is a far better option.

With Remote Installation Services, this goal is achievable, and we will be going into a lot more detail about how to do this in later chapters, where the "One Image Fits All" concept is discussed.

1.2 Deployment methods and technologies

In this section, we'll discuss the most common deployment methods and technologies used for the Microsoft Windows operating systems: manual installation, unattended installation, the Sysprep method, imaging, and Remote Installation Services.

1.2.1 Manual installations and upgrades

This method is all about manually inserting the CD-ROM containing your new operating system code drop and then deciding whether to upgrade the existing operating system or to make a fresh installation. Needless to say, making a fresh installation will involve formatting the hard disk and then installing the operating system in question. This is possible with all Microsoft Windows operating systems.

The upgrade option is even easier than performing a completely manual installation. Inserting the Windows XP CD-ROM will allow you to upgrade to Windows XP from an existing Windows 95, Windows 98, Windows ME, Windows NT 4.0 Workstation, or Windows 2000 operating system platform. Inserting the Windows Server 2003 CD-ROM will allow you to upgrade from an existing Windows NT 4.0 Server or Windows 2000 Server operating system platform. Note that if you are upgrading an existing Windows NT 4.0 PDC/BDC or a Windows 2000 Domain Controller, special rules and conditions apply. Any upgrade will prompt you for a valid license code for your new operating system.

Note: Remember that when upgrading, any problem or issue you might have faced using the previous operating system in question will not be resolved or removed after an upgrade.

Good things about manual installations and upgrades

- You are manually in control of the entire installation process; therefore, every installation is individual and can be tailored to suit any individual need.
- Manual upgrades are easier and more intelligent than ever before. Setup wizards for Windows XP and Windows Server 2003 can even check the Web for known application compliance issues.
- They are great for coffee breaks.

Bad things about manual installations and upgrades

- Manual installations are a lot more time consuming than automated deployments.

- When upgrading, existing operating system problems and operation issues are not removed or resolved.
- Service packs and hotfixes must, in most cases, be applied manually.

1.2.2 Unattended installations

A manual installation can be made unattended. An unattended installation is basically the same type of installation as a manual installation, but with an unattended installation, the user is not prompted for the usual installation questions such as hard disk formatting, time zones, keyboard layout, license code, and so forth. All of the information the user would normally have to input during installation is written into a file instead, a so-called unattended text file. This file is divided into sections, and a special context of keys and values is inserted below each section.

The unattended text file can be created either manually or by using the Setup Manager wizard. Normally, it is the responsibility of the system administrators to create this file. The process of creating this file using either method will be covered in later chapters. When setup begins, using the setup executable, a parameter is added, and the path to the unattended text file should be provided. Windows XP and Windows Server 2003 support unattended installations.

Good things about unattended installations

- User-/computer-specific information does not need to be manually input during installation.
- They are faster than manual installations, yet slower than automated deployment.

Bad things about unattended installations

- No deployment automation is possible when deploying a large number of computers. You must still sit in front of the individual computer to start and perform an unattended installation.
- More often than not, several unattended text files must be maintained and administered.
- Preinstalled applications cannot be administered from the Active Directory.

1.2.3 The Sysprep method

Sysprep is short for System Preparation Tool and, as the name implies, it is a tool that prepares your operating system for deployment. The Sysprep Tool was originally introduced for Windows NT 4.0, and new versions shipped with Windows 2000 and Windows XP. The tool is designed for wiping the SID and user-specific information off a template computer to prepare it for imaging.

A Sysprep installation is unattended, but instead of the unattended text file, another file, sysprep.inf, is used. As with the unattended text file, the sysprep.inf file can be created either manually or by using the Setup Manager wizard. Then, when the computer is configured, and you have created the sysprep.inf file, you run the Sysprep Tool (sysprep.exe). When sysprep.exe finishes, the computer will shut down.

It is now ready to be cloned by imaging software of your choice. When this image is downloaded to other computers, the first time the computer starts up, it will prompt the user to input only the information not prepared in the sysprep.inf file, and every deployed computer will be given its own individual user information, computer name, and SID identifier.

Good things about Sysprep installations

- They are great for original equipment manufacturer (OEM) businesses wishing to preload operating systems onto computers.
- They are great for preparing computers for future deployments.
- None or very little user interaction is needed when the end user starts the computer for the first time.
- They interact with imaging software.

Bad things about Sysprep installations

- No deployment automation is possible when deploying a large number of computers unless you also use imaging software. You must still sit in front of the individual computer to start and perform a Sysprep'd installation.
- More often than not, several sysprep.inf files must be maintained and administered.
- Preinstalled applications cannot be administered from the Active Directory.

1.2.4 Imaging

Imaging is a technology that basically allows you to build a PC with an operating system along with applications, customizations, and registry changes. The PC is then referred to as a *donor* PC because it will be the donor of many other PCs (clones) having the same setup and characteristics. The imaging software (such as Symantec Norton Ghost) allows the donor computer setup and characteristics to be uploaded to a file share, thus becoming what is referred to as an *image*. Usually this is done by uploading a sector-by-sector copy of the hard disk.

The uploaded image can then be downloaded from this file share on several other computers, now referred to as *clones*, because they are really cloned images of the original donor computer. Downloading a clone is normally a pretty fast procedure. It is usually done by booting the computer using a floppy disk or boot CD, after which you are given entry to the share that holds the image. All you then need to do is download the image file. Again, this is done using a special sector-by-sector download technology.

Imaging is a great deployment technology by some terms, yet by other terms, a not-so-great technology. Let's take a look at the benefits of imaging.

Good things about imaging

- It's very fast to download an image (approximately 10 minutes).
- It works great for identical hardware platforms.
- Building an image is as fast as installing a PC manually from scratch and then uploading it using imaging software.
- It interacts with Sysprep'd computers.

All this is truly great stuff. Imaging was great in the days of Windows NT 3.5, Windows NT 3.51, Windows NT 4.0, and Windows 95/98. In those days, Microsoft did not provide any operating system–specific deployment tools, but things have changed now. It all changed with the introduction of Windows 2000 Server, and it is even better now that Microsoft has understood that client computer deployment is important for businesses, small or large.

Surely there are drawbacks to imaging technology. As discussed earlier, imaging technology is based on a simple one-to-one, disk sector-per-sector upload/download technology. Although this might work fast, there are issues concerning scalability and flexibility.

Not-so-great things about imaging

- Every clone computer is *exactly* 100% hardware-dependent on the donor computer where the image was originally produced. Any device not matching that of the donor computer can produce an unknown device. In other words, you are *100% dependent* on your hardware manufacturer delivering *exactly identical computers* over the period of time you buy the computer type in question. Even minimal differences between the donor computer and the clone computer, such as chipsets, SCSI/RAID controllers, or even the simplest video card, can lead to functionality failures or performance issues.
- You *must* maintain an image for every single hardware platform (machine type) in your business.
- It is impossible to maintain one single image that will match different computer machine types unless a lot of postoperative manual work is included in the process.
- Given that it is impossible to maintain one single image that will match different computer machine types, it will always be necessary to make manual customizations to an image.
- Imaging software and cloned images do not integrate with the Windows Active Directory.
- From a server administration point of view, imaging will only reduce total cost of ownership (TCO) if you compare it with manual installations.
- Imaging software costs money.
- Imaging can potentially become a costly affair given these points.

Please note that we're not attempting to be negative about imaging technology at all. Imaging software is great for deployment in very small organizations and businesses, and imaging is often the preferred deployment method for Citrix server specialists for cloning different Citrix servers.

1.2.5 Remote Installation Services

Remote Installation Services first saw daylight with the release of Windows 2000 Server. Remote Installation Services was an integrated part of the operating system and contained only very few errors, even in the initial release. Strangely enough, Microsoft seemed to not make a very big deal out of promoting the powerful features of Remote Installation Services. Additionally, many IT professionals had a hair-tearing experience getting it to do what it does—deploying client and server operating systems—not because it didn't work, but because information on setting up prerequisites for making it work seemed sparse.

So what is Remote Installation Services?

In a nutshell, Remote Installation Services is a server component that is included with Windows Server 2003 and Windows 2000 Server. In Windows Server 2003, it is installed as a service and provides a central administrative point for automated deployment of client/server Windows operating systems. Having said that Remote Installation Services is installed as a service, it should also be noted that in Windows Server 2003, this service really consists of different components on which it is dependent. In Windows 2000 Server, it is not installed as a single service but as a collection of service components. With Remote Installation Services, tools to help deploy software, scripts, printers, and so on are provided.

How does it work?

Remote Installation Services is *not* imaging. Imaging is a completely different technology. Remote Installation Services performs a real client installation in the same manner that you would install an operating system manually. Only with Remote Installation Services, the process is not manual, but fully automated and unattended. You get the best of both worlds—real installations and no user input during deployment.

With a Remote Installation Services client installation, files are downloaded once only; all other installation tasks are performed locally on the client computer. All you need to do is to go to the computer, turn it on, press F12, enter your username and password, select an installation, and away you go. The beauty of this is that each computer is installed individually, allowing businesses to maintain different types of computers regardless of their hardware specifications.

Unlike imaging, there are no hardware dependencies to the donor computer on which the image was originally made, because with Remote Installation Services there is no donor computer. In addition, SID and computer name is generated automatically in accordance with your definitions.

Why should I use Remote Installation Services?

Building a Remote Installation Services environment will take a tad longer than installing imaging software, building an image, and then deploying it. Nevertheless, the extra time spent will eventually provide you and your organization with a much more flexible and powerful deployment environment than would be similarly achievable using imaging technology.

Also, even if installing a client computer using Remote Installation Services takes slightly longer than performing an image download, the benefit is that you will be independent of hardware-related incompatibility issues plus a lot of other stuff that would normally require manual work to be carried out. In the end, Remote Installation Services is a lot more TCO friendly than imaging. There are several other good reasons why you should use Remote Installation Services. Here are some of them:

- Client installations are real installations; an individual computer installation is performed.
- Hardware differences are not an issue because an individual computer installation is performed.
- There is no need for boot disks; the preboot execution environment (PXE) network boot protocol is used instead.
- Less peak network bandwidth is used. With Remote Installation Services, when you perform a client installation, all of the files are downloaded only once; every other installation task is performed locally on the computer in question.
- Smarter functionality is used in deploying additional software, registry changes, and general installation setup characteristics using cmdlines.txt and GuiRunOnce.
- Administration and maintenance are performed centrally from the Active Directory Users and Computers console and through Windows Explorer.
- Different images do not need to be maintained and updated. You can use one image for all computers and maintain that through the Remote Installation Services server.
- It is easy to test. Testing additional images with Remote Installation Services does not affect production images.
- It integrates with Windows Active Directory Users and Computers and the dynamic host configuration protocol (DHCP) console.
- Users will be happier. Deployment is fast, and it is unlikely that you will ever have to make manual customizations on a client computer unless you change the original scope of your deployment criteria during the deployment process.

- Active Directory maintenance is streamlined.
- ***IT'S FREE!*** Yes! Microsoft is giving it to us free of charge as long as you pay for your Windows Server License.

With Remote Installation Services, you can build a deployment infrastructure that is powerful, flexible, and scalable. Using this wonderful technology, you can build a deployment infrastructure that will leverage the "One Image Fits All" concept by maintaining one client installation profile that will fit all computers in your organization.

2

The Big Picture

The intent of this chapter is to explain the fundamental technological terms that are used when discussing Remote Installation Services. It is important to have just a brief understanding about these terms before proceeding with other chapters. In some chapters we refer to certain terms or technologies, such as OCR, TFTP, SIF, and so forth. We do not want you to get lost in the midst of terminologies and grammatical shortcuts throughout this book, so read this chapter before reading anything else. Consider the content in this chapter a brief introduction to getting started with understanding Remote Installation Services.

2.1 Remote Installation Services Windows services

Remote Installation Services is an additional server component that can be installed in Windows Server 2003 and Windows 2000 Server. No matter which of the two server platforms you run, Remote Installation Services can be added using the Control Panel, Add/Remove Programs, selecting Add/Remove Windows Component, and then selecting Remote Installation Services.

Remote Installation Services displays itself as a single server service in Windows Server 2003, and as a collection of services in Windows 2000 Server. In Windows Server 2003, the Remote Installation Services entry is apparent when you view the services component in Administrative Tools. In Windows 2000 Server, Remote Installation Services does not exist as a single service; instead, it is compromised of two services: Boot Information Negotiation Layer and Trivial File Transfer Protocol.

In terms of Windows services, the only difference between Windows Server 2003 and Windows 2000 Server is that in Windows Server 2003, the Remote Installation Services service is really only a shortcut to the Boot

Information Negotiation Layer and Trivial File Transfer Protocol services. In addition to this, Remote Installation Services depends on several other services and components to run. These are DHCP Server, Trivial File Transfer Protocol, and Boot Information Negotiation Layer.

2.2 DHCP

DHCP is the short term for Dynamic Host Configuration Protocol. DHCP is a core TCP/IP network component. A DHCP server distributes IP addresses to several TCP/IP clients in specific subnets in compliance with the TCP/IP address scopes you have defined. Alternatively, if you do not use DHCP in your Local Area Network (LAN) environment, the only other option is to assign static IP addresses to every single computer on your LAN. In that case, Remote Installation Services will not work because it relies on DHCP to perform PXE communication.

2.3 PXE

PXE is short for Preboot Execution Environment. PXE does not run as a Windows service. PXE refers to ways of getting a computer to boot without the need for a hard drive or boot diskette. In most cases, the boot process is performed using the network adapter of the computer. In order to do this, the computer must have a PXE-enabled network adapter, and before booting, the network adapter must be configured to boot to the network. This is almost always preset.

When a PXE client is turned on, it sends out a DHCP discovery packet as part of the initial DHCP discovery request and identifies itself as being PXE-enabled. It requests an IP address and the IP address of a Remote Installation Services server through the PXE extensions added to the DHCP protocol.

2.4 BINLSVC

BINL is short for Boot Information Negotiation Layer. The Windows service name is BINLSVC. The service runs on the Remote Installation Services server and acts on client boot requests. When booting a client, the client receives an IP address from the DHCP server and the IP address of the Remote Installation Services server. The client then contacts the Remote Installation Services server, using the BINL, which then provides the location and filename of the bootstrap image to the client.

2.5 TFTP

TFTP is short for Trivial File Transfer Protocol. The Windows service name is TFTPD. TFTP is used to transfer data files to the Remote Installation Services client. TFTP is a little similar to File Transfer Protocol (FTP), a protocol that (as the name indicates) transfers files from one computer to another. It is used where user authentication and directory visibility are not required You could say that TFTP is the simple and trivial version of FTP. TFTP is not as capable as its big brother FTP. TFTP uses the User Datagram Protocol (UDP) rather than the Transmission Control Protocol (TCP) and provides no security features.

2.6 SIF

SIF is short for Setup Information File. As the name implies, this is a text file, not a Windows service or program component. Naturally, when deploying a heavy amount of operating systems to computers, you need the benefits of doing it automated and unattended. To do this, you must use a method of telling the computer being installed exactly what to do, how to do it, and when to do it. That is exactly what an SIF does. All instructions and definitions written into the SIF are executed by the client during installation.

2.7 OSC files

OSC files are Operating System Chooser files. These are the files that are displayed when starting a client installation from Remote Installation Services. By default, the standard OSC files display a number of DOS-style screens, which prompt you for input prior to installing a client computer. OSC files are written in a simple code called OSChooser Markup Language (OSCML), which is similar to HTML version 2. OSC files can be modified to suit special functionality (e.g., which language and Active Directory Organizational Units to use) prior to client installation.

2.8 Summary

Remote Installation Services consists of different technologies that all work together and perform different tasks at different times. To avoid confusion when reading later chapters, this chapter provides an overview of the most important components used. All of the technologies mentioned in this chapter will be discussed in much greater detail throughout this book.

3

Installing Remote Installation Services Server

This chapter will explain how to install and configure Remote Installation Services. The chapter will walk you through a basic installation of the Remote Installation Services server component and guide you through the process of uploading the first image to the Remote Installation Services server. The configuration of DHCP will also be covered in this chapter. After doing this, it is important to verify the Remote Installation Services installation, and this chapter will guide you through the right way to verify that Remote Installation Services is configured correctly and running smoothly.

As mentioned in Chapter 2, Remote Installation Services servers provide the option of unattended installation of Remote Installation Services server images; this chapter will cover this option in detail. In the last section of this chapter, we will take a quick look at the standard Setup Information File (SIF) and make some minor modifications to it. The SIF is an answer file in which all unattended installation options are defined. This ensures that the Remote Installation Services server images will be installed without any dialog boxes prompted before the user.

Highlights:

- Hardware and software requirements
- Configuration of DHCP server
- Installation of Remote Installation Services
- Basic Remote Installation Services configuration
- How to add additional Remote Installation Services images
- Unattended Remote Installation Services image installations
- Verifying Remote Installation Services installations
- The standard SIF at a glance

3.1 Remote Installation Services server requirements

Before installing Remote Installation Services server, some prerequisites must be in place. The following hardware and software requirements must be met before installing Remote Installation Services.

3.1.1 Software and services requirements

- *Microsoft Windows 2003 server.* Three versions of Microsoft Windows Server 2003 can install Remote Installation Services: Windows 2003 standard, Windows 2003 Enterprise server, and Windows 2003 Datacenter server.
- *A minimum 2 GB volume formatted with NTFS.* The size can vary depending on the number of Remote Installation Services images being deployed in your organization.
- *DHCP.* A DHCP server must be present in the environment before Remote Installation Services can serve client computers. If the DHCP server is a Microsoft DHCP service, it must be authenticated ether manually or through Remote Installation Services.
- *Enterprise admin group.* To install Remote Installation Services, membership in the Enterprise Admin group is required for the account installing it.
- *DNS.* DNS services are used to find a domain controller to validate the user account, prestaging client computers, and a Remote Installation Services server in your site.
- *Active Directory.* Active Directory is used to validate and authenticate the user account.
- *Services:*

  — Remote Installation Services (captures PXE boot)
  — TFTP. Transfers the Welcome.OSC file as well as the image to the client
  — SIS. Housecleaning on the images volume

  All three services must run before the Remote Installation Services server will distribute Remote Installation Services images to clients.

3.1.2 Hardware requirements (single server specification)

CPU	A Pentium II 166-MHz processor
RAM	A memory of minimum 64 MB RAM (if additional services such as Active Directory, DHCP, and DNS are installed, then the minimum amount of memory required is 128 MB RAM)
Hard disk	A minimum of 2 GB hard disk space dedicated to the Remote Installation Service directory tree
Other	A 10/100/1000 Mbit network adapter card

These are the minimum hardware requirements as indicated by Microsoft. Normally, we'd recommend the following minimum hardware specification to ensure that Remote Installation Services server runs optimally:

CPU	A Pentium P III 800-GHz processor
RAM	512 MB RAM
Hard disk	20 GB to Remote Installation Services images
Other	100/1000 Mbit network adapter card

3.1.3 Client computer hardware requirements

CPU	A Pentium 166-MHz (or faster) processor
RAM	A minimum memory of 64 MB RAM
Hard disk	A minimum of 800 MB hard disk space
Other	PXE .99c-compatible network card. If the client's network adapter doesn't support PXE boot, it is possible to create a boot disk with standard network adapter drivers on it. The RBFG tool is used to create the RBFG boot disk. The RBFG tool will be discussed in a later chapter.

Real-life implementations of Microsoft Remote Installation Services servers and client computers often prove that hardware requirements are different from the Microsoft minimum requirements. The requirements are the following:

CPU	A Pentium P III 500-Mhz processor
RAM	A minimum memory of 128 MB RAM
Hard disk	8 GB hard disk space
Other	A network adapter supporting the PXE 0.99c standard.

3.2 DHCP configuration

The DHCP server must be installed, authenticated, and configured for the network topology. You must manually install DHCP services and configure scopes and options at either server level or scope level. The standard scope options are the following:

- 03 Gateway
- 06 DNS servers
- 15 DNS suffix
- 44 Wins servers
- 46 Nodetype

In most networks, these options will already be set (Figure 3.1).

In a switched network, it can be a requirement to use two more options:

- 66 Remote Installation Services server
- 67 Startrom.com file

These options must be used if PXE discovery packets aren't allowed by the switches on the network. By using the first option, the client is forced to use unicast to discover the Remote Installation Services server, and the second option is the path to the *Startrom.com* file. The *Startrom.com* file is used to transfer the first welcome client screen to the client computer. In some cases, it is required to enable Cisco switches to use *Spanning Tree Port Fast*, which allows Remote Installation Services servers to function properly. (See Figure 3.2.)

The next step is authentication of the DHCP server. This can be done manually, or the Remote Installation Services server can make this adjust-

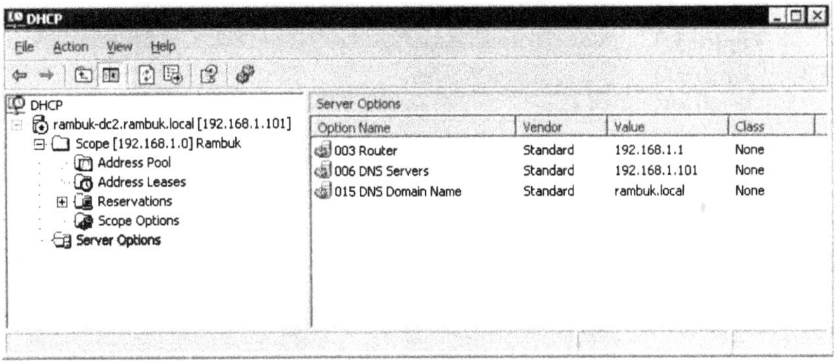

Figure 3.1 *Standard DHCP server options.*

ment. You must be a member of the Enterprise Admin group to perform this action. Only Windows 2003 Remote Installation Services server can automatically make this adjustment.

The authentication of DHCP server is a new function that was introduced with Microsoft Windows 2000 server. This mechanism will automatically query Active Directory for a list of authenticated DHCP servers. If the server is not on the list, the DHCP server will automatically close the DHCP services and thereby not respond to client requests for an IP address. (See Figure 3.3.)

Installing a Remote Installation Services server on the same server as the DHCP means the server hostname is already on the DHCP list in Active Directory and therefore does not need to be authenticated again. To authorize an RIS server in DHCP, go to the DHCP server, select properties for the DHCP server, and click to authorize the new RIS server.

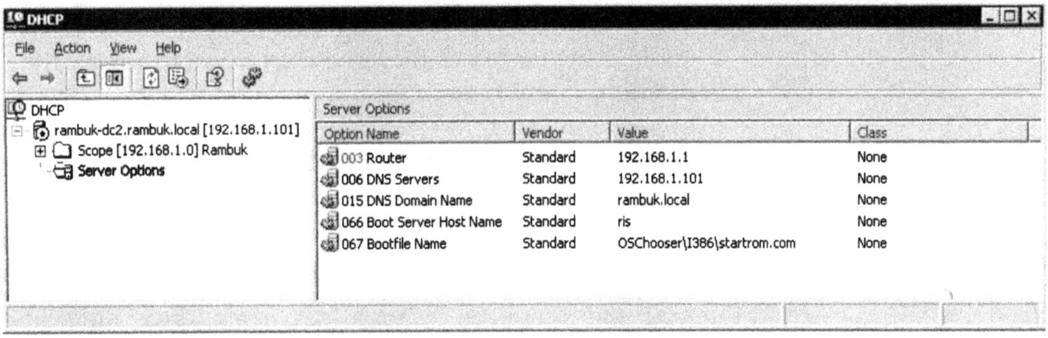

Figure 3.2 *Standard DHCP server options. Option 066 is the name of the RIS server and option 067 it the path to the startrom.com file.*

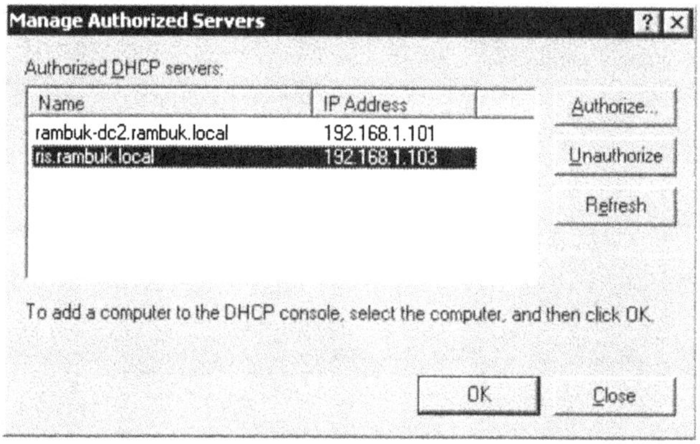

Figure 3.3
A list of authorized DHCP and RIS servers in Active Directory.

3.3 Installing Remote Installation Services

The process of installing Remote Installation Services can be divided into two steps:

1. Installation of Remote Installation Services, during which the three services (i.e., BINL, TFTPD, and SIS) are activated and started
2. Configuration of the Remote Installation Services service and upload of the first image

3.3.1 Install Remote Installation Services service

1. Open Add/Remove programs in control panel (Figure 3.4).
2. Click to select the Remote Installation Services checkbox. The server will need the installation files from the Windows 2003 CD-ROM. After the install, the server must reboot to activate the three services.

3.3.2 Configure Remote Installation Services

1. Open Add/Remove programs in the control panel or write *RISetup* in run or in a command prompt (Figure 3.5).

   Running the command *RISetup* can apply three different switches:

   - */Add.* Adds an image to the Remote Installation Services server

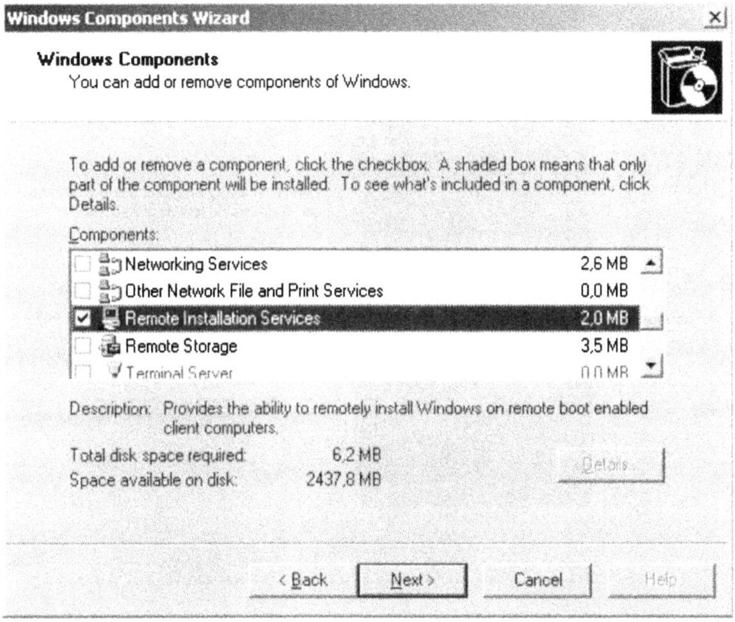

Figure 3.4 *The Remote Installation Services are found in Windows Components in the Add/Remove Programs Wizard.*

- */Check.* Verifies the state of the Remote Installation Services server
- */Auto.* Uses an unattended file to upload and configure a new image. The unattended method will be covered later in this chapter.

2. Click Remote Installation Services Setup from administrative tools.
3. In Welcome screen, click next (Figure 3.6).
4. In the *Remote Installation Folder Location* screen (Figure 3.7), write the path to where the Remote Installation Services images

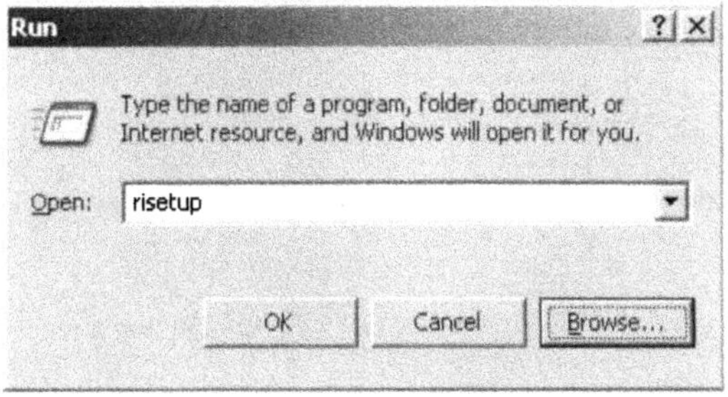

Figure 3.5 *To begin configuration of the RIS server, type "risetup" in the Run box.*

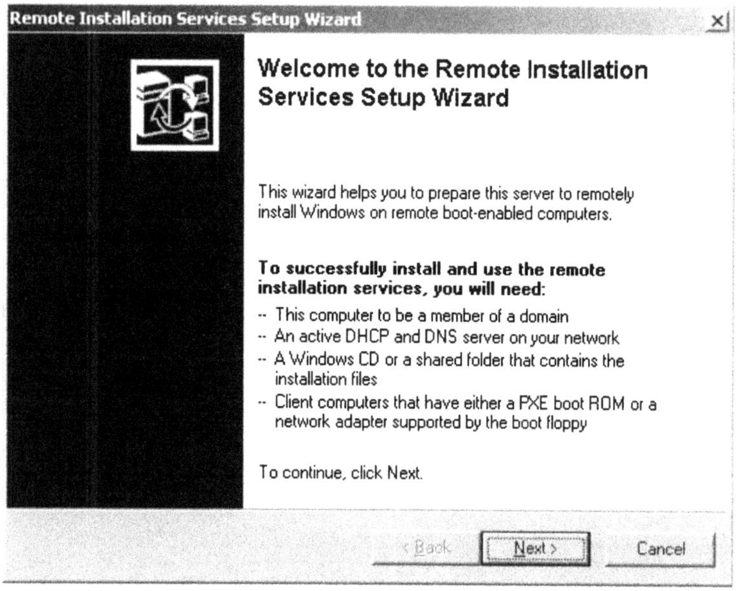

Figure 3.6 *The Remote Installation Services Setup Wizard screen displays an overview of the components needed to perform a successful RIS installation.*

will be installed. Remember, the drive must be formatted with NTFS version 5 and must be at least 2 GB in size. Normally, the RIS server will require a 20-GB hard drive or more depending on the numbers and sizes of images. The partition cannot be on the

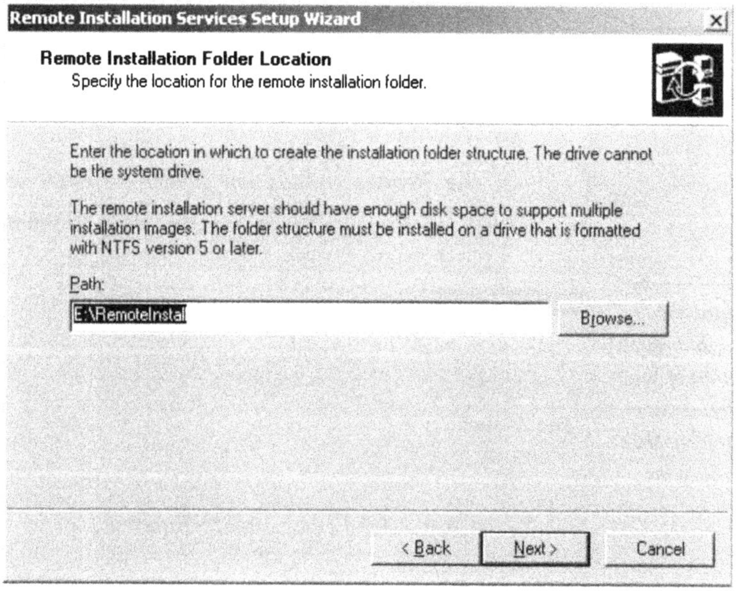

Figure 3.7 *Specify the volume where the RIS images will be stored.*

system root. The installation will automatically share this installation point as *REMINST.*

5. In the *Initial Settings* screen (Figure 3.8), there is an option called *Respond to client computers requesting services.* If this checkbox isn't checked, client computers cannot connect to the Remote Installation Services server and thereby start installing Remote Installation Services images. This is a good option, when maintenance of the Remote Installation Services server is required, to ensure that client computers are not connecting and installing images that are not finished. If this option is enabled, the Remote Installation Services server begins responding to clients requesting Remote Installation Services images. There is a second option when responding to clients: *Do not respond to unknown client computers.* In the short term this means that if the computer account isn't prestaged in Active Directory, then the Remote Installation Services server won't respond to Remote Installation Services clients. Prestaging will be covered later in Chapter 9. Select the checkbox and continue configuring the Remote Installation Services server.

6. In the *Installation Source Files Location* screen (Figure 3.9), the path to the installation source will be entered; this could be Windows 2000 Professional with service pack 4 or Windows XP Professional with service pack 2 CD-ROM. If the media doesn't

Figure 3.8
By default, the RIS server does not support client computers. Click the checkbox to enable RIS to respond to client computer requests.

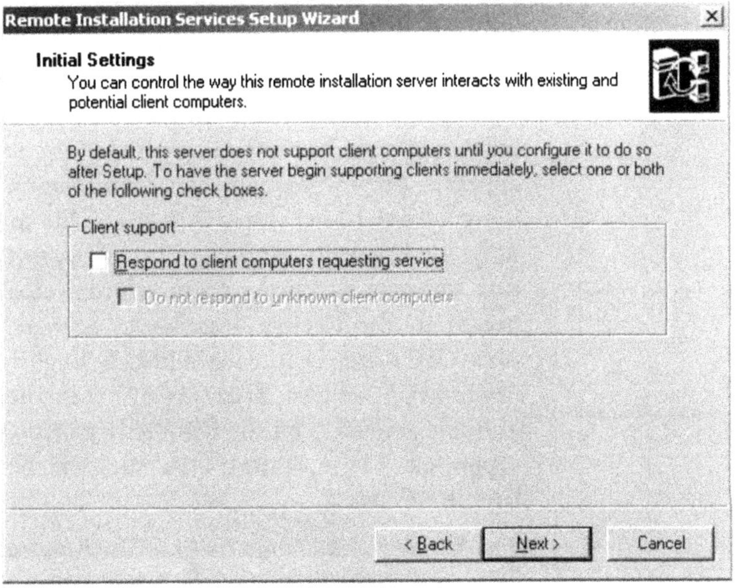

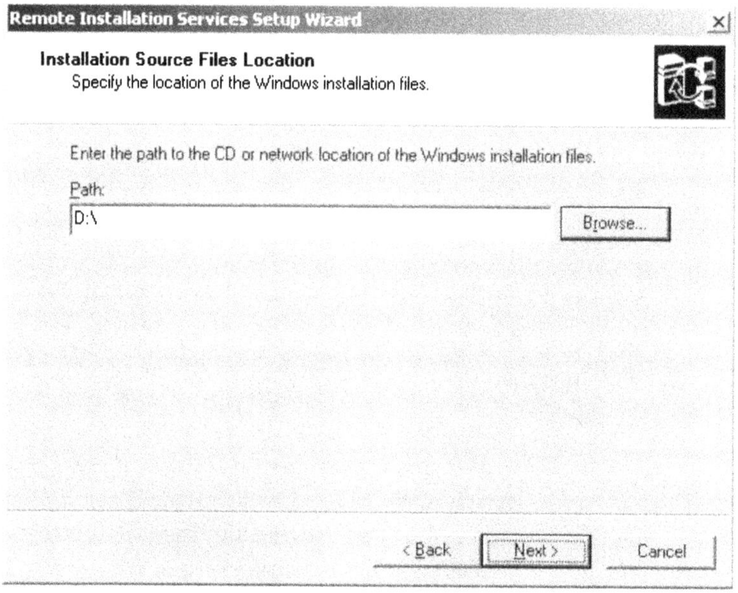

Figure 3.9 *Specify the location of Windows 2000, Windows 2003, or Windows XP media. This can be on a CD-ROM, hard disk, or network share.*

include an integrated service pack, then the option to manually slipstream the operation system with a service pack is possible. The slipstreaming process must be done before the configuration of the Remote Installation Services server (e.g., Windows XP Professional integrated with service pack 2). The slipstreaming process will be covered later in this book.

7. The *Language Mismatch* screen (Figure 3.10) will only appear if you are using a different language from client computers (e.g., the server could be in U.S. English and the client operating system could be in Danish). If that is the case, then this screen will appear to provide you with some information. The information is a guideline to use the *Multilng.OSC* file to install clients in a different language. Normally, the *Welcome.OSC* screen is the first standard screen the client will download when first connected to the Remote Installation Services server. The *Welcome.OSC* screen is only listed in U.S. English. By renaming the *Multilng.OSC* file to *Welcome.OSC*, then the possibility to use multiple languages on the Remote Installation Services server is supported. The operating OSC files will be covered in detail later in this book.

8. The *Windows Installation Image Folder Name* screen (Figure 3.11) will query for the name of the folder where the image must be

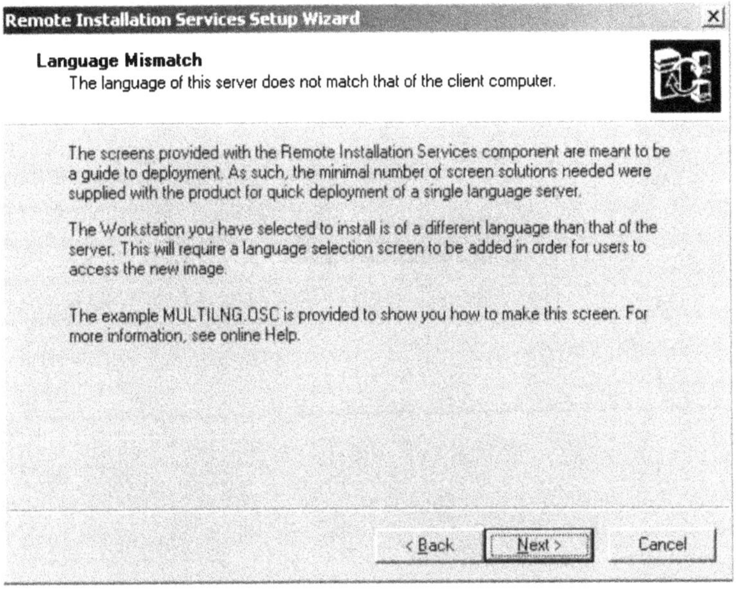

Figure 3.10 *The Language Mismatch page will be displayed only if the OS deployed is in a language different from the server OS language.*

uploaded. Best practice is to use a naming standard that is easy to read and provide the correct information of the image installing.

9. In *the Friendly Description and Help Text* screen (Figure 3.12), there will be a short description of the image (e.g., Windows XP

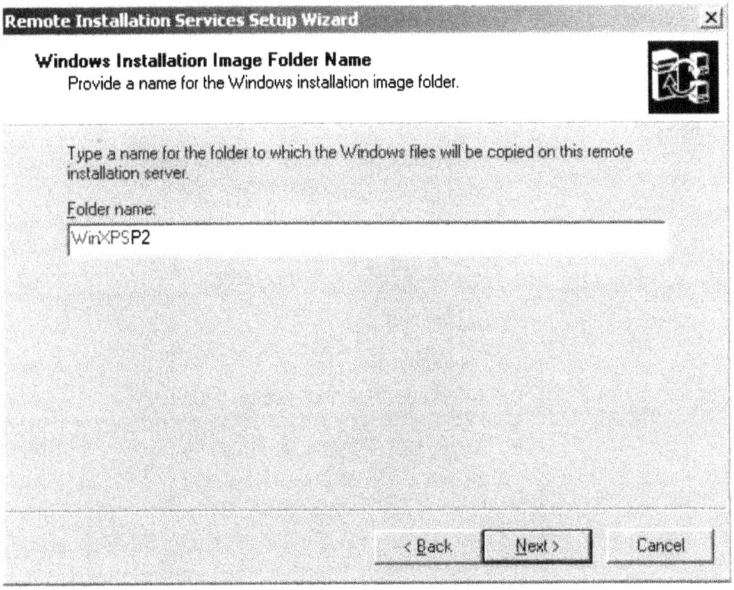

Figure 3.11 *Provide a name for the image folder.*

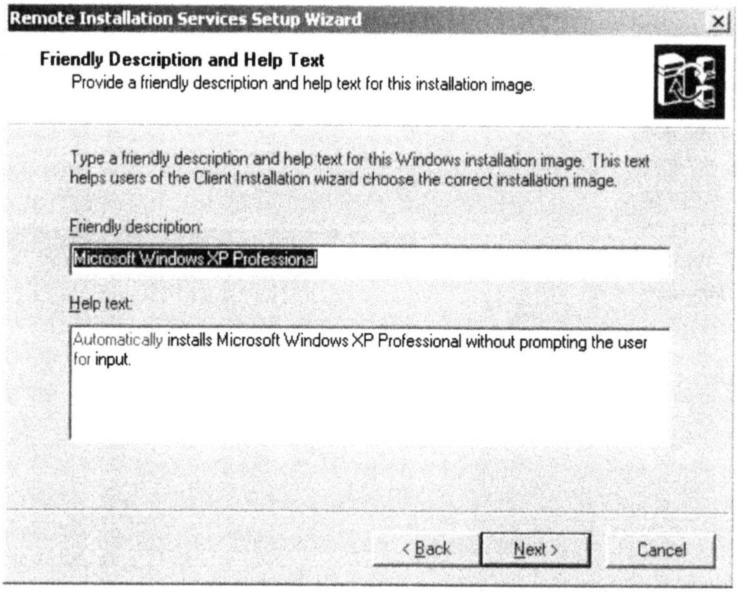

Figure 3.12 *Type an image description and help text. The text will be merged into the SIF.*

SP2), and under Help text there will be a more accurate text description. This information will be provided to the client in the first Client Installation Wizard (CIW) pages, when a connection is made to the Remote Installation Services server.

10. The *Review Settings* screen (Figure 3.13) provides a summary of the choices made in the wizard and gives the option to go back and correct any mistakes made in previous options.

11. When finish is clicked, the wizard begins the following tasks (see Figure 3.14):

    - Creating the remote installation folder and sharing it under the sharename *REMINST.*
    - Copying the files needed to run the Remote Installation Services. These services are:

      — TFTP
      — SIS
      — Remote Installation Services

    - Copying the installation files (e.g., Windows XP SP2 or Windows 2003 standard Server).

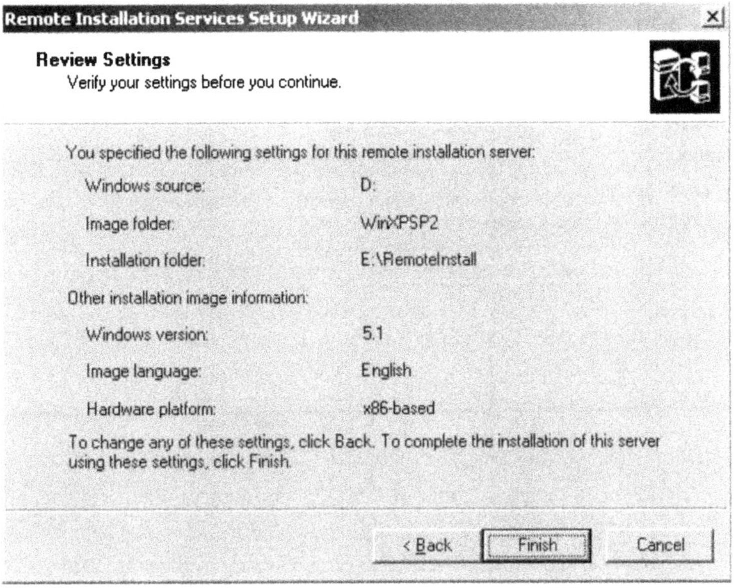

Figure 3.13 *The Review Settings screen displays the choices made in the wizard.*

- Updating the client installation wizard screens. If a second image is made, the wizard will prompt for overwriting or keep the original CIW screens.
- Creating an unattended SIF with the name *Ristndr.SIF.* There needs to be some minor modification in the file before the image works. This can be done either by using the Setup Manager or manually. Both topics will be covered in further detail later in this book.
- Updating the registry to start acting as a Remote Installation Services server.
- Creating a Single-Instance-Store (SIS) Volume on the drive that was specified to contain the Remote Installation Services image. The drive will contain two hidden files and a hidden folder; otherwise, the SIS service can't run.
- Starting the *Remote Installation Services* and *TFTP service.*
- Authorizing the DHCP server. To authorize a DHCP server, membership in the Enterprise Admin group is required.

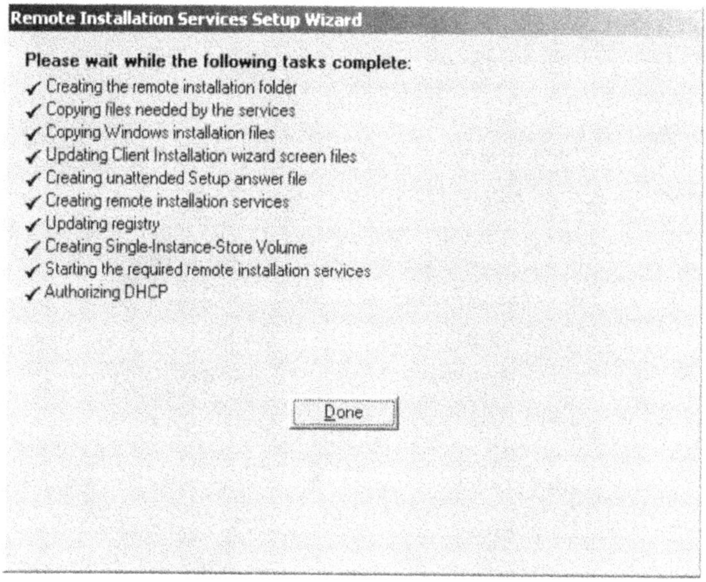
Remote Installation Services Setup Wizard
Please wait while the following tasks complete:
✓ Creating the remote installation folder
✓ Copying files needed by the services
✓ Copying Windows installation files
✓ Updating Client Installation wizard screen files
✓ Creating unattended Setup answer file
✓ Creating remote installation services
✓ Updating registry
✓ Creating Single-Instance-Store Volume
✓ Starting the required remote installation services
✓ Authorizing DHCP
Done

Figure 3.14 *When the wizard has finished collecting information, the process of creating the image begins.*

Note: Automatic authorizing of the DHCP server is not part of a Windows 2000 Remote Installation Services configuration. If using a Windows 2000 Remote Installation Services server, then authorizing the DHCP server must be done manually. This action is performed in the DHCP Microsoft Management Console (MMC): Right-click on the DHCP root and choose authorize. Membership in the Enterprise Admin group is required to perform this action.

3.4 Other configuration options

There are other options to configure when the wizard is finished. These options are covered in this section. To configure these options, choose Properties in the Remote Installation Services server in Active Directory Users and Computers (Figure 3.15) and click the Remote Installation tab.

In *Client Support* (Figure 3.16), there is the option to enable or disable client request from the Remote Installation Services server or the option to only reply to prestaged clients in Active Directory.

In *Check server*, the option to *Verify Server* is given. By using this option, the Remote Installation Services server will provide a status of the *Remote*

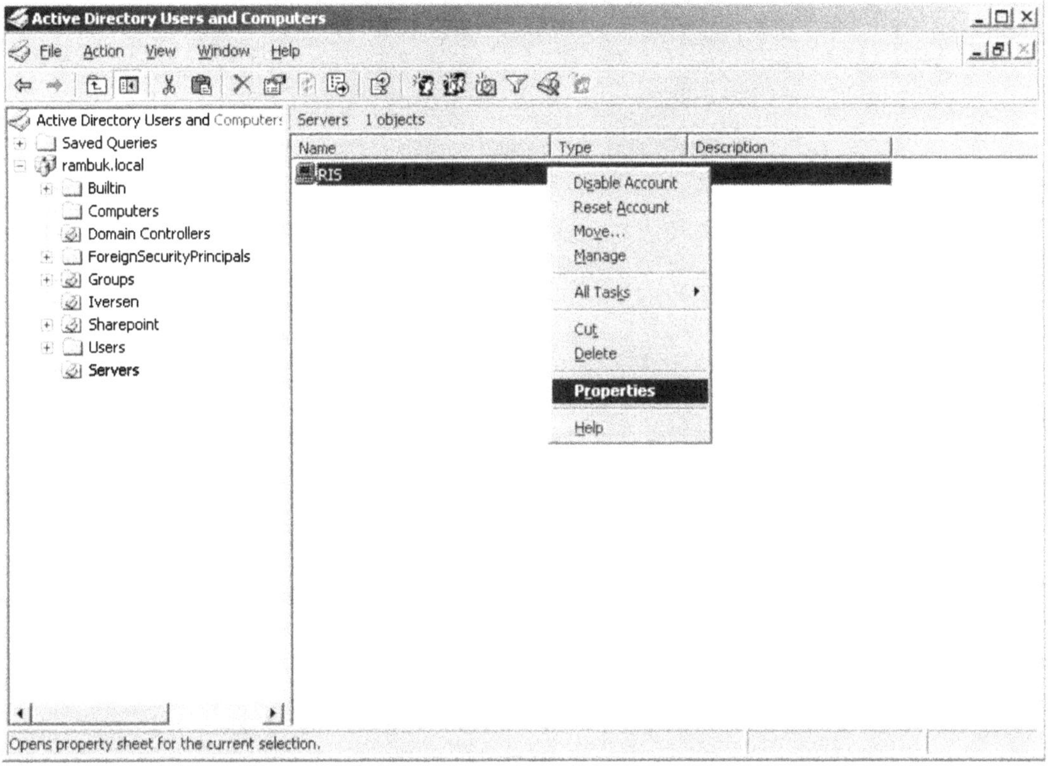

Figure 3.15 *Right-click the RIS server and select Properties to access the Remote Installation settings.*

Installation services that are running correctly and the DHCP server that is authorized (Figure 3.17).

The *show client* button will show the client in Active Directory that has been rolled out with Remote Installation Services. It will also provide information about which Remote Installation Services server the client belongs in if it is prestaged.

Advanced Settings will give an overview of the advanced options for predefined computer naming conversion and predefined standard container/organization unit where the computer account must be installed into active directory. Also the possibility to change the standard text provided in the CIW screens can be modified in this section. (See Figure 3.18.)

On the *New Clients* tab (Figure 3.19), there are two options to customize Remote Installation Services clients; the first option is to generate the computer name automatically. There are different options to structure the naming convention. Standard naming convention is *Username* of the user

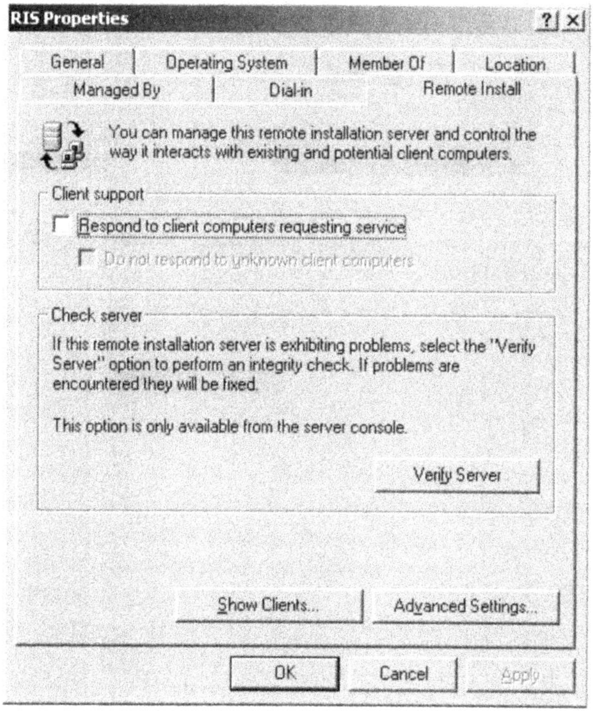

Figure 3.16
On the Remote Install tab, note the option to "Respond to client computers requesting service." By default, the option is disabled.

that performs the actual Remote Installation Services installation on the client computer. If only Remote Installation Services installations are performed by using a single Remote Installation Services account, then the Remote Installation Services server will automatically assign a number after the username. There are also other options to the naming conventions.

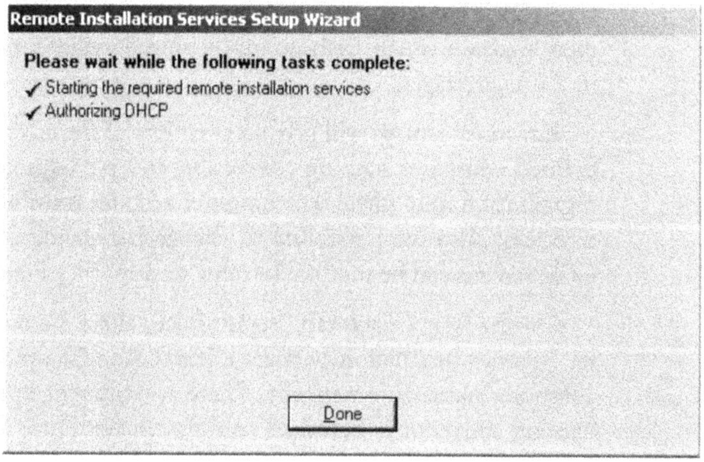

Figure 3.17
Verify Server checks the services that are running and authorizes the DHCP server.

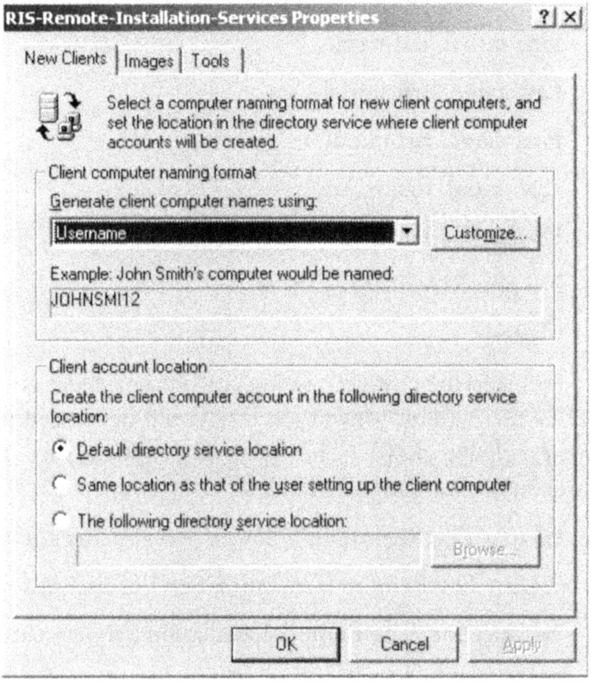

Figure 3.18 *On the New Clients tab, note the option to generate computer names and to choose the location into which the client computer will be installed.*

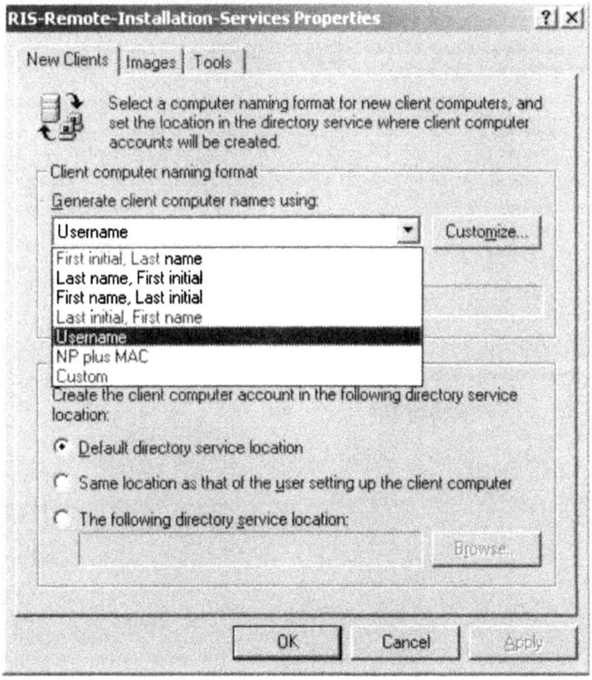

Figure 3.19 *There are some predefined naming conventions and the option to create a custom naming convention on the New Clients tab.*

Standard naming convention is the following:

- First initial, last name
- Last name, first initial
- First name, last initial
- Last initial, first name
- Username (default)
- NP plus MAC
- Custom

By using the custom naming convention, there are more options to predefine the naming convention that could be needed in a network environment (Figure 3.20). The following options are available to Remote Installation Services installations:

- %First. The Remote Installation Services user first name
- %Last. The Remote Installation Services user last name
- %Username. The Remote Installation Services user username
- %MAC. The MAC address of the netcard on the Remote Installation Services client computer

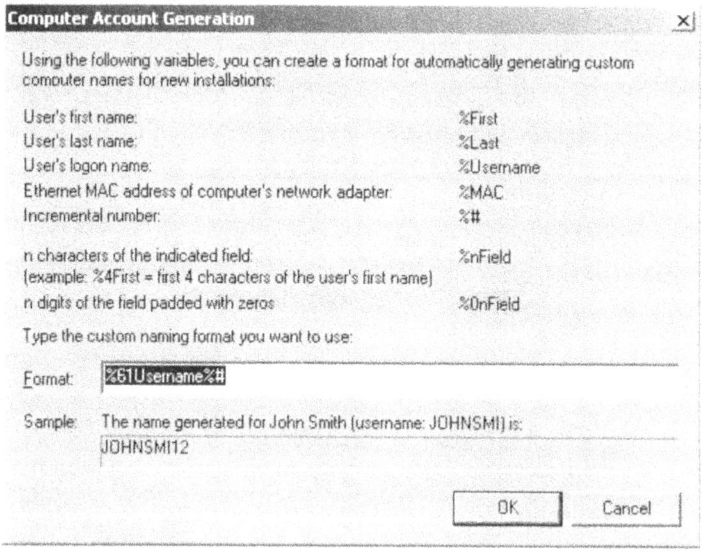

Figure 3.20
An example of a custom naming standard.

- %#. A number updating by one within every Remote Installation Services installation on that client computer
- %nField. The number of characters to be within the name (e.g., %n2Username will give the first two characters of the account installing the Remote Installation Services image)
- %0nField. Number of zeros provided in the computer name, working the same way as %nField

If the standard or custom naming convention doesn't fit organization standards, then there is an option to manually provide the computer name when starting the Remote Installation Services installation. Read more about this option in Chapter 5. The second setting on the *New Clients* tab is where the new computer account must be installed in the Active Directory structure (Figure 3.21). There are three options:

1. *Default directory service location (Default).* Using this option means to install in the *Computers* container. The *Computers* container is the standard container in Microsoft Active Directory where all computer accounts are created by default.

Figure 3.21 *A predefined OU location, into which all client computers will be installed.*

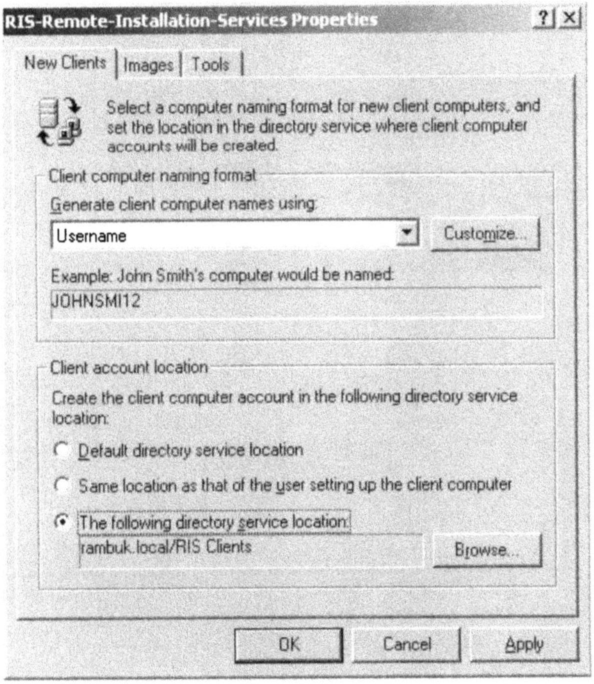

2. *Same location as the user installing this computer.* If the user account is placed in an Organization Unit (OU) called Sales, then the computer account will be placed in the same location.
3. *The following directory service location.* A predefined OU where all new computer accounts will be installed.

If these three options aren't sufficient, then there is an option to define where the computer account must be placed during the client installation. To apply this option, a Group Policy must be applied. There will be more about Group Policy later in Chapter 5.

The *Image* tab (Figure 3.22) will provide an overview of all images provided by this Remote Installation Services server. There will be information about the operating system, the platform, and the language.

Clicking the *Properties* button on this page will provide an overview of the *friendly description* and the *help text* (Figure 3.23). This text is presented to the client when beginning the installation of a Remote Installation Services image. This information comes from the standard SIF created automatically by the Remote Installation Services server when uploading the first image. Modification to the text will automatically be applied to the SIF.

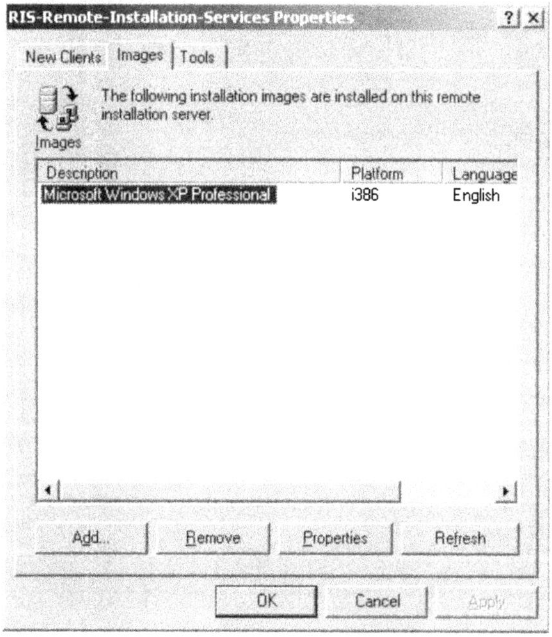

Figure 3.22
The Images tab lists all images on the RIS server.

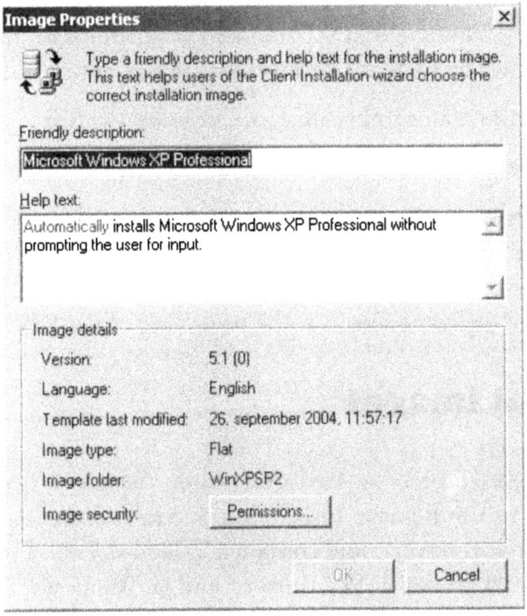

Figure 3.23 *On the Image Properties page is the option to change the description and help text of the image.*

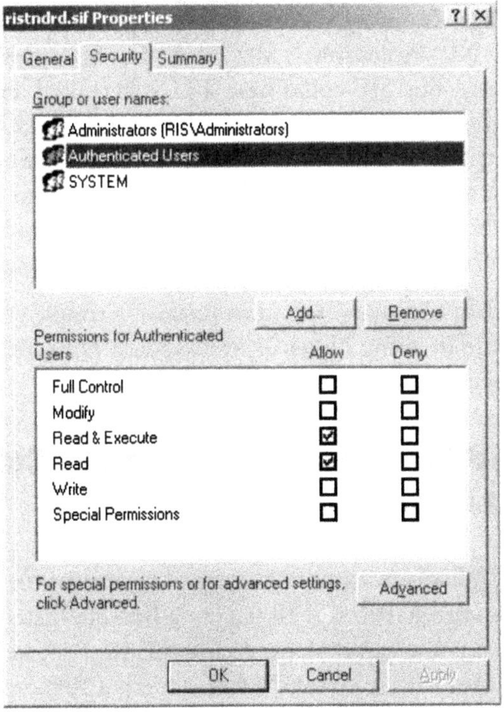

Figure 3.24 *Standard access rights on the SIF. The installation user needs Read permission to get the image listed prior to the RIS client installation.*

On the *Image Properties* page, there is the option to click *Permissions* to give information about the standard permissions on the standard SIF (Ristndr.SIF). The standard permissions are (see Figure 3.24):

- Administrator rights are *Full Control* of the SIF.
- System rights are *Full Control* of the SIF.
- Authenticated user rights are *Read* and *Read and Execute* of the SIF. If a user doesn't have *Read* rights to an SIF, then the user won't have the option to install that image, because the SIF won't be displayed in the client welcome screen at the beginning of the RIS installation.

3.5 Additional images

The wizard can be started every time there is a need to add additional images to the Remote Installation Services server (e.g., a Remote Installation Services server could contain a Windows 2000 Professional SP4 image, an XP Professional SP2 image, and a Windows 2003 standard server image). Every time the wizard is started, the option to create a brand-new image is displayed. There is also an option to attach an additional SIF to a single image. By using this method, it's possible to have one image with Windows XP Professional SP2, and the SIF provides different client options (e.g., one SIF could have a U.S. keyboard and 800 × 600 display settings; the second SIF could have a DK keyboard layout, 1200 × 1024 display settings, and a mass storage device driver defined in the SIF). There is no limit to the number of SIFs a single image can have, and there is no limit to the number and size of images the Remote Installation Services server can contain. The only limit is the size of the hard drive.

To add an additional SIF to an image is a simple creation process, which can be done by using Notepad or the Setup Manager. Setup Manager will be discussed in more detail later in Chapter 7.

3.6 Unattended Remote Installation Services image installation

Microsoft Windows supports the use of an answer file to automate the process of adding a base image flat file to a Remote Installation Services server. *RISetup.exe* is the stand-alone version of the Remote Installation Services Setup Wizard that is invoked when adding a Remote Installation Services image by using the Active Directory Users and Computers MMC snap-in.

RISetup.exe can be run without command-line arguments to invoke the Setup Wizard, or it can be run with the /auto switch if an answer file is specified on the command line.

The command-line syntax when you start RISetup.exe using an answer file is:

```
RISetup /auto c:\answerfiles\XPPRO.inf
```

The following is a sample answer file and command-line syntax for adding a Windows XP Professional base image unattended to an RIS server:

```
[version]
signature = "$Windows NT$"

[Risetup]
RootDir = "f:\remoteinstall"
Source = "\\server\WinXP\pro\i386"
Directory = "XPPro"
Description = "Windows XP Pro base image"
HelpText = "This will install the base Windows XP Pro.
This will support all x86 hardware."
Screens = "leavealone"
```

The configurable items in the answer file are:

```
[Version]
Signature = "$Windows NT$"
```

Required. Heading and version line.

```
[Risetup]
```

Required. Heading.

```
RootDir = "f:\RemoteInstall"
```

Required. Drive and folder that contain the Remote Installation files and folders. It must include this line every time RISetup is run. If Remote Installation Services is already installed, the path must remain unchanged from the current path for the Remote Installation Services installation. The maximum number of bytes is 127.

```
Source ="e:\"
```

Required. Path to the source CD or shared folder from which to create an installation image. The maximum number of bytes allowed for this line is 260.

```
Directory = "WinXPro"
```

Required. Directory in which to place the new installation image. The maximum number of bytes is 39.

```
Description = "Windows XP"
```

Required. Short description of the installation image. The maximum number of bytes is 65.

```
HelpText = "For English-speaking users."
```

Required. Long description of the installation image. The maximum number of bytes is 260.

```
Screens = "overwrite"
```

Required. Action to perform on existing .OSC files, which contain text that displays in screens seen by users of the Client Installation Wizard. Specify only one of the following choices:

```
"overwrite"
"backup"
"leavealone"
```

```
Architecture = "x86"
```

Required. Either x86 for an image that will be installed on x86 computers or ia64 for an image that will be installed on Itanium-based computers.

```
Language = "English"
```

Required. Language of the image.

3.7 Verifying Remote Installation Services

To begin verifying Remote Installation Services servers, the first place to check is the physical file structure. Under the *RemoteInstall* folder, there will be four new libraries called:

- *Admin* (Figure 3.25). The admin folder will hold four files (Figure 3.26):
  - — *RBFG.exe.* RBFG is used to create a boot disk to Remote Installation Services clients, if the Remote Installation Services client doesn't support PXE boot. More about this tool later in Chapter 5.

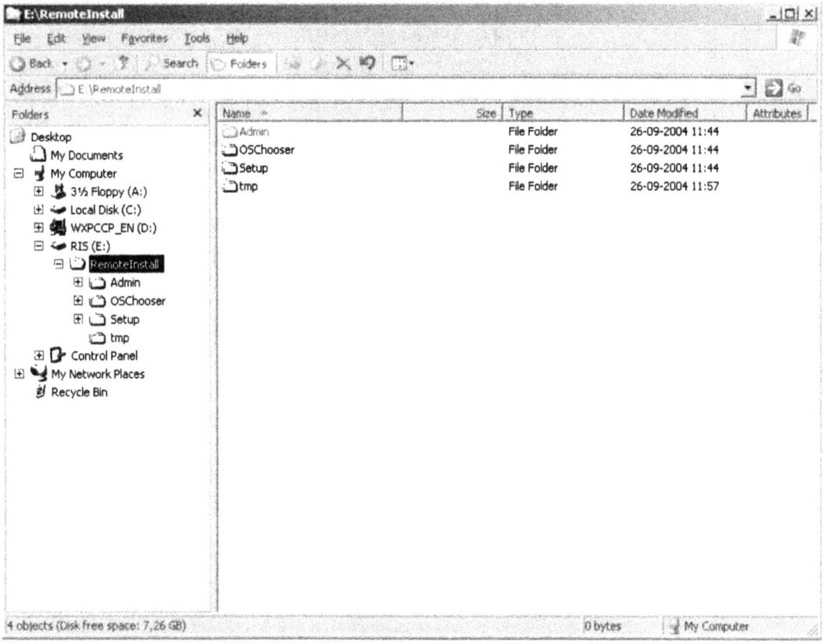

Figure 3.25
Four default folders are created when the RIS server is installed. The folders are: Admin, OSChooser, Setup, and tmp.

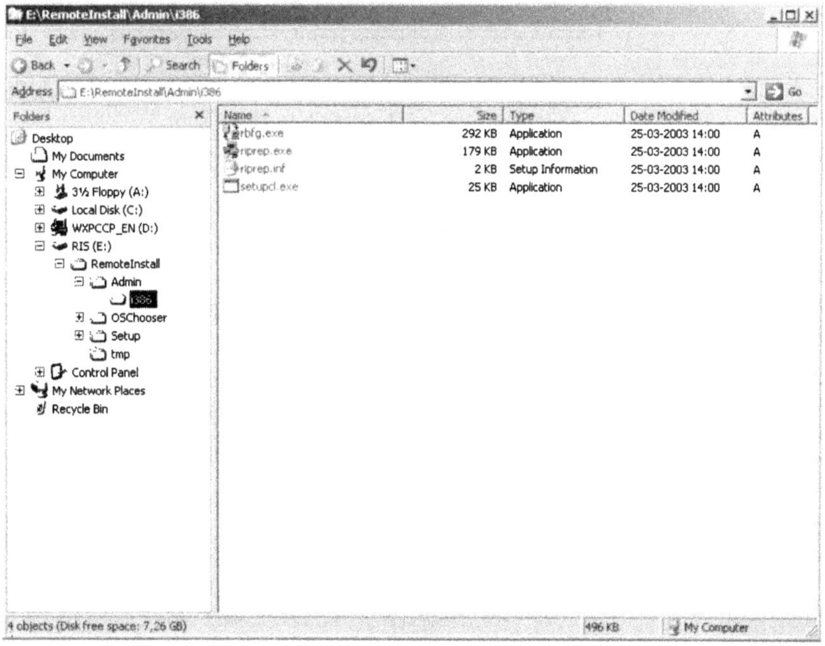

Figure 3.26
The tools installed automatically by the RIS server in the Admin\I386 folder are displayed.

— *RIPrep.exe.* RIPrep is used to create new images that include software packages, drivers, or special client configurations. The RIPrep tool will be covered later in Chapter 8.
— *RIPrep.inf.* Part of the RIPRep.exe file
— *Setupcl.exe.* Used for ripping all unique information from images (e.g., hostname, IP address, or SID-related information).

- *OSChooser* [Figure 3.27(a)]. The OSChooser folder has all of the client screens (OSC files), including the first welcome screen, the password screen, and all error screens.
- *Setup.* The Setup folder holds all images and SIFs [Figure 3.27(b)].
- *Tmp.* The tmp folder is used to temporarily hold a copy of the SIF under the client installation.

The next step is to verify and check the status of the three new services, which should all be running, as follows:

- *Remote Installation* (Figure 3.28). Needed to respond to client computers.

Note: In Windows 2000 RIS server, the service is called *BINL Service.* This service must be restarted every time a change is done in the I386 folder.

- *TFTPD (Trivial FTP Daemon)* (Figure 3.29). This service will transfer the first CIW screen to the client.
- *SIS (Single Instance Storage Groveler)* (Figure 3.30). Housecleaning services on the Remote Installation Services server. This service will run every 12 hours and check all images to find duplicate filenames. If a duplicate filename is found, then the HASH will be checked, and if it is the same, the SIS services will delete one of the files and create a pointer to the file that is left. In practice this means that a lot of images will take up a small amount of disk space. This special mechanism will require a backup program that can back up pointers. The built-in NT backup program supports this feature.

To verify that the Remote Installation Services server is installed correctly, the Remote Installation Services server functionality and connectivity can be validated by using these simple steps:

1. Open Active Directory Users and Computers.
2. Right-click the Remote Installation Services server you need to verify.

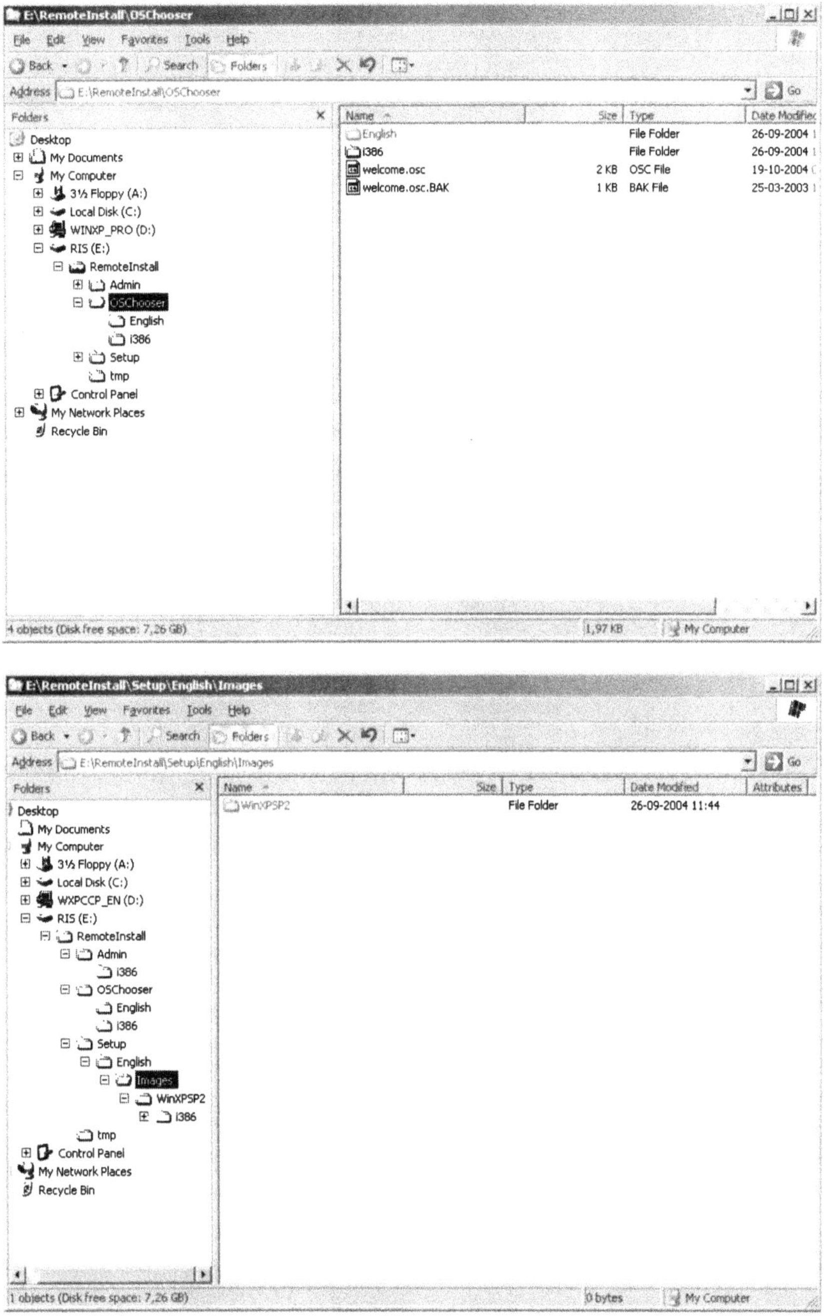

(a)

(b)

Figure 3.27 *(a) The welcome.osc and the multilng.osc files are in the OSChooser folder. welcome.osc was renamed welcome.osc.BAK, and multilng.osc was renamed welcome.osc. (b) The Images folder contains all images that are on the RIS server; in this case, there is only one image.*

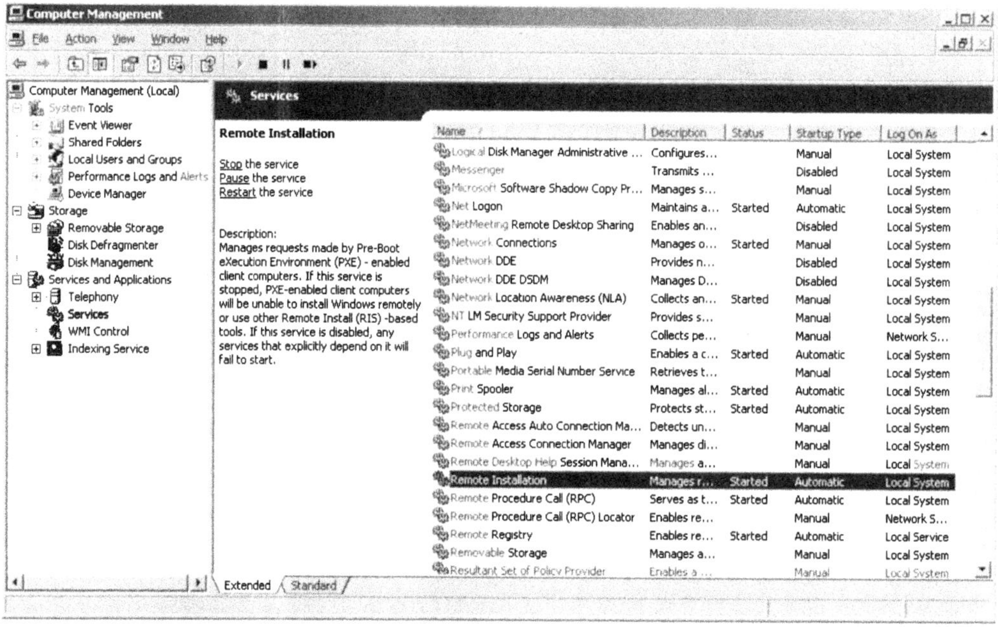

Figure 3.28 *The remote installation services are started. The services must be restarted when changes are made to the I386 folder.*

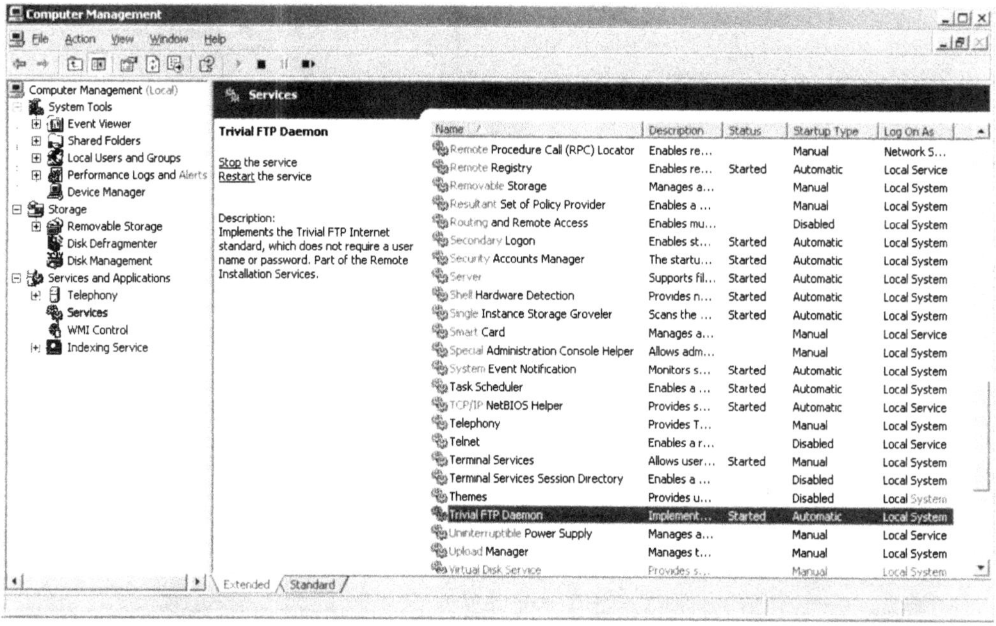

Figure 3.29 *The TFPTD services are used to transfer the welcome.osc file to the client computer.*

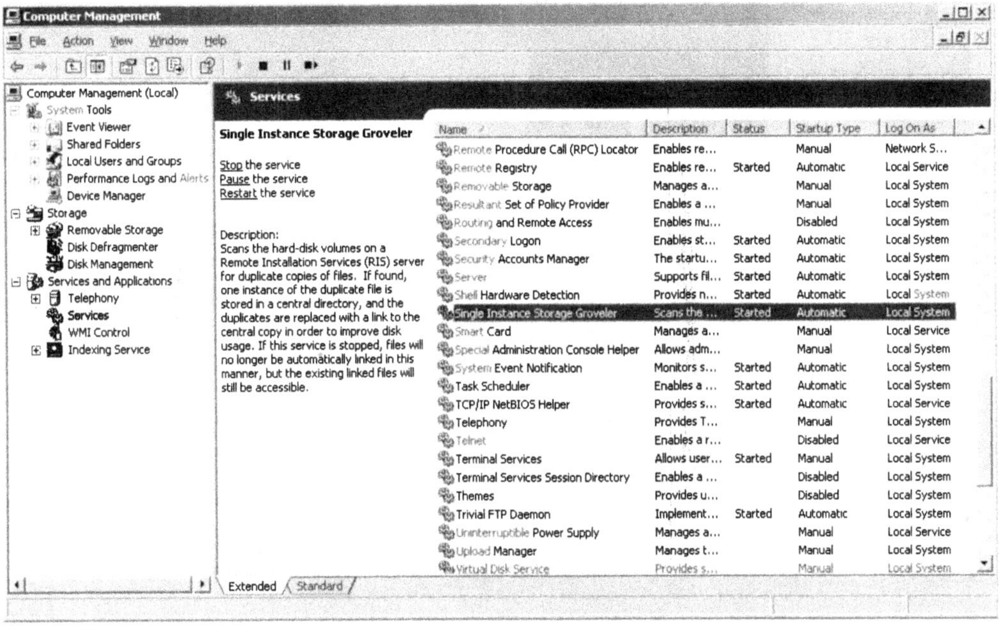

Figure 3.30 *The Single Instance Storage Groveler services are "housecleaning" all images.*

3. Click properties, Remote Install tab.
4. Click verify server.

Or simply write *RISetup /check* in the run box (Figure 3.31). The wizard will test that the Remote Installation Services server is working and will provide a status screen in the end, where all information is gathered in a simple interface (Figures 3.32 and 3.33).

Please notice that it doesn't check the integrity of images on the RIS server or the client (OSC files) screens.

Figure 3.31 *To perform a check on the RIS server, run the command "risetup /check."*

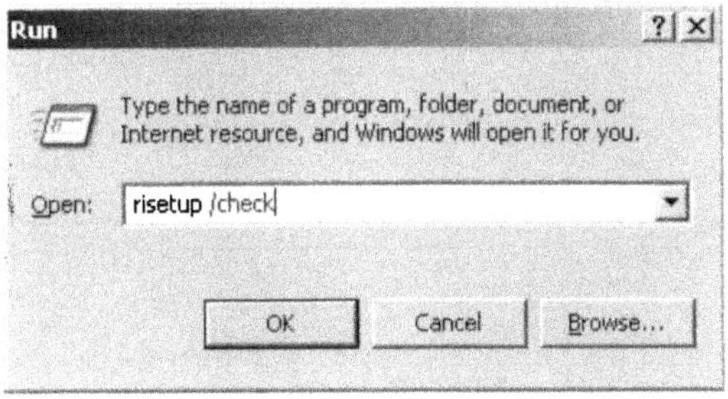

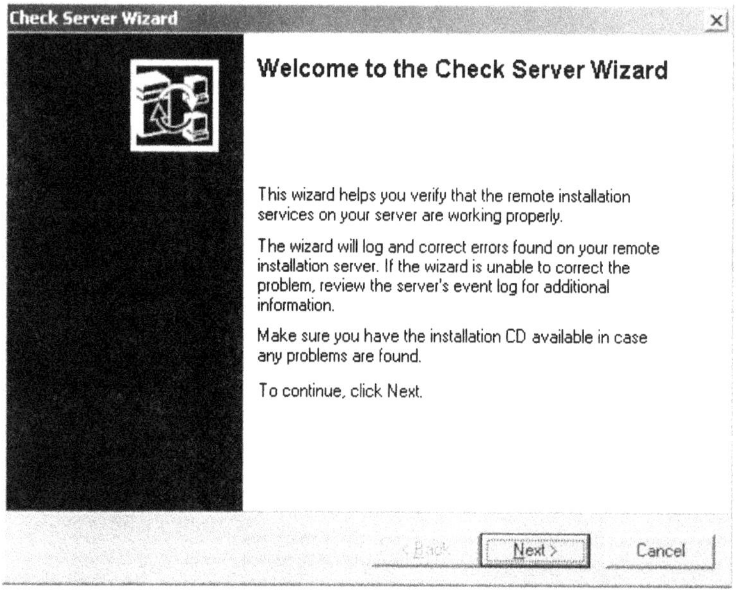

Figure 3.32
The Check Server Wizard.

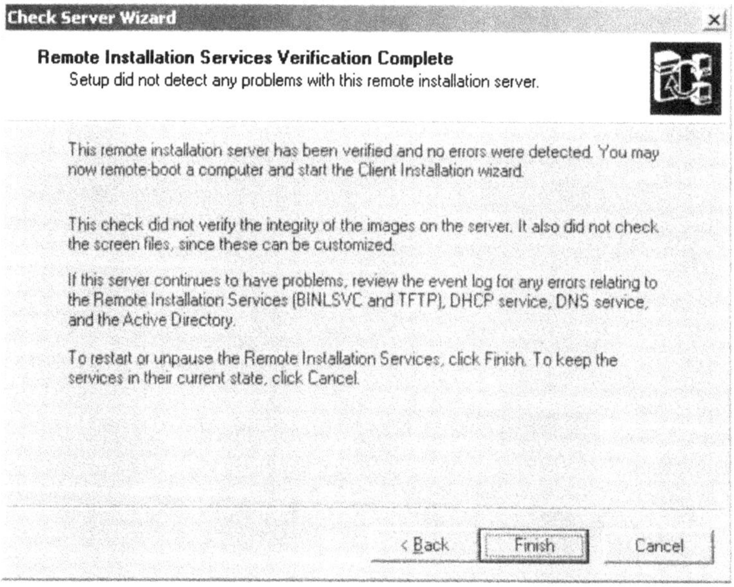

Figure 3.33
The "no errors detected" screen.

3.8 Check the SIF and apply standard modifications

After installing, configuring, and verifying the Remote Installation Services server, let's take a look at the standard SIF the installation procedure provided. The SIFs will be covered in detail in Chapter 6. An SIF is a simple answer file containing sections, keys, and values. This is the SIF provided by the Remote Installation Services server under the standard installation. The comments in bold are standard changes that need to be modified before testing the first image. The changes can be done in Notepad or using the Setup Manager. The Setup Manager will be covered later. If no modifications are made to the standard SIF, then the first image will not run completely without user interaction, and the computer will not automatically be joined to the domain.

The SIF is located in the *X:\RemoteInstall\Setup\Language\Images\imagename\Templates*

X is the RIS image drive, *Language* is the Language folder, and the *imagename* is the name of the folder holding the image.

This section is a walk through the standard SIF created by the RISetup wizard, and the settings there must be changed before the image is ready to be deployed.

```
[data]
floppyless = "1"
msdosinitiated = "1"
ORiSrc = "\\%SERVERNAME%\RemInst\%INSTALLPATH%\
%MACHINETYPE%"
OriTyp = "4"
LocalSourceOnCD = 1
DisableAdminAccountOnDomainJoin = 1 ; Remark this setting
to enable the local administrator account.

[SetupData]
OsLoadOptions = "/noguiboot /fastdetect"
SetupSourceDevice = "\Device\LanmanRedirector\
%SERVERNAME%\RemInst\%INSTALLPATH%"

[Unattended]
OemPreinstall = no
FileSystem = LeaveAlone
ExtendOEMPartition = 0
TargetPath = \WINDOWS
```

```
OemSkipEula = yes
InstallFilesPath = "\\%SERVERNAME%\RemInst\
%INSTALLPATH%\%MACHINETYPE%"
LegacyNIC = 1

[UserData]
FullName = "%USERFIRSTNAME% %USERLASTNAME%" Change this
setting to one single name.
OrgName = "%ORGNAME%" Change this setting to a company
name.
ComputerName = %MACHINENAME%
Productid = "XXXXX-XXXXX-XXXXX-XXXXX-XXXXX" This setting
must be manually added to the SIF.

[GuiUnattended]
OemSkipWelcome = 1
OemSkipRegional = 1
TimeZone = %TIMEZONE%
AdminPassword = "*" Set the local admin password. (Clear
text) or use Setup Manager, which will encrypt it.

[Display]
BitsPerPel = 16
XResolution = 800
YResolution = 600
VRefresh = 60

[Networking]

[NetServices]
MS_Server=params.MS_PSched

[Identification]
JoinDomain = %MACHINEDOMAIN% Change to the NETBIOS name
of your domain.
DoOldStyleDomainJoin = Yes

[RemoteInstall]
Repartition = Yes
UseWholeDisk = Yes

[OSChooser]
Description ="Microsoft Windows XP Professional"
Help ="Automatically installs Microsoft Windows XP
Professional without prompting the user for input."
LaunchFile = "%INSTALLPATH%\%MACHINETYPE%\templates\
startrom.com"
ImageType =Flat
Version="5.1 (0)"
```

After modifying the standard SIF, the first Remote Installation Services image is ready to be deployed to client computers.

3.9 Summary

Before installing a Remote Installation Services server, all prerequisites (e.g., DHCP) must be in place so the process can continue uploading the first Remote Installation Services image. After installing the first image, understanding the process and verifying the Remote Installation Services server are very important. Before the first image can be deployed, minor modifications must be made to the standard SIF. If the Remote Installation Services image is in a language other than U.S. English, then renaming the *Multilng.OSC* file to *Welcome.OSC* will allow use of multiple languages in Remote Installation Services installations. The *Multilng.OSC* file can be found in the *OSChooser* folder.

4

Client Installation

This chapter is about the client installation procedure and provides a walk-through of the different options clients have when using RIS server images. Before an RIS installation can begin, there must be some understanding about the services and process flow that are involved in deploying RIS clients. Verifying the client installations, drivers, and checking for common errors will all be covered in this chapter.

Highlights:

- Flow in RIS installations
- Client installation
- Verifying the client installation
- Verifying the drivers
- Common errors

4.1 Overview

Before going into the client installation, it is important to understand what is happening on the network and the different services involved; if there is an understanding of this process, then troubleshooting will be easier. The flow in RIS installations, from the client pressing F12 to the final installation of a brand-new Windows 2000 professional, Windows XP professional computer, or a new Windows 2002 server, will involve different kinds of services to interact with RIS and different packets on the network. Let's take a look at the flow in RIS installations, from the first boot to the final image working.

4.2 The flow in RIS installations

1. *The client presses F12* (Figure 4.1). The client presses F12 to start a PXE boot. This option must be enabled in the client basic input/output system (BIOS). Different vendors will have different options and interfaces in BIOS. If the client doesn't support PXE boot, then there is an option to use a boot disk, created by the RBFG tool. More about the tool will be discussed later.

2. *The client broadcasts a DHCP discovery packet (including the client GUID)* (Figure 4.2). If the DHCP server is in a switched network, then the two DHCP options 66 and 67 must be enabled. Option 66 is the hostname of the RIS server, and option 67 is the physical path to the *Startrom.com* file. The *Startrom.com* file is used to start the TFTP and transfer the Welcome.OSC file to the RIS client. If using Cisco switches, then the option *Spanning Tree Port Fast* must in some cases be enabled. If the option is disabled, then the DHCP packets could be delayed, and therefore the RIS installation doesn't begin.

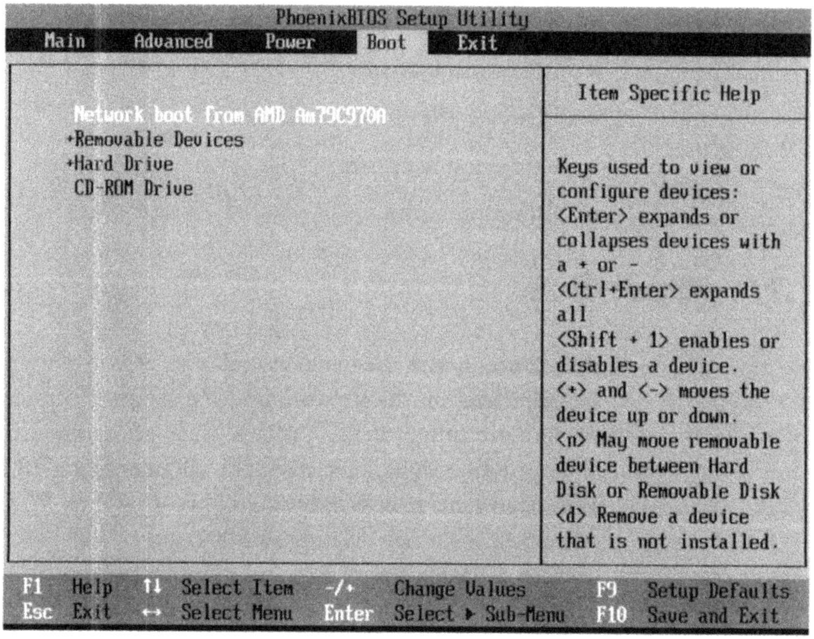

Figure 4.1 *BIOS options. A network boot is needed to perform a PXE boot. Different BIOS can have different options.*

Figure 4.2 *The client waiting for a DHCP discovery packet.*

3. *The DHCP server broadcasts a DHCP Offer packet.* All DHCP servers will pick up the DHCP discovery packet and send a DHCP Offer packet return to the client. This packet will only include a subset of a full DHCP packet.
4. *The client sends a DHCP Request packet.* The client will receive multiple DHCP Offer packets and will only send a DHCP Request packet to the first DHCP Offer received.
5. *The DHCP sends a DHCPACK packet* (Figure 4.3). The DHCP server sends either a DHCPACK packet return, including all information, to the client or a DHCPNACK packet refusing the DHCP Request, forcing the client to start the DHCP Discover process again. The process will continue until the client receives a DHCPACK packet.

Figure 4.3 *The client computer received an IP address from the DHCP server. The next step is to press F12 to start the TFTPD services and download the Startrom.com file.*

6. *The client asks the DNS server for a Kerberos server and updates the client information in the DNS.* The client will update the DNS server with the A record (Hostname to IP address), and the DHCP server will update the client PTR record (IP address to Hostname). The client will also ask the DNS server for the location of the nearest Kerberos server.

7. *The client asks Active Directory about prestaging.* The client asks Active Directory about his status. If the client computer is prestaged, then the client will be redirected to that specific RIS server. If not, the process continues.

8. *The client looks for an RIS server on its own site.* The RIS client will always try to use an RIS server on its own site first. If no RIS server is present in the client's site, then the client will choose the nearest site and continue the process.

9. *The client asks the RIS server for OSChooser.* The client asks the RIS server for *Startrom.com,* and the RIS server transfers the *Welcome.OSC* file by TFTP to the client.

10. *The client applies Username, Password, and domain* (Figure 4.4). For security reasons, the user must provide Username, Password, and Domain name before the RIS installation can continue.

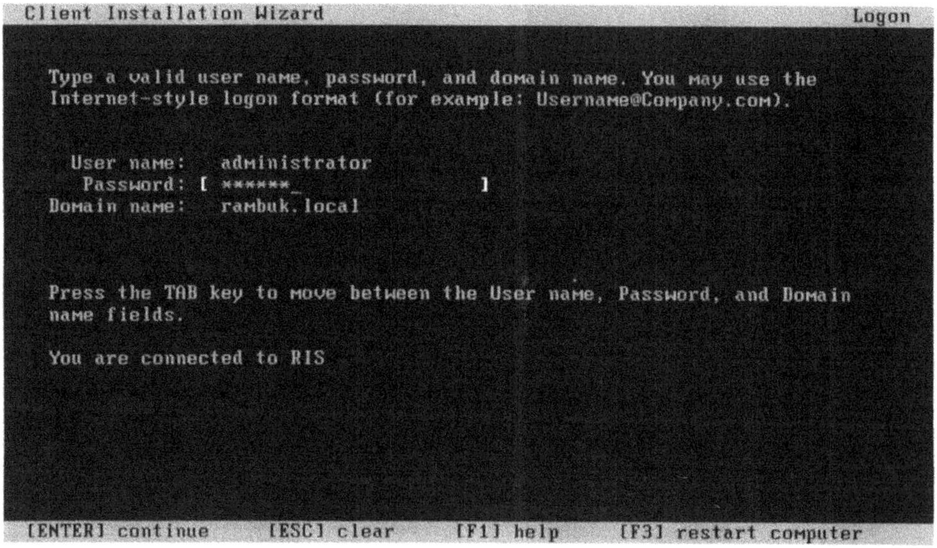
Client Installation Wizard
Logon
Type a valid user name, password, and domain name. You may use the Internet-style logon format (for example: Username@Company.com).
User name: administrator
Password: [******_]
Domain name: rambuk.local
Press the TAB key to move between the User name, Password, and Domain name fields.
You are connected to RIS
[ENTER] continue [ESC] clear [F1] help [F3] restart computer

Figure 4.4 *Before the RIS client installation can begin, the user must provide a user name, password, and domain name. The username/password are validated in Active Directory*

11. *Active Directory validates the security credentials.* If the Username, Password, and Domain name are correct, then the process will continue.

12. *Active Directory reads the Group Policy.* If there are modifications to the standard Group Policy for RIS, then they will be applied now. More about RIS Group Policy later.

13. *Active Directory displays the right SIFs to the user.* Depending on the security rights on the SIFs, the client will be provided with a list of SIFs to choose from. The client needs *Read* and *Read and Execute* rights to get the SIF listed.

14. RIS installation begins.

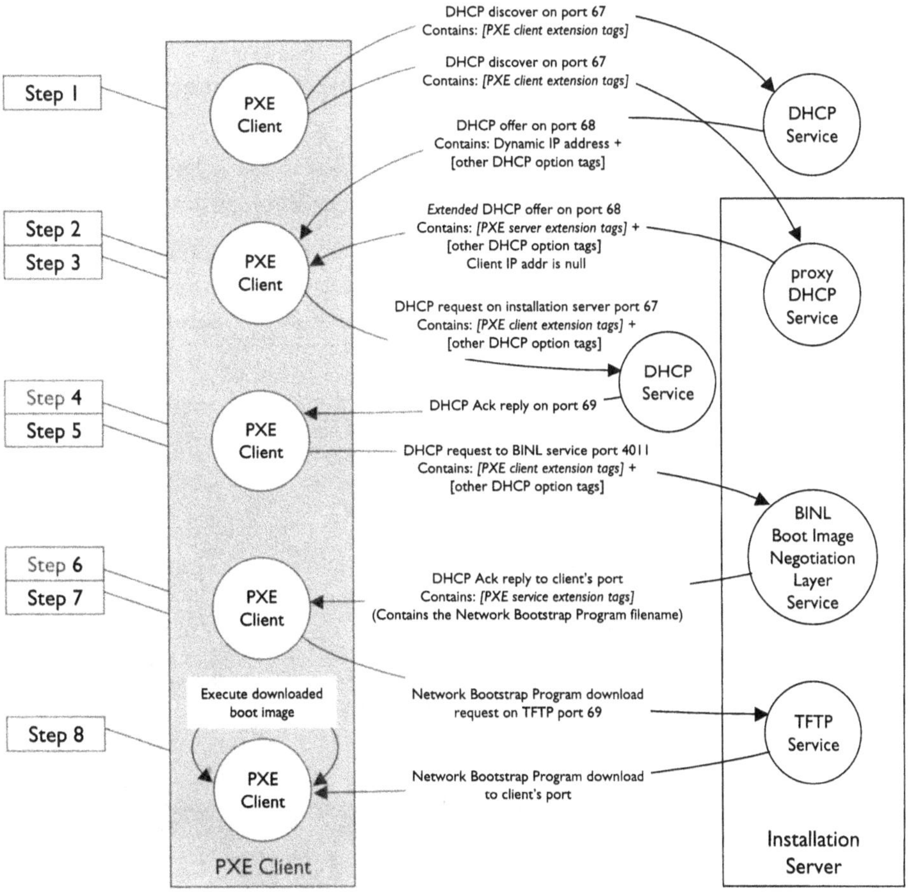

Figure 4.5 *PXE operation: Client–Server interaction.*

4.2.1 Open ports in the process

Some standard ports must be opened when deploying RIS images to clients on the network:

- 67. DHCP Discovery packets, DHCP Request packets
- 68. DHCP Offer packets, DHCPACK Packets
- 69. TFTP
- 4011. BINL Service (Remote Installation Services in Windows 2003)

There must also be open ports to Active Directory (e.g., LDAP (389), DNS (53). A full overview of the PXE boot process is shown in Figure 4.5.

4.3 Client installation

Let's continue with the client installation and see if the first RIS image will be installed successfully.

1. *After pressing F12, the CIW screen is presented to the client* (Figure 4.6). This screen is only an information screen.
2. *The next screen is the Validation screen* (Figure 4.7). On this screen, the Username, Password, and the Domain Name must be entered before the installation process can continue.

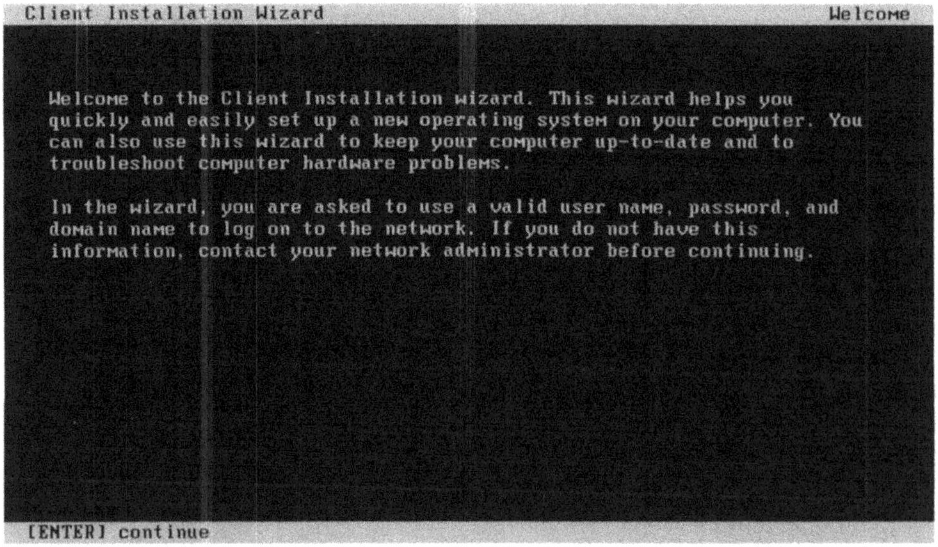
Client Installation Wizard
Welcome
Welcome to the Client Installation wizard. This wizard helps you quickly and easily set up a new operating system on your computer. You can also use this wizard to keep your computer up-to-date and to troubleshoot computer hardware problems.
In the wizard, you are asked to use a valid user name, password, and domain name to log on to the network. If you do not have this information, contact your network administrator before continuing.
[ENTER] continue

Figure 4.6 *The first screen displayed on the client computer.*

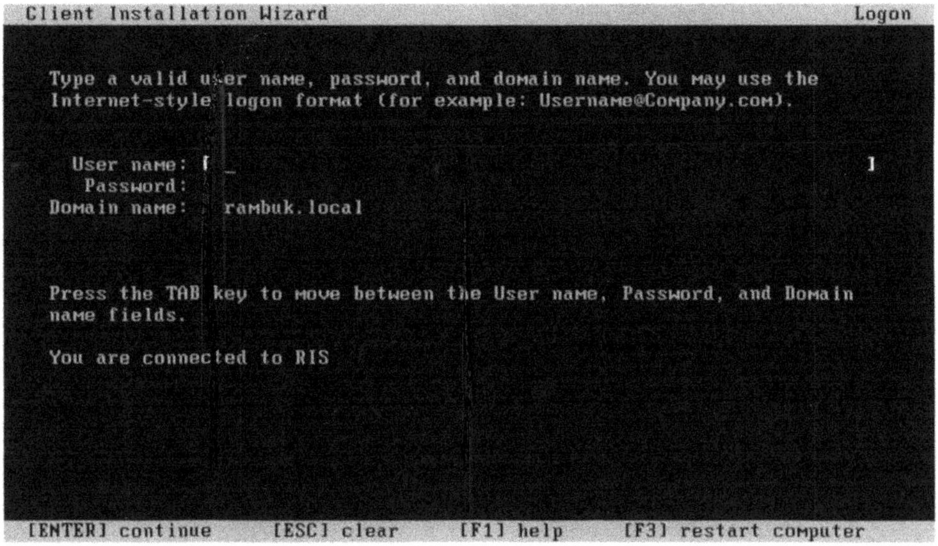
Client Installation Wizard
Logon
Type a valid user name, password, and domain name. You may use the
Internet-style logon format (for example: Username@Company.com).
User name: [_]
Password:
Domain name: rambuk.local
Press the TAB key to move between the User name, Password, and Domain
name fields.
You are connected to RIS
[ENTER] continue
[ESC] clear
[F1] help
[F3] restart computer

Figure 4.7 *On the Logon page, the user must enter a correct user name and password before the process continues.*

3. *The client will be provided with a multilanguage screen if the RIS server has multiple images in different languages installed* (Figure 4.8). This screen is not the typical screen and is only used if the RIS server has more than one language. If the images aren't in U.S. English, then this screen will be presented for the client. To use multiple languages on the RIS server, change the original *Welcome.OSC* file to something different and rename the *Multilang.OSC* to *Welcome.OSC*. The files can be found in the *Templates* folder. The standard *Welcome.OSC* file will only contain information about U.S. English OS. *Multilang.OSC* will contain information in more languages. More about OSC files in a later chapter.

4. *The next screen is the GPO screen* (Figure 4.9). Here the options set in RIS Group Policy will be displayed. More about Group Policy later.

5. *The next option is to choose from the list of images to apply to the client.* An RIS server can hold multiple images or one image with multiple SIFs (e.g., an RIS image could have an SIF for different types of keyboard layout, display options, or local admin account password).

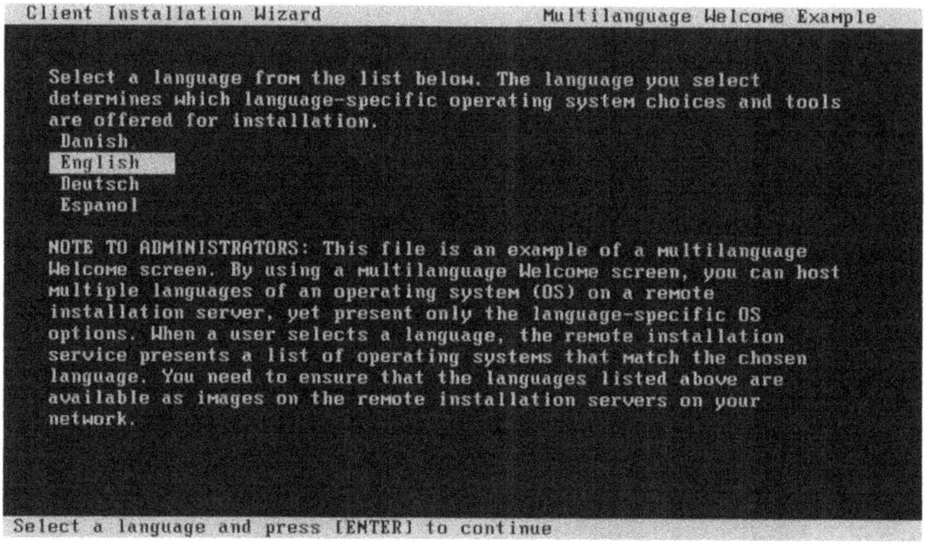

Figure 4.8 *An example multilanguage page.*

6. *The next screen is the information screen* (Figure 4.10). This screen provides information about the computer name, GUID number, and which RIS server to install from. The GUID can be used if a computer account needs to be prestaged in Active Directory.

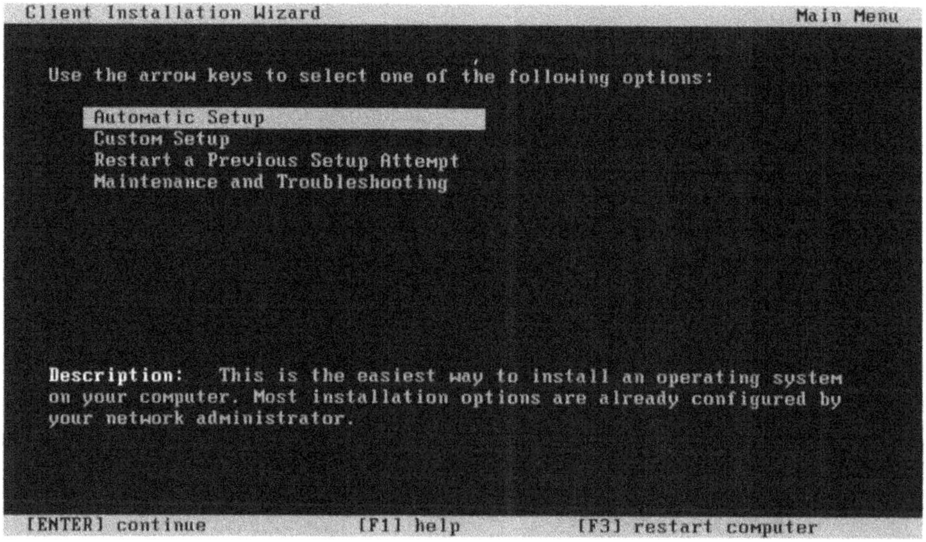

Figure 4.9 *The Main Menu page shows the options set by Group Policy in Active Directory. The page will reflect the settings in the policy.*

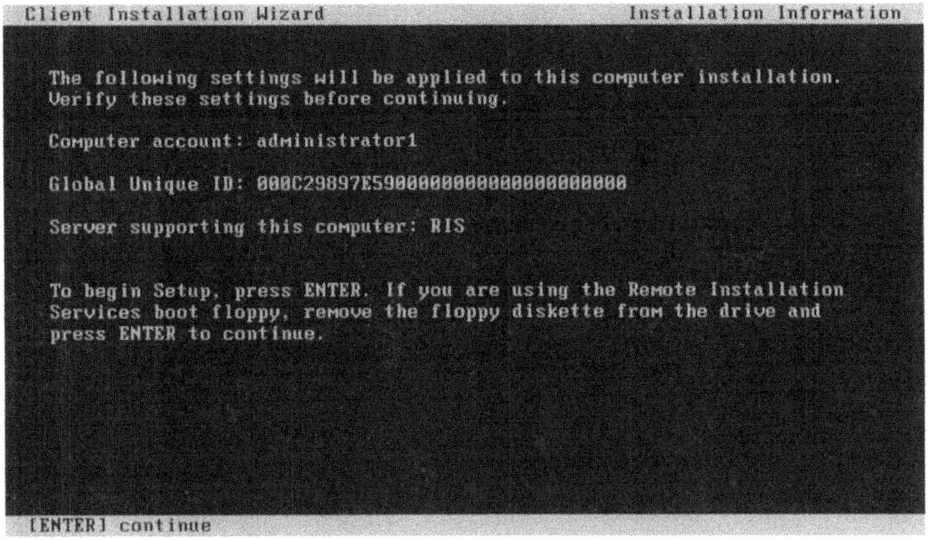

Figure 4.10 *The information page will display the name of the computer that will be created in Active Directory, the GUID number, and the server that will install the RIS client.*

7. *The last screen is a warning screen* (Figure 4.11). The screen explains that the hard drive will be formatted and all data will be lost.

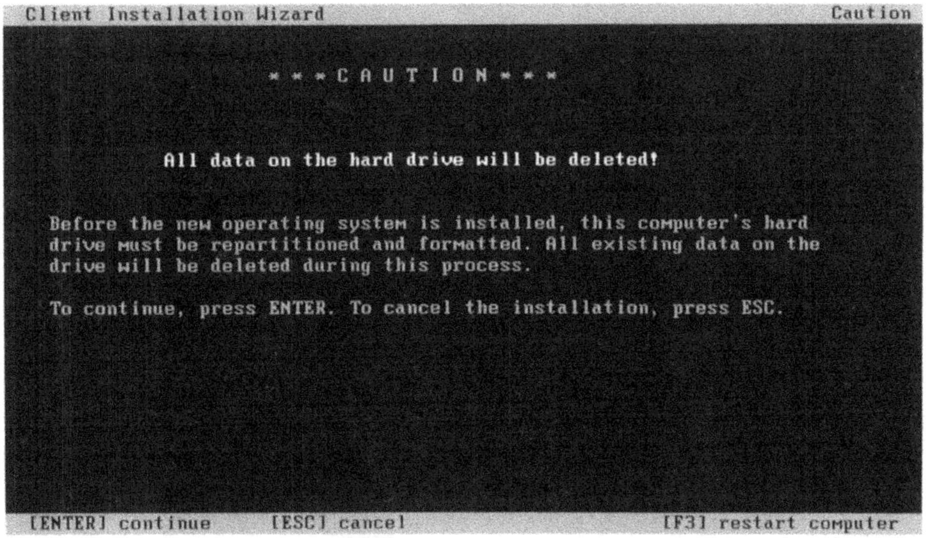
Client Installation Wizard
Caution
* * * C A U T I O N * * *
All data on the hard drive will be deleted!
Before the new operating system is installed, this computer's hard drive must be repartitioned and formatted. All existing data on the drive will be deleted during this process.
To continue, press ENTER. To cancel the installation, press ESC.
[ENTER] continue
[ESC] cancel
[F3] restart computer

Figure 4.11 *The Caution page. By pressing Enter the C hard drive will be formatted and all information lost.*

When the installation starts, it will try to find the netword interface card (NIC) driver for the client computer on the RIS image. If successful, the RIS server will copy all files down locally and start the installation when the copying process is finished. If the NIC driver doesn't exist on the RIS server, then the installation will stop with an error, and the troubleshooting process starts. More about applying NIC drivers into RIS images in a later chapter.

4.4 Verifying the client installations

There are different places to check to verify that the installation is working correctly. Remember, this first image was a standard image without any modifications other than the small adjustment in the standard SIF. Let's look at the client computer and check the client, using the following questions:

- *Is the computer joined to the domain?* On the logon screen there is information about domain membership; otherwise, the information can be found on the *System properties* page (Figures 4.12 and 4.13).
- *Is the service pack integrated?* Check this in *System properties* under *General.* Figure 4.14 shows the information about the operating system and service pack.
- *Does the client computer have an IP address?* Check the computer IP address with the command: *ipconfig /all* (Figure 4.15).

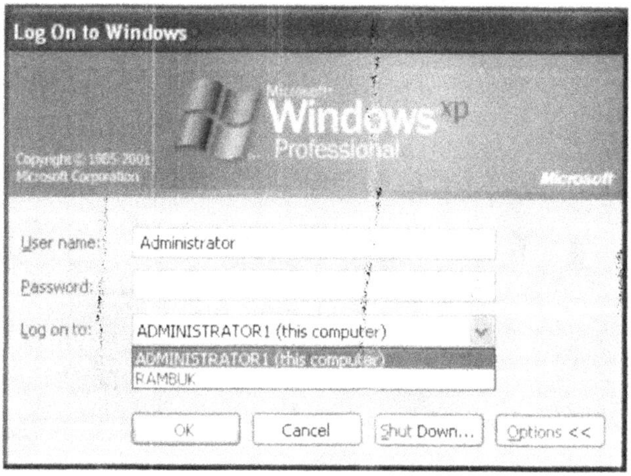

Figure 4.12 *The Log On to Windows screen gives you the option to log on to the local computer or the domain.*

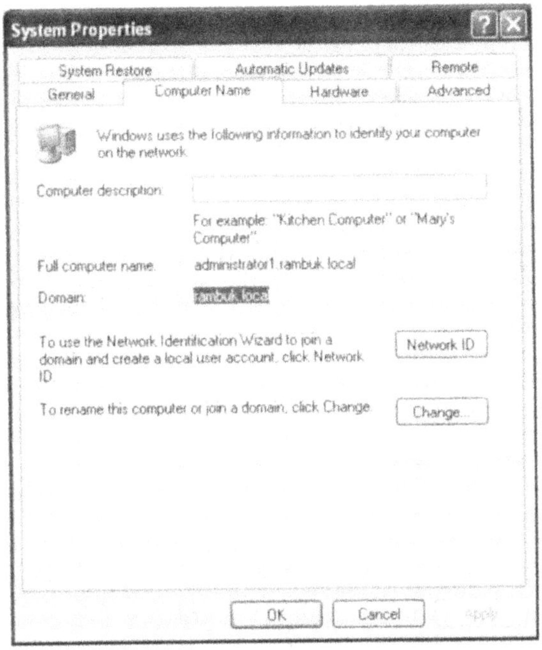

Figure 4.13
The domain name is rambuk.local.

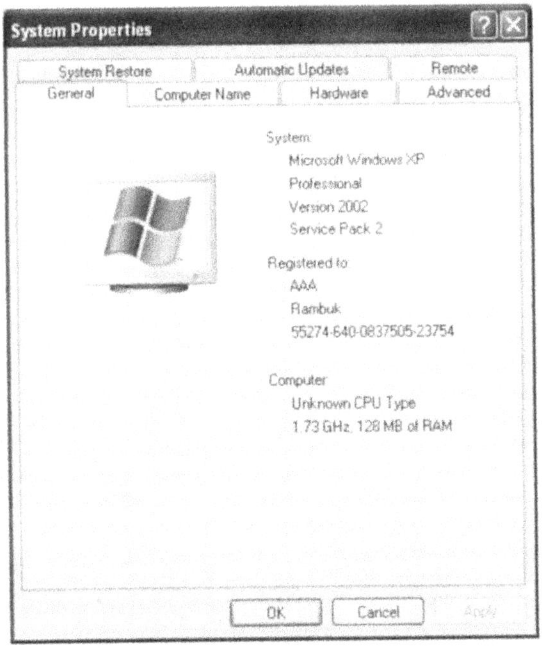

Figure 4.14
The OS is Windows XP with Service Pack 2 installed.

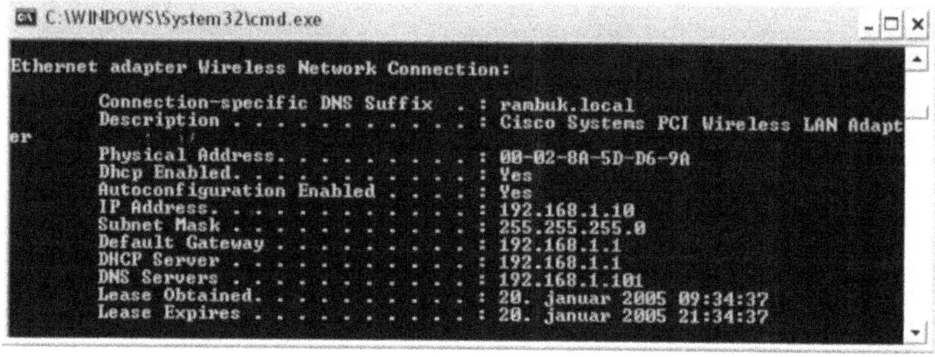

Figure 4.15 *IPCONFIG command output.*

4.5 Verifying drivers

Drivers are important for all OS installations. If the NIC driver isn't installed, then the client computer can't join a domain, and if the video driver is missing, then the display settings will be wrong. Or maybe there are unknown device drivers. These issues will be covered in detail in a later chapter.

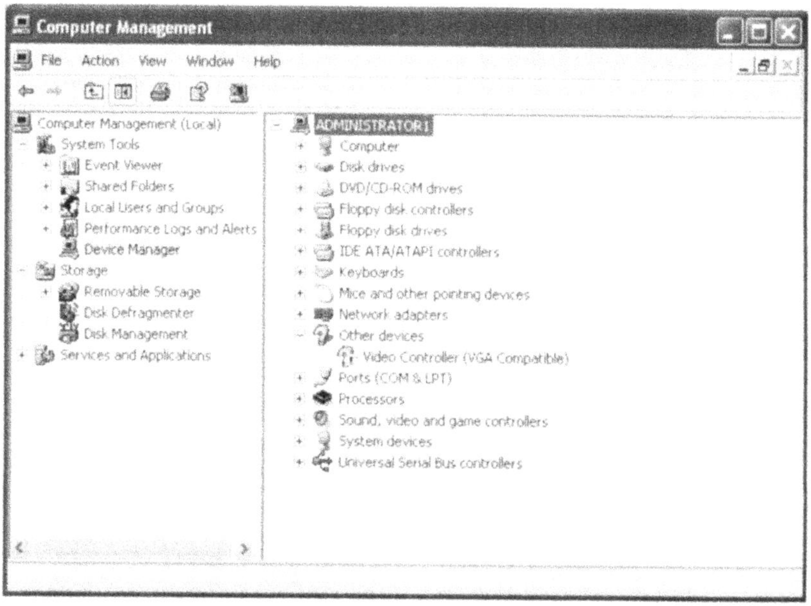

Figure 4.16 *Device Manager indicates that the video controller driver isn't correctly installed.*

Let's look at this standard RIS image on the client and check the driver status in *Device Manager.* Checking the *Device Manager* shows that the video driver isn't the correct one, so the RIS image needs to contain these video drivers. Often, in preloaded computers from different vendors, there will be a drivers library containing the driver specific for that computer model. This place is often a good starting point to begin finding the correct or missing drivers (Figure 4.16).

4.6 Common errors

There are some common errors in RIS installations that are easy to fix if an understanding of the process is in place. Let's look at some of the common mistakes in RIS installations:

- *Language Mismatch* screen (Error 00000003). If the screen (Figure 4.17) is presented by the RIS server, then renaming *Welcome.OSC* to something different and renaming the *Multilng.OSC* to *Welcome.OSC* will fix this problem.
- *Personalize Your Software.* If this screen (Figure 4.18) is presented, the client installation will stop and the information must by provided

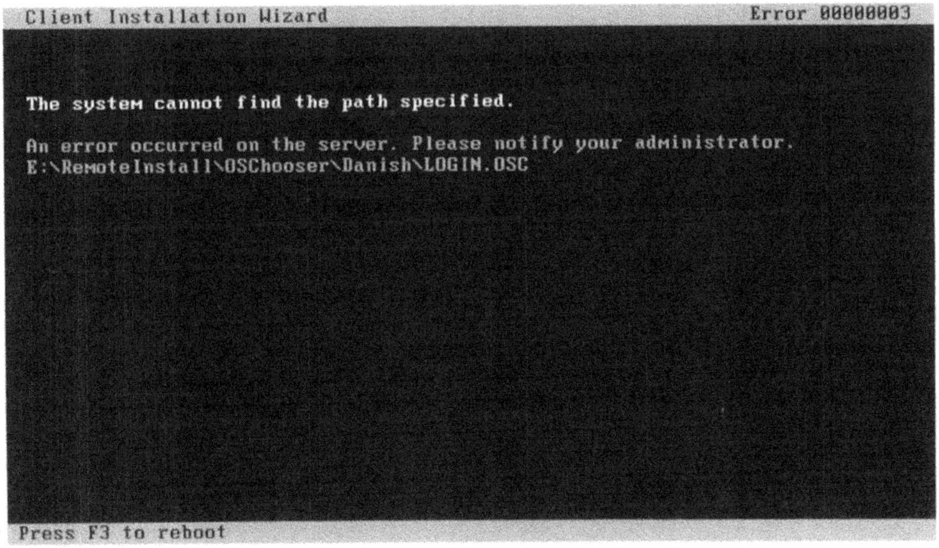
Client Installation Wizard
Error 00000003
The system cannot find the path specified.
An error occurred on the server. Please notify your administrator.
E:\RemoteInstall\OSChooser\Danish\LOGIN.OSC
Press F3 to reboot

Figure 4.17 *The error message displayed if there are images in a different language on the RIS server and the multilanguage.osc file isn't used.*

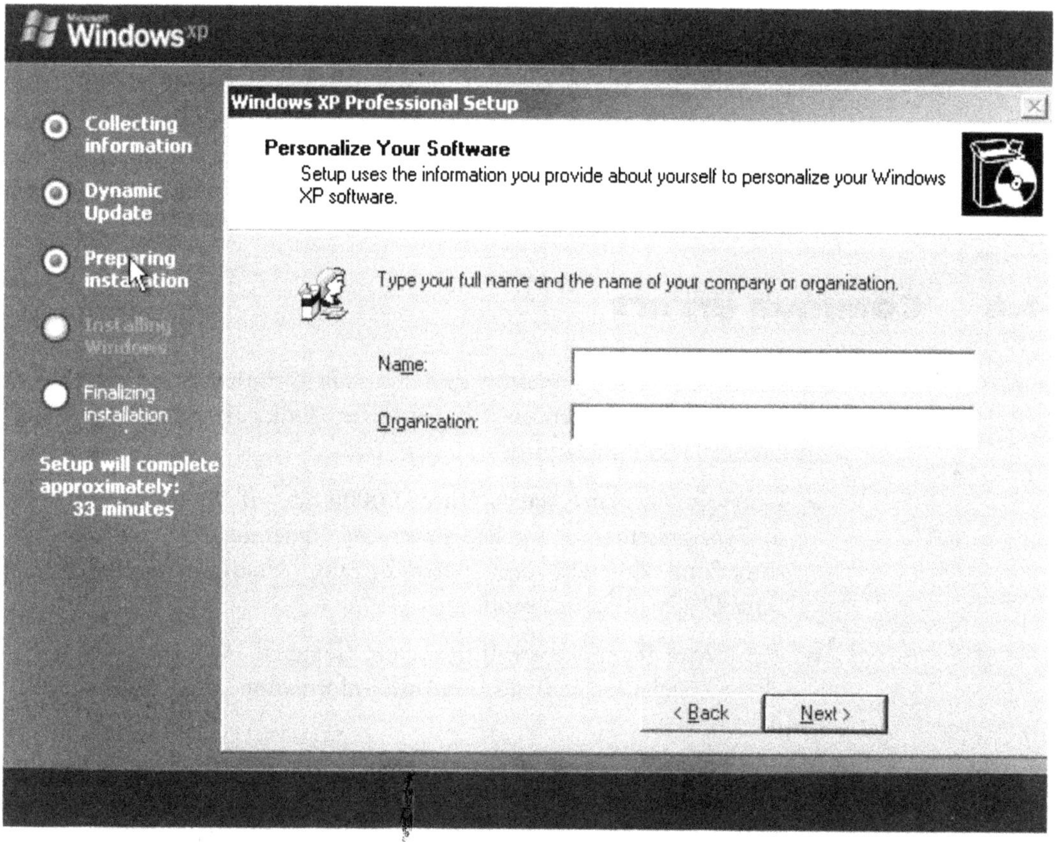

Figure 4.18 *If the name and organization aren't formatted correctly in the SIF, this page will be displayed. The installation can continue, but the information must be filled in manually.*

manually. To fully automate this screen, a minor change in the SIF must be made:

```
[UserData]
FullName = "%USERFIRSTNAME% %USERLASTNAME%" Change
this setting to one single name.
OrgName = "%ORGNAME%" Change this setting to a company
name.
```

- *Your Product Key screen.* If the installation stops on this screen (Figure 4.19), the product key can be provided manually. To fully automate the screen, a new entry must be created in the SIF.

```
[User Data]
Productkey = "XXXXX-XXXXX-XXXXX-XXXXX-XXXXX" This
setting must be manually added to the SIF.
```

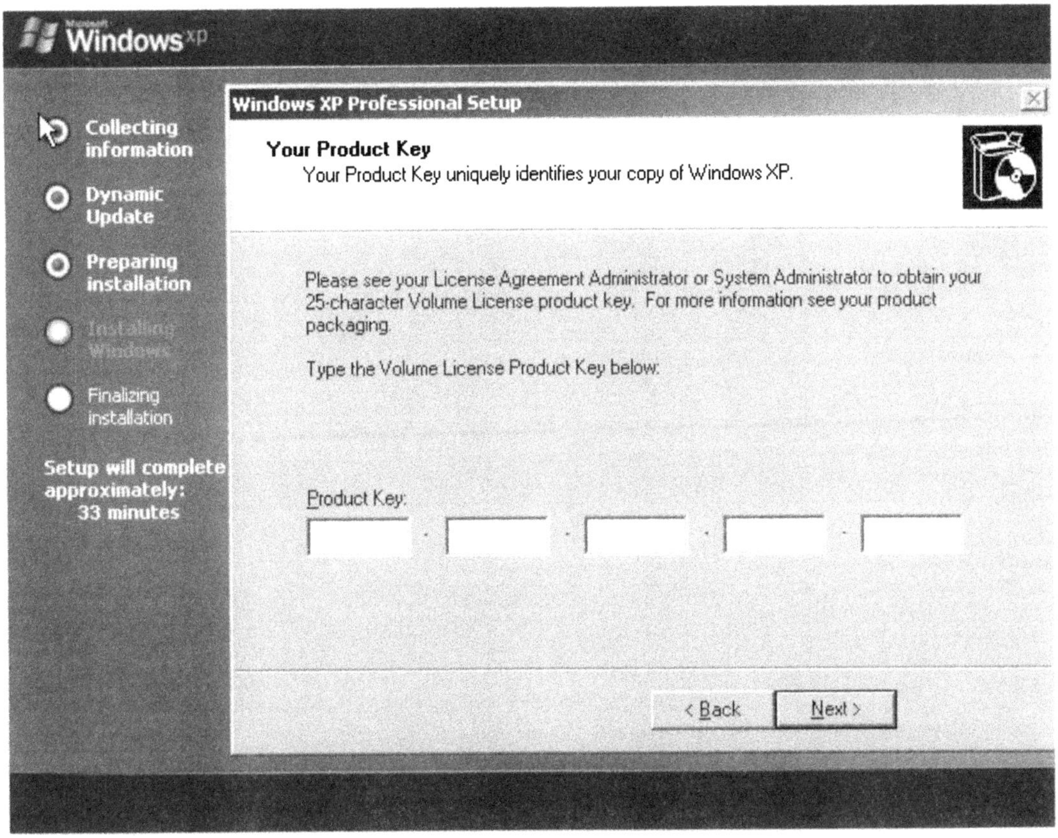

Figure 4.19 *If the product key has not been manually entered in the SIF, this page will be displayed. The installation process can continue, but the product key must be entered manually. The product key must always be provided manually in the SIF file.*

4.7 Summary

Now an understanding of the flow in RIS installations is in place and the installation of the first client computer has been completed with success. The book continues with the RBFG tool, which can be used if the client computer doesn't support the PXE .99c standard.

5

Slipstreaming, RBFG, and Group Policy

This chapter provides an overview of the slipstreaming process. By slipstreaming an OS, an RIS image can be installed, including a service pack. The RBFG tool can be used to create a boot disk for client computers that don't support the PXE .99c standard. This section also walks through the process to create the RBFG disk. Last in this chapter, a guideline to RIS Group Policy in Microsoft Active Directory is presented.

Highlights:

- Slipstreaming process
- RBFG
- RIS Group Policy

5.1 Slipstreaming

The OS image on the RIS server has the possibility to integrate a service pack into that image (e.g., Windows XP Professional will have service pack 2 integrated), so there is no need to deploy that package later in the process. Unfortunately, it's not possible to integrate a service pack after an image is uploaded to the server, so the process needs to be applied before the RIS image is being uploaded.

Over time, Microsoft will develop new service packs to various operating systems such as Windows XP. When new service packs are published to the public, the service pack must be tested on the network against business applications, and when the test is successful, a new image with Windows XP Professional with SP X can be integrated into one image. The new image can then be uploaded to the RIS server, ready to deploy to thousands of client computers.

If the service pack hasn't been integrated into the OS image, then it must be deployed later in the process by another mechanism. There is the possibility to use Software Update Service (SUS), Systems Management Server (SMS), or to deploy the service pack via Group Policy in Active Directory. If the service pack isn't integrated into the image, then there is no guarantee of the integrity of the installation. Every time the client computer uses files from the installation point, it will be necessary to ensure the integrity of the service pack. Best practice is to integrate the service pack with the basic OS.

The process to integrate a service pack is called *slipstreaming* and is fairly simple; just follow these steps:

1. Copy the entire Windows CD-ROM to a folder on the local hard drive.
2. Download the latest service pack from Microsoft's Web site. The network version is needed and must be in a localized version.
3. Extract the service pack with the command: *Service pack name /x* (Figure 5.1(a)).

   Specify a folder into which the service pack will extract (Figure 5.1(b)).

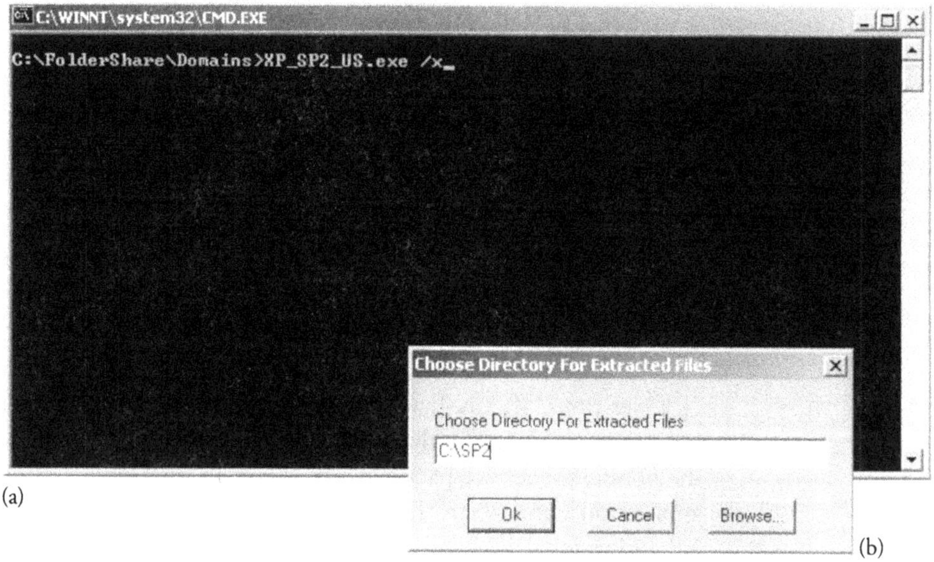

(a) (b)

Figure 5.1 *The command to extract the service pack (a); specify the directory for the service pack files (b).*

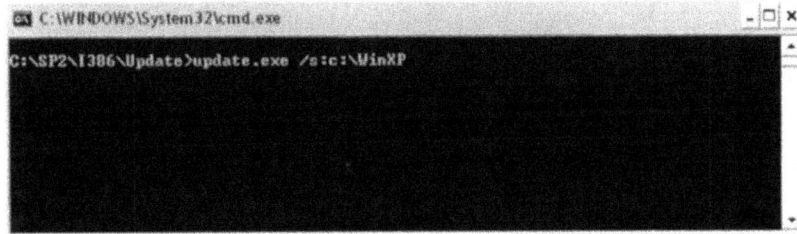

Figure 5.2 *The update.exe /s:c:\WinXP command will begin the slipstream process. The I386 folder must not appear in the command. The slipstreaming process will automatically detect the I386 folder.*

4. Start a command prompt and navigate to the update folder beneath the extracted service pack folder. Then run the command: *update.exe /s:c:\osimage*, where *osimage* is the location of the Windows installation files. This command will start the slipstreaming process. Don't specify the I386 folder under the CD-ROM image. The setup program will automatically look for I386 in the path specification (Figure 5.2).

After the slipstreaming process is finished, the images are ready to be uploaded to the RIS server by using the command *RISetup /add* from the *RUN* menu.

The command will begin the slipstreaming process and start integrating the service pack into the basic OS (Figures 5.3 and 5.4).

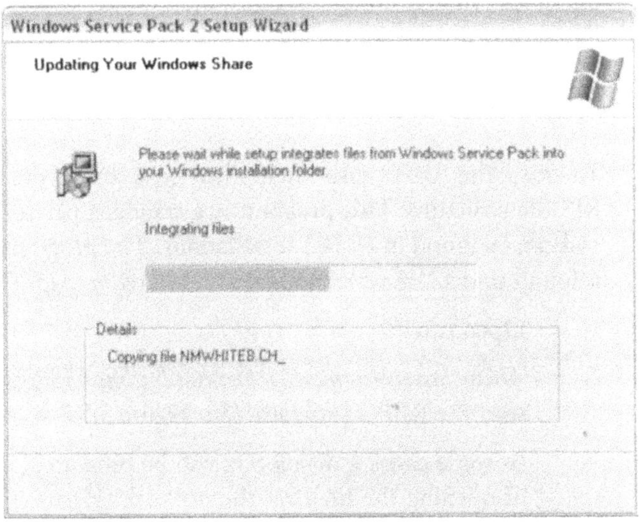

Figure 5.3 *The slipstreaming process integrates the service pack into the OS.*

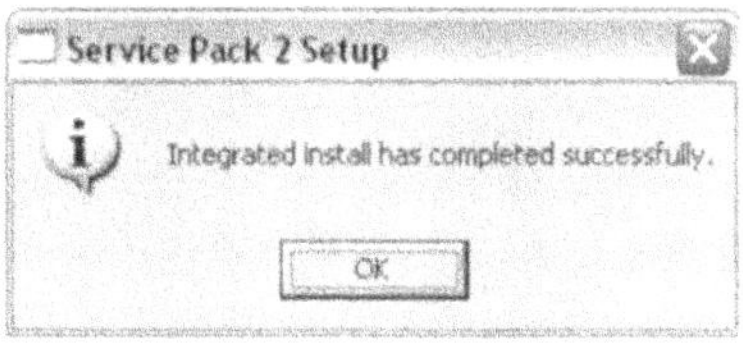

Figure 5.4
The slipstreaming process finishes with success.

5.2 Remote Boot Floppy Generator (RBFG)

If there are clients on the network whose NIC doesn't support the PXE .99c standard, then it isn't possible to use the standard RIS installation procedure. The NIC must support the PXE .99c standard. One way to address this problem is to create a remote boot floppy generator (RBFG) disk. The RBFG disk gives the possibility to deploy RIS images to clients via this boot disk. The RBFG disk only knows about 20 standard chipsets. If the chipset isn't on the list, it will not work. It is unfortunately not possible to add additional chipsets to the RBFG disk. This may change in later versions of the RBFG tool. Nearly all new NICs support the PXE .99c standard today.

5.2.1 How it works

Put the disk in a client computer, make sure the BIOS boots on the floppy disk first, and press F12 when the PXE boot is finished. After the boot disk has initiated the first connection to the RIS server, the RBFG boot disk can be removed, and the installation process continues to install. The RGFG boot disk can help companies with old NIC computers to take advantage of RIS servers quickly and easily.

5.2.2 How to create the RBFG disk

To create the RBFG disk, there must be access to the right program in the RIS file structure. This program is a standard part of the RIS installation and can be found in all RIS installations. The program is called *rbfg.exe* and is found under *\\servername\Remoteinstall\admin\I386:*

1. Open run.
2. Write *\\servername\Remoteinstall\admin\I386\rbfg.exe*. This will start the RBFG program. (See Figure 5.5.)

   In some cases, a dialog box will be presented, explaining the risk of opening the file over the network (Figure 5.6). Press Open to continue with the RBFG tool.

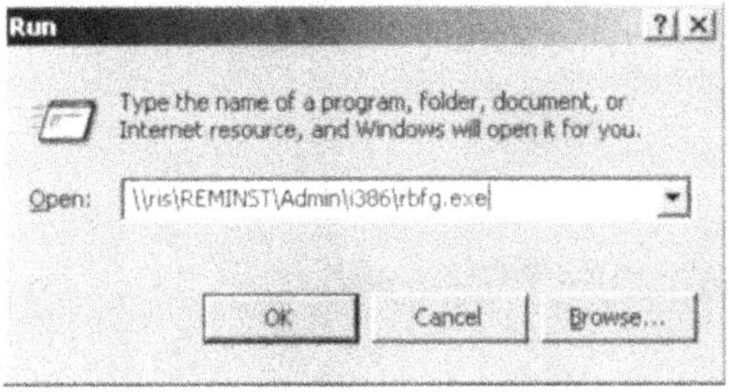

Figure 5.5 *The command to begin creation of the RBFG boot disk*

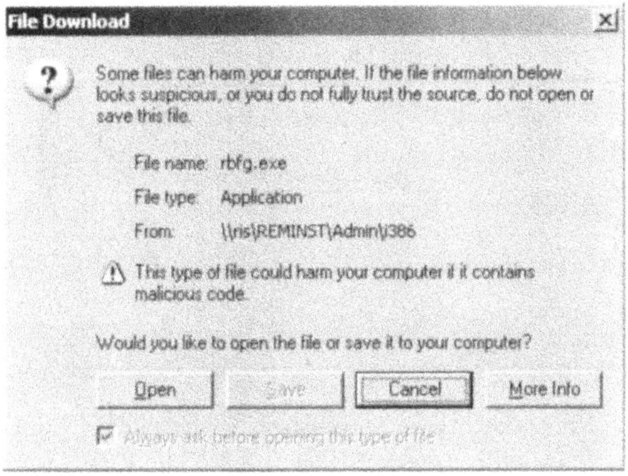

Figure 5.6 *The download dialog box for opening or saving the RBFG.exe file, or canceling the process. Press Open to continue creation of the RBFG boot disk.*

3. Click Create Disk (Figure 5.7).
4. Insert a floppy disk when asked.
5. The RBFG tool will verify the floppy disk, delete all information on the disk, and create the boot disk (Figure 5.8).

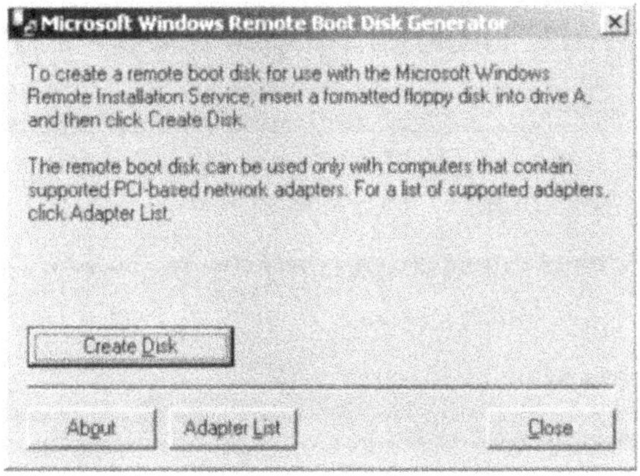

Figure 5.7 *The RBFG program dialog box. Press Create Disk to create a boot disk. The adapter list will produce an overview of all chipsets supported by the RBFG tool.*

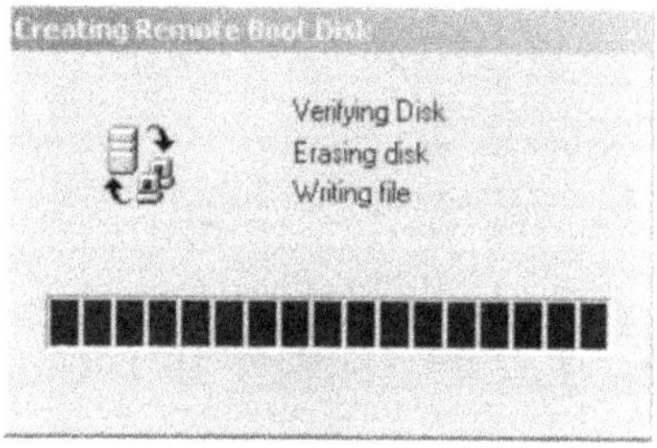

Figure 5.8 *When creating a RBFG boot disk, the Wizard will first delete all information on the disk.*

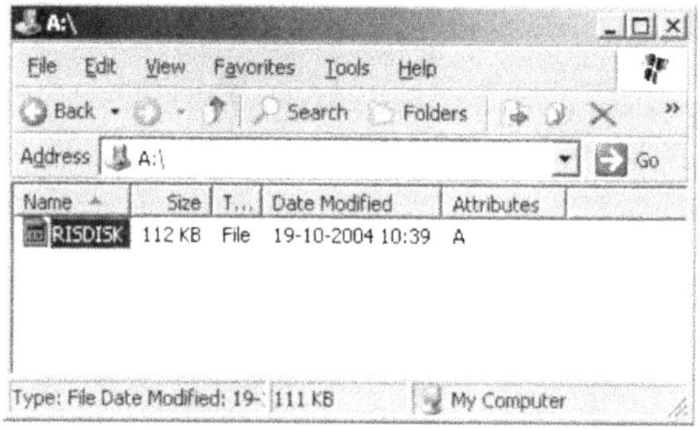

Figure 5.9 *Contents of a new RBFG boot disk*

When the process is finished, a new RBFG boot disk containing only one binary file is created (Figure 5.9). The RBFG boot disk is now ready to be tested on the client's computers that don't support the PXE .99c standard. Remember, it is not possible to add additional chipsets to the RBFG disk.

When using the RBFG tool, no Global Unique Identifier (GUID) number is involved. The RBFG tool covers this issue by using the MAC address on the NIC and applying 20 zeroes to the MAC address.

5.2.3 Network chipset supported by RIS boot disk

The RBFG boot disk isn't compatible with all chipsets. The RBFG tool can handle approximately 20 chipsets—there is no way to extend the RBFG boot disk to contain more chipsets.

The chipsets that are supported are listed below.

- 3Com 3C900B-Combo
- 3Com 3C900B-FL
- 3Com 3C900B-TPC

- 3Com 3C900B-TPO
- 3Com 3C900-Combo
- 3Com 3C900-TPO
- 3Com 3C905B-Combo
- 3Com 3C905B-FX
- 3Com 3C905B-TX
- 3Com 3C905C-TX
- 3Com 3C905-T4
- 3Com 3C905-TX
- 3Com MiniPCI
- Accton MPX5030
- Allied Telesyn 2500TX
- AMD PCnet Adapters
- Compaq NetFlex 100
- Compaq NetFlex 110
- Compaq NetFlex 3
- DEC DE450
- DEC DE500
- HP DeskDirect 10/100TX
- Intel Pro 10+
- Intel Pro 100+
- Intel Pro 100B
- Realtek RTL8029
- Realtek RTL8139
- SMC 1211TX
- SMC 8432
- SMC 9332
- SMC 9432
- SMC EN1209D-TX5

Note: The RIS boot disk generator only supports PCI-based network cards (i.e., ISA, EISA, and Token Ring cards are not supported).

Wireless NICs aren't supported in RIS installations. This may change in later versions of the wireless standard.

5.3 RIS Group Policy

There exists only one Group Policy with four options, which can be used in Active Directory regarding RIS services. This section covers these options and settings. The Policy is located under *User Configuration\Windows Settings\Remote Installation Services* and has the following four options (see Figure 5.10):

- *Automatic Setup.* Using this option, the client only needs to provide a username, password, and domain for a full RIS installation. The client doesn't need to know anything about RIS or images.
- *Custom Setup.* Using this option, the client has the choice to provide a computer name and the OU location of the computer account. It's possible to modify the screen by changing the standard OSC file to,

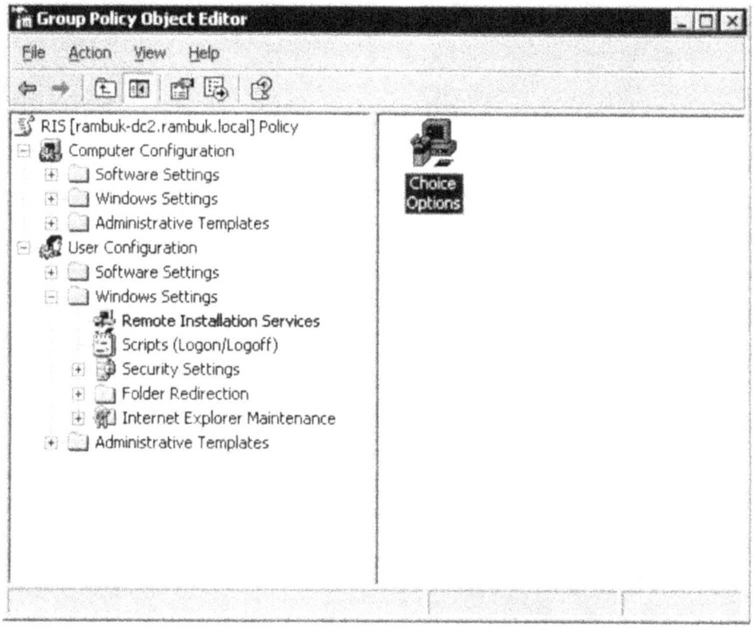

Figure 5.10
The location for the RIS Group Policy.

for example, IP address, subnet mask, and so on. More about that topic will be discussed later.

- *Restart Setup.* Using this option, the client must be allowed to restart an RIS installation if the first installation fails.
- *Tools.* This option can be used in conjunction with third-party tools. For example, we could apply a BIOS update by using the RIS server or configure a RAID controller.

All of these Group Policy options can have three states (see Figure 5.11):

1. *Enabled.* The policy will be applied.
2. *Disabled.* The policy will not be applied.
3. *Not Configured.* The policy is neutral.

These policies can be applied on all levels in Active Directory from domain level to a single OU, or the RIS policy can be linked to multiple OUs. For example, one OU could have an automatic policy for standard users, and the IT Support OU could have Automatic, Custom, and Restart. This will give the option to provide different interfaces to different users.

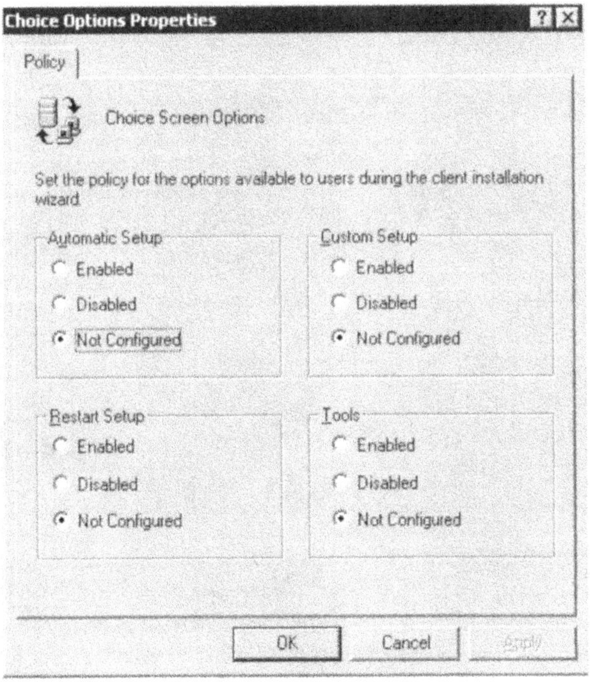

Figure 5.11 *The four installation options for RIS Group Policy.*

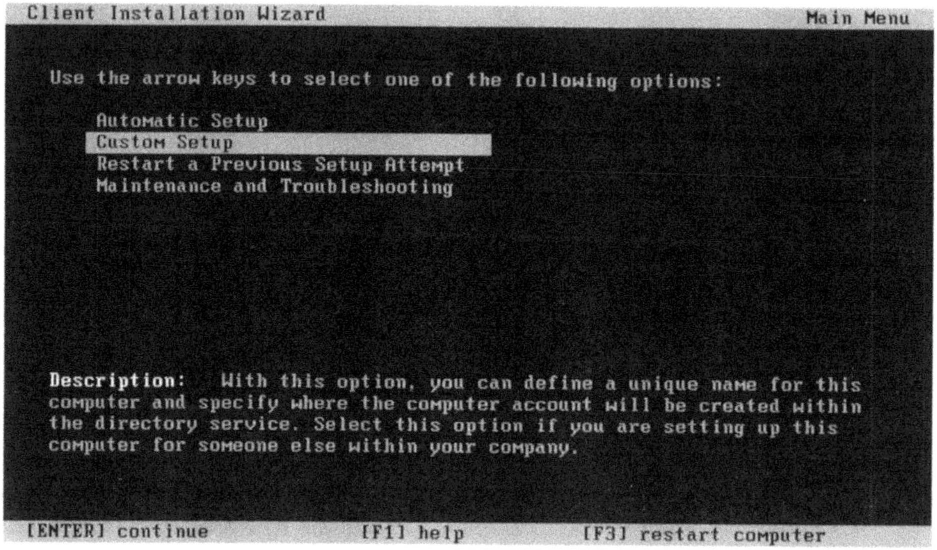

Client Installation Wizard
Main Menu
Use the arrow keys to select one of the following options:
Automatic Setup
Custom Setup
Restart a Previous Setup Attempt
Maintenance and Troubleshooting
Description: With this option, you can define a unique name for this computer and specify where the computer account will be created within the directory service. Select this option if you are setting up this computer for someone else within your company.
[ENTER] continue
[F1] help
[F3] restart computer

Figure 5.12 *The Main Menu page reflects the settings made in RIS Group Policy.*

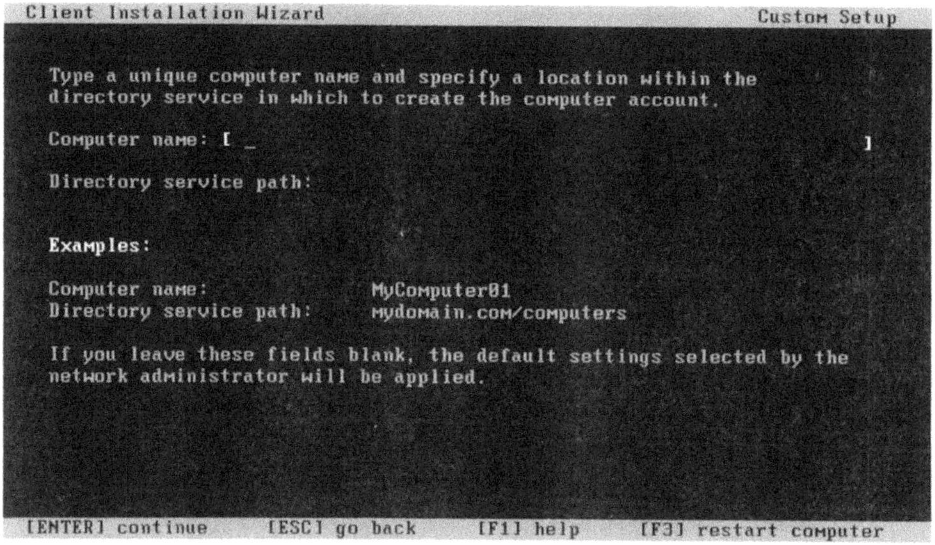

Client Installation Wizard
Custom Setup
Type a unique computer name and specify a location within the directory service in which to create the computer account.
Computer name: [_]
Directory service path:
Examples:
Computer name: MyComputer01
Directory service path: mydomain.com/computers
If you leave these fields blank, the default settings selected by the network administrator will be applied.
[ENTER] continue
[ESC] go back
[F1] help
[F3] restart computer

Figure 5.13 *By selecting the Custom Setup, the user can name the client computer account and enter the location of the client computer in Active Directory. If the fields are left blank, the standard naming convention and location are used.*

Changing any of these policies affects the layout of the standard OSC screen. If RIS Group Policy isn't used, then the standard screen will only display automatically for a brief moment; too fast for the human eye. By changing the standard RIS policy, then the layout of the CIW screens is presented in another order. Let's look at the changes. The first screen gives the option to use all of the possibilities that were specified in the RIS policy. Let's go through the *Custom Policy.* (See Figure 5.12.)

By choosing *Custom Setup,* there is an option to specify the computer name and the location of the OU, where the computer account must be placed (Figure 5.13). If any of the options aren't specified, then the default settings are applied.

5.4 Summary

In most cases, a service pack needs to be integrated into a basic OS image. The process is fairly simple and must be done before the image is ready to be added to the RIS server. It must be a network and localized version of the service pack.

The RBFG tool is essential when the client's computer doesn't support PXE .99c. The RBFG disk contains multiple hardware chipsets from a large variety of hardware vendors. There is no tool to extend the RBFG disk to contain more chipsets, but perhaps Microsoft will change this in an updated version of the tool.

Changing the standard RIS Group Policy will provide more options for how the RIS installations will behave. The possibility of having more than one RIS Group Policy can also give the IT staff the ability to restart an RIS installation if it fails or use a custom setup in the RIS installation.

6

The Setup Information File

In the previous chapter we looked briefly at the SIF, and we showed you how to edit it to add support for OEM drivers, how to set up a path to your OEM drivers, and how to ignore driver signing. These were the three key changes we had to make in order to extend the driver support for client installations. However, there is a lot more to the SIF than what we have shown you previously.

In this chapter, we'll explore the many possibilities of configuring a client installation using the answer file. We will explain how to use it, how to edit it, and how to tune it to address your specific requirements.

Highlights:

- Understanding what an answer file is
- Diving into answer file sections
- Understanding how to modify installation options

6.1 SIF architecture and functionality

The SIF is the basic building block of deploying a client installation using Remote Installation Services; look at it as a sort of "menu card" for the client installation you are making. This is where you choose, select, and deselect from a variety of options, settings, and the like to create a computer that looks exactly how you want it to look.

In other words, it lists the characteristics applied to a client installation. It is maintained in a single text file and uses the .sif context. A standard SIF is automatically generated upon having applied an image to the Remote Installation Services server; it is named ristndrd.sif. The SIF can be created and edited manually, or you can create an answer file automatically using Setup Manager. Using Setup Manager to create an answer file and then editing it manually after creation can be an easy way to get around addressing specific needs of setup. Use of Setup Manager is discussed in Chapter 7. In this chapter, we go into detail about editing the default answer file manually.

The SIF is used to configure a client installation in the following ways:

- OEM drivers are defined.
- GUIRunOnce commands are defined.
- General settings for the image are defined.
- Components (e.g., games, accessories) can be selected or deselected from the image.

6.2 SIF directory

The SIF is located in the RemoteInstall\Setup\[Language]\Images\[Friendly name of image]\I386\Templates folder. This is the default location of the file, and whenever an image is added to the Remote Installation Services server, a default SIF will be written to this location below the image in question. One default SIF is made on a per-image basis. It is possible to maintain multiple (different) SIFs in the \Templates folder belonging to the image in question.

6.3 How the SIF works

The SIF is divided into sections. Each section contains entries defining different characteristics and settings, which are applied to the image. The structure of the SIF is illustrated as follows:

```
[Section description 1]
Key 1 = Value 1
Key 1 = Value 2
[Section description 2]
Key 1 = Value 1
Key 1 = Value 2
[Section description n]
Key 1 = Value 1
Key 1 = Value 2
```

- A *section* is a description of a specific subset of settings.
- The *Key* term represents a definition of a characteristic functionality, which is applied to the client installation in question. The *Value* term represents the setting of the given key.

- The same key cannot be entered more than once.
- The semicolon (;) is used to remark a key, thus disabling it.
- Upon adding an OS to the RIS installation, a default answer file, ristrnd.sif, is created.

  The default sections provided are the following:

- [Data] defines how to handle disk partitions on the client computer.
- [Unattended] defines that the client installation is unattended and which folder will be used to host the operating system.
- [User data] defines the computer name and contains name/company field information.
- [GuiUnattended] defines the local administrator password and sets the time zone.
- [Networking] defines which networking components to install.
- [Identification] defines whether to join a workgroup or a domain.

  This is an example of a default SIF for a Windows XP client installation:

```
[data]
floppyless = "1"
msdosinitiated = "1"
OriSrc = "\\%SERVERNAME%\RemInst\%INSTALLPATH%\
%MACHINETYPE%"
OriTyp = "4"
LocalSourceOnCD = 1
DisableAdminAccountOnDomainJoin = 1

[SetupData]
OsLoadOptions = "/noguiboot /fastdetect"
SetupSourceDevice = "\Device\LanmanRedirector\
%SERVERNAME%\RemInst\%INSTALLPATH%"

[Unattended]
OemPreinstall = no
FileSystem = LeaveAlone
ExtendOEMPartition = 0
TargetPath = \WINDOWS
OemSkipEula = yes
InstallFilesPath = "\\%SERVERNAME%\RemInst\
%INSTALLPATH%\%MACHINETYPE%"
LegacyNIC = 1
```

```
[UserData]
FullName = "%USERFIRSTNAME% %USERLASTNAME%"
OrgName = "%ORGNAME%"
ComputerName = %MACHINENAME%

[GuiUnattended]
OemSkipWelcome = 1
OemSkipRegional = 1
TimeZone = %TIMEZONE%
AdminPassword = "*"

[Display]
BitsPerPel = 16
XResolution = 800
YResolution = 600
VRefresh = 60

[Networking]

[NetServices]
MS_Server=params.MS_PSched

[Identification]
JoinDomain = %MACHINEDOMAIN%
DoOldStyleDomainJoin = Yes

[RemoteInstall]
Repartition = Yes
UseWholeDisk = Yes

[OSChooser]
Description ="Microsoft Windows XP Professional"
Help ="Automatically installs Microsoft Windows XP
Professional without prompting the user for input."
LaunchFile = "%INSTALLPATH%\%MACHINETYPE%\templates\
startrom.com"
ImageType =Flat
Version="5.1 (0)"
```

6.4 SIF best practices

A few words about maintaining SIFs in a structured manner:

- Remove or remark unnecessary entries or sections.
- Include remarks so that you know why you created an additional entry.

- Use as few answer files as possible for ease of understanding and logistics.
- Always keep an originally created answer file for reference to default values and sections.

6.5 Editing default SIF keys and values

In this section we'll look at the different sections provided in the default SIF. We'll explain what the most important keys define and show examples of how to change the values.

6.5.1 The Data section

There's really not much editing to make in this section; the data here is mostly information for the setup process whenever an image using this SIF is downloaded. It is a good idea, however, to remark the *DisableAdminAccountOnDomainJoin* key, otherwise the local computer administrator account will be disabled. Here's an example with the *DisableAdminAcocuntOnDomainJoin* key disabled using the remark ";":

```
floppyless = "1"
msdosinitiated = "1"
OriSrc = "\\%SERVERNAME%\RemInst\%INSTALLPATH%\
%MACHINETYPE%"
OriTyp = "4"
LocalSourceOnCD = 1
;DisableAdminAccountOnDomainJoin = 1
```

6.5.2 The SetupData section

The data in this section should not be edited. Again, it is used during installation initialization of the image to which the SIF applies.

6.5.3 The Unattended section

The `[Unattended]` section can contain a huge amount of keys and values that control how the computer handles tasks that would normally require user attention during installation. In Appendix C, all of these keys are described. Some of the most popular keys and values to change or add are as follows:

- *OEMPreinstall.* Change this value to yes to specify whether installation will install files and OEM drivers from the distribution folder (OEM).
- *DriverSigningPolicy.* This key specifies how to process unsigned drivers during installation. The value can be either warn, block, or ignore. You must choose the "ignore" value, otherwise installation will either not install the device driver (if the value is "block") or will stop and require user intervention (if value is "warn").
- *OEMPnPDriversPath.* This key specifies the path to one or more folders that contain OEM drivers not distributed in Drivers.cab on the Windows product CD. This would most often be the distribution folder (OEM).

Here's an example of a modified Unattended section:

```
OemPreinstall = Yes
DriverSigningPolicy = Ignore
OemPnpDriversPath = drivers\audio;drivers\nic;drivers\
video
FileSystem = LeaveAlone
ExtendOEMPartition = 0
TargetPath = \WINDOWS
OemSkipEula = yes
InstallFilesPath = "\\%SERVERNAME%\RemInst\
%INSTALLPATH%\%MACHINETYPE%"
LegacyNIC = 1
```

Please refer to Appendix C for a full list of keys available for this section.

6.5.4 The UserData section

In this section, the name/company fields are defined, and the default SIF values set these values using the variables `%USERFIRSTNAME%`, `%USERLASTNAME%`, and `%ORGNAME%`. This means that every computer installed with this image to which this SIF applies will be installed with the credentials of the installation account. If you want to avoid this, replace the variables with real names, as illustrated in the following example.

A key missing from this section in the default SIF is the *ProductID* key, which, for some reason, must always be set manually. The value for this key should be the 30-character volume license key for your Windows client. The following example shows how these changes are applied to this section. The *ProductID* in the example has been replaced by Xs.

```
FullName = "Section West"
OrgName = "Acme"
ComputerName = %MACHINENAME%
ProductID = "XXXXX-XXXXX-XXXXX-XXXXX-XXXXX"
```

Please refer to Appendix D for a full list of keys available for this section.

6.5.5 The GuiUnattended section

The *OemSkipRegional* key specifies whether to skip the Regional and Language Options page in the Mini-Setup stage. The default value of "1" means that the user will not be prompted to input regional and language options. The *OemSkipWelcome* key specifies whether to skip the Welcome page in the Mini-Setup stage. The default value of "1" means that the welcome page will not display.

The *TimeZone* key specifies the time zone of the computer. If the entry is not present, the user will be prompted to select a time zone. If you do not configure a specific time zone setting, the default time zone depends on the language version of Windows that is installed. For example, in the Japanese version, the default time zone is "GMT+9 (Osaka, Sapporo, Tokyo)." The values can also be to a fixed zone number, an index number. To learn more about index numbers for time zones, please refer to Appendix B.

In this section, the most important key is *AdminPassword.* The password value can be set manually, and it then appears in clear text. If you generate the SIF using Setup Manager, the password will become encrypted and displayed as "*". Values in this section are seldom changed, although some of the most popular keys in this section are *AutoLogon* and *AutoLogonCount* used in connection with the optional GuiRunOnce section. You can read a lot more about GuiRunOnce, *AutoLogon,* and *AutoLogonCount* in Chapter 14.

```
[GuiUnattended]
OemSkipWelcome = 1
OemSkipRegional = 1
TimeZone = %TIMEZONE%
AdminPassword = "*"
```

Please refer to Appendix B for a full list of keys available for this section.

6.5.6 The Display section

This section sets the default monitor/screen settings in the following ways:

- *BitPerPel* sets the color quality in bits.

- *XRsolution* sets the horizontal screen resolution.
- *YResolution* sets the vertical screen resolution.
- *VRefresh* sets the screen refresh rate in Hertz.

  Following is an example of modifications made to this section:

```
[Display]
BitsPerPel = 32
XResolution = 1024
YResolution = 768
VRefresh = 75
```

6.5.7 The Networking, Identification, and RemoteInstall sections

The *Networking* section generated in the default SIF contains no keys itself. However, to configure network protocols or network settings, one or more of the following sections must be included:

- *adapter_specific_protocol_section*
- Identification
- *MS_AppleTalk parameters*
- *MS_ATMArps parameters*
- *MS_ATMLANE parameters*
- *MS_ATMUni parameters*
- *MS_L2TP parameters*
- *MS_MSClient parameters*
- *MS_NetMon parameters*
- *MS_NWClient parameters*
- *MS_NWIPX parameters*
- *MS_NwSapAgent parameters*
- *MS_PPTP parameters*
- *MS_Psched parameters*
- *MS_RAS parameters*
- *MS_RasSrv parameters*
- *MS_Server parameters*

- *MS_TCPIP parameters*
- *MS_WLBS parameters*
- NetAdapters
- NetBindings
- NetClients
- NetOptionalComponents
- NetProtocols
- NetServices
- Networking
- *params.adapter instance*
- *protocol parameters section*

Note: As you can see, the networking section can contain a huge amount of stub sections, keys, values, and parameters. Using this section, you can manually configure any networking component or networking service for specific functionality. This can be essential when preparing an SIF for servers, for example. To obtain a full list of keys and stub sections that can be used, please refer to the Microsoft Windows Preinstallation Reference (ref.chm) found on the Windows XP SP2 CD.

The *NetServices* stub of the networking section generated in the default SIF section contains entries for installing network services. The *MS_Server=params.MS_PSched* entry installs the QoS Packet Scheduler.

In the identification stub of the networking section, *JoinDomain* specifies the name of the domain in which the computer participates. It is a good idea to change the variable to a real domain name. Use the NETBIOS domain name if the *DoOldStyleDomainJoin* key is set to a value of Yes.

If you do not wish to join a domain, you can join a workgroup. To do that, remark the *JoinDomain* key and add a *JoinWorkgroup* key. *JoinWorkgroup* specifies the name of the workgroup in which the computer participates. You can specify either this entry or the *JoinWorkgroup* entry, but you cannot specify both. You can also add the *MachineObjectOU* key, which specifies the full Lightweight Directory Access Protocol (LDAP) path name of the organizational unit (OU) in which the computer belongs. *Repartition* specifies whether to delete all partitions on the first drive of the client computer and reformat it with the NTFS file system. The *UseWholeDisk* key is valid only for Sysprep images.

Here's an example of the sections with only the *JoinDomain* key modified:

```
[Networking]

[NetServices]
MS_Server=params.MS_PSched

[Identification]
JoinDomain = ACME
DoOldStyleDomainJoin = Yes

[RemoteInstall]
Repartition = Yes
UseWholeDisk = Yes
```

6.5.8 The OSChooser section

The content in the OSChooser section is automatically generated from the information gathered when you added the OS in question to the Remote Installation Services server. This includes the friendly description of the image, the additional help text, which startrom to use, the image type, and the version of the operating system.

The friendly description of the image and the additional help text can be modified if you wish. It is not recommended that you modify other values.

```
[OSChooser]
Description ="Microsoft Windows XP Professional"
Help ="Automatically installs Microsoft Windows XP
Professional without prompting the user for input."
LaunchFile = "%INSTALLPATH%\%MACHINETYPE%\templates\
startrom.com"
ImageType =Flat
Version="5.1 (0)"
```

6.6 Optional sections

6.6.1 The Components section

Using this section, you can select or deselect components to be installed on the client computer. This way you can leave out unwanted features from the installation. It uses a simple context based on a simple on/off value, where on means that the feature in question will be installed, and if the value is set to off, the feature in question will not be installed. In the SIF the context is as follows:

```
[Components]
Feature name = on/off
```

Please refer to Appendix A for a full list of feature keys available for this section.

6.6.2 The GUIRunOnce section

Using the `[GuiRunOnce]` section, you can run commands to install applications, files, and so on the first time a user logs onto the computer after final installation is complete. It works together with the *Autologon* and *AutologonCount* keys from the GuiUnattended section. In the SIF, a GuiRunOnce section uses this context:

```
[GuiRunOnce]
Command0 = [command string 0]
Command1 = [command string 1]
Commandn = [command string n]
```

You can learn a lot more about GuiRunOnce in Chapter 14.

6.6.3 The RegionalSettings section

The `[RegionalSettings]` section is used to define regional settings for language, keyboard, and specific input locales. This is an example of a RegionalSettings entry in the SIF:

```
[RegionalSettings]
LanguageGroup=1
SystemLocale=00000406
UserLocale=00000406
InputLocale=0406:00000406
```

To see all options for the RegionalSettings section, please refer to the Microsoft Windows Preinstallation Reference (ref.chm) found on the Windows XP SP2 CD.

6.6.4 The TapiLocation section

Adding this section to the SIF would set up a modem using the predefined values of your choice; for example:

```
[TapiLocation]
CountryCode = 45
Dialing = Tone
AreaCode = 38
LongDistanceAccess = "0"
```

To see all options for the `[TapiLocation]` section, please refer to the Microsoft Windows Preinstallation Reference (ref.chm) found on the Windows XP SP2 CD.

6.7 Reference material

For ease of understanding, all keys and their respective values for the `[Unattended]`, `[GuiUnattended]`, `[Components]`, and `[UserData]` sections are listed in Appendices A to D at the end of this book. To see key and value options for all SIF sections, please refer to the Microsoft Windows Preinstallation Reference (ref.chm) found on the Windows XP SP2 CD. Updated reference files can be downloaded from *www.microsoft.com/windows*.

6.8 Summary

The SIF is an essential and integrated part of any Remote Installation Services installation. The SIF glues every detail together of a client installation. The file can be created either manually or by using Setup Manager, but any editing must be done manually. Different sections, keys, and values can be made to tailor every aspect of the client computer installation. Use the reference material to understand which options apply to your organization.

7

Setup Manager

This chapter covers how to install Setup Manager and how use it to create or modify SIFs. Setup Manager is a powerful tool that can help create good and correctly formatted SIFs in minutes. Setup Manager is a graphical user interface (GUI) tool that is easy to install and use. The only way to encrypt the local admin password in the SIF is using the Setup Manager; otherwise the local admin password will be on the network in clear text. The Setup Manager has changed from Windows 2000 to Windows 2003 server, and some additional features have been implemented in Windows XP Professional Service Pack 2. By using the latest version of the Setup Manager, some common tasks are easier to manage.

Highlights:

- Installing Setup Manager
- Inside Setup Manager
- Changes in the SIF

7.1 Installing Setup Manager

Microsoft has provided a fully functional Setup Manager to help deploy unattended installations, Sysprep installations, and RIS images. The Setup Manager has a GUI interface in which most parameters in the SIF are set by using a wizard. SIFs are used by RIS to determine how the client should be installed. The SIF is a basic text file in which all parameters in an RIS installation can be specified.

The Setup Manager is not installed by default, but can be extracted from the CD-ROM media containing Windows 2003 Standard or Enterprise edition. (An old version of the Setup Manager is on the Windows 2000 or Windows XP CD-ROM.) To use the Setup Manager from Windows XP

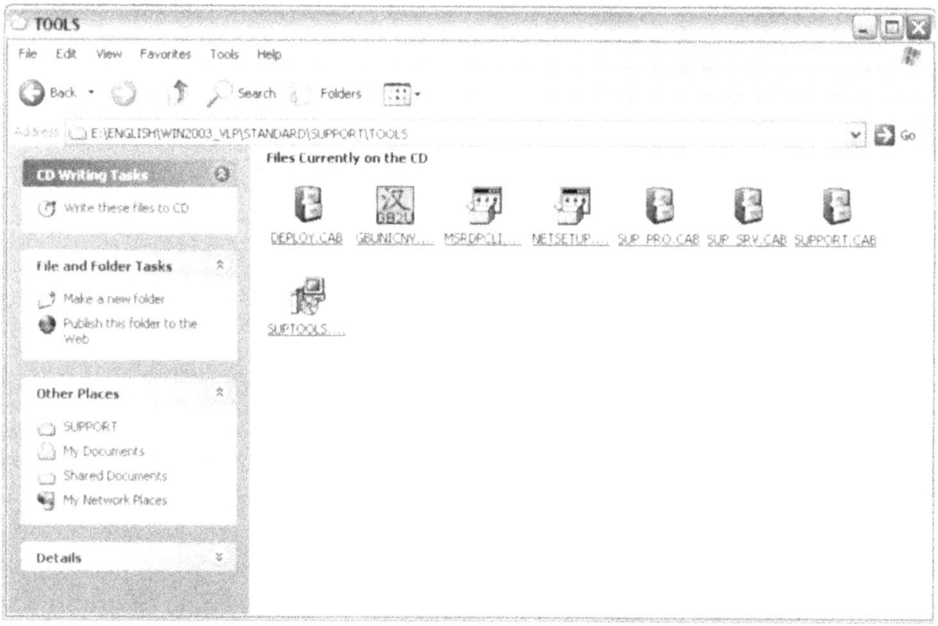

Figure 7.1 *To install the Setup Manager, double-click on Deploy.cab.*

Professional Service Pack 2, a download of the deployment pack from Microsoft's Web site is required. The download is free.

To install the Setup Manager, follow these simple steps:

1. Insert the Windows 2003 Standard or Enterprise CD-ROM.
2. Open the *Support\Tools* folder on the CD-ROM (Figure 7.1).
3. Double-click the *Deploy.cab* file to extract it to your local hard drive.
4. Start the program by clicking *Setupmgr.exe*. The Setup Manager wizard starts. Follow the wizard to create the SIF.

There are three more files to extract; these files have all the detailed information about the Setup Manager and unattended installations. The three files' names and locations are listed here:

- I386\Unattend.txt
- Support\Tools\Deploy.cab\Ref.chm
- Support\Tools\Deploy.cab\Deploy.chm

These three files contain information about unattended installation, Sysprep, and RIS installations. The most important file is Ref.chm, which has all entries that can be used in SIFs, Sysprep files, or unattended files.

Note: If using the Setup Manager from Windows 2000 or Windows XP, then the Setup Manager will automatically apply ProductID key in the UserData section to define the license key. In Windows 2003, the right key is ProductKey. Today both settings are acceptable, but this could change in the future.

Microsoft has released a new version of Setup Manager in the release of Windows XP Professional Service Pack 2. This deploy package can be downloaded directly from Microsoft's Web site, free of charge. This version of Setup Manager corrects minor mistakes in the Proxy, FavoritesEx, Branding, URL, and GuiRunOnce sections. Also, the Ref.chm and Deploy.chm files are updated with new information about Windows XP Professional Service Pack 2. These files have updated information about settings for the new firewall in Windows XP SP2, the enhanced IE security in Windows 2003 servers, and the pop-up blocker in Windows XP SP2 Internet Explorer. In future releases of Microsoft clients and servers OS, these files will be updated to reflect the new technology and services in these new products.

7.2 Inside Setup Manager

This section will provide a walkthrough of Setup Manager. To run the program, double-click *Setupmgr.exe.*

1. The first entry in Setup Manager is the *Welcome* page, and the only choice is to click Next (Figure 7.2).
2. The *New or Existing Answer file* page will ask you to create a new answer file or modify an existing one (Figure 7.3). It's possible to open an existing SIF and correct entries in that file.
3. The *Type of Setup* page gives three choices: to create an unattended setup file, to create a Sysprep file, or to create an RIS SIF (Figure 7.4).

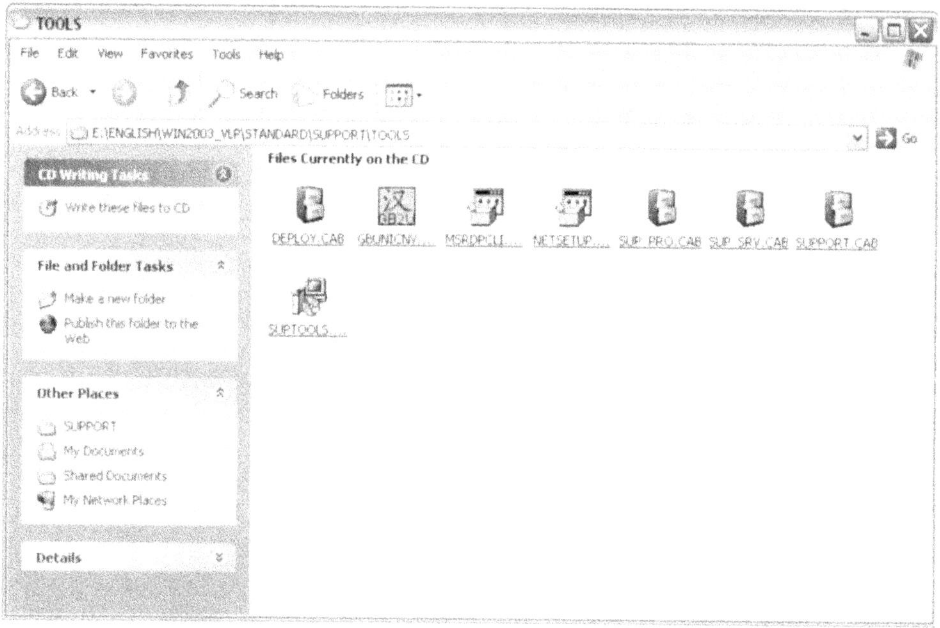

Figure 7.1 *To install the Setup Manager, double-click on Deploy.cab.*

Professional Service Pack 2, a download of the deployment pack from Microsoft's Web site is required. The download is free.

To install the Setup Manager, follow these simple steps:

1. Insert the Windows 2003 Standard or Enterprise CD-ROM.
2. Open the *Support\Tools* folder on the CD-ROM (Figure 7.1).
3. Double-click the *Deploy.cab* file to extract it to your local hard drive.
4. Start the program by clicking *Setupmgr.exe.* The Setup Manager wizard starts. Follow the wizard to create the SIF.

There are three more files to extract; these files have all the detailed information about the Setup Manager and unattended installations. The three files' names and locations are listed here:

- I386\Unattend.txt
- Support\Tools\Deploy.cab\Ref.chm
- Support\Tools\Deploy.cab\Deploy.chm

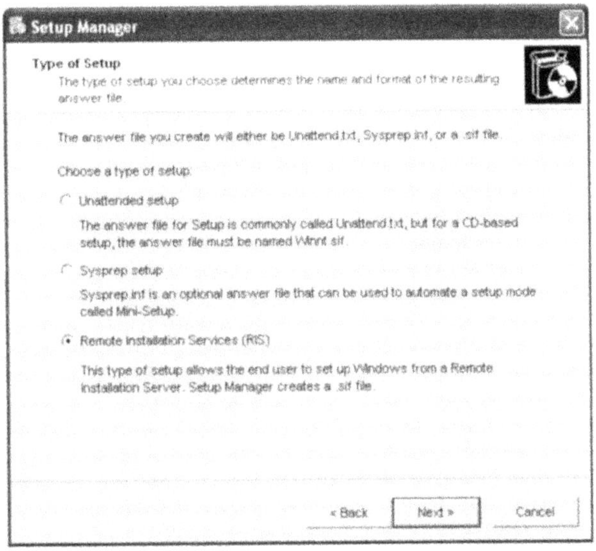

Figure 7.4
The Setup Manager allows you three types: Unattended, Sysprep, or RIS.

5. The *User Interactive* page gives different options for how the user can interact under the RIS installation (Figure 7.6):
   - *User controlled.* The user can change default options.
   - *Fully automated.* All answers are described and the user can't change them. This option is the most common.

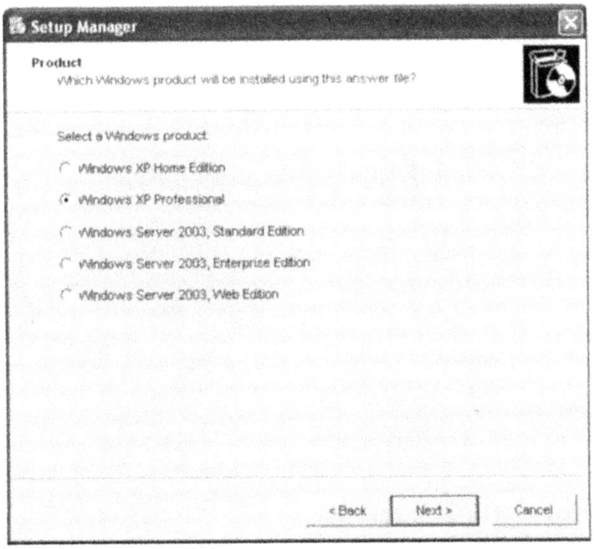

Figure 7.5
The supported OSs are displayed on the Product page.

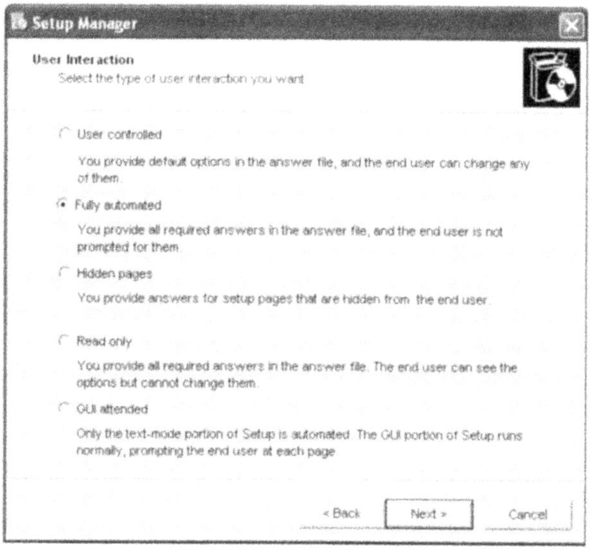

Figure 7.6 *User interaction options.*

- *Hidden pages.* Default answers are hidden from the user.
- *Read only.* The user can see all of the default settings from the answer file but cannot change any of them.
- *GUI attended.* Only the text mode is automated. The GUI mode runs manually, but the user must provide the answers to each page.

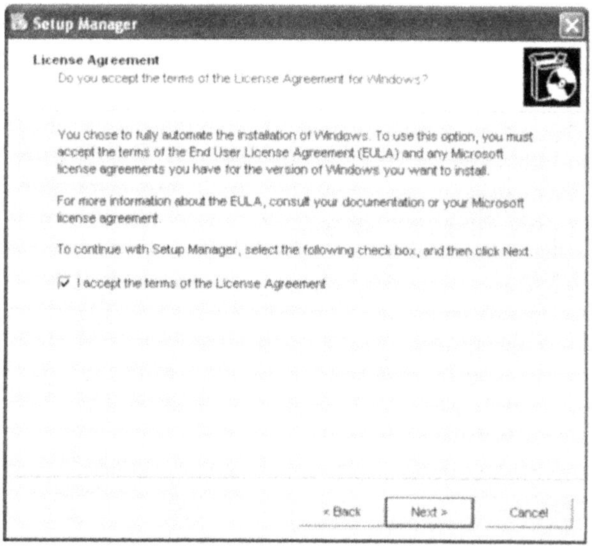

Figure 7.7 *Before the wizard can continue, the terms of the License Agreement must be accepted.*

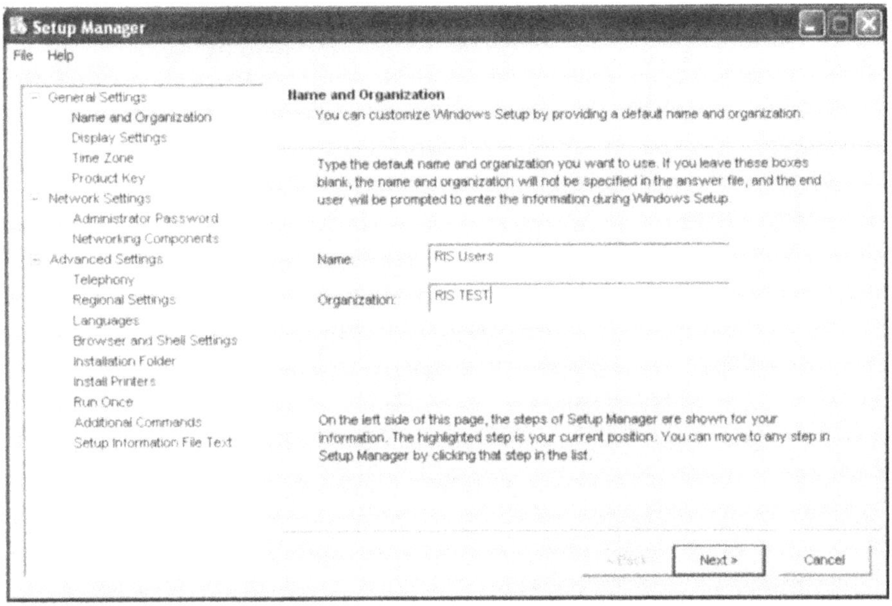

Figure 7.8 *Provide a name and an organization name to the wizard.*

6. To continue the process, the "accept the license" checkbox on the *License Agreement* page must be checked off (Figure 7.7).

7. Next is the Name and Organization page (Figure 7.8). The installation and organization names must be provided.

8. The next page is *Display Settings*. Provide the settings that will apply to all computers in your network (e.g., 600 × 800 with 32-bit colors). There is an option to add additional customization on this page by clicking *Custom*. (See Figure 7.9.)

9. The next setting is the *Time Zone* page (Figure 7.10). The default setting is Set Same as Server; otherwise the correct time zone can be set here.

10. The next page is the *Product Key* (Figure 7.11). A multivolume License key is normally entered here when deploying Windows XP Professional clients, or a standard product key to Windows 2000 clients. A multivolume license key is used to prevent a client's computer from registering over the Internet. To ensure a fully automated installation, a correct license key is needed.

11. The next page is the *Administrator Password* page (Figure 7.12). This page allows you to create an admin password and provides

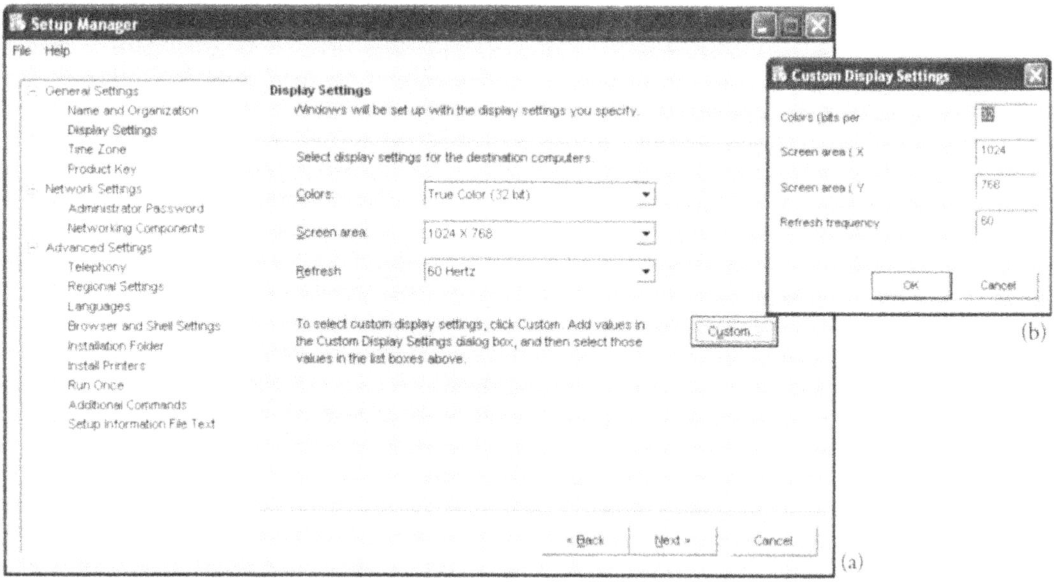

Figure 7.9 *The Display Settings page (a). Video layout is defined here. Press Custom to further customize video settings (b).*

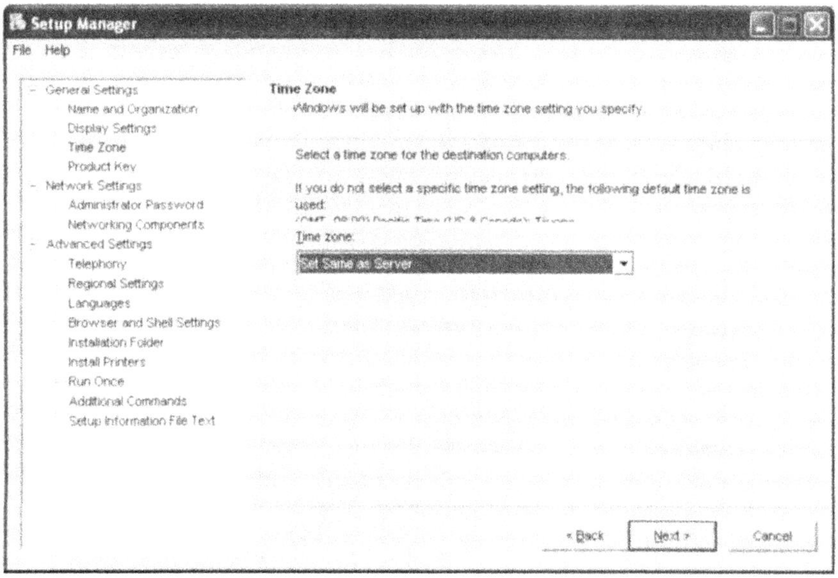

Figure 7.10 *The Time Zone page. By default, the wizard uses the same time zone as the server.*

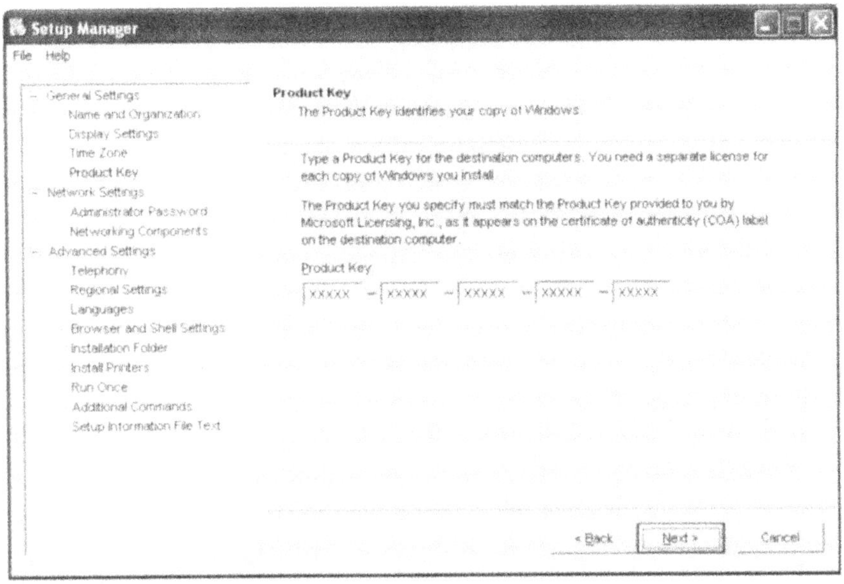

Figure 7.11 *The product key must be correct or the RIS client installation process will stop. The product key is written into the SIF.*

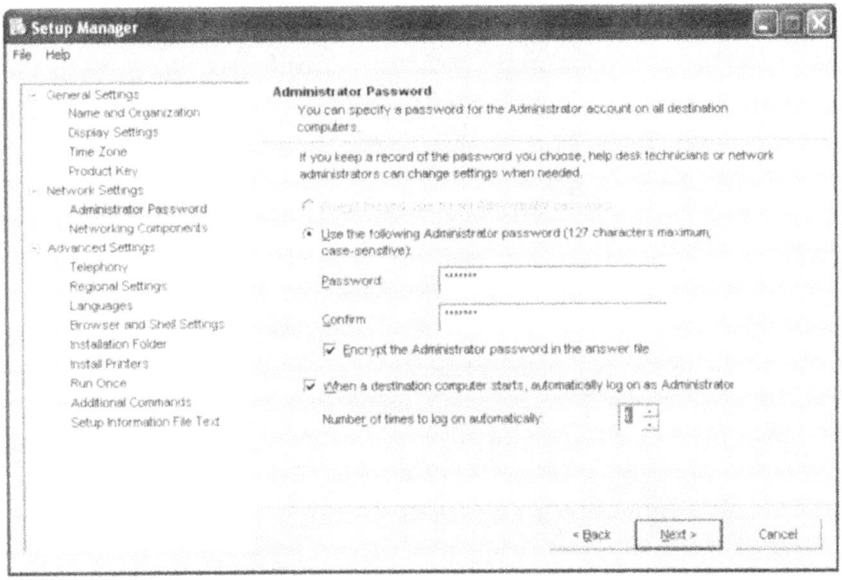

Figure 7.12 *The Administrator Password page.*

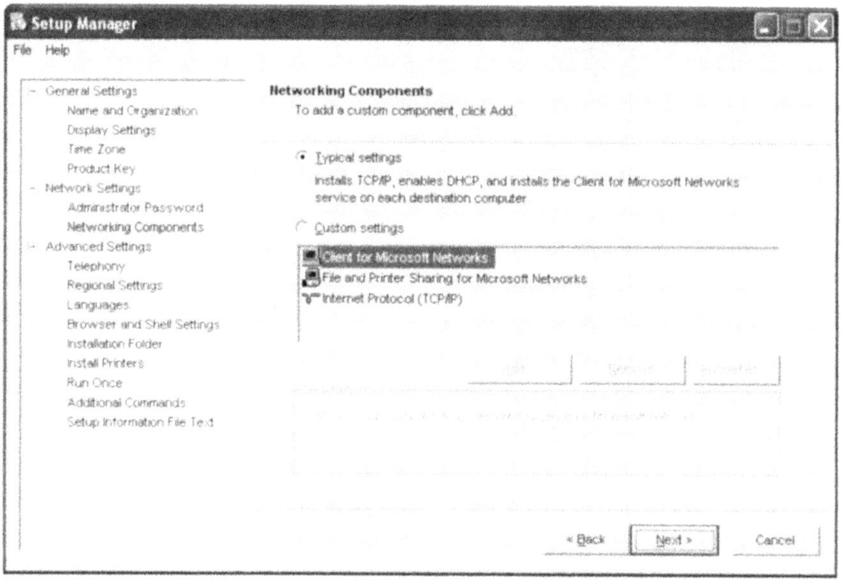

Figure 7.13 *The Network Components page, where all options about network protocols are defined.*

the option to encrypt the password in the SIF. Only with Setup Manager can the Administrator password be encrypted. Another option is to set "auto-logon" with the first computer boot. By using "auto-logon" with the first reboot, the option to use *GuiRunOnce* in the SIF is ready. More about *GuiRunOnce* later. Also, the number of "auto-logons allowed" is specified on this page.

12. The next page is the *Network Components* settings (Figure 7.13). In most cases, the default settings will be correct. It is possible to provide custom settings (e.g., see Figure 7.14, TCP/IP settings).

13. The next page is *Telephony* (Figure 7.15). Apply any choice and click Next.

14. The *Regional Settings* page uses three different settings:

    - Use the default setting from your OS version (Figure 7.16).
    - Specify the settings in the SIF (Figure 7.17).
    - Customize the regional settings by clicking the Custom button (Figure 7.18).

15. The next page setting is to install *Additional Languages* into the OS (Figure 7.19).

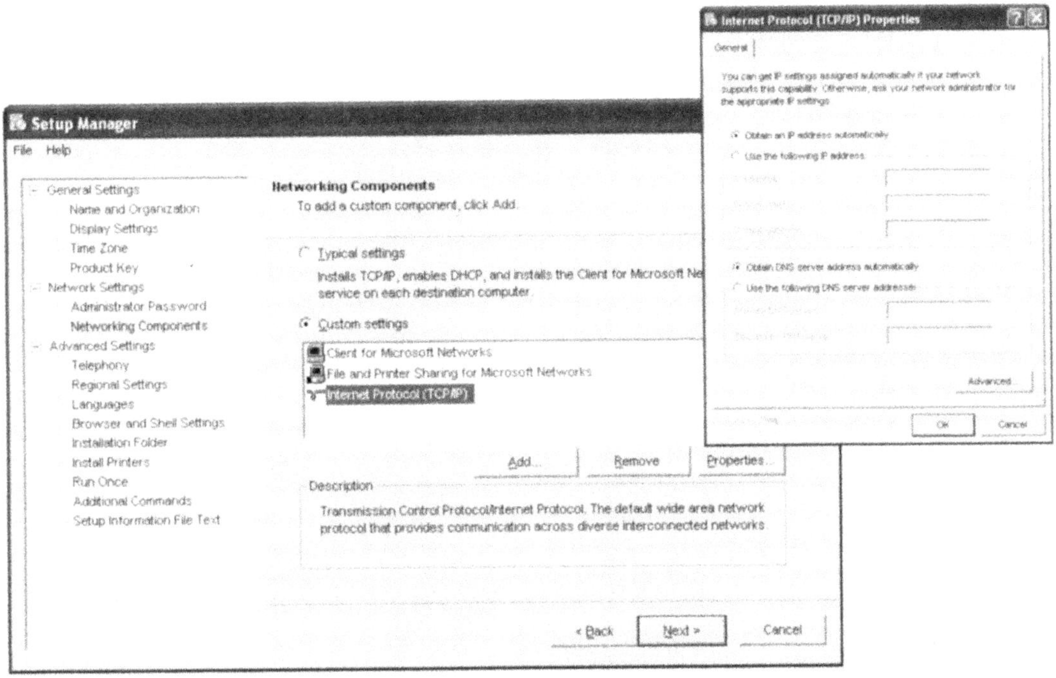

Figure 7.14 *Choosing Internet Protocols (TCP/IP) Properties gives the option to automatically obtain IP and DNS addresses or manually enter specific settings.*

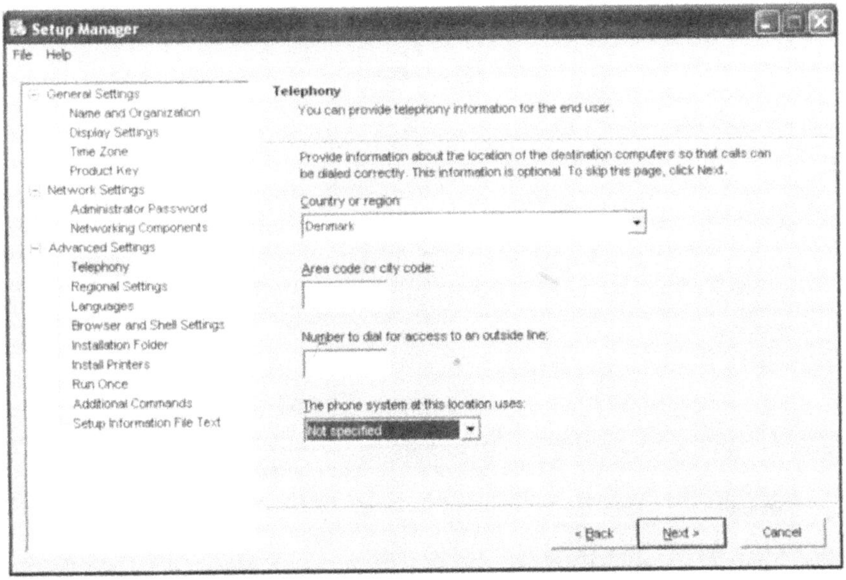

Figure 7.15 *The Telephony page. All dialout information can be configured here.*

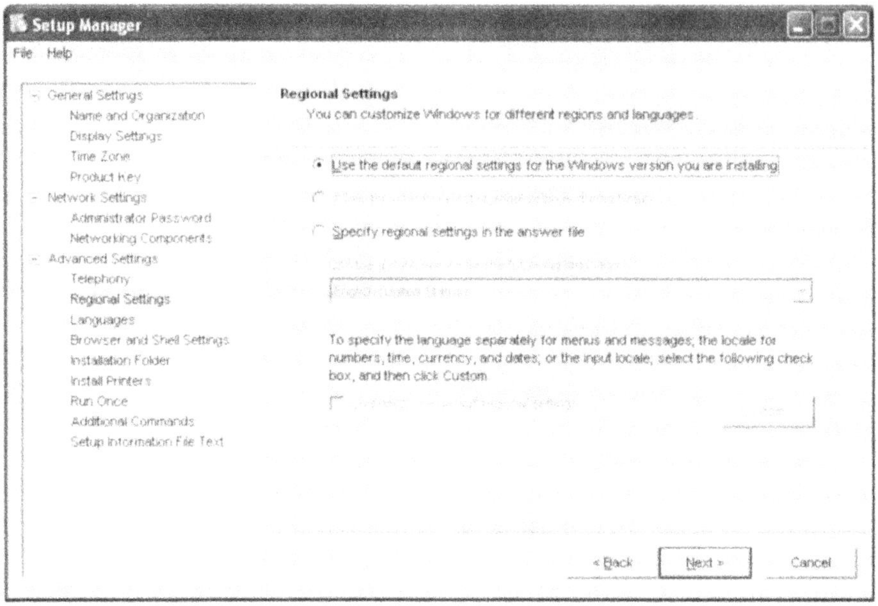

Figure 7.16 *Regional settings can be defined here.*

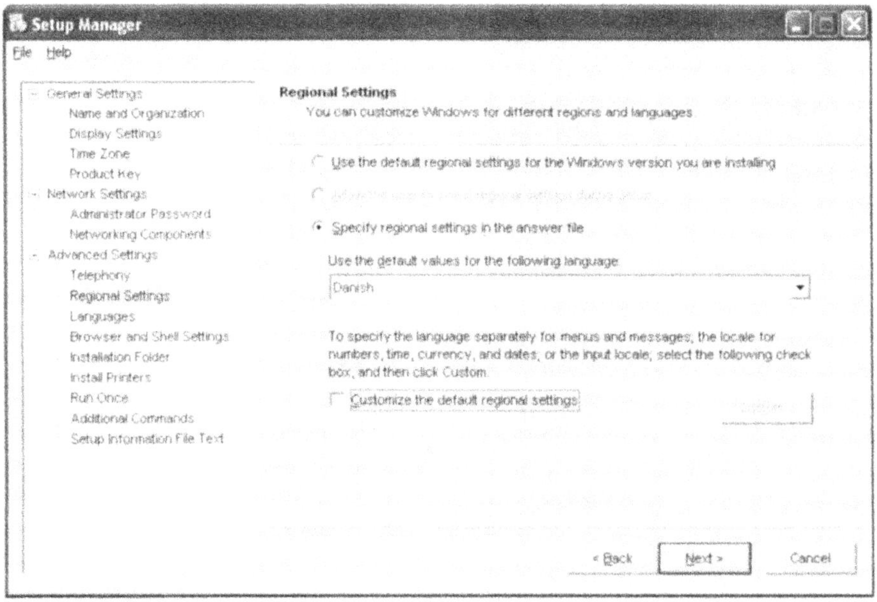

Figure 7.17 *The Danish language is set to be the standard language on all client computers that are deployed by RIS.*

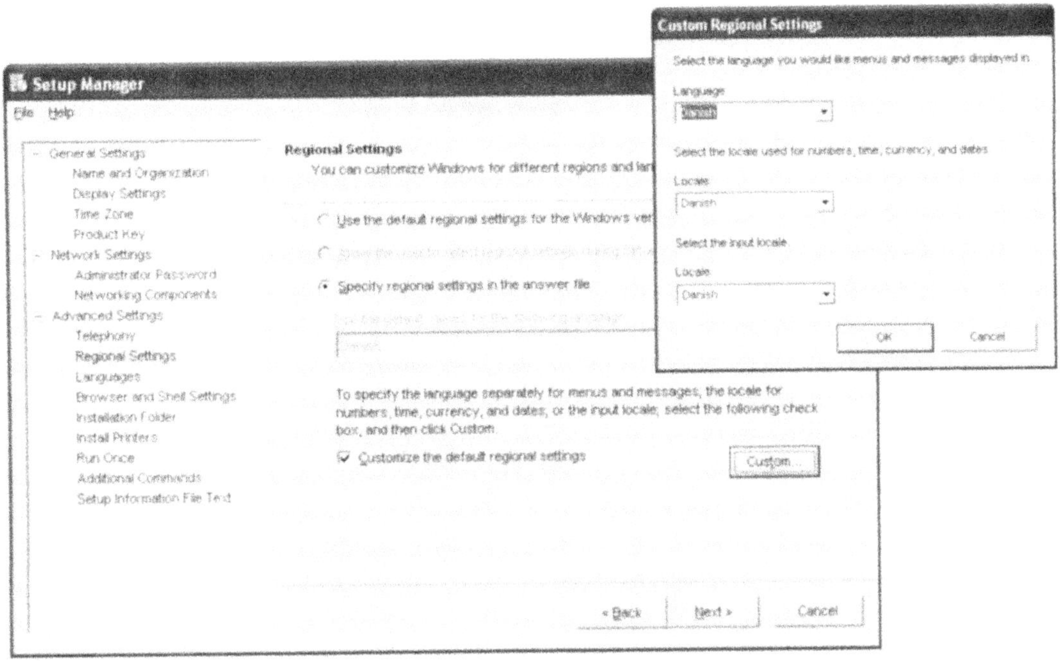

Figure 7.18 *Press Custom for more options when configuring the SIF file.*

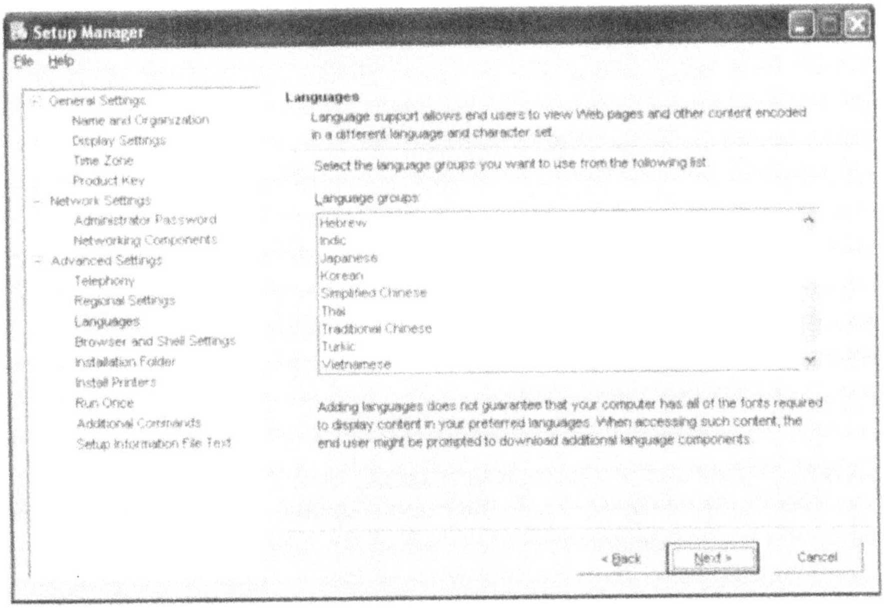

Figure 7.19 *A list of the different language groups the RIS client can have installed.*

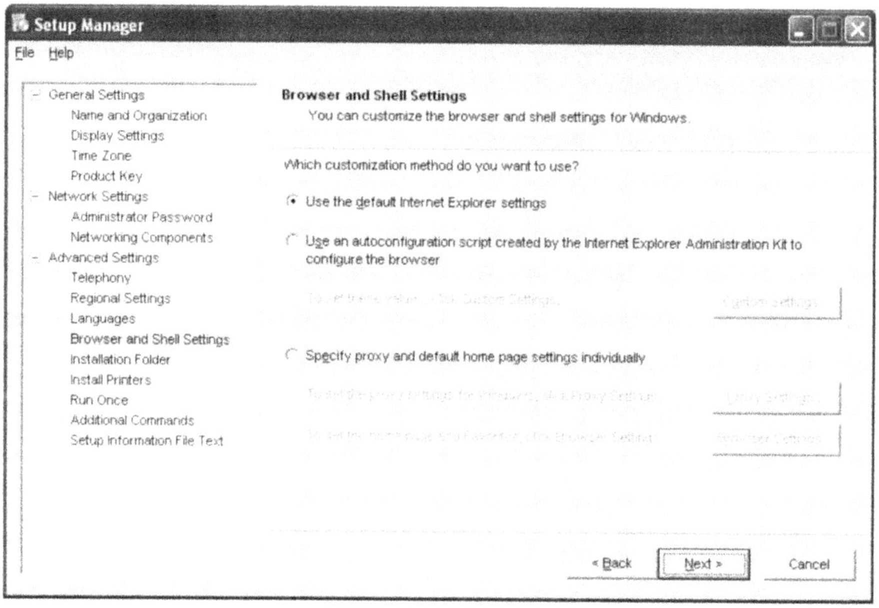

Figure 7.20 *The Browser and Shell Settings page for customizing your browser settings.*

16. The next option is the *Browser and Shell Settings* page. There are three options on this page:
    - Use the default Internet Explorer settings (Figure 7.20).
    - Use the Internet Explorer Administration Kit to configure Internet Explorer (Figure 7.21).
    - Specify proxy and default home page settings individually (Figures 7.22 through 7.24).
17. The *Installation Folder* page (Figure 7.25) gives three options to the SIF:
    - Default is a folder called Windows
    - A folder with a unique name generated by Setup
    - A folder name specified in the wizard (Figure 7.26)
18. The next page gives the option to *Install Printers* in the SIF (Figure 7.27). There is no limit to the number of printers that can be specified on this page. The syntax is *Servername**Printershare.*

    The *Run Once* setting page (Figure 7.28) will run the first time a user logs on to the computer.

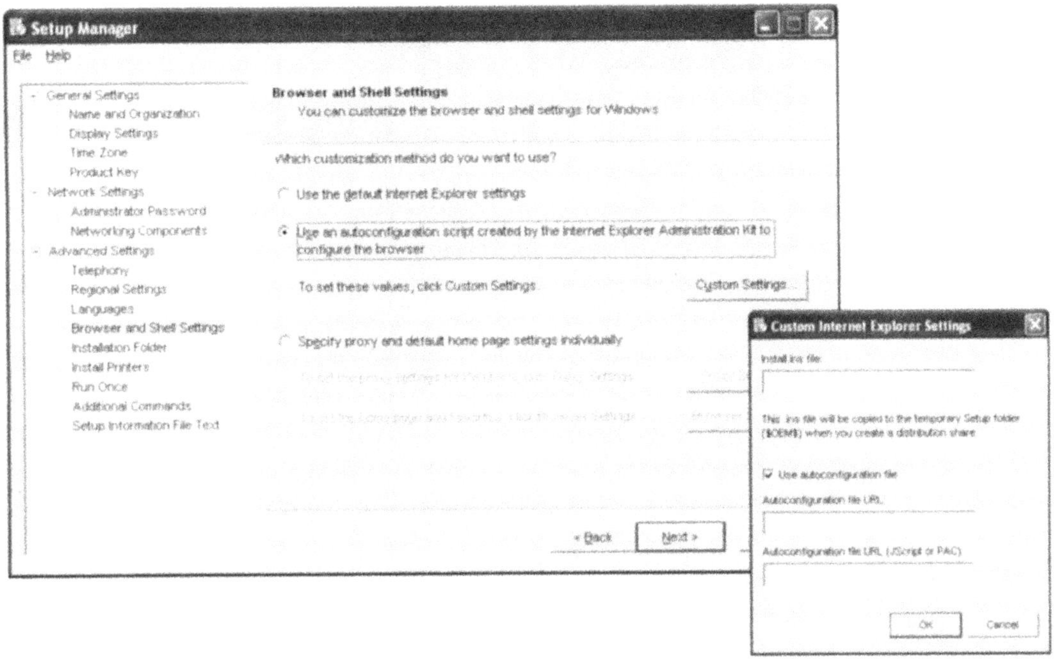

Figure 7.21 *It's possible to use a browser configuration file built by the Internet Explorer Administration Kit (IEAK) tool.*

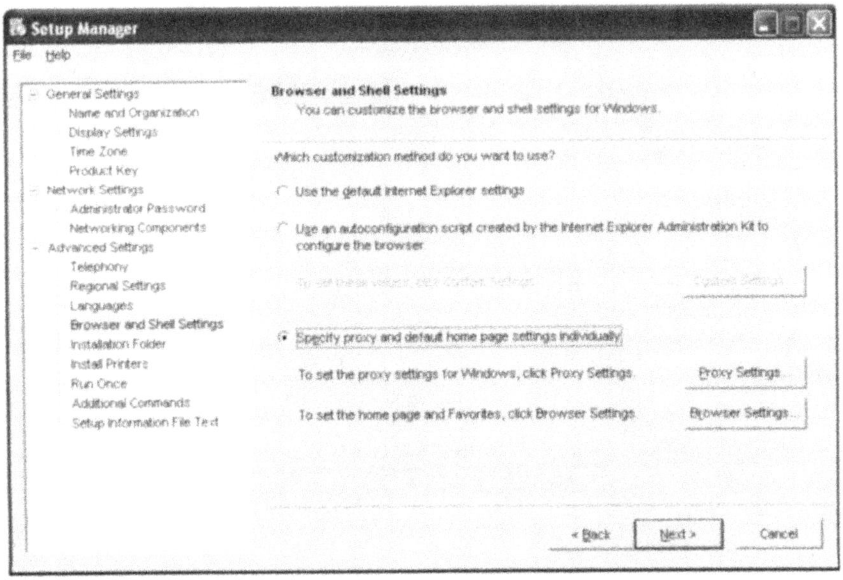

Figure 7.22 *Specifying custom Internet Explorer settings.*

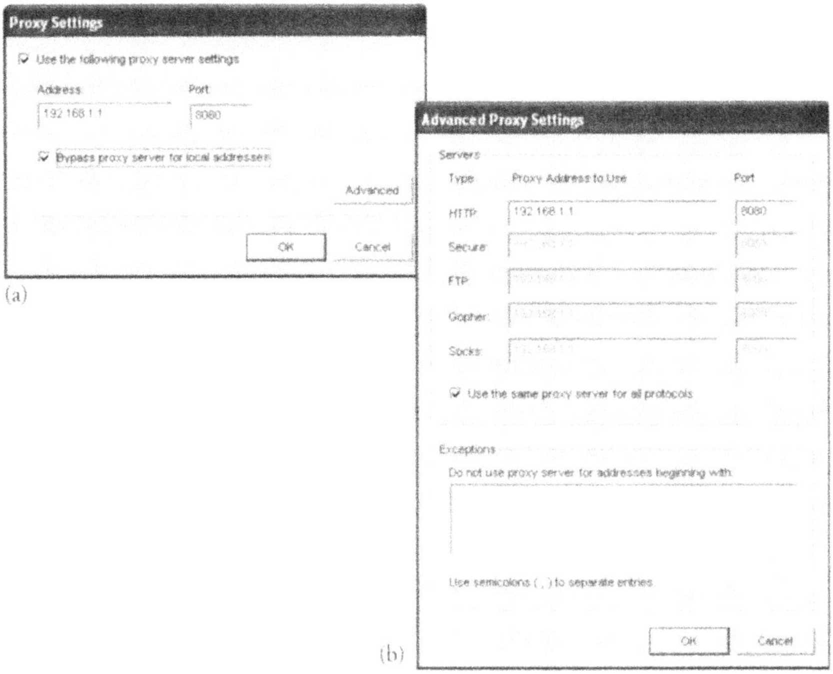

Figure 7.23 *Custom settings provides the opportunity to specify the proxy address and bypass local addresses.*

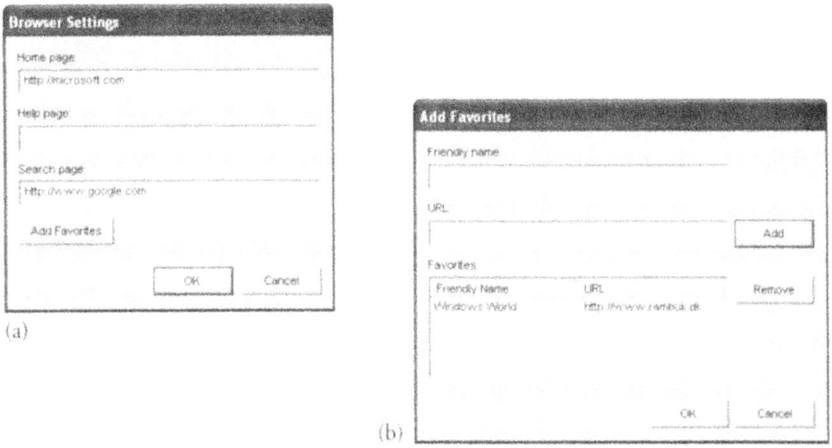

Figure 7.24 *The default home and search pages defined in the SIF (a). The list of Web sites that will populate the client's Favorites folder in Internet Explorer (b).*

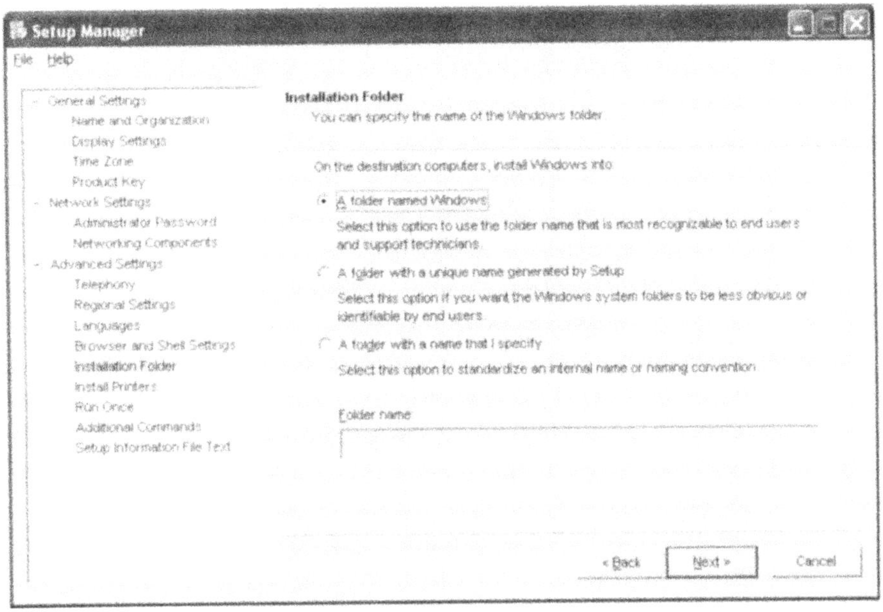

Figure 7.25 *Specify the Windows installation folder. The default is a folder named "Windows."*

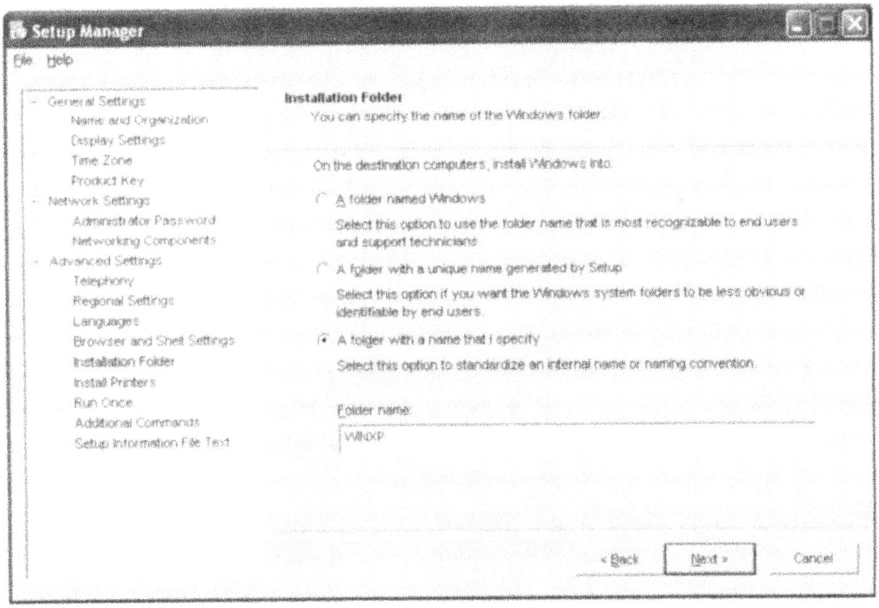

Figure 7.26 *A custom folder name is chosen in the wizard. All client computers will be installed in the folder named "WINXP."*

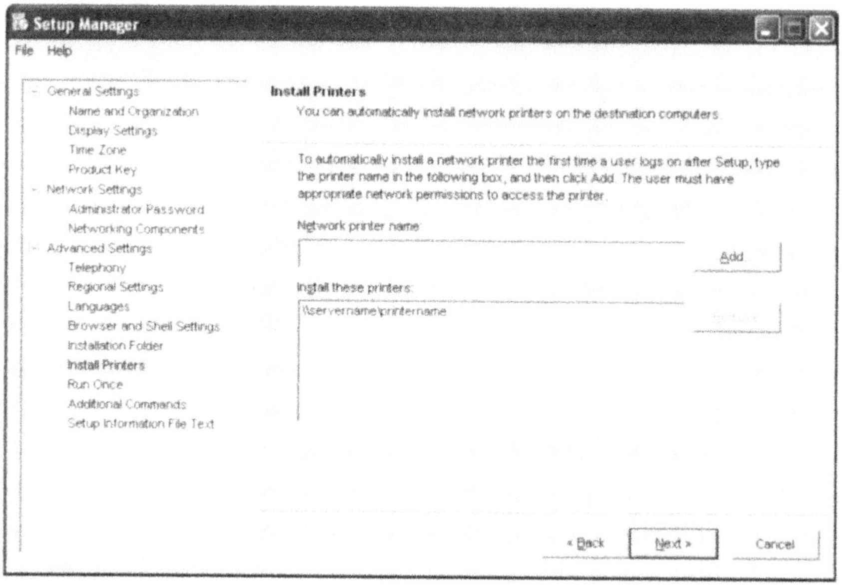

Figure 7.27 *Installing network printers in Setup Manager.*

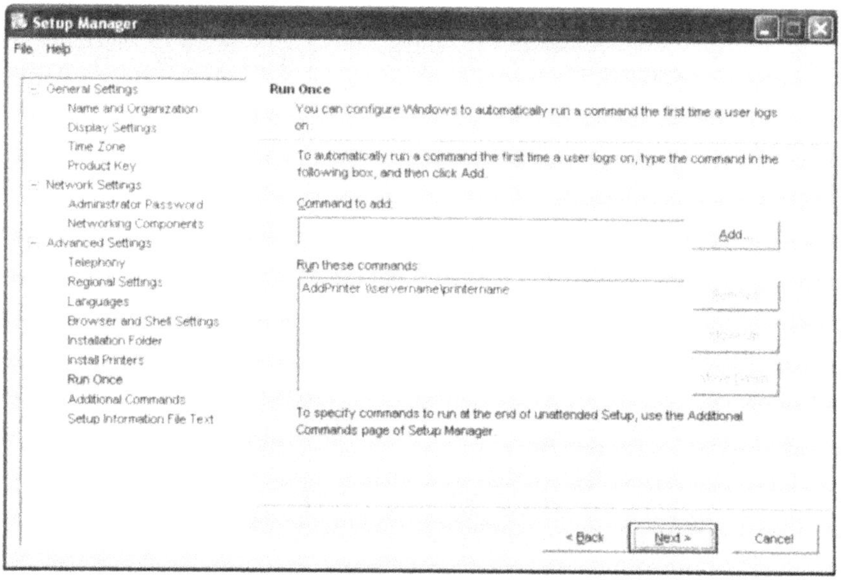

Figure 7.28 *The Run Once page gives the option to add additional commands to the standard RIS installation. The selected command will only run once, after installation is complete.*

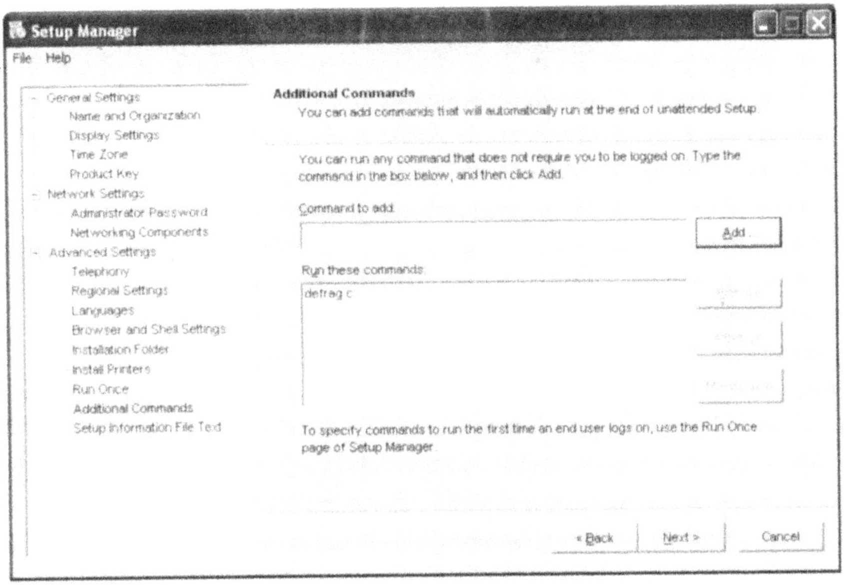

Figure 7.29 *The Additional Command page.*

19. The *Additional Commands* page (Figure 7.29) gives the option to run programs without logging on to the computer.

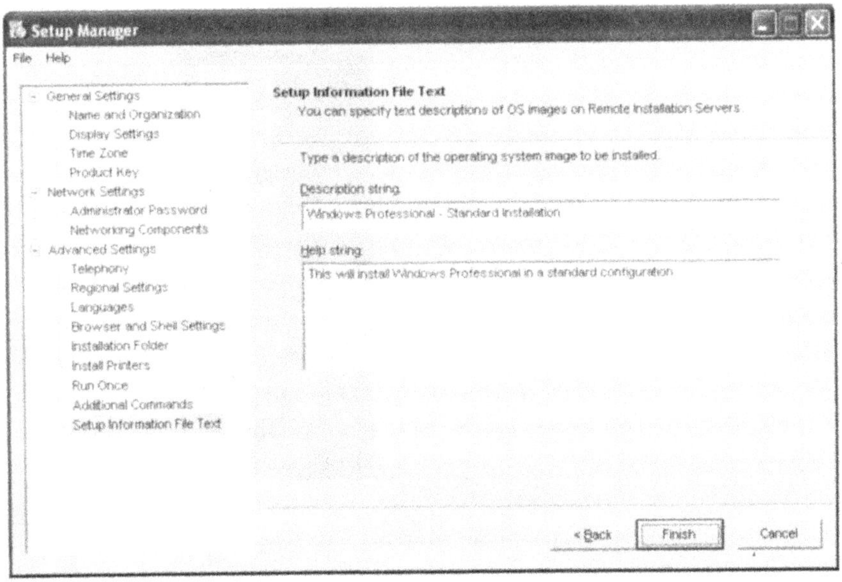

Figure 7.30 *Enter a description of the operating system image and relevant help text.*

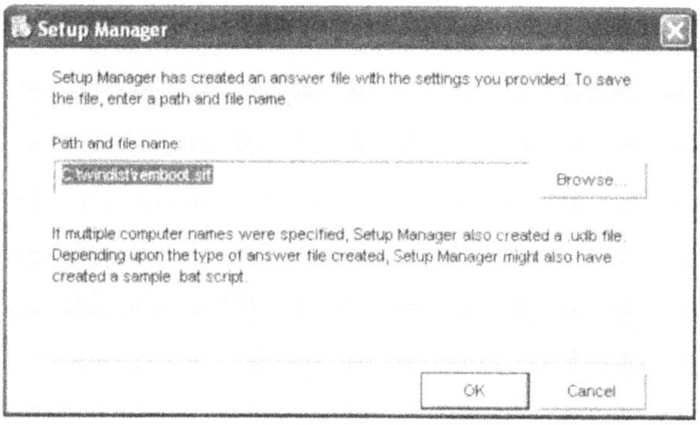

Figure 7.31 *Enter the name and location of the new SIF.*

20. The *Setup Information File Text* page (Figure 7.30) is the standard text the user will see in the Client Installation Wizard (CIW) when installing an RIS image.

21. The next page (Figure 7.31) is used to provide the path and name of the SIF.

22. The last page is the end of the road (Figure 7.32). Microsoft has forgotten to add a finish button, but click the "X" button in the upper right-hand corner to close Setup Manager.

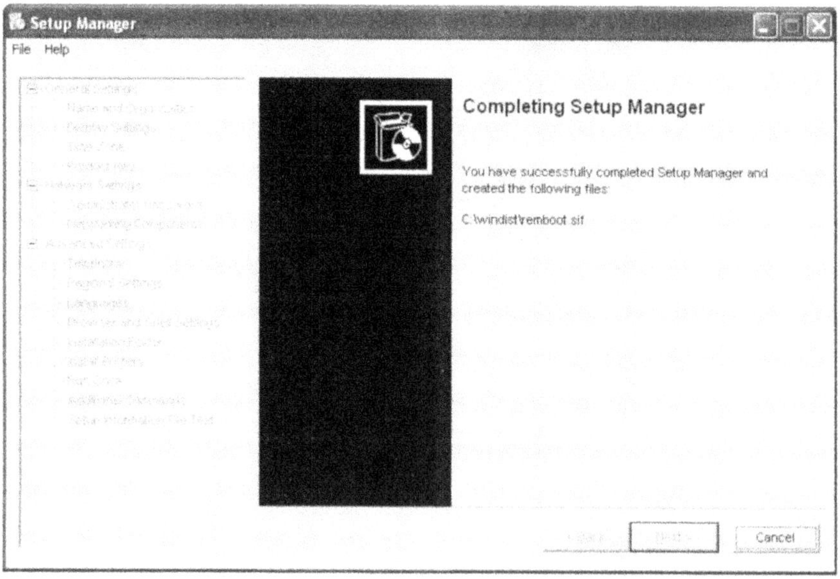

Figure 7.32 *On the last page, the only options are to cancel or close. All changes have been made and nothing will be lost.*

7.3 Changes in the SIF

The Setup Manager did create the following entries in the new SIF. In this section there are no settings coming from the wizard. These settings are standard SIF settings.

```
;SetupMgrTag
[Data]
    AutoPartition=1
    MsDosInitiated="1"
    UnattendedInstall="Yes"
    floppyless="1"
    OriSrc="\\%SERVERNAME%\RemInst\%INSTALLPATH%"
    OriTyp="4"
    LocalSourceOnCD=1

-------------------------------------------------------
In this section, the Wizard does not modify the settings;
standard settings are used
-------------------------------------------------------

[SetupData]
    OsLoadOptions="/noguiboot /fastdetect"
    SetupSourceDevice="\Device\LanmanRedirector\%SERVERNAME%\
RemInst\%INSTALLPATH%"

-------------------------------------------------------
The settings in bold are set by the Wizard.
-------------------------------------------------------

[Unattended]
    UnattendMode=FullUnattended   From User Interactive page
    OemSkipEula=Yes               From License Agreement Page
    OemPreinstall=No
    TargetPath=WINXP              From Installation folder page
    FileSystem=LeaveAlone
    NtUpgrade=No
    OverwriteOemFilesOnUpgrade=No

-------------------------------------------------------
The settings in bold are set by the Wizard.
-------------------------------------------------------

[GuiUnattended]
    AdminPassword=14efc108a634a787aad3b435b51404eecab068
    e094889e667e6d94bec6abb575
    EncryptedAdminPassword=Yes
    AutoLogon=Yes
    AutoLogonCount=1
          All settings come from Administrator Password page
    OEMSkipRegional=1
          Setting comes from Regional Setting page
```

```
    TimeZone=%TIMEZONE%
    OemSkipWelcome=1

--------------------------------------------------------
The settings in bold are set by the Wizard.
--------------------------------------------------------

[UserData]
    ProductKey=XXXXX-XXXXX-XXXXX-XXXXX-XXXXX
          From Product key page
    FullName="RIS Users"     From Name and Organization page
    OrgName="RIS TEST"
    ComputerName=%MACHINENAME%

--------------------------------------------------------
The settings in bold are set by the Wizard.
--------------------------------------------------------

[Display]
    BitsPerPel=32     All settings come from Display Settings page
    Xresolution=1024
    YResolution=768
    Vrefresh=60

--------------------------------------------------------
The settings in bold are set by the Wizard.
--------------------------------------------------------

[TapiLocation]
    CountryCode=45    Setting comes from Telephony page

--------------------------------------------------------
The settings in bold are set by the Wizard.
--------------------------------------------------------

[RegionalSettings]
    LanguageGroup=1
          All settings comes from Regional Settings page
    SystemLocale=00000406
    UserLocale=00000406
    InputLocale=0406:00000406

--------------------------------------------------------
The settings in bold are set by the Wizard.
--------------------------------------------------------

[SetupMgr]
    DistFolder=C:\windist     Settings from path and filename page
    DistShare=windiest
```

```
-------------------------------------------------------
The settings in bold are set by the Wizard.
-------------------------------------------------------

[Branding]
    BrandIEUsingUnattended=Yes
          Setting from Browser and Shell settings

[Proxy]
    Proxy_Enable=0
          Setting from Browser and Shell custom settings
    Use_Same_Proxy=1
    HTTP_Proxy_Server=192.168.1.1:8080

-------------------------------------------------------
The settings in bold are set by the Wizard.
-------------------------------------------------------

[GuiRunOnce]
    Command0="rundll32 printui.dll,PrintUIEntry /in /n \\
servername\printername"
          Comes from Run Once page

-------------------------------------------------------
In this section, the Wizard does not modify the settings;
standard settings are used
-------------------------------------------------------

[Identification]
    JoinDomain=%MACHINEDOMAIN%
    DoOldStyleDomainJoin=Yes

-------------------------------------------------------
The settings in bold are set by the Wizard.
-------------------------------------------------------

[Networking]
    InstallDefaultComponents=Yes
          Comes from Network Components page
    ProcessPageSections=Yes

-------------------------------------------------------
In this section, the Wizard does not modify the settings;
standard settings are used
-------------------------------------------------------

[RemoteInstall]
    Repartition=Yes
```

```
-------------------------------------------------------
The settings in bold are set by the Wizard.
-------------------------------------------------------

[OSChooser]
    Description="Windows Professional - Standard Installation"
    Help="This will install Windows Professional in a standard
configuration."
          Comes from Setup File Text page
    LaunchFile="%INSTALLPATH%\%MACHINETYPE%\templates\
startrom.com"
    ImageType=Flat
...
```

7.4 Summary

The Setup Manager provides an easy method to create complex SIFs. The SIF Setup Manager does not cover all options, so it may be necessary to use information from the *REF.cmd* help file to create additional options in the SIF (e.g., the Setup Manager cannot remove components from the basic RIS image). To remove components, the SIF needs additional entries. Always use the latest version of the Setup Manager. The latest version is part of the Windows XP Professional Service Pack 2.

8

Using RIPrep

This chapter covers the process of RIPrep and gives an overview of CD (flat) images versus RIPrep images. By using an RIPrep image, it's possible to include applications, drivers, and specific configured desktops to the image and then upload it back to the RIS server. Deploying an RIPrep image can be a fast way to deploy a full business platform to clients. This chapter also covers the prerequisites for RIPrep, how to create RIPrep images, and how to validate RIPrep images. There will also be some common entries that must be changed in the RIPrep SIF. These settings are covered in this chapter.

Highlights:

- Overview of RIPrep
- RIPrep prerequisites
- Creating RIPrep images
- Standard changes to be modified in the SIF
- Validating RIPrep images

8.1 Overview

By using RIPrep, it's possible to deploy an image with applications built into it, deploying special drivers or special configurations. This approach gives a full-blown image deployed to clients in a time-saving way. The only two catches are maintains of all images and the dependence of the hardware abstraction layer (HAL); if a computer needs an RIPrep image and the image doesn't have the same HAL, then the image installation will not show in the image list on the OSC screen. By using RIPrep images, it's possible to deploy the same image to multiple computers. This can be done because the RIPrep process strips out unique information in the image (e.g., SID, hostname).

The RIPrep image uses the same file structure as the original image and keeps track of files that are changed, added, or removed by checking the hash value. The RIPrep image is always built from a CD or an RIS image, and it must be in the same language and regional settings as the original image. The regional settings can easily be changed in the SIF after the image is built. An easy way to find the correct settings for keyboard layout and regional settings is to use the Setup Manager.

After installing the base image to a client computer, applications can be installed and customizations can be made to the computer. After the modifications to the client computer are complete, the profile that was used to install applications will be copied to the default profile to ensure that all settings in the profile are in place. The last step is to upload the new customized image to the RIS server. After the upload is finished, minor adjustments to the new SIF are needed. The new SIF is automatically created by the RIPrep tool. The changes could, for example, be Productkey and DisableAdminAccountOnDomainJoin.

After building the RIPrep image and uploading it to the RIS server, the image can be installed again to make more modifications. Only three builds of an RIPrep image can be made before the Windows XP product activation program will kick in and reset the grace period. The Windows XP Volume License Key allows RIPrep images to be modified more then three times. Best practice is to install a basic image and make all modifications to that image and then upload it back to the RIS server.

By default RIPrep doesn't use plug-and-play detection. This behavior can be changed by using the command *RIPrep.exe –PnP;* after the use of *RIPrep.exe –PnP* the image will always use plug-and-play detection. To disable this feature again, a new image must be created.

An RIPrep image will always use at a minimum the same size hard drive to install the image. For example, if the client donor computer has a hard drive that is 4 GB, then all of the destination client computers' hard drives will be formatted, even if that hard drive is 10 GB. This behavior can be changed in the SIF by changing the setting UseWholeDisk. By changing the *UseWholeDisk* parameter setting to equal No, the default behavior will only format the hard drive to match the capacity of the source computer, and the remainder of the destination computer's disk will be unformatted.

Note: In Windows 2000 RIS server, the basic image must always be installed from the RIS server.

64-Bit OS doesn't support RIPrep images.

8.2 Prerequisites

Before the RIPrep technology can be used, there are some prerequisites that must be in place—they are listed below.

- To create an RIPrep image, membership in the local admin group on the client computer or membership in the domain admin group on the network is required.
- Write permissions to the RIS folder structure are explicitly required, or membership in the local admin group on that local server is required.
- Client computers must use the same HAL.
- The hard drives on client computers must be at least the same size or bigger as the donor computer.
- The client computer, with the basic image, must have only one partition.
- An RIS image must exist on the RIS server before RIPrep is working.
- Encrypted files are not supported in RIPrep images.
- Modifications to RIPrep images are not supported.
- RIPrep images can only be uploaded to RIS servers, not to a CD-ROM or network shares.
- Software licenses for all client computers are required.
- A NIC driver must exist in the basic image.
- 64-Bit systems don't support RIPrep.

8.3 Making an RIPrep image

To make an RIPrep image, follow these simple steps:

1. *Deploy an image from the RIS server or CD-ROM.* Start the client computer with F12 and pick an image containing the appropriate

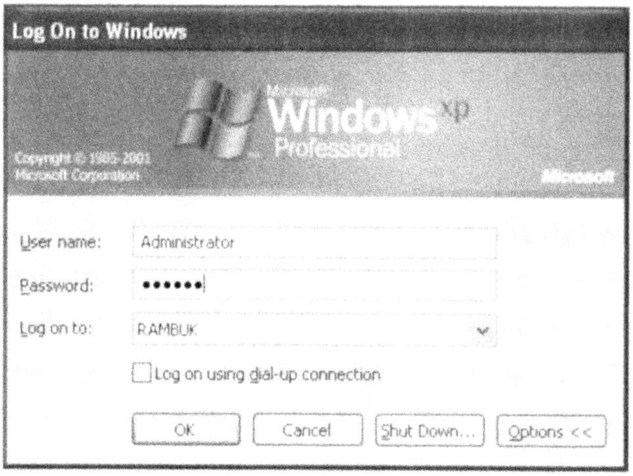

Figure 8.1 *Log on to the client computer that will be donor for the RIPrep.*

drivers for this hardware platform or install the basic OS from a CD-ROM media.

2. *Log on as local administrator* (Figure 8.1). After the image has been deployed, log on as a local admin or domain admin.

3. *Apply applications, update drivers, and make changes to the standard configuration.* Install applications, update drivers, and install hot/security fixes. Do not start any of the installed applications because they will change the application profile. In this case, Adobe 6.1 is installed; installation of a hotfix and a video driver is used. Figures 8.2 and 8.3 show the desktop install applications and a screenshot of the missing video driver.

4. *Reboot the client computer.* To make sure that all settings are written to the registry, a reboot of the client computer is required so that all registry writes can be applied to HKEY_LOCAL_MACHINE. In some applications, these settings are first written with the first reboot.

5. *Make a new admin account* (Figure 8.4). The new admin account will be used to copy the profile to "default user." The profile on the old admin account will be locked, so this is the only solution to address this problem.

6. *Log on with the new admin account* (Figure 8.5). When logging on with the new account, a new profile will be created, and the old admin account profile will not be used and will be locked.

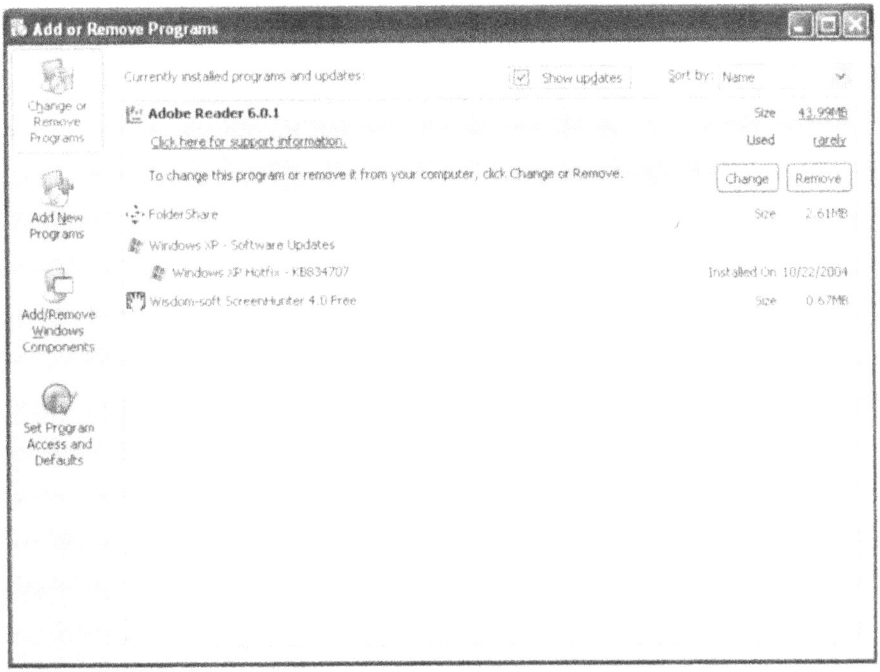

Figure 8.2 *Updates and applications installed on the client computer.*

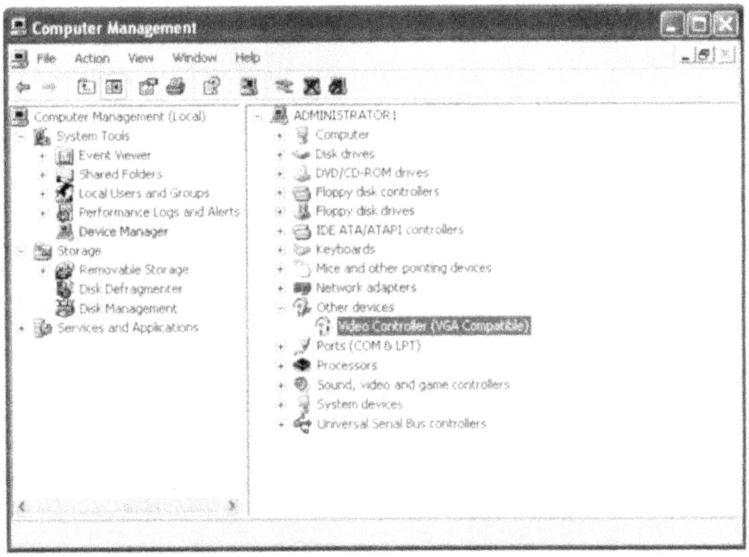

Figure 8.3 *There is a problem with the video driver on the client computer.*

Figure 8.4
Create a new administrator on the client computer.

7. *Change the folder settings to "Show hidden files and folders"* (Figure 8.6). By changing the setting to *Show hidden files and folders*, it's possible to explore the "Default User" profile. The "Default User" profile is hidden by default. By changing the standard setting, it is possible to copy the profile where the application is installed to the "Default User" profile, meaning that all new users on the computer will always have the correct shortcuts and start menu.

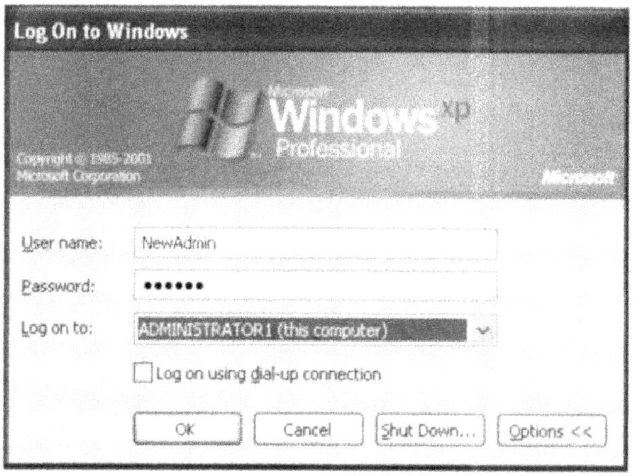

Figure 8.5
Log on to the client computer with the new administrator account.

Figure 8.6
The "Default User" profile is accessible by enabling the "Show hidden files and folders" option.

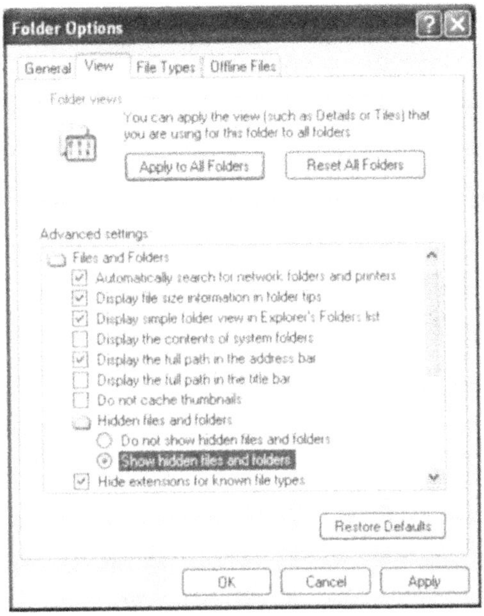

8. *Copy the local administrator profile to the default user profile.* Go to user profiles and give *Permitted to use* rights to everybody who uses the admin account profile (Figure 8.7). Copy the profile to "Default User" (C:\Document and Settings\Default User). Click yes to overwrite the profile. (Figure 8.8)

Figure 8.7
Copy the profile to the "Default User" profile and give permission to "Everyone."

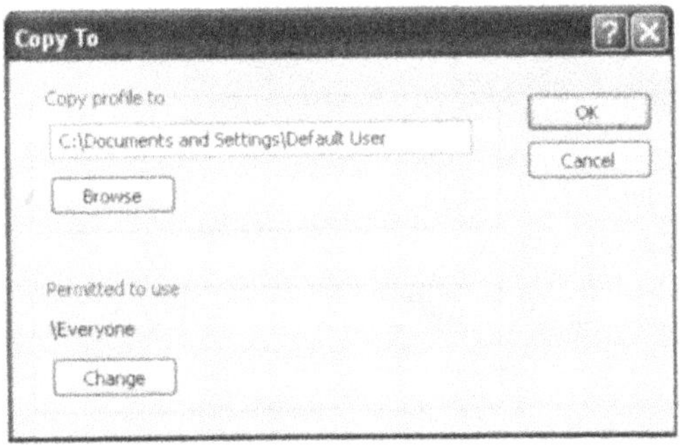

Figure 8.8
Click "Yes" to overwrite the preexisting "Default User" profile

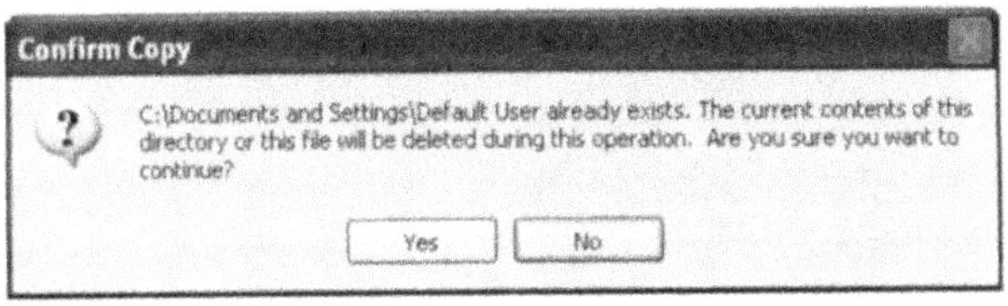

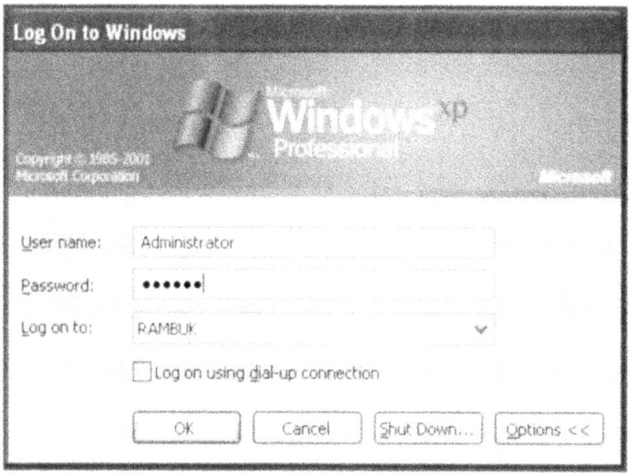

Figure 8.9 *Log on to the client computer with the Domain Administrator account.*

9. *Log on as the old admin account* (Figure 8.9). Log on with the old admin account to start the image upload.

10. *Delete the new admin account and remove the user profile for this account.* Go to profile settings and delete the new admin account profile, so that profile isn't part of the RIPrep image.

11. *Run the RIPrep program from this connection: \\servername\reminst\admin\i386\riprep.exe* (Figure 8.10). From the run command, connect to *\\servername\reminst\admin\i386\riprep.exe* to start the the new image upload. Do not make a persistent network connection to this location because it will be part of the image.

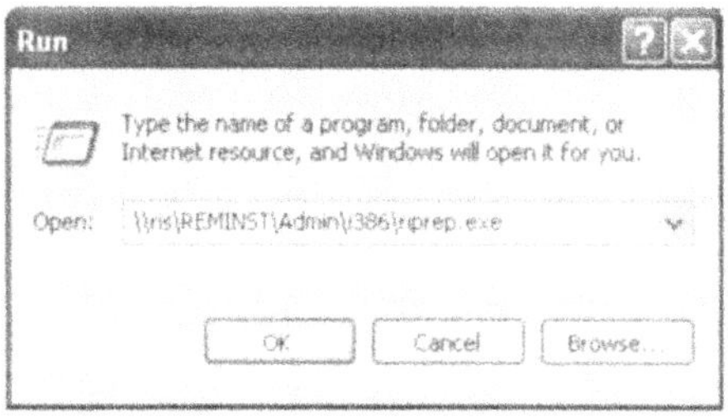

Figure 8.10 *Run riprep.exe to begin the RIPrep process.*

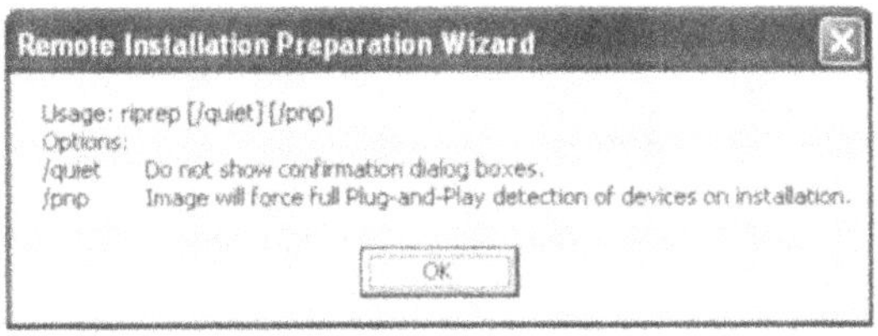

Figure 8.11
The different command switches to use with RIPrep: /Quiet and /PnP.

There are two parameters to use with the command *RIPrep.exe* (Figure 8.11). The two switches are:

- *Quiet* to install without confirmation dialog boxes
- *PnP* to force full plug-and-play detection

12. The first page is the *Welcome* page (Figure 8.12); the only option is to click Next.
13. The next page is the *Server Name* page (Figure 8.13); on this page, the server name of the RIS server where the RIPrep image will be uploaded must be applied.

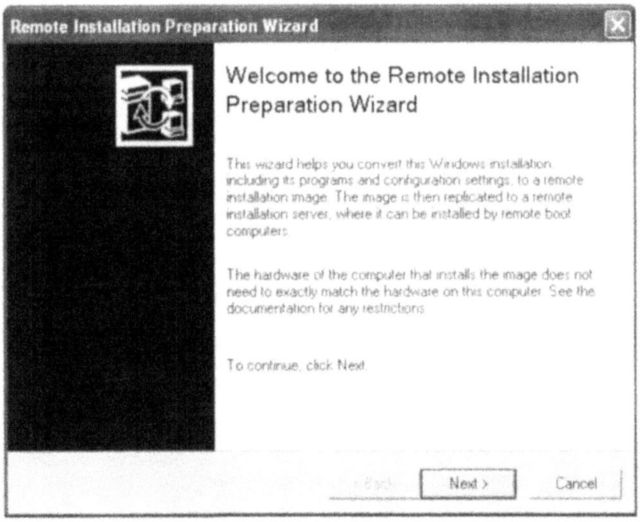

Figure 8.12
The RIPrep wizard begins; click Next to begin the process.

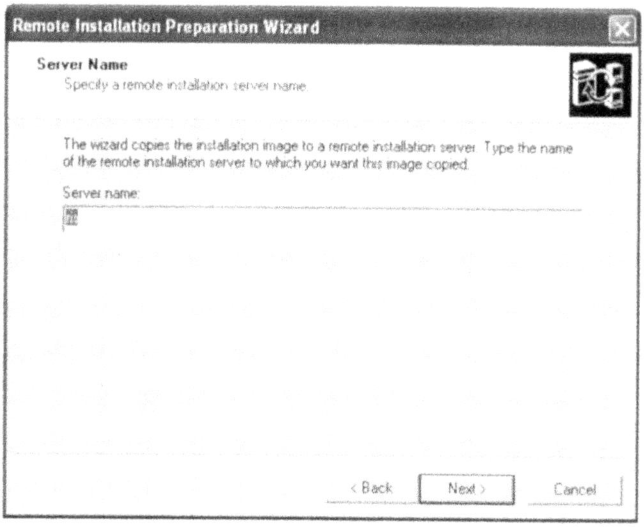

Figure 8.13
Type the name of the RIS server that will hold the new RIPrep image.

14. In the *Folder Name* page (Figure 8.14), the folder name will be applied. This folder will contain all of the files needed for the RIPrep image. Keep the naming conversion simple and easy to read.

15. On the *Friendly Description and Help Text* page (Figure 8.15), the wizard will apply a friendly name and some help text. This information will be written to the SIF and will be used when the client

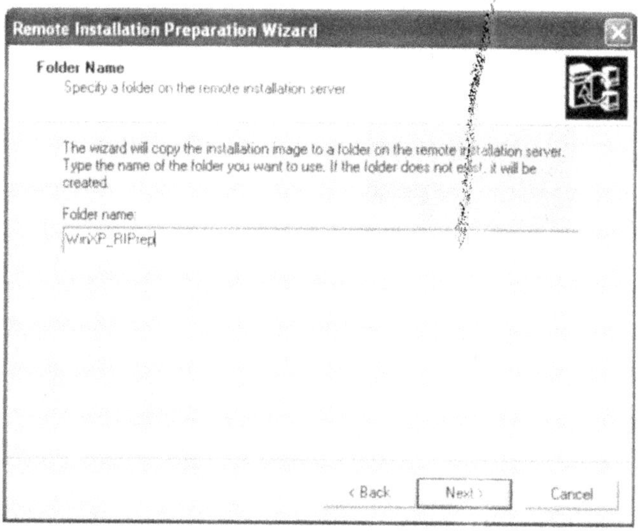

Figure 8.14
Provide a folder name on the RIS server to contain the new RIPrep image.

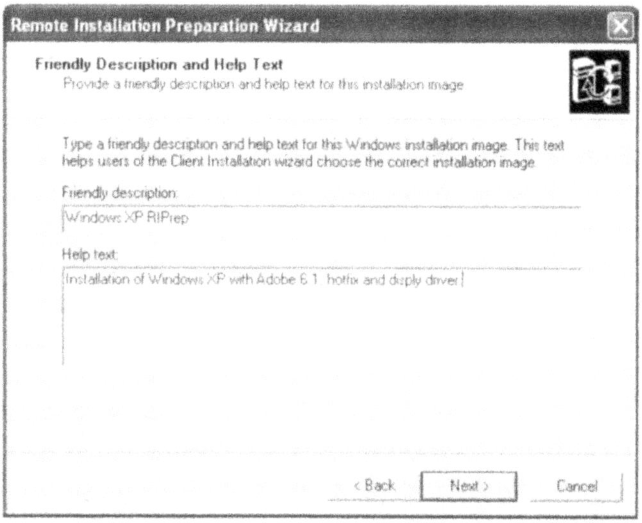

Figure 8.15
Add a description and help text to the image.

starts an installation of the RIPrep image. This description and help text can always be changed later either by modifying the SIF or by using the GUI Active Directory.

16. The *Stop Services* page (Figure 8.16) is a warning page that will list all services running and must be stopped before the RIPrep imaging will continue.

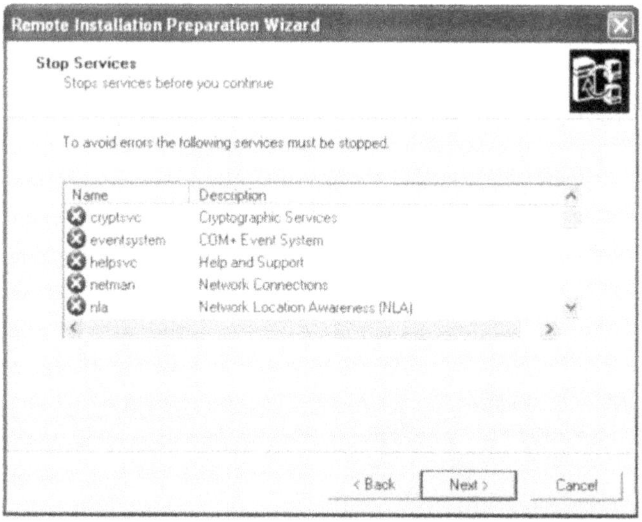

Figure 8.16
An overview of the services running on the client computer.

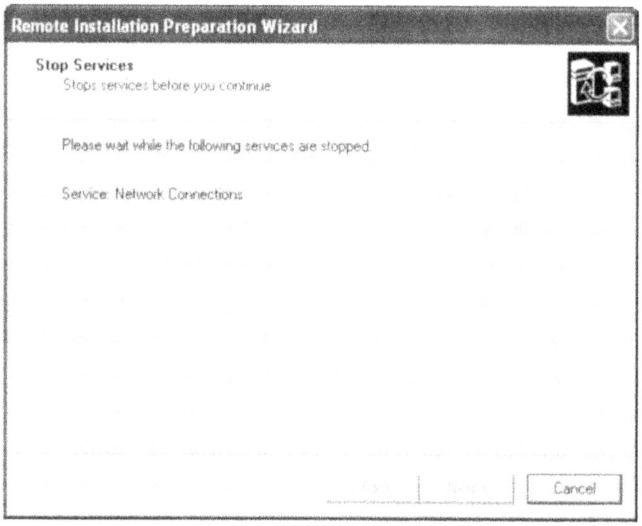

Figure 8.17 *RIPrep trying to stop the service from running.*

17. The RIPrep process will automatically try to shut down the listed services (Figure 8.17), but if the services cannot be shut down automatically, then use *Task Manager* to manually stop these services.

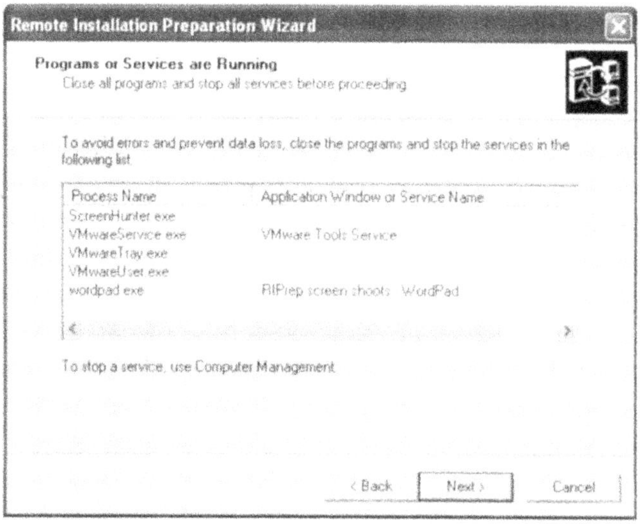

Figure 8.18 *The services that cannot be stopped by the RIPrep services. Use the Computer Management screen to stop the service manually.*

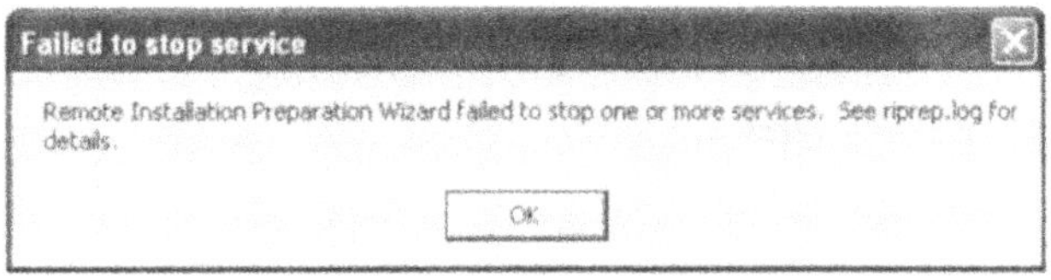

Figure 8.19 *If the RIPrep process failed to stop a service, an entry is written in the riprep.log file.*

18. If there are services the RIPrep wizard can't stop and that aren't stopped manually, then the process will create an entry in the Riprep.log. The log file is placed on the RIS server in the RIPrep image folder (e.g., *\\Server\reminst\setup\images\riprepimage\I386*). (See Figures 8.18 through 8.20.)

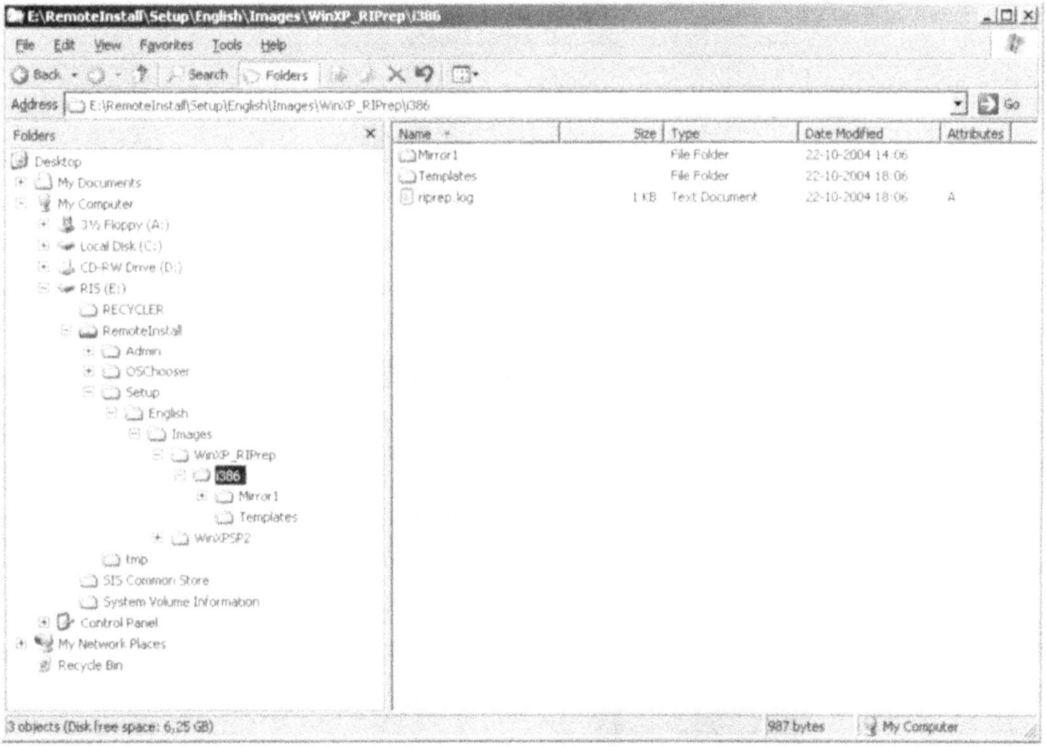

Figure 8.20 *The new image folder structure. There are only two folders and a log file.*

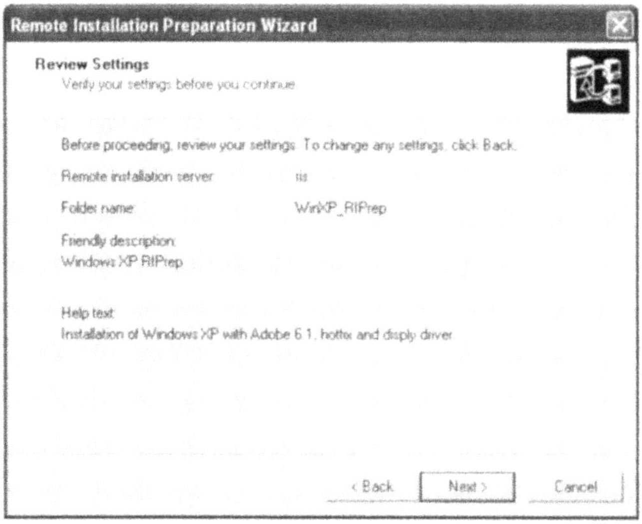

Figure 8.21
A summary of the choices made in the RIPrep process.

19. The *Review Settings* page (Figure 8.21) will provide an overview of the choices made with the wizard. There is always the option to go back and correct entries, if any mistakes were made in previous pages.

20. The *Completing the Remote Installation Preparation Wizard* page (Figure 8.22) is a summary before the actual process begins.

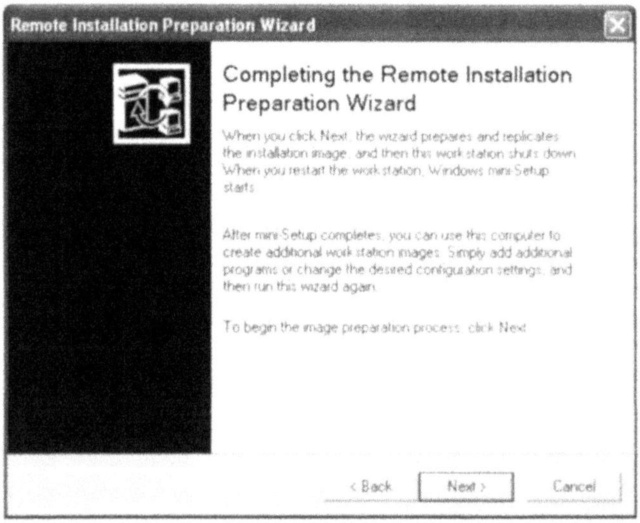

Figure 8.22
Clicking Next begins the RIPrep process and the new image is uploaded to the RIS server.

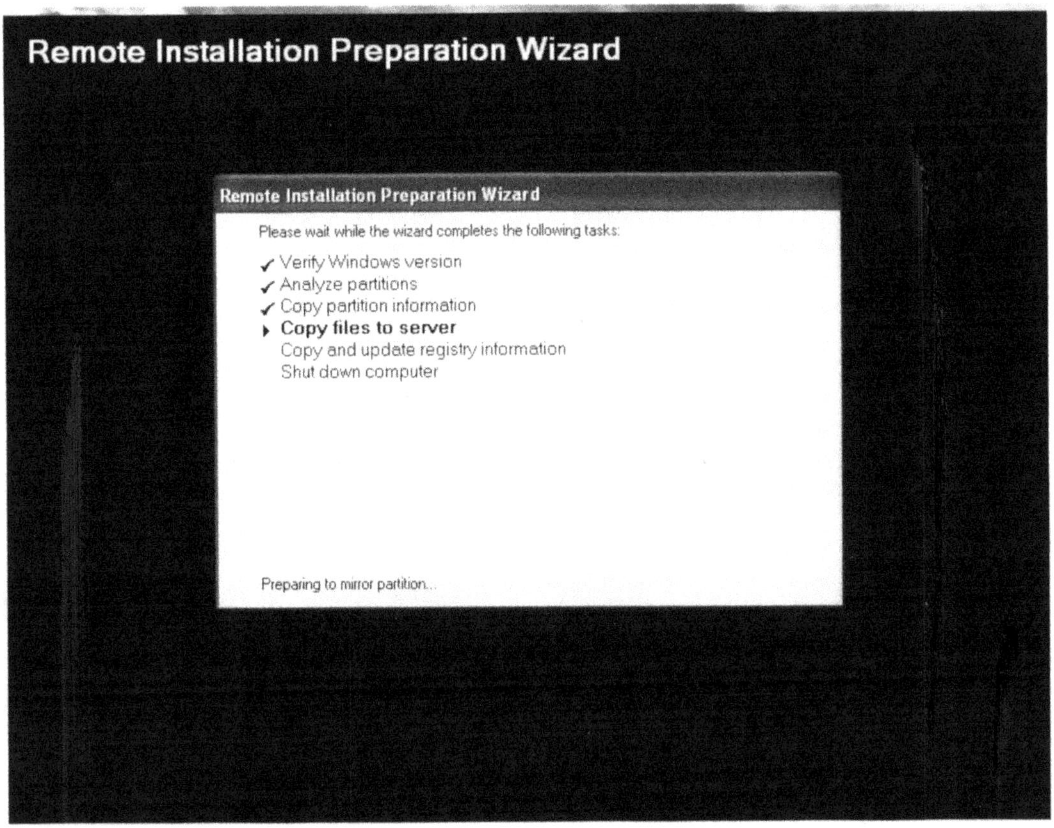

Figure 8.23 *The RIPrep process in action.*

21. The Wizard continues with the following tasks (Figure 8.23):
    - Verify Windows version. The RIPrep image checks the RIS server for a basic image before the process continues.
    - Analyze partitions. Checks the size and numbers of partitions on the client donor computer.
    - Copy partition information to the RIS server.
    - Copy files to server. All files are copied to the RIS server in the right location.
    - Copy and update registry information. All information in the registry is corrected and unique entries (e.g., SID, hostname, and domain information) are stripped out.
    - Shut down computer. After the process is finished, the client donor computer is automatically shut down.

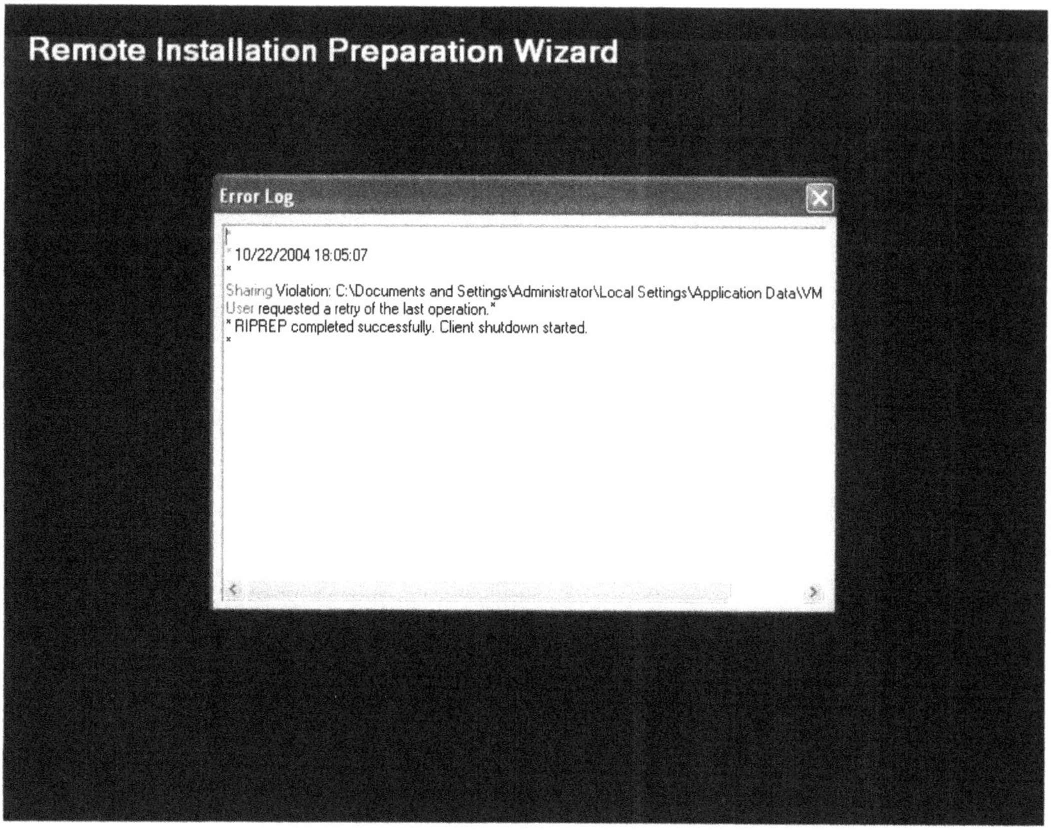

Figure 8.24 *The last step in the RIPrep process.*

22. Just before shutdown, the RIPrep wizard will display an error log, which lists any errors in the RIPrep process (Figure 8.24).

8.4 Changing the SIF

Let's look at the new SIF created by the RIPrep tool:

```
[data]
floppyless = "1"
msdosinitiated = "1"
OriSrc = "\\%SERVERNAME%\RemInst\%INSTALLPATH%\
%MACHINETYPE%"
OriTyp = "4"
LocalSourceOnCD = 1
DisableAdminAccountOnDomainJoin = 1
```

```
[SetupData]
OsLoadOptions = "/noguiboot /fastdetect"
SetupSourceDevice ="\Device\LanmanRedirector\%SERVERNAME%\
RemInst\%INSTALLPATH%"
SysPrepDevice="\Device\LanmanRedirector\%SERVERNAME%\
RemInst\%SYSPREPPATH%"
SysPrepDriversDevice="\Device\LanmanRedirector\
%SERVERNAME%\RemInst\%SYSPREPDRIVERS%"

[Unattended]
OemPreinstall = no
FileSystem = LeaveAlone
ExtendOEMPartition = 0
TargetPath = \WINDOWS
OemSkipEula = yes
InstallFilesPath = "\\%SERVERNAME%\RemInst\%INSTALLPATH%\
%MACHINETYPE%"
LegacyNIC = 1

[UserData]
FullName = "%USERFIRSTNAME% %USERLASTNAME%"
OrgName = "%ORGNAME%"
ComputerName ="%MACHINENAME%"

[GuiUnattended]
OemSkipWelcome = 1
OemSkipRegional = 1
TimeZone = %TIMEZONE%
AdminPassword = "*"

[Display]
BitsPerPel = 16
XResolution = 800
YResolution = 600
VRefresh = 60

[Networking]

[NetServices]
MS_Server=params.MS_PSched

[Identification]
JoinDomain = %MACHINEDOMAIN%
DoOldStyleDomainJoin = Yes

[RemoteInstall]
Repartition = Yes
UseWholeDisk = Yes
```

```
[OSChooser]
Description ="Windows XP RIPrep"
Help ="Installation of Windows XP with Adobe 6.1, hotfix and
display driver."
LaunchFile ="%INSTALLPATH%\%MACHINETYPE%\templates\
startrom.com"
ImageType =SYSPREP
Version="5.1 (2600)"
SysPrepSystemRoot="Mirror1\UserData\WINDOWS"
HalName=halaacpi.dll
ProductType=0
```

Some minor changes in the standard SIF must be made before the new RIPrep image is ready to be tested:

- *Remark DisableAdminAccountJoinDomain.* Remarking this setting will not allow the RIS installation to disable the admin account after the join to the domain.

Note: The DisableAdminAccountJoinDomain isn't used on Microsoft Windows 2000 RIS server.

- *Full name.* Provide a name to the installation.
- *Org name.* Provide the company name.
- *Product key.* Provide the product key to the client image.
- *Regional settings.* Specify your regional settings.
- *Display layout.* Provide information about screen resolution and refresh rate.

The RIPrep process will always use the first CD images found in the file structure on the RIS server. This fact is important when there is more than one CD image on the RIS server. To force an RIPrep to use the right image, just rename the folder to a name that will be first in the alphabet. If the folder isn't renamed, then the RIPrep image will use a wrong basic image that contains wrong drivers and an incorrect SIF. *This behavior is by design and cannot be changed.*

Note: If using RIPrep from a Windows 2000 RIS server with *no* service pack installed, then install the updated RIPrep tool to deploy Windows XP. This tool can be downloaded from Microsoft: look for Q313069.

8.5 Verifying the RIPrep image

The first step is to read the riprep.log; to find the log file, go to *\\Server\reminst\setup\language\images\RIPrep image\I386*. It's important to read and verify the log file and understand which services or files weren't processed correctly. The next step is to roll out a new client computer, with the new RIPrep image to test the functionality and test for errors in the image. In most cases, the RIPrep process will work perfectly even with minor errors in the riprep.log file! The riprep log file looks like this:

```
*
* 10/22/2004 13:49:01          Date the RIPrep process started
*
Failed to stop service: netman Two services the RIPrep process
                               couldn't stop
Failed to stop service: webclient
Server       : ris             RIS Server name
Image Dir    : WinXP_RIPrep    Name of RIPrep folders
Language     : English         Language of image
Architecture: i386             Processor type
Description : Windows XP RIPrep Short description and help text
HelpText    : Installation of Windows XP with Adobe 6.1, hotfix and
disply driver.
SystemRoot   : Mirror1\userdata\winntLocation of primary data
Winnt Dir    : C:\WINDOWS      Name of Windows systemroot
*
* 10/22/2004 14:30:12          Description of a lock in the RIPrep
                               process. In the first entry the
                               user retries the operation; the
                               second time the user chooses to
                               ignore the error.
*
Sharing Violation: C:\WINDOWS\system32\CatRoot2\edb.log
User requested a retry of the last operation.*
* 10/22/2004 14:30:17
*
Sharing Violation: C:\WINDOWS\system32\CatRoot2\tmp.edb
Error ignored. Operation continuing.*
* 10/22/2004 17:49:01
*
Error 0x00000040: C:\WINDOWS\inf\mdmsun2.PNF
User requested a retry of the last operation.*
* 10/22/2004 18:05:07
*
Sharing Violation: C:\Documents and Settings\Administrator\Local
Settings\Application Data\VMware\hgfs.dat
User requested a retry of the last operation.*
* RIPREP completed successfully. Client shutdown started.
                               RIPrep finish
*
```

The next step is to validate the physical location of the RIPrep files. The place to look is *\\Server\reminst\setup\language\images*, where *images* is the name of the RIPrep image.

A I386 folder must exist, with two subfolders called Mirror1 and Templates. The Template folder is the same as normal, holding, for example, the SIF. The Mirror1 folder contains all files that are part of the RIPrep image.

Remember, to install a RIPrep image, the RIS server will start installing the first basic image on the RIS server, and after the process is finished, the RIPrep image will be applied by checking the hash values on all files. The checking of the hash value is the reason why it isn't possible to directly modify the RIPrep image files. For example, there is no way to apply Service Pack 2 or add new drivers to this image. The only option is to make these modifications to the basic image.

The fact of always installing from the first basic image from the RIS server will create some challenges in scenarios where multiple basic RIS images exist. There is no way to force a basic image to be installed. Be sure that all the drivers needed to install the images are in the first basic image. (See Figures 8.25 through 8.27.)

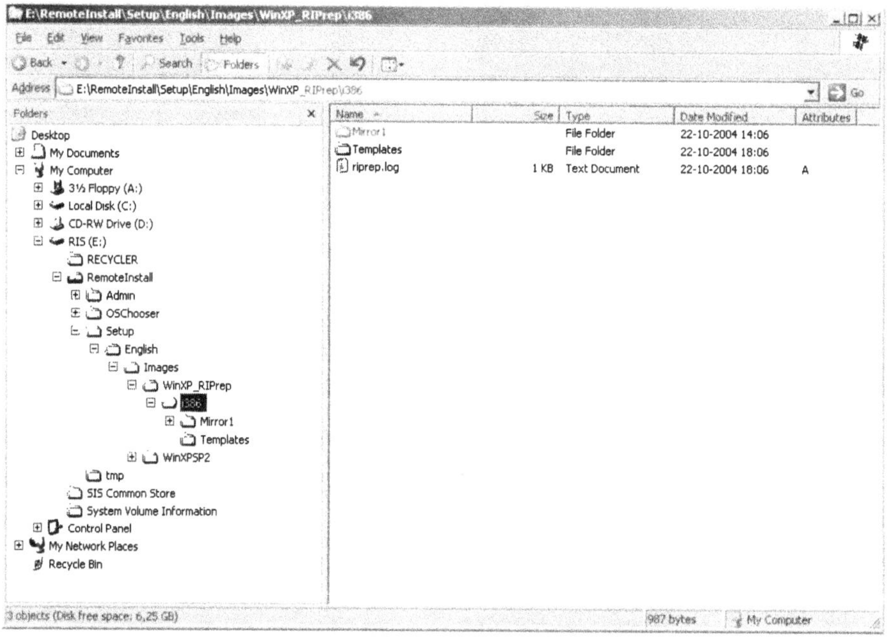

Figure 8.25 *When verifying the RIPrep image, begin by checking the riprep.log file.*

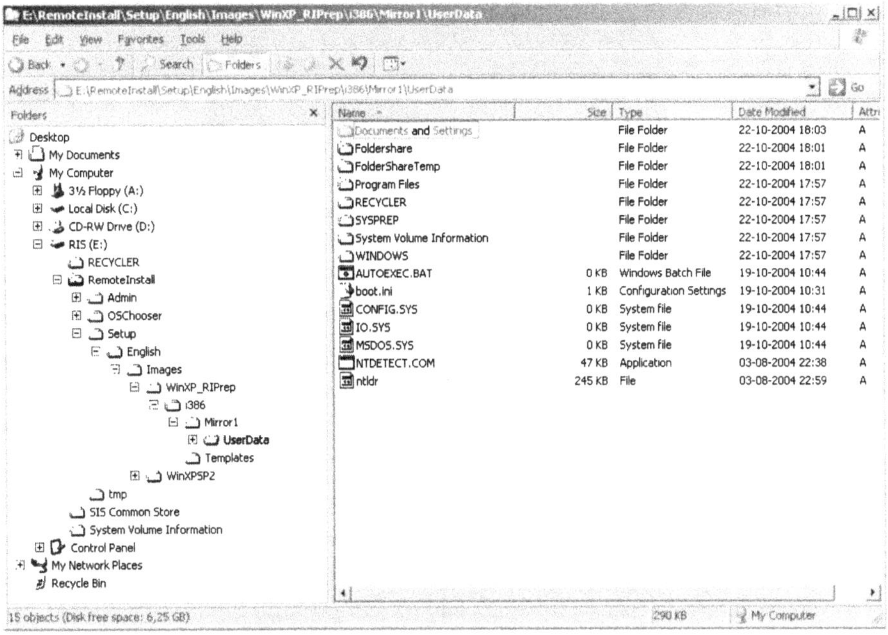

Figure 8.26 *The UserData created by RIPrep.*

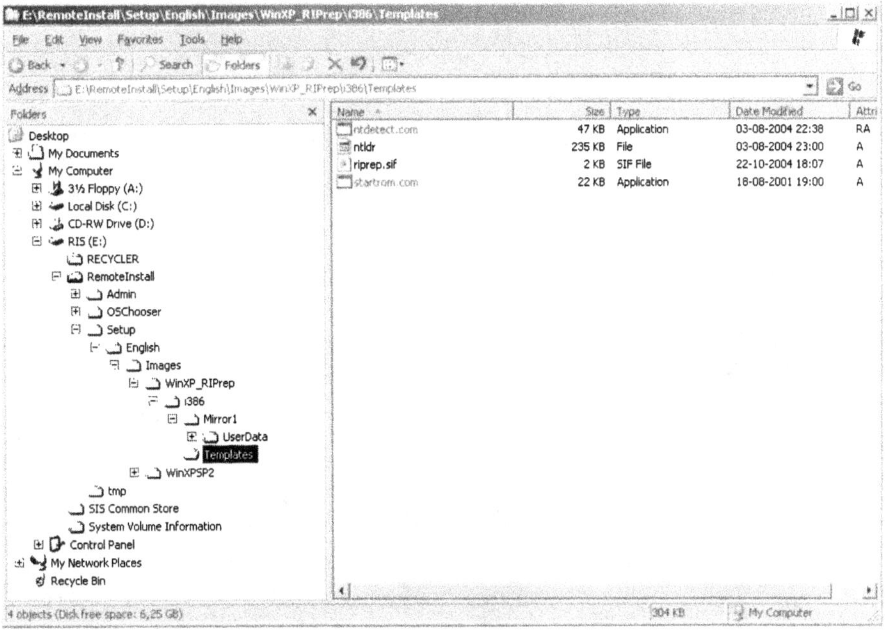

Figure 8.27 *In the Template folder, is the SIF created by the RIPrep process.*

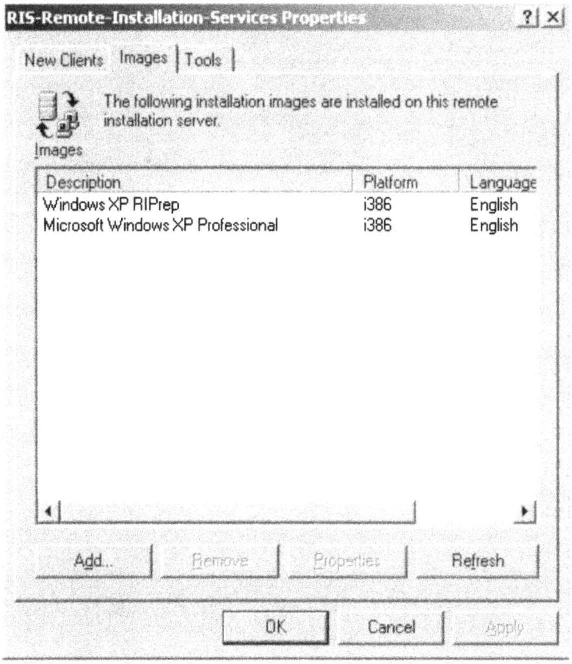

Figure 8.28 *Select the Images tab to check and edit the new RIPrep image information.*

The next step is to check the RIS server interface to ensure that the correct information is present in the GUI (Figure 8.28). Remember that it's possible to change the description and help text from this location.

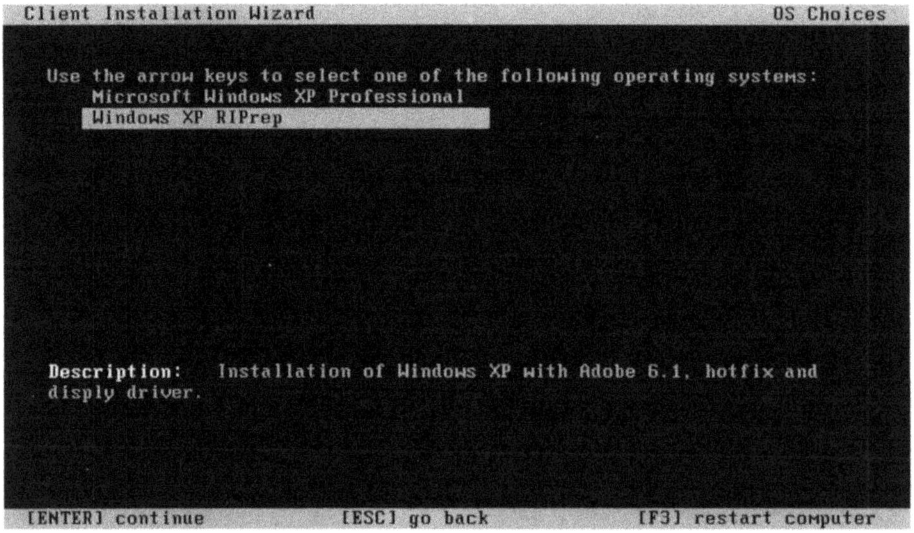

Figure 8.29 *Begin an RIS client installation and check that the RIPrep image is displayed.*

After the minor modifications to the SIF are made, the RIPrep image is ready to be tested. Fire up a new client computer, and hit F12 to begin the RIS installation process. There will now be a new entry on the list of images to choose from. The description and help text are correct, and the image is ready to be deployed.

After installing the new RIPrep image, a test of all applications is needed to verify that the image is working correctly. In some cases, a rebuild of the RIPrep image must be done, perhaps because an application isn't working properly or something is forgotten in the RIPrep image. (See Figure 8.29.)

8.6 Summary

The RIPrep process is fairly simple and a quick way to provide a business platform to multiple client computers in a fast and time-saving way. The RIPrep image can contain applications, drivers, and special configurations on the client computer. The only requirement is that the HAL must be the same for deploying the RIPrep image to multiple computers.

The RIPrep image will always use the first basic image on the RIS server to apply drivers and settings in the OEM file structure. This setting is by design and cannot be changed in this version of RIS. There is no way to directly modify the RIPrep image; all modifications must be made in the basic image. Before the RIPrep image can be used, some minor modifications must be made to the SIF that are automatically created by the RIPrep tool.

9

Prestaging

Prestaging is the ability to create a network infrastructure in which all client computers will use specified RIS servers. This option can be used with success when there are multiple RIS servers in the same site in the Active Directory. A client computer will always try to connect to an RIS server in the same site as it belongs. If prestaging isn't used, then there is a possibility that all clients will contact an RIS server in another physical location and thereby use all of the bandwidth available on the WAN lines. If there is only one RIS server in the network, then there is no need for prestaging. If there isn't an RIS server in the client's site, then the client computer will automatically go to the nearest site possible to connect to an RIS server.

Imagine this scenario: There is one site covering two locations, with a 2-Mbit line, and there is an RIS server in each location. Both locations serve 350 client computers. In this scenario, there is a reason to make sure that the client computers always use the RIS server in their own locations and thereby save bandwidth between the two sites. There are two possible solutions to this scenario:

1. Change the site structure from one site to two sites.
2. Prestage computers to the RIS server in their own locations.

Another reason is security. If all computer accounts in the Active Directory are prestaged, then only known client computers can download RIS images. Before this will work, the option "Do not respond to unknown client computers" must be enabled. This option can be found in the properties of the RIS server under Remote installation.

Highlights:

- How prestaging works
- How to find the GUID number

- Setup of prestaging
- Enabled prestaging on the RIS server
- Finding prestaged computer accounts

9.1 How it works

When the client computer contacts the Active Directory in the RIS installation process, the Active Directory looks at the client's Globally Unique Identifier (GUID) number. If the GUID number is prestaged to a specific RIS server, then the Active Directory will respond with that RIS server.

9.2 How to find the GUID number

There are different ways to find the computer's GUID number. One way is to capture the DHCP discovery broadcast packet in a network monitor when the client computer fires up (Figure 9.1). Another method is to start the RIS installation process; the GUID number will be displayed on the last CIW page. The GUID number is a 32-Bit unique number stored in the Active Directory with the computer object. Client computers there don't support the PXE standard and can't supply the GUID number to RIS servers; instead they supply the MAC address and add 20 zeros to it. In some

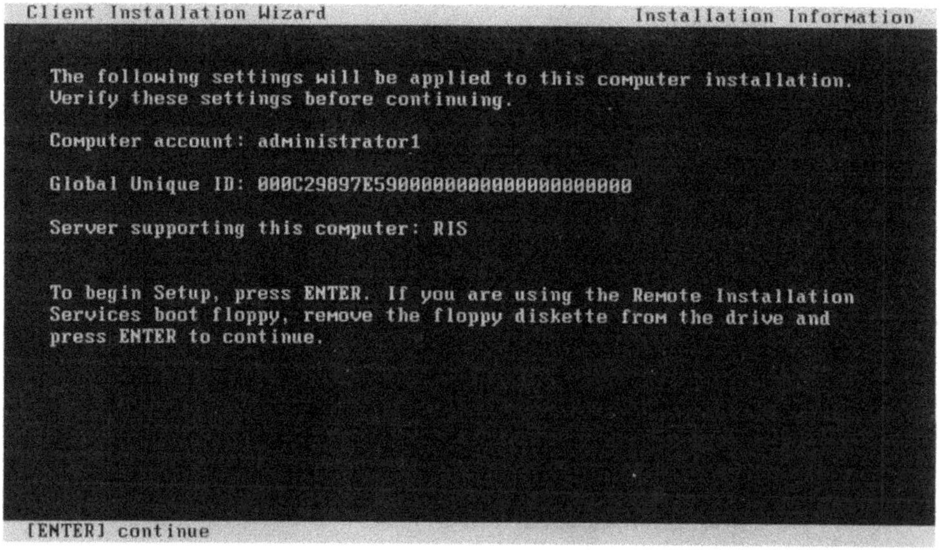
Client Installation Wizard
Installation Information
The following settings will be applied to this computer installation.
Verify these settings before continuing.
Computer account: administrator1
Global Unique ID: 000C29097E5900000000000000000000
Server supporting this computer: RIS
To begin Setup, press ENTER. If you are using the Remote Installation
Services boot floppy, remove the floppy diskette from the drive and
press ENTER to continue.
[ENTER] continue

Figure 9.1 *The GUID can be read from the RIS client installation pages.*

cases, the GUID number is also stored in the computer BIOS or labeled on the computer cases.

Before prestaging a computer account in the Active Directory, the GUID number must already be discovered and ready to be applied to the computer account when it is created in the Active Directory. There is no way to take already existing computer accounts and make them manageable by RIS in the Active Directory. The prestaging must be done before the RIS installation begins.

9.3 Setup prestaging

1. Locate the container in the Active Directory service in which you want your client accounts to be created.
2. Right-click the container, click New, and then choose Computer. The New Object-Computer dialog box is displayed (Figure 9.2).

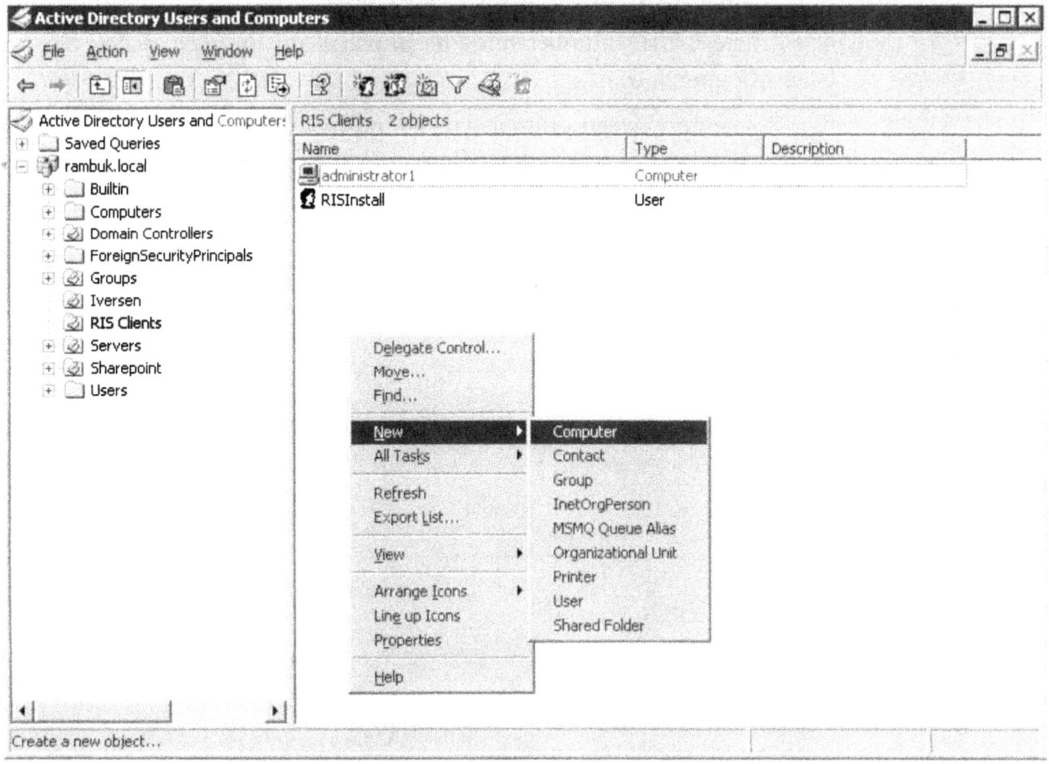

Figure 9.2 *Create a new computer in Active Directory.*

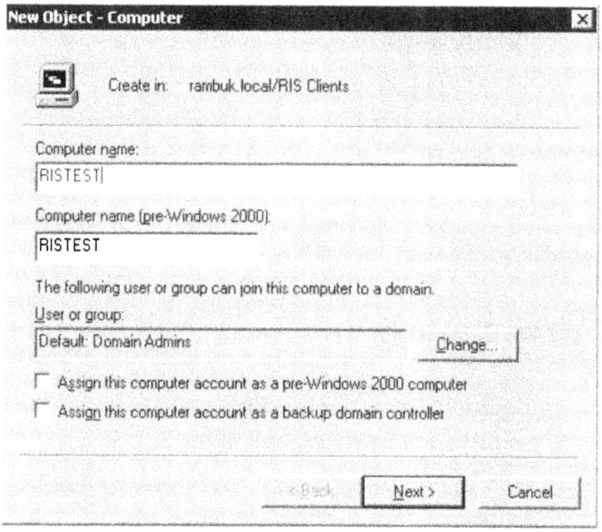

Figure 9.3 *Give the new computer a name.*

3. Enter the computer name (Figure 9.3).
4. The GUID number must be provided on the next dialog box (Figure 9.4).
5. The next screen prompts you to indicate the RIS server that this computer is serviced by (Figure 9.5). This option can be left blank to indicate that any available RIS server can answer and

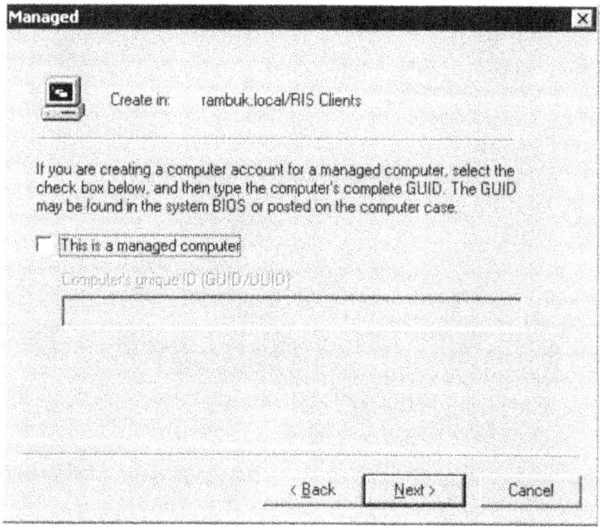

Figure 9.4 *The checkbox is specific for the RIS service.*

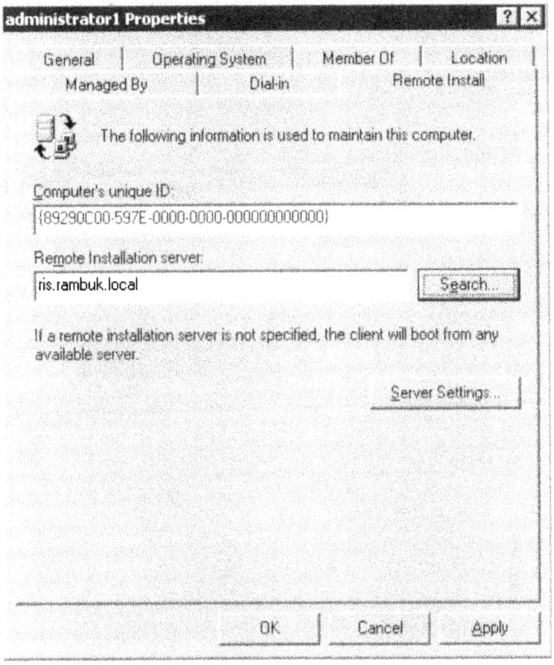

Figure 9.5 *Type the GUID number of the client computer and the RIS server that will manage this computer account.*

service this client. Prestaging the client computer to a specific RIS server will give the option to control network bandwidth and provide more security to the RIS installation process.

9.4 Enabled prestaging on the RIS server

After the process of prestaging client computers to specific RIS servers is complete, then the option *Do not respond to unknown clients* can be enabled. By enabling this option on the RIS server, the RIS server will only respond to prestaged client computers and thereby raise the security on the RIS server.

To enable this feature, follow these steps:

1. Right-click the RIS server and choose properties, then go to the *Remote Installation* tab (Figure 9.6).
2. Click the *Do not respond to unknown clients* checkbox (Figure 9.7). After clicking this option on, the RIS server will only answer prestaged clients.

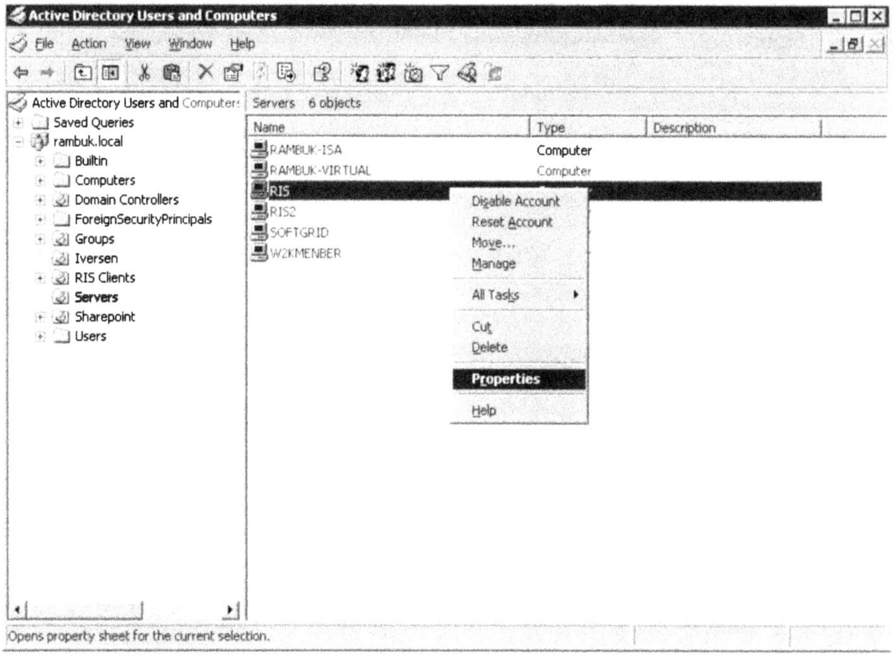

Figure 9.6 *Select Properties on the RIS server to access the Remote Install settings.*

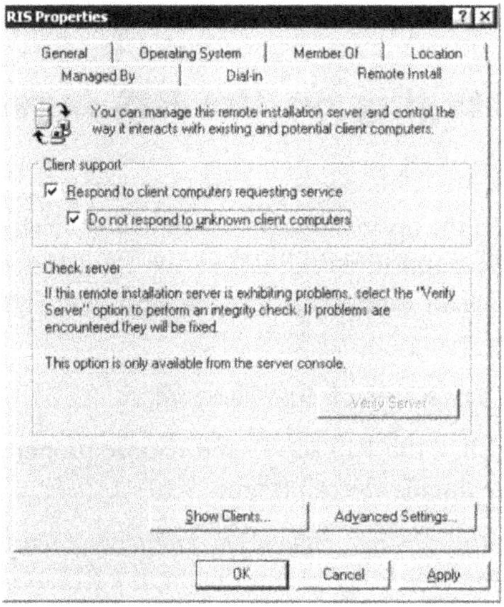

Figure 9.7 *Selecting "Do not respond to unknown client computers," causes the RIS server to only respond to prestaged client computers.*

9.5 Finding prestaged computers in the Active Directory

In a large network environment, it may be necessary to get an overview of which RIS server images to which client computers. By using the search functionality in the Active Directory, prestaged computers can be quickly discovered and managed.

Use these steps to find prestaged computer accounts in the Active Directory:

1. Start an Active Directory search from any Domain Controller.
2. Use the dropdown box to locate *Remote Installation Clients* in the Find box (Figure 9.8).
3. Search the *Entire Directory* to find all RIS clients in the Enterprise and click Find Now (Figure 9.9).
4. After clicking Find Now, the search engine will list all prestaged computers in the Enterprise (Figure 9.10). This picture lists two machine accounts, their names, and GUID numbers.
5. Change the search query by adding an RIS server Full Qualify Domain Name (FQDN) in the *RI server* text box to make the query specific to a single RIS server client (Figure 9.11).

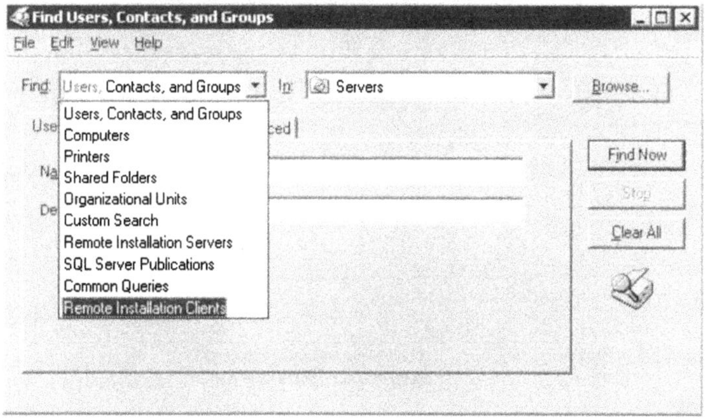

Figure 9.8
The different options for searching in Active Directory. Last on the list is "Remote Installation Clients."

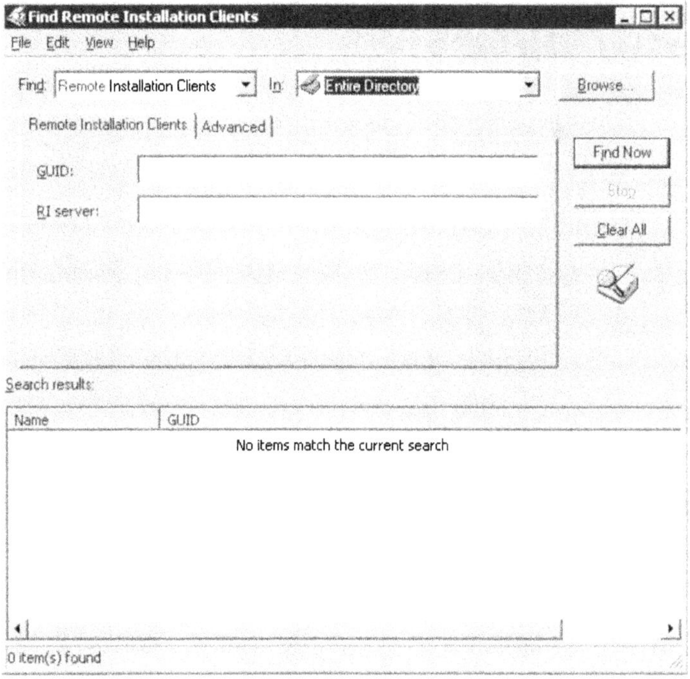

Figure 9.9
Enter a GUID or RIS server name to find clients in Active Directory.

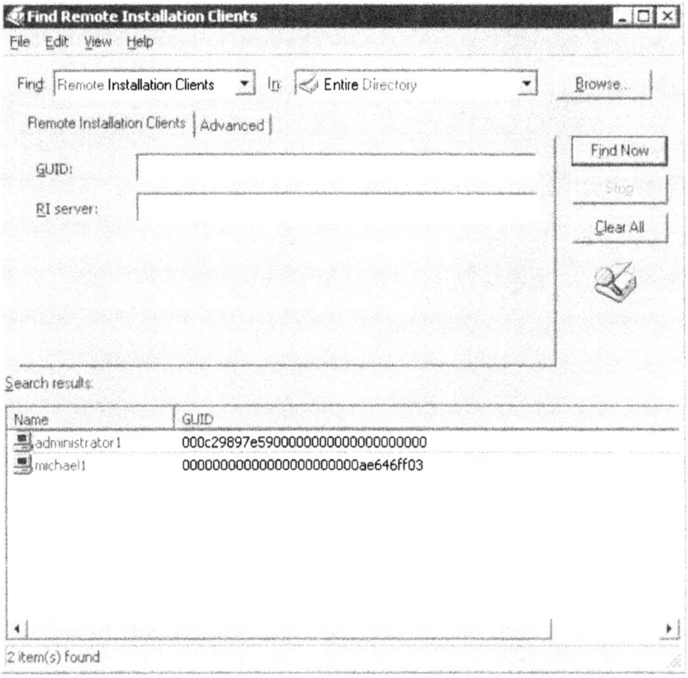

Figure 9.10
A list of RIS server clients in the directory.

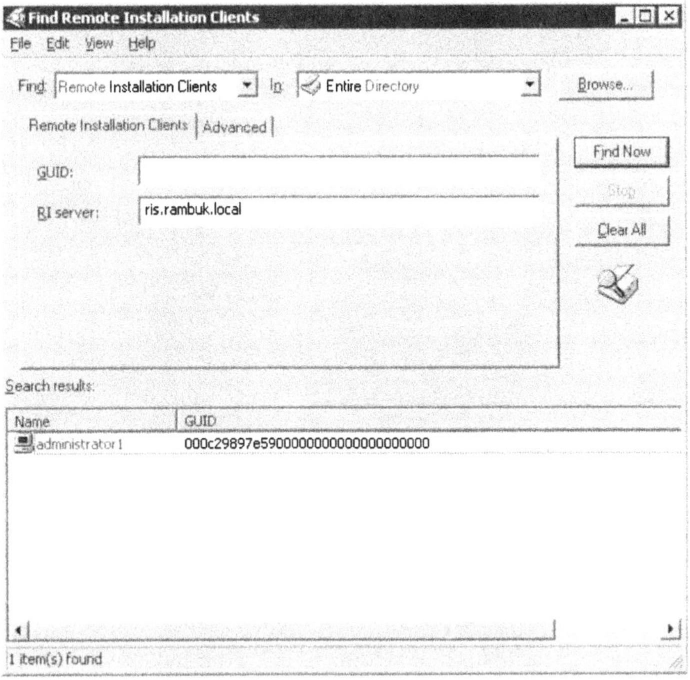

Figure 9.11 *A list of client computers that are managed by a RIS server called "ris.rambuk.local."*

9.6 Summary

Prestaging can be used in corporate networks to control which RIS server the client computers must use. By prestaging computer accounts, the security model on the RIS server can be made stronger, by not responding to unknown clients. The Active Directory supports the search for prestaged RIS clients in the search engine.

10

Move and Backup of RIS Servers

This chapter describes how to move RIS images between volumes and servers. It also covers the process of moving an RIS server between domains and the steps involved in keeping the RIS images functioning correctly when they are moved. The backup and restore process is covered in the last section.

Highlights:

- Moving RIS images between volumes
- Moving RIS images between RIS servers
- Moving RIS servers between domains
- Backup and restore of RIS servers

10.1 Move RIS images between volumes

Sometimes it's required to move the RIS images from one volume to a different volume. Maybe the volume is running out of space, or the disk is beginning to contain bad blocks, or maybe the RIS volume is moved to a SAN.

To move the RIS images from one location to a new location, the target volume must be formatted with NTFS and must at least have the same space available as the source volume. The method to move RIS images from one volume to a different volume does not require new images to be installed and does not require any reboots.

Follow these simple steps to move between different volumes:

1. Stop the following services:
   - Remote Installation Services (BINLSRV) (in Windows 2000, this is called BINL services)
   - Trivial FTP Daemon (TFTPD)

By stopping these services, the Remote Installation directory isn't locked, and therefore the process to copy the directory structure can be done without problems. Another reason to stop the two services is to ensure that no client computer will attempt to download an image from the RIS server while the RIS images are being moved.

2. Stop sharing the *RemoteInstall* folder; there is no need to share the *RemoteInstall* folder after the RIS file structure has been moved. (See Figure 10.1.)

3. Move or copy the *RemoteInstall* directory to the new location. Move the RIS file structure to the new volume by using any kind of copy/move mechanism.

4. Share the *RemoteInstall* folder on the new location as *Reminst* (Figure 10.2). By sharing the folder, the clients will have access to the new location of the RIS images. The permissions must at least be READ, so the clients can copy the files down locally.

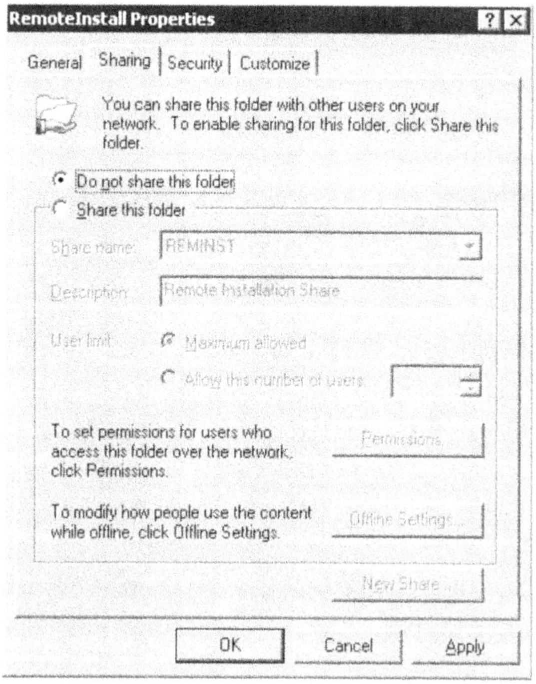

Figure 10.1
Stop sharing of the REMINST folder.

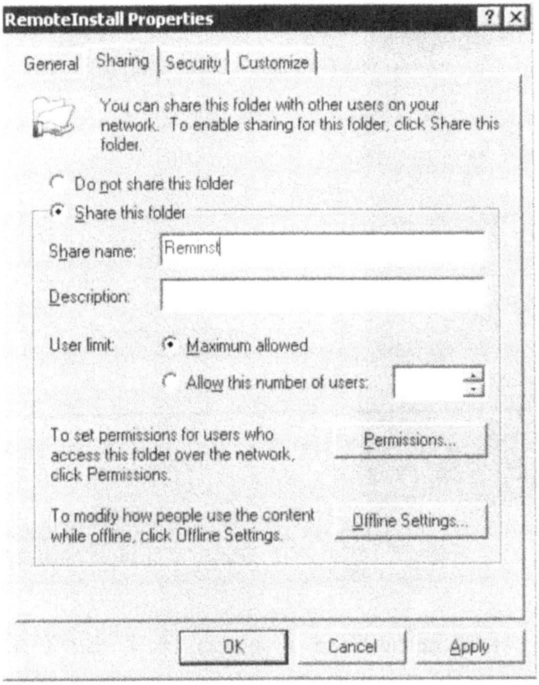

Figure 10.2 *Share the folder with the name "Reminst."*

5. Run the *RISetup –check* command (Figure 10.3). By running the RISetup command with the switch *–check*, the RIS server will begin a wizard to ensure the health of the server.

   The *Check Server Wizard* page is only a welcome screen, where the only option is to click Next. (See Figure 10.4.)

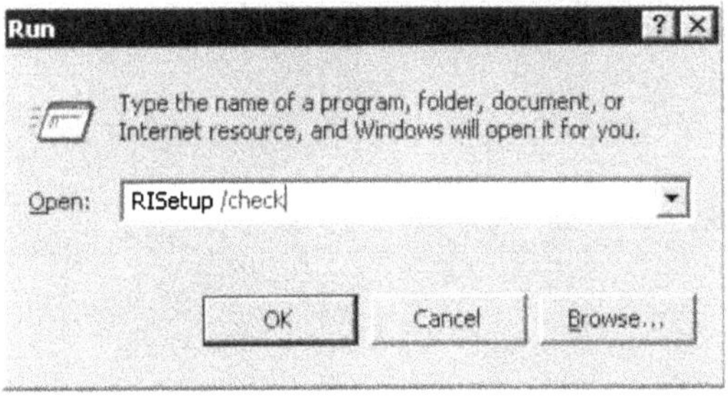

Figure 10.3 *Run "Risetup/ check" to validate the RIS server.*

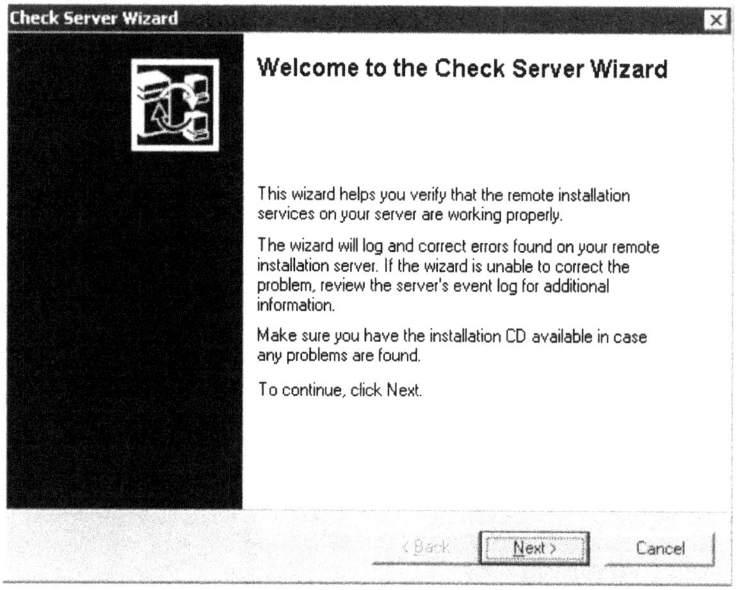

Figure 10.4 *The first page in the Wizard is an information page.*

On the next screen (Figure 10.5), the Wizard will automatically detect errors and ask you to have the RIS server installation CD-ROM ready.

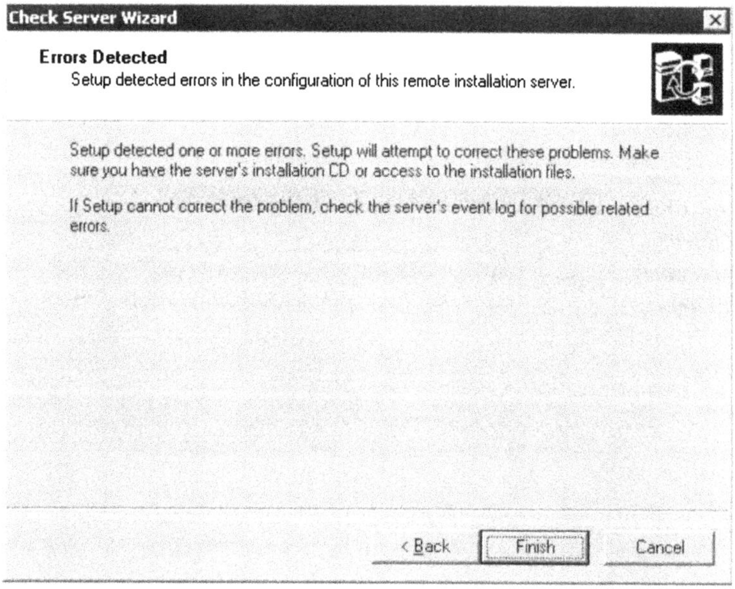

Figure 10.5 *If the Wizard discovers errors, it will try to correct them.*

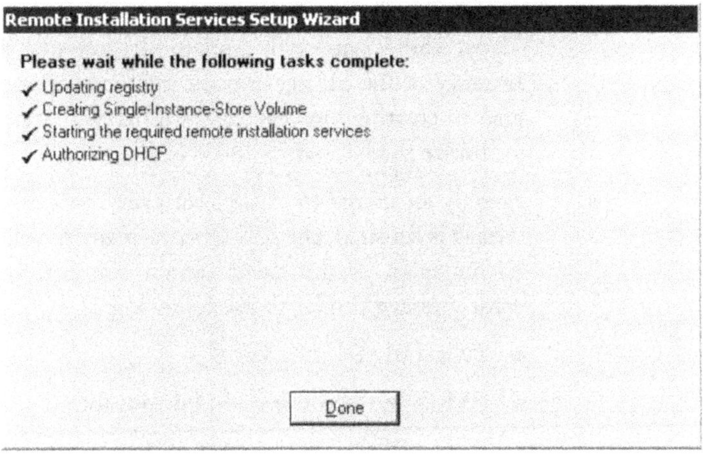

Figure 10.6 *A summary of the repair process.*

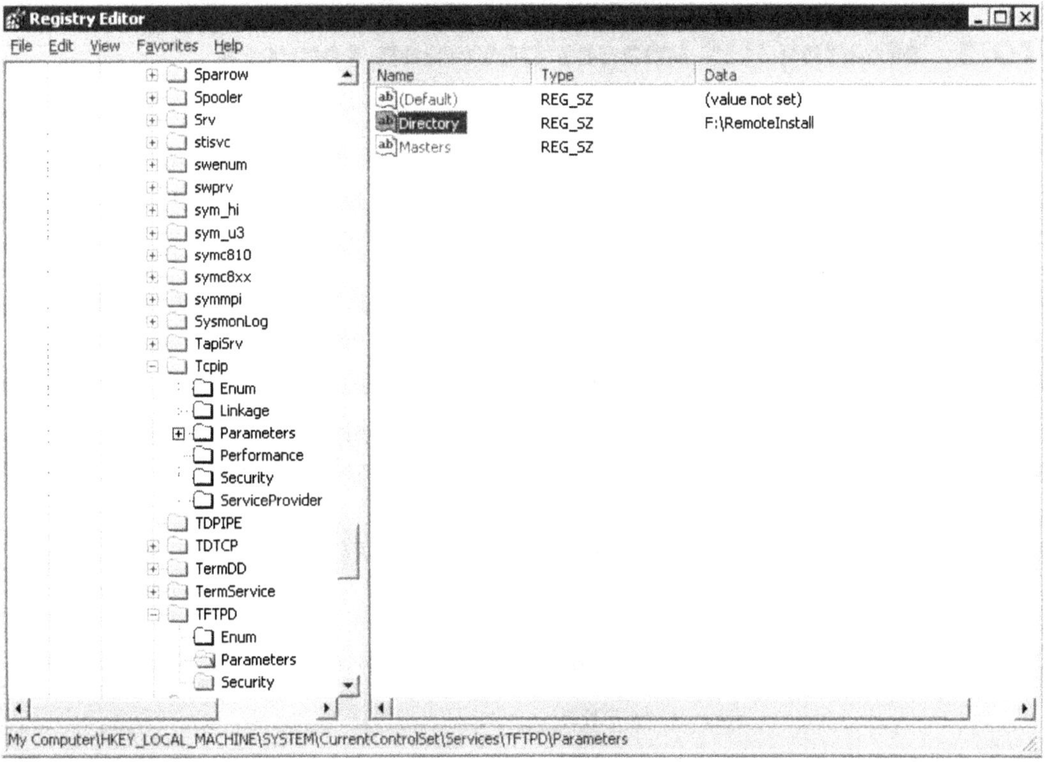

Figure 10.7 *The TFTP service can be checked in the registry.*

On the *Remote Installation Services Setup Wizard* page (Figure 10.6), the wizard will update the registry and create a new instance of the SIS services on the new volume. After the update and re-creating process, the wizard will start the services and authorize the RIS server in DHCP.

6. Deploy an image to check that everything is working. After the wizard is finished, the RIS server is ready to roll out RIS images to clients again. If the client cannot connect, you may receive an error message similar to the following:

   - PXE-T01: File not found
   - PXE-E3B: TFTP Error – File not found

   If the client receives either of these errors, check the following registry location to make sure the TFTPD is pointing to the new location: *HKEY_LOCAL_MACHINE\System\CurrentControlSet\Services\Tftpd\Parameters\Directory* (See Figure 10.7.).

10.2 Moving RIS images between servers

When installing the RIS server, one part of the setup process will set up and configure the appropriate services, and it will determine which drive or volume will hold the different RIS images. Sometimes it's necessary to move the RIS images from one RIS server to a new RIS server. The reasons could be newer hardware, more disk space, or a new topology in the network infrastructure. To ensure that the RIS images will work successfully after the move process, there are some simple steps to go through:

1. Install the RIS on the new server. (See Figure 10.8.)
2. Run *RISetup* and follow the wizard to create a new image. The new image is only temporary and will be deleted later in the process.
3. Move the file structure from the *REMINST* folder from the old server to the new directory on the new server. Delete the temporary image created in step 2.
4. Authorize the RIS server in DHCP.
5. Restart the BINL services.
6. Test that the images are working.

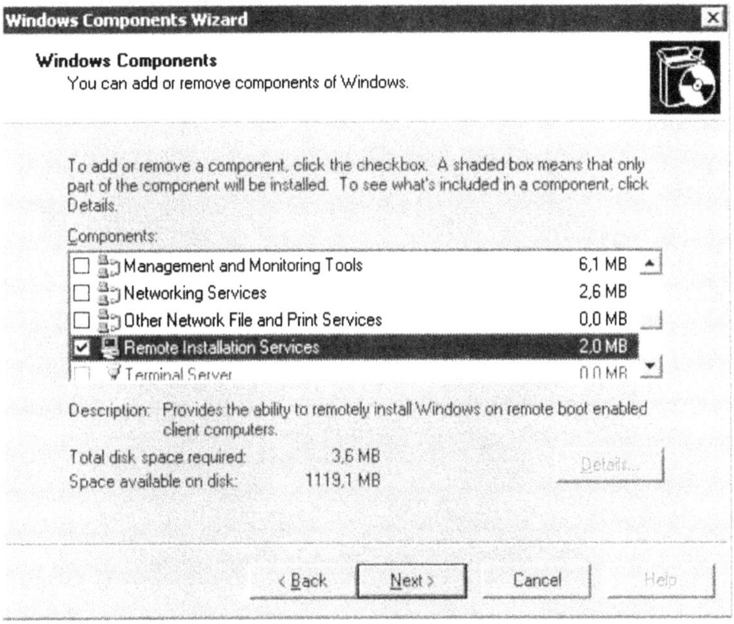

Figure 10.8 *Install the RIS service from "Add/Remove Programs" in the control panel.*

10.3 Moving RIS servers between domains

If RIS servers need to be moved between domains, some additional steps are required to ensure success in the process. It is not possible to simply join the Remote Installation Services server to a new domain; if you do that, there will be an error saying: *"BINL Services could not read its settings from Active Directory"* during the Client Installation Wizard.

This behavior is by design. During installation of an RIS server, it creates RIS-specific subobjects below the RIS server's Machine Account Object (MAO). When moving the RIS server between domains, these subobjects aren't created automatically in the target domain, so to ensure that these sub objects are created correctly in the target domain, these simple steps must be followed:

1. Remove the RIS server from the old domain and put it in a temporary workgroup, as shown in Figure 10.9. Restart the server.
2. After the server restarts, log on and join the new domain. Restart the server.
3. Authorize the RIS server from the DHCP management snap-in.

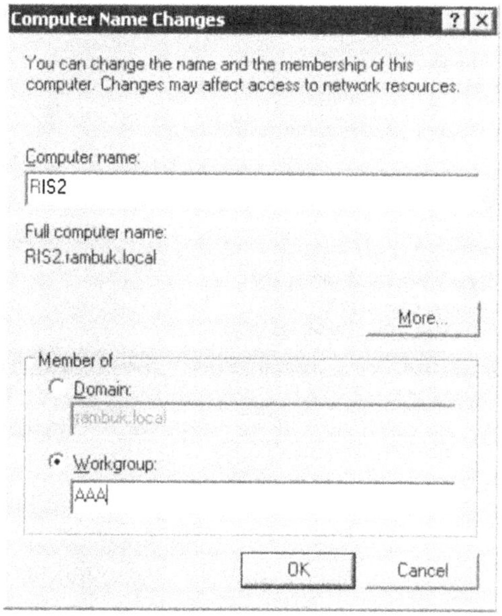

Figure 10.9 *The RIS server moves to the workgroup "AAA."*

4. On the RIS server, type the following command: *RISetup –check;* this command starts RISetup.exe in check mode. Follow the prompts on the screen until setup is finished. This process adds the required subobjects back into the RIS server's MAO, and the RIS server is fully functional.

10.4 Backup and restore of RIS servers

To ensure full backup capability, the backup program must support backup of SIS pointers and must back up the whole volume containing the RIS images. There are a lot of backup programs on the market. They are all good and provide the functionality required to back up RIS images. In this chapter, the built-in NT backup program is used.

To ensure recovery from an RIS server failure, there must be a full Automatic System Recovery (ASR) backup of the operating system and a full backup of the RIS volume. The ASR backup will be used to recover the operating system and must be done before the RIS images can be restored. The backup program must also back up the whole volume that contains the RIS images.

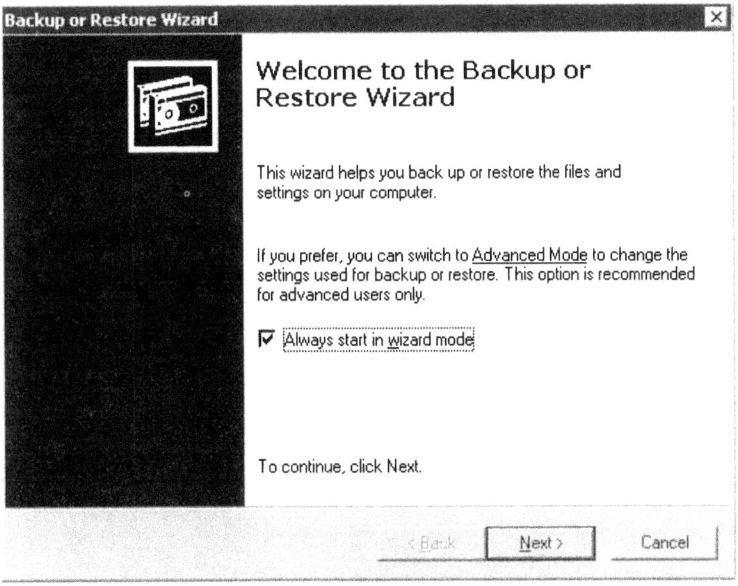

Figure 10.10 *The first information page presented when starting the backup wizard.*

So to simplify, the steps needed are as follows:

1. Perform an ASR backup of the RIS server.
2. Perform a complete backup of the RIS volume.

Let's go through the process of backup of RIS volumes:

1. Start the backup program. The first screen is the *Backup or Restore Wizard* (Figure 10.10). The only option is whether or not to start in Wizard mode.
2. On the *Backup or Restore* screen (Figure 10.11), choose *Back up files and settings* and continue to the next screen.
3. On the *What to Back Up* page (Figure 10.12), use the option *Let me choose what to back up.*
4. On the *Items to Back Up* page (Figure 10.13), choose the entire volume containing the RIS images.
5. On the *Back Up Type, Destination, and Name* page (Figure 10.14), choose where to place your backup and the name for the backup.

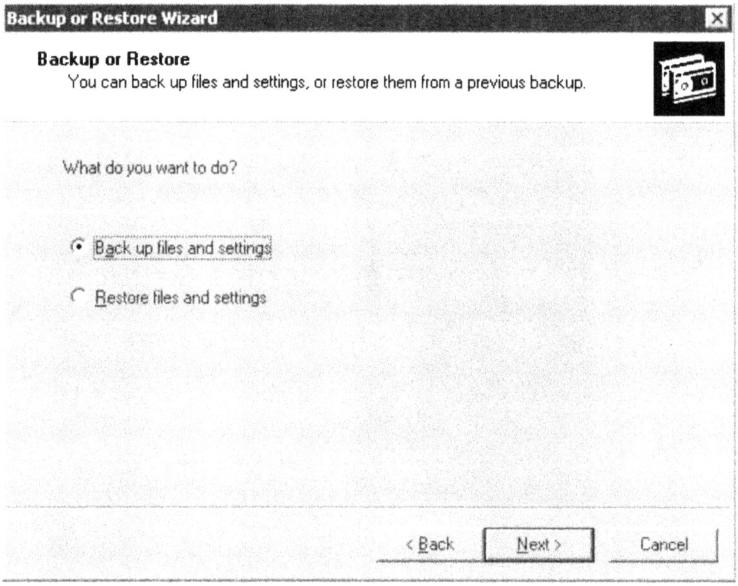

Figure 10.11 *Choose to backup files and settings.*

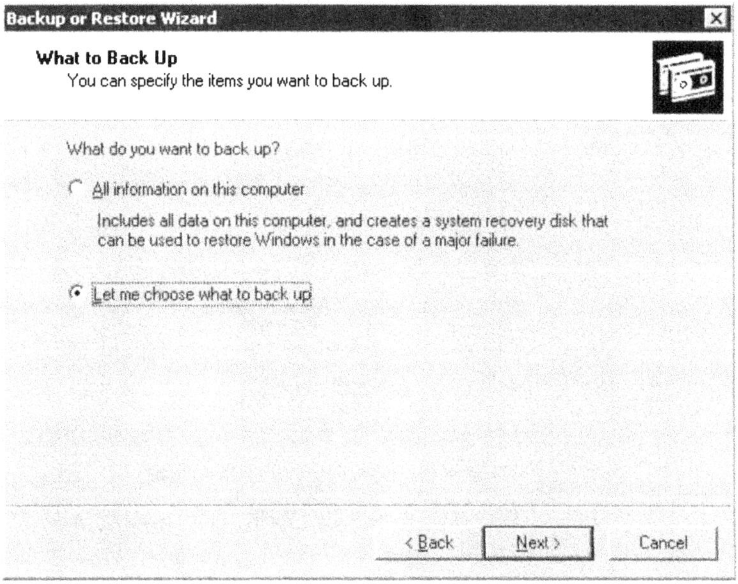

Figure 10.12 *Choose which files and folders to back up.*

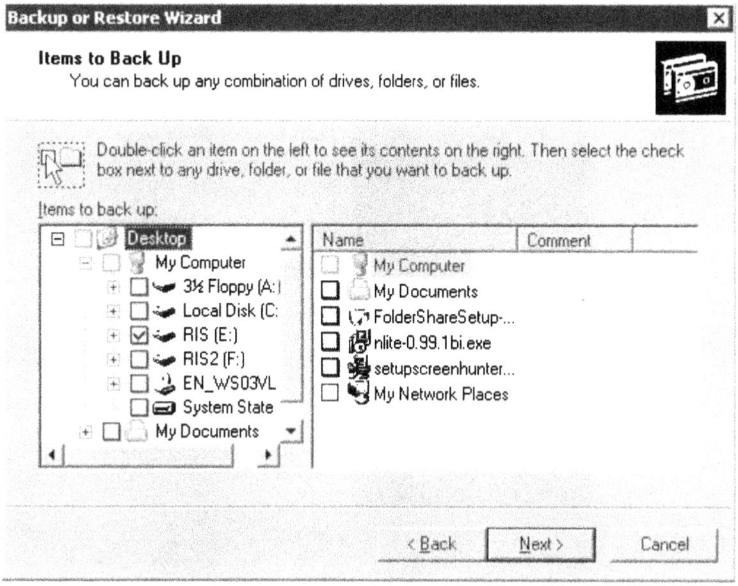

Figure 10.13 *An entire E: volume backup.*

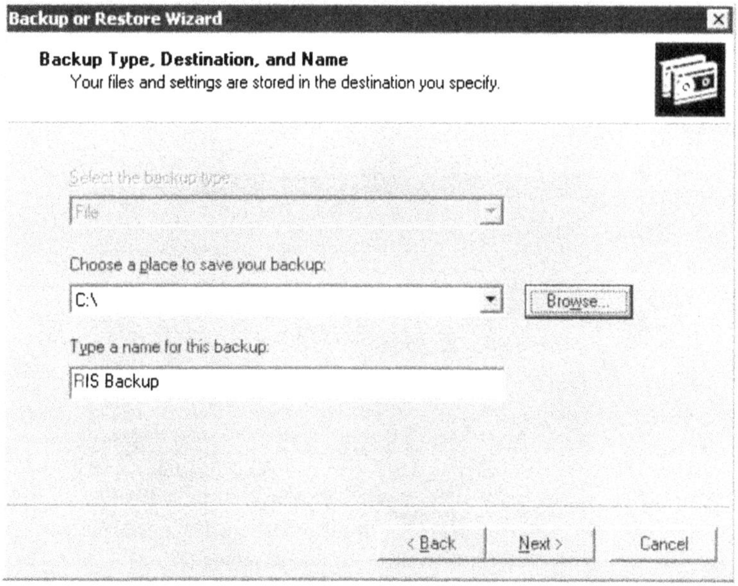

Figure 10.14 *Choose where the backup must be placed. Here the backup is placed on the C volume and given the name "RIS Backup."*

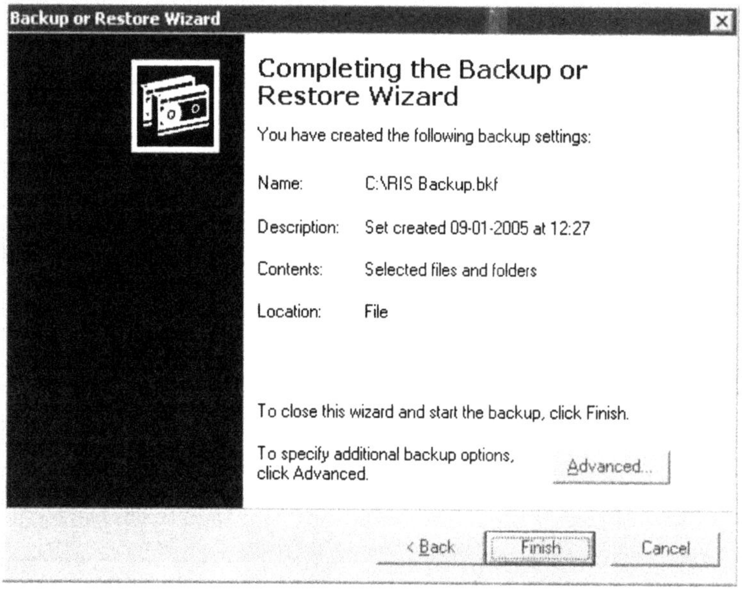

Figure 10.15
A summary displayed by the wizard.

6. On the *Completing the Backup or Restore Wizard* page (Figure 10.15), a summary is presented, and the option to go back and change any option is available. When you click Finish, the backup process begins. When the backup process completes, the report shown in Figure 10.16 is displayed.

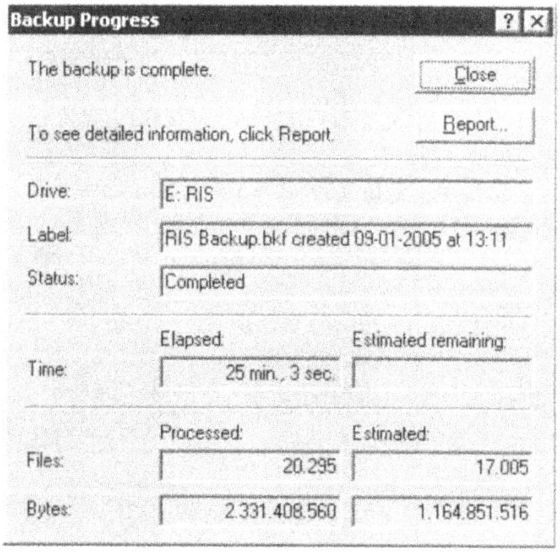

Figure 10.16
After the backup process is finished, a status screen is displayed.

To recover from a server breakdown, these simple steps are required:

1. Initiate an ASR recovery of the failed RIS server.
2. Install a CD-ROM-based image by running the *RISetup.exe* command. This step creates a clean *RemoteInstall* folder structure.
3. Restore the backup of the original SIS volumes data to the newly created *RemoteInstall* folder. After this process, there is access to the original images, and the RIS server is fully operational.

Let's go through the process of restoring RIS images:

1. On the *Welcome to the Backup or Restore Wizard* page (Figure 10.17), click Next.
2. On the *Backup or Restore* page (Figure 10.18), choose to *Restore files and settings.*
3. On the *What to Restore* page (Figure 10.19), choose the latest backup of the RIS volume.
4. On the *Completing the Backup or Restore Wizard* page (Figure 10.20), there is a summary about the choices made in the previous pages. Click *Finish*, and the restore process begins. After the restore process is finished, the report shown in Figure 10.21 is displayed and the RIS images are ready to be used.

Figure 10.17 *The restore wizard information page.*

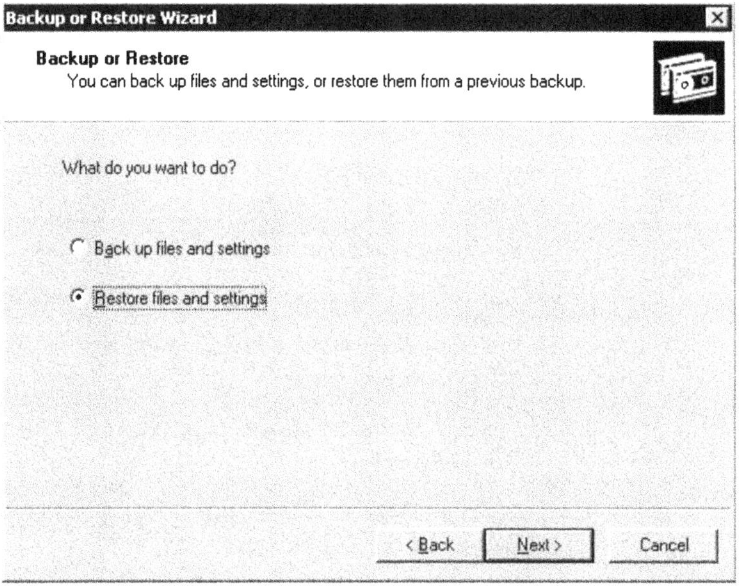

Figure 10.18
Choose "Restore file and settings."

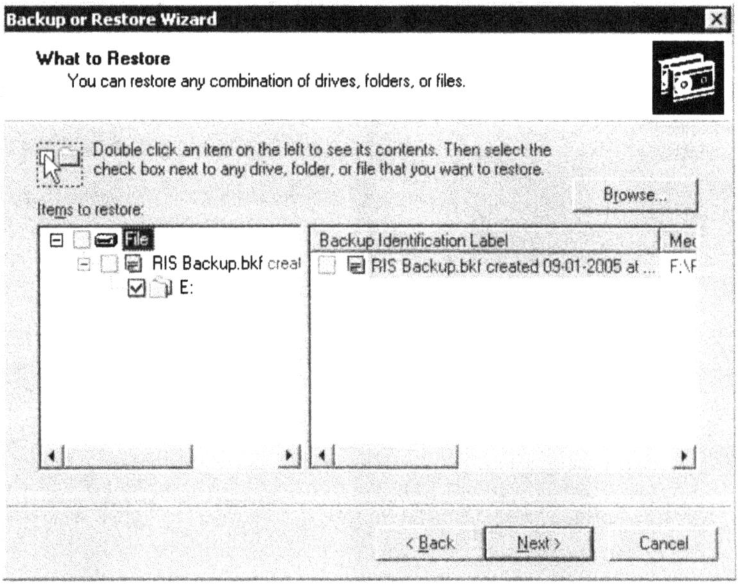

Figure 10.19
Choose the desired backup set.

Figure 10.20
A summary page displayed before the restore process begins.

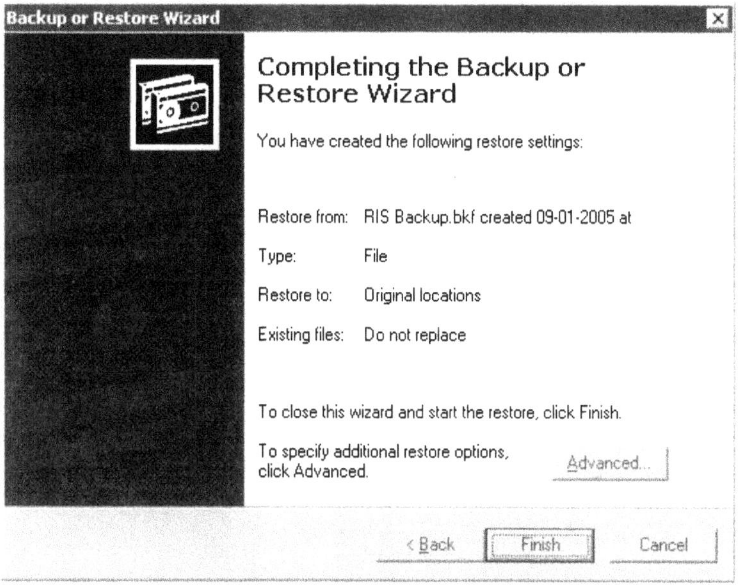

Figure 10.21
After the restore process is finished, a summary page is displayed.

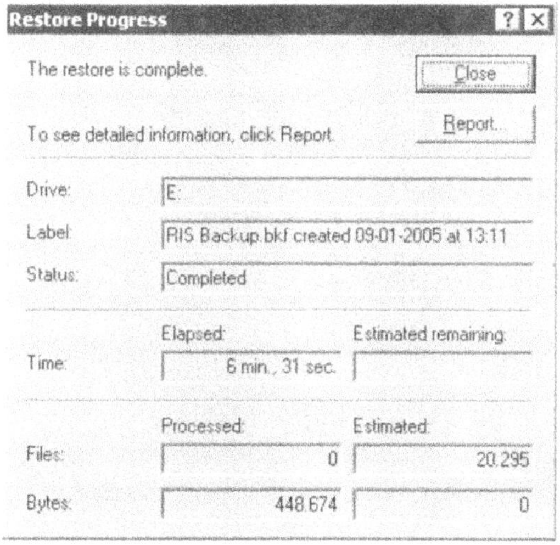

10.5 Summary

This chapter shows how easy it is to move RIS images between volumes, servers, and even domains. Last in this chapter was a quick overview of backup and restore of RIS servers and images. There must be an ASR backup in order to fully recover an RIS server from a hardware failure.

11

Understanding and Identifying Devices and Drivers

This chapter discusses some of the more theoretical terms of understanding what drivers do and how they work with Microsoft Windows and with Remote Installation Services. We'll also be showing some real-world examples of how to work with drivers more practically. The focus is not on hardware-specific issues. You don't need to be a hardware expert to understand this chapter. Instead, the focus is on how driver software interacts when deploying an operating system using Remote Installation Services. It is important to understand the interaction between devices, driver software, and the operating system if you want to make a successful client or server deployment using Remote Installation Services.

Highlights:

- Understand why drivers are important
- Understand why adding additional OEM driver support to client and server installations is essential
- Understand how drivers are built
- Get familiar with inf and sys files
- Understand how to identify unknown devices

11.1 Understanding driver inclusion

The drivers available in an OS image consist of the drivers supplied with that OS at the time of its release. This means that if you have added a Microsoft Windows XP image to your Remote Installation Services server, by default only the drivers supplied with Microsoft Windows XP are available with the image in question unless you manually include the additional correct drivers. This is the case for all operating systems supported with Remote Installation Services, including Microsoft Windows 2000 Professional or Server,

Microsoft Windows Server 2003, and Microsoft Windows XP. However, the drivers supplied with the OS are often not up-to-date, or the specific drivers you need for a certain device might not be there at all. There may be hardware devices in your hardware that are not supported with the default drivers, including audio cards, video cards, modems, power-saving units, chipsets, and so on.

Most important is the support for the network interface card (NIC) in the computer. The reason for this is that the network driver must be available in the image to make it possible to start loading the image onto the client computer in the first portion of Remote Installation Services Setup. To work around this issue of nonexisting or outdated drivers, it is possible to add new drivers to the Remote Installation Services image, thus supporting the hardware in question.

Using the previous example, your computer might contain an NIC that is not supported in the default image. In such a situation, it is possible to extract the correct drivers supplied from the hardware provider and include them on the image by merging the drivers into the basic image for the specific operating system. We will go into a lot of detail about how to do this in a later chapter.

11.2 Drivers included with Microsoft Windows

Microsoft Windows XP and Microsoft Windows Server 2003 ship with a much larger quantity of drivers out of the box than Microsoft Windows 2000. Also, significantly more devices are supported. This makes Microsoft Windows XP or Microsoft Windows Server 2003 easier operating systems to deploy using Remote Installation Services, because the number of drivers to manually merge into the basic image will be smaller. However, there are no general rules for this process, because hardware manufacturers keep developing new hardware all the time, thus making the default hardware support in Microsoft Windows XP or Microsoft Windows Server 2003 less compatible with new hardware over time.

When Microsoft Windows 2000 shipped some years ago, it supported almost all hardware, but things change, hardware gets better all the time, and new hardware devices are invented. Today, because new hardware has been developed, Microsoft Windows 2000 does not support the same amount of hardware that it did some years ago. This will eventually also happen with Microsoft Windows XP or Microsoft Windows Server 2003 over the next few years, and therefore it is important to understand how to make a Remote Installation Services image support new hardware. There is a common misunderstanding that Microsoft Windows Service Packs extend the driver support of the OS by adding new drivers, but this is not the case.

11.3 What is OEM?

This section explains what OEM is. It's important to understand, because when working with Remote Installation Services, there are many references to the terms OEM or OEM driver. OEM is short for Original Equipment Manufacturer, which is a misleading term for a company that has a special relationship with computer manufacturers. OEMs buy computers in bulk and customize them for a particular application or purpose. They then sell the customized computer using their own brand name. The term OEM is really a misnomer because OEMs are not the *original* manufacturers; they are the customizers.

To make it short, when referring to the term OEM in connection with Remote Installation Services, we refer to a producer of driver software that is not included with Microsoft Windows by default; the driver is written or even just branded by an OEM provider. The driver could be digitally signed by Microsoft, but, in some cases, it might not be. Also remember that if a driver isn't signed by Microsoft, it doesn't mean that the driver doesn't work.

11.4 Including OEM drivers in the installation

The starting point for adding driver support to your Remote Installation Services image is to identify the hardware devices for which we need to add support. To simplify the concept of devices and drivers, you need to understand this context:

- A device is a hardware unit (e.g., an audio card).
- A driver makes the operating system identify and support the device, thus making the device available to the operating system and to applications.

Identifying unsupported hardware devices can at times be a time-consuming process, and it is heavily dependent on the hardware providers' documentation. Whereas some hardware providers and vendors provide great publicly available documentation, others do not.

11.5 Identifying devices and drivers

Quality hardware manufacturers provide detailed documentation for all devices in their computers and have publicly available resources for downloading the appropriate drivers for these devices. If this documentation is not in place, it can become more of a hit-and-miss affair to obtain the correct drivers. Try the Web first. This is normally the best entry point to find a hardware manufacturer. Unfortunately, some OEM providers do not have a Web site at all.

Never conclude anything by the brand name on the front of your computer hardware box. The name there could be only your local dealer's brand name or the whole idea or approach to maintaining an OEM brand name. The computer might be assembled from several hardware devices found on the spot on the day of putting it together. Or even worse, things might be thrown inside that are incompatible with the operating system you wish to load onto it.

In general, we urge businesses to look for brand names when purchasing computers. Buying a quality brand computer might cost you a tad more, but it's well worth the effort in the long run because of the available resources and documentation (and because these companies actually make good computers and also invest in R&D).

11.5.1 The trial-and-error method

One way of identifying computer devices is to perform a standard, manual CD-based Microsoft Windows installation on the computer, and then just see what happens. You can then identify the unsupported devices appearing as being unavailable devices in the Microsoft Windows Device Manager. However, Microsoft Windows Device Manager does not clearly identify which type of device is unsupported; it only identifies the device as "Unknown" or as an "Unknown PCI Device." Other descriptions are used too. An unknown device is also identified with a yellow mark in the Microsoft Windows Device Manager. Other than this way, the only way to find out which devices are unavailable is to actually test them using different device drivers. Again, documentation is the key to success.

11.5.2 The use-the-preload method

A slightly easier way to work around identifying unknown devices is to simply turn on the computer and start it up with its preinstalled operating

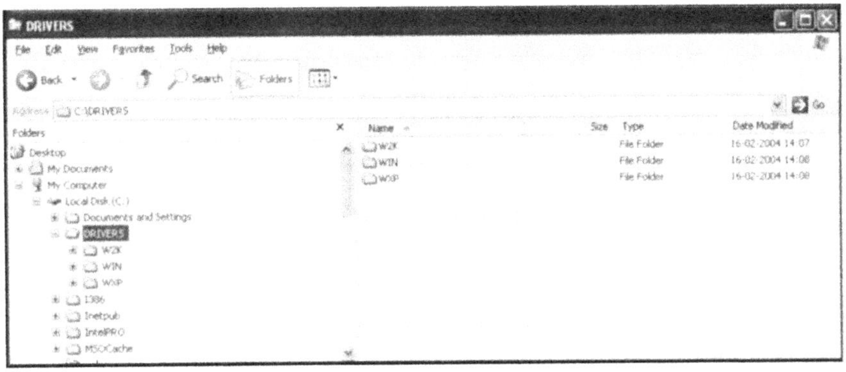

Figure 11.1 *An example of drivers included with an OS preload. They are all on the hard disk ready to copy. In this example, drivers are included for several operating systems.*

system (provided there is one, of course). You will often find that the drivers for all hardware devices are available from the hard disk, ready to copy and reuse in your Remote Installation Services environment. (See Figure 11.1.) However, not all computers ship with a preinstalled OS, or the preinstalled OS might not be similar to the OS you wish to deploy using Remote Installation Services.

11.6 Identifying unknown devices using the registry

If you do not want to go through the hassle of trial and error in attempting to identify an unknown device, there is another possibility. This method requires using the registry editor. First a little background: When your computer boots, the Peripheral Component Interconnect (PCI) devices are polled for the following information:

- Vendor ID
- Device ID
- Subsystem ID
- Hardware Revision ID

This information is stored in the following Microsoft Windows registry location:

```
HKEY_LOCAL_MACHINE\System\CurrentControlSet\Enum\PCI\
```

A number of subkeys will be present and use this context:

```
VEN_<vendorID>&DEV_<deviceID>&SUBSYS_<subsystemID>&REV_
<hardwarerevisionID>
```

`<VendorID>` is a four-digit hexadecimal vendor ID number.

`<DeviceID>` is a four-digit hexadecimal device ID number.

`<SubsystemID>` is a subsystem ID number.

`<HardwarerevisionID>` is a hardware revision ID number.

All of these ID numbers are unique for any PCI device type that has ever been made. To use this information to help you identify the unknown device, follow these steps:

1. Open the registry editor (regedit.exe) and expand the following registry subkey:

   ```
   HKEY_LOCAL_MACHINE\System\CurrentControlSet\Enum\
   PCI
   ```

2. Under PCI, expand one of the following subkeys:

   ```
   VEN_vendorID&DEV_deviceID&SUBSYS_subsystemID&REV_
   hardwarerevisionID
   ```

   For example:

   ```
   VEN_11C1&DEV_0442&SUBSYS_04401668&REV_01
   ```

Now click the subkey below it. You will notice different values.

From Figure 11.2, note these values:

1. *Class* is the hardware class of the device, such as "MEDIA." The Class value varies, and it describes the hardware class.
2. *DeviceDesc* is the description of the device, such as "SoundMAX Integrated Digital Audio." The device description varies according to what device is in question.
3. *Mfg* is the device manufacturer, such as "Analog Devices, Inc." This value also varies depending on the name of the manufacturer.

To identify the unknown PCI device, follow these steps:

1. View the registry entries in the folder that appears in each of the registry subkeys under the following registry key: *HKEY_LOCAL_MACHINE\System\CurrentControlSet\Enum\PCI.*
2. Note the `Class` registry entry with the `Data` value of `Unknown`.
3. Write down the following information for the parent registry subkey where these values are located:

- Vendor ID
- Device ID
- Subsystem ID
- Hardware Revision ID

For example, if the `Unknown` data value is found in the subfolder of the following registry subkey, write down the following information:

Registry subkey:

```
HKEY_LOCAL_MACHINE\Enum\PCI\VEN_11C1&DEV_0442&SUBSYS_
04401668&REV_01
```

In that case, you should write down the following information:

- Vendor ID: 11C1
- Device ID: 0442
- Subsystem ID: 04401668
- Hardware Revision ID: 01

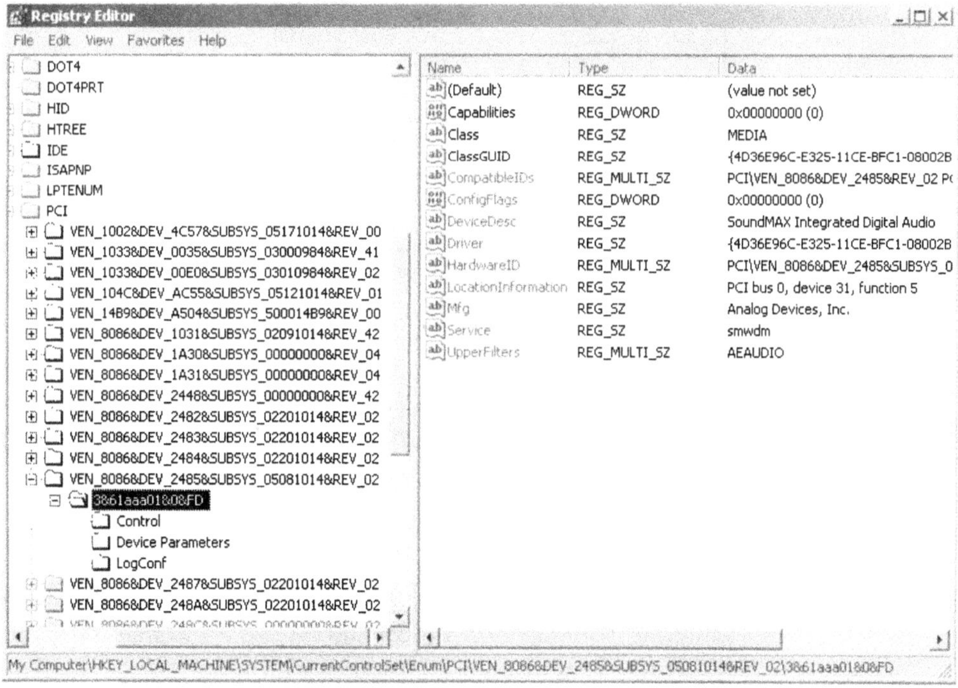

Figure 11.2 *An example of a PCI device known to the operating system.*

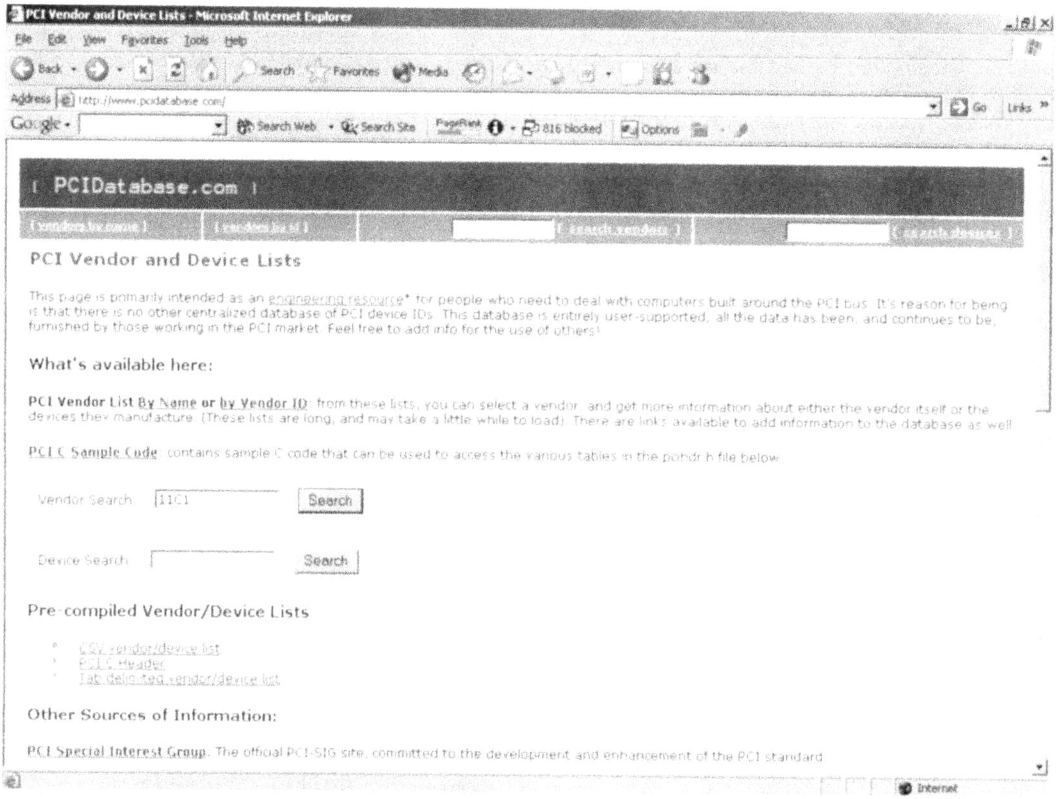

Figure 11.3 *Entering a search criteria using www.pcidatabase.com.*

Now that you have this information in place, go to the PCI Vendor and Device Lists Web site to find matches to your unknown device: *www.pcidatabase.com.* (See Figure 11.3.)

The search result using the `<Vendor ID>` data is shown in Figure 11.4.

Afterward, based on the information you get, obtain the driver software for the device. The next steps in including OEM drivers in the Remote Installation Services installation are to test the driver manually on a reference computer, save the driver software you have found in a safe place, and analyze how the driver software is built.

In the next chapter we will go into detail about how to specifically do it, but before doing that, it is important to understand how a driver is built and how Remote Installation Services identifies a driver. Read on.

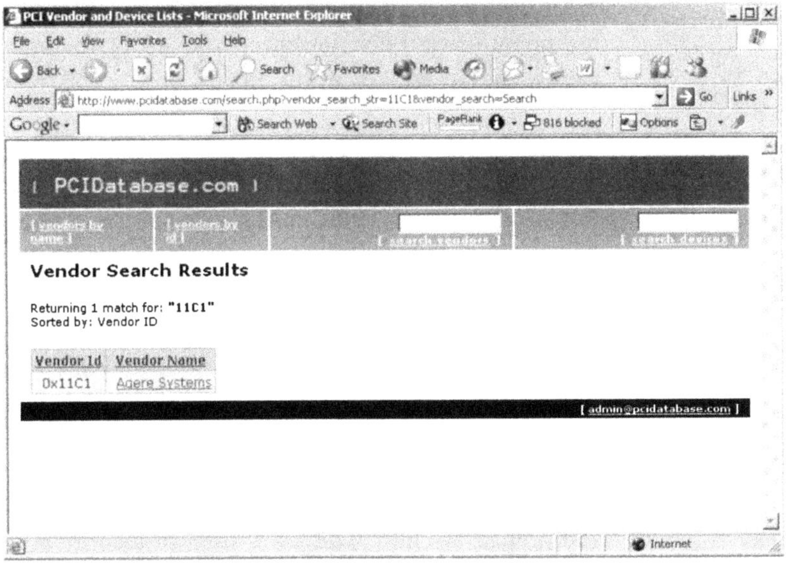

Figure 11.4 *The return result of the search. You can now refine the information you need.*

11.7 Driver file essentials

You've heard of drivers, and you've probably heard of (or experienced) how a poorly written or implemented driver can become a frustrating experience. In most cases, there's bound to be a completely rational explanation for driver problems. In other cases, there might not be. Some drivers are poorly written (which, apparently, occurs every now and then), and some drivers are simply implemented incorrectly. No matter what the case, drivers that work incorrectly are a moment of irritation. Therefore, it's important to understand some basic things about how a driver works and how it is built.

As mentioned earlier, a driver has one purpose: To add support for a specific device. It makes the operating system consult the device so that it becomes operational for the operating system and for applications installed on the operating system platform. In other words, the driver is a genuine middle man. It takes orders from the operating system (or from an application through the operating system) and passes on the orders to the device to make the device perform an instruction.

For example, suppose you're writing a Microsoft Word document. Now you want to print it. You click *Print*. This instruction is now passed on to the driver, which in return orders the printer to do the job of printing the document using the various properties set by the user. It's so basic, but still somewhat complicated if this process isn't carried out correctly.

11.7.1 What's in a driver?

At a bare minimum, a driver basically consists of two files:

- The system information file (.inf)
- The actual driver binary file (.sys)

Other files might be included in a driver build (e.g., executables, DLLs, and proprietary files), but the system information file and driver binary file are really the most important files. The system information file is essentially a text file. The file contains device identification numbers, vendor IDs, and pointers to the driver binary file and in some cases to DLLs, executables, and proprietary files. The file is used to identify a device using the driver binary file, which in effect performs the actual device identification task. This way, a printer, for example, can never be identified as an audio card. The driver binary file contains the driver binary code. It's coded by enthusiastic code dwarves who know a lot about devices and machine code.

Remote Installation Services identifies a device by analyzing the system information file for information about the device in question and then parses the information to the driver binary file during installation. The driver binary file then returns information to the operating system about the device. It also matches the driver files for compliance with the device. The system information file and driver binary file are the files you need to identify and to make available to eventually make a driver work with Remote Installation Services.

11.7.2 Catalog files

Sometimes you will also see .cat files included in the set of files of the driver. A .cat file is a catalog file. Encryptions of the driver binary and other relevant information are stored in a catalog file. A catalog file is a collection of tags. Each tag corresponds to a file that is installed by the driver package. Each driver package that is submitted to Windows Hardware Quality Logo (WHQL) for cryptographic signing has a catalog file entry in the .inf file that specifies the name of the catalog file. During WHQL tests, a digitally signed catalog file is created that corresponds to the catalog file entry in the .inf file of the driver package. During driver package installation, the catalog file is registered with the operating system. The operating system references the registered catalog file during the installation of driver files that are contained in the driver package.

11.8 Other files and folder structures

As mentioned earlier, it is important to save the other files that came with the driver software, not just the .inf and .sys files. If an extracted driver is made up in a logical folder structure, it is important too to leave that folder structure untouched, with all the right files in the right folder structures. Never rename folders and *never* rename files. The reason for not renaming folders is that the system information file often points to files inside the driver software folder structure, thus requiring the files in question to be present in exactly those specific locations.

11.9 Setup.exe programs

Installing a specific driver usually seems to only involve downloading a file and then running the setup.exe program from that file. Although this process works fine for already installed computers, it does not provide any support in Remote Installation Services. The first reason for this is that, as mentioned earlier, Remote Installation Services will only extend its driver support capability by identifying .inf and .sys files, nothing else. Running a setup.exe program can never be integrated into a Remote Installation Services driver structure to be extended. Second, most setup programs that install drivers are in fact install packages that do a whole wealth of things: they extract and install the drivers and additionally install supporting software or actual applications as well. These setup programs are designed to satisfy the needs of home users, making it easy to install a driver. There is an option to install drivers silently using *cmdlines* or *GUIRunOnce* when the driver software package allows it. This option is addressed in Chapter 14.

11.10 Extracting drivers

Nevertheless, most setup programs are designed so that core driver files can be extracted. If that is the case, you will be able to run the setup program of the downloaded file with one or more options or parameters, which allow you to extract the drivers into a directory structure of your own choice. Some setup programs will prompt you to indicate whether you want to

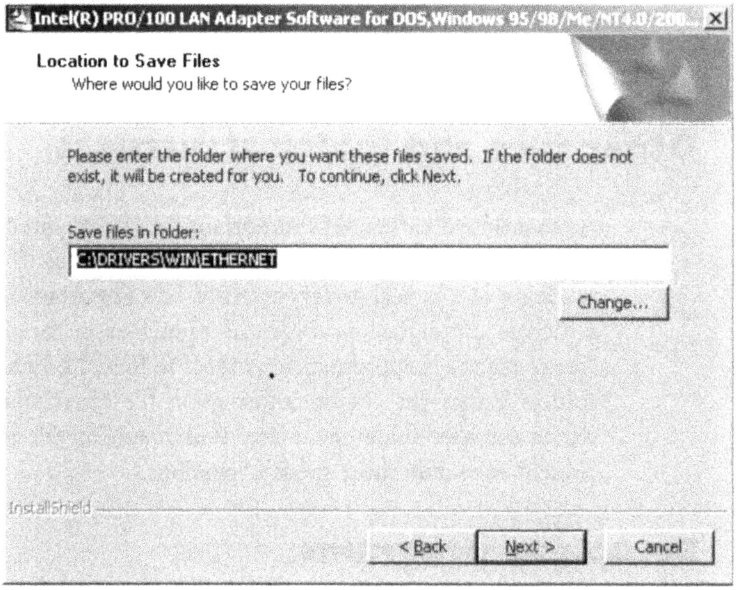

Figure 11.5 *This is an example of one of the better setup.exe install packages. You just double-click setup.exe, and it automatically prompts you to extract driver files to a location of your choosing. Not all setup.exe programs are this friendly though.*

install the software or extract the files, but others will not. If you are given such an option, always choose to extract files for later installation and inclusion in Remote Installation Services. (See Figure 11.5.)

If your setup.exe program isn't as friendly as the one in Figure 11.5, you must go to a command prompt and try different possibilities. Extraction of files from a setup.exe program is often done using hidden parameters. You will have to run the setup program from a command line running setup.exe followed by the parameter. The /x parameter is widely used for this purpose. The extraction parameters vary. Using the /? parameter will usually cause the setup program to display a list of all parameters available. Reading

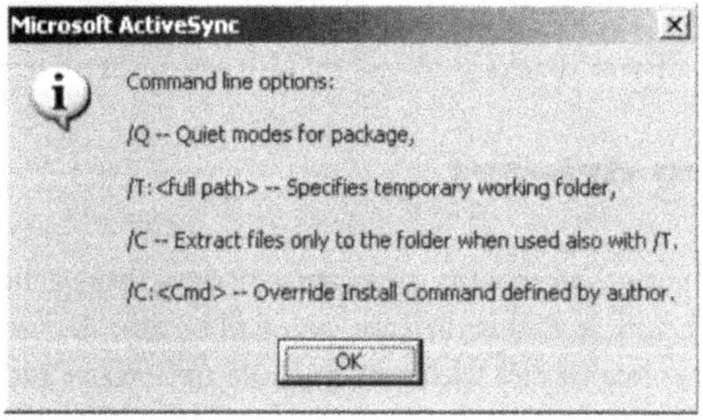

Figure 11.6 *Command line options.*

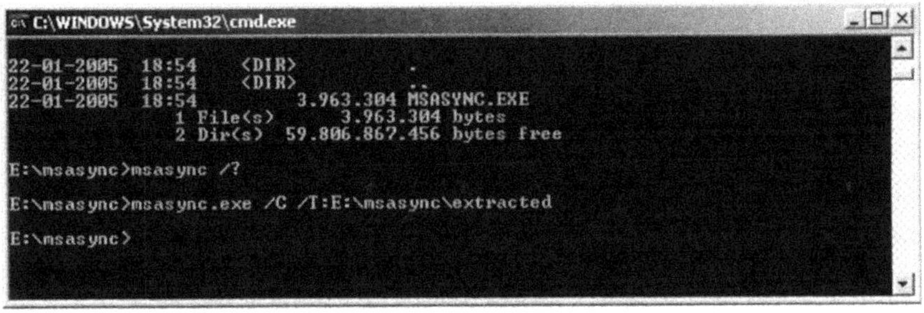

Figure 11.7 *Application file extraction command.*

the readme.txt file, which is often bundled with the software driver files, can sometimes turn out to be useful.

Following is a discription of a simple extraction—it shows how you first run the /? parameter after the executable.

After opening a command prompt, write the command "msasync.exe / ?" (msasync.exe is the name of the application executable in this example only). After having written this command, the computer produces the output shown in Figure 11.6.

From this information window, we now see that in order to extract the program files, we must use the /C parameter. However, it also shows that we must use the /T parameter to specify the directory in which we wish to extract the files. So the final command to extract the files of this application is shown in Figure 11.7.

Always extract driver/application files to some file location where it is possible to work freely with the driver software without interfering with production systems. Again, there are no rules about whether the extraction option is available other than those defined by the driver software provider. Once extracted, the files might look as those shown in Figure 11.8.

As mentioned earlier, the file names and folder hierarchy of the extracted files must never be changed, given the pointers in the .inf and .sys files. (See Figure 11.9.)

For the same audio driver as illustrated before, we found the .inf and .sys files in this subfolder. These are the files we need to make available to Remote Installation Services. However, the entire folder hierarchy, including the folders and files above the level of the .inf and .sys files, must be included in the Remote Installation Services installation. *In such case, note this location for later inclusion in the answer file.*

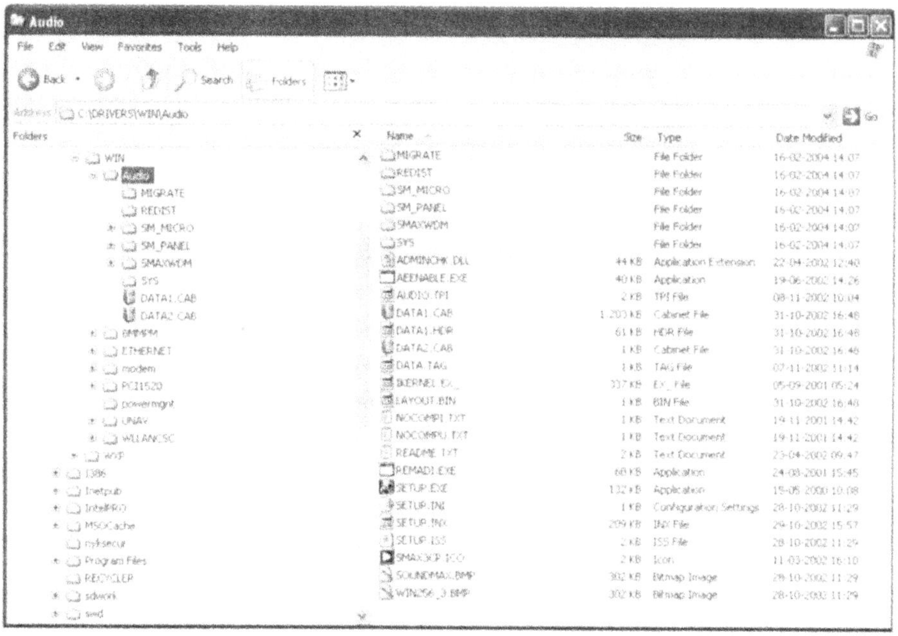

Figure 11.8 *An example of an extracted audio driver. As you see, there are no .inf and .sys files present in this top-level folder hierarchy, only a setup.exe file.*

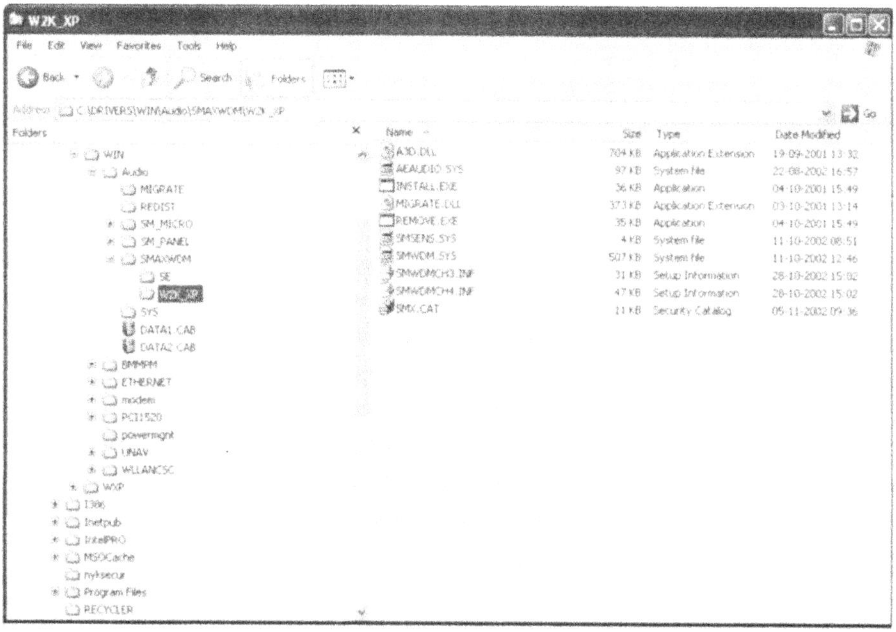

Figure 11.9 *The .sys and .inf files are placed in a lower-level folder.*

11.11 Multiple device support

You will sometimes find that an extracted setup program extracts several .inf and .sys files. The reason for this is that the driver in question may support multiple devices. At other times, one single .inf and .sys file might support multiple devices. There might even be several .inf and .sys files in multiple folders. Most commonly, the driver files at the top level of the driver folder hierarchy are authoritative for the entire structure. The .inf file will point to the correct .sys file, or even point to another .inf file in a different folder, which alternatively points to the correct .sys file in its own folder or yet another folder.

There is little logic in how .inf files point to .sys files in multiple folders. The only logic is that of the developer who has written the driver binaries and its structure. Digging deeper into this logic, it is, however, perfectly possible to open .inf files for viewing and editing with a text editor such as the incredible Notepad. Editing a system information file is not recommended (unless you're a code dwarf or just bored), however, because one comma or dot (let alone, a dash) in the wrong place in the file could mean the difference been success or fiasco in applying a driver.

Network drivers and chipset drivers can be particularly difficult to include in Remote Installation Services installations. We will go into detail about network card drivers in a later chapter. Eventually, the driver files will have to be made available to the Remote Installation Services server. This is done by including the files in the OEM folder structure and creating an entry for the .inf and .sys files in the answer. This process will be discussed from Chapter 12 and on.

11.12 Summary

In order to eliminate the infamous *Unknown PCI Device* warning, which is not uncommon to appear on a newly installed computer, it is absolutely essential to use the correct OEM drivers if Windows does not have built-in support for the device. OEM drivers are sometimes supplied with an operating system preload, but you can never be sure. Use documentation or the Windows registry to identify the drivers. To be able to identify the drivers, it is helpful to understand the fundamentals of what the system information file and the driver binary file do.

12

Creating and Understanding the OEM Structure

Now that we have discussed driver essentials and the importance of the system information file and the driver file, let's go into detail about how to actually make them available in Remote Installation Services, where to include the files, and how to work with Remote Installation Services once the files are available.

Highlights:

- Understand what a distribution point is
- Understand the content of different folders
- Understand specific use of OEM subfolders
- Understand what "one-image-fits-all" really means

The Remote Installation Services file share is by default shared as "REMINST." The default folder name is "RemoteInstall." The real structure indicates a rather logical setup:

```
RemoteInstall (shared as REMINST, all Remote Installation Services
               files are placed below)
    Admin (this is where the global administration tools are
           located)
    OSChooser (this is where options for text-mode setup
               are defined)
        Setup (top-level folder for all images)
             [Language of image] (a language folder is created for
                                  images of different languages)
                 Images (top-level folder for images for the
                        language in question)
                    [Friendly name of image] (this is the name that
                                              identifies the image)
                        I386 (containing the operating system code
                             drop)
                            lang
                            system32
                              templates
```

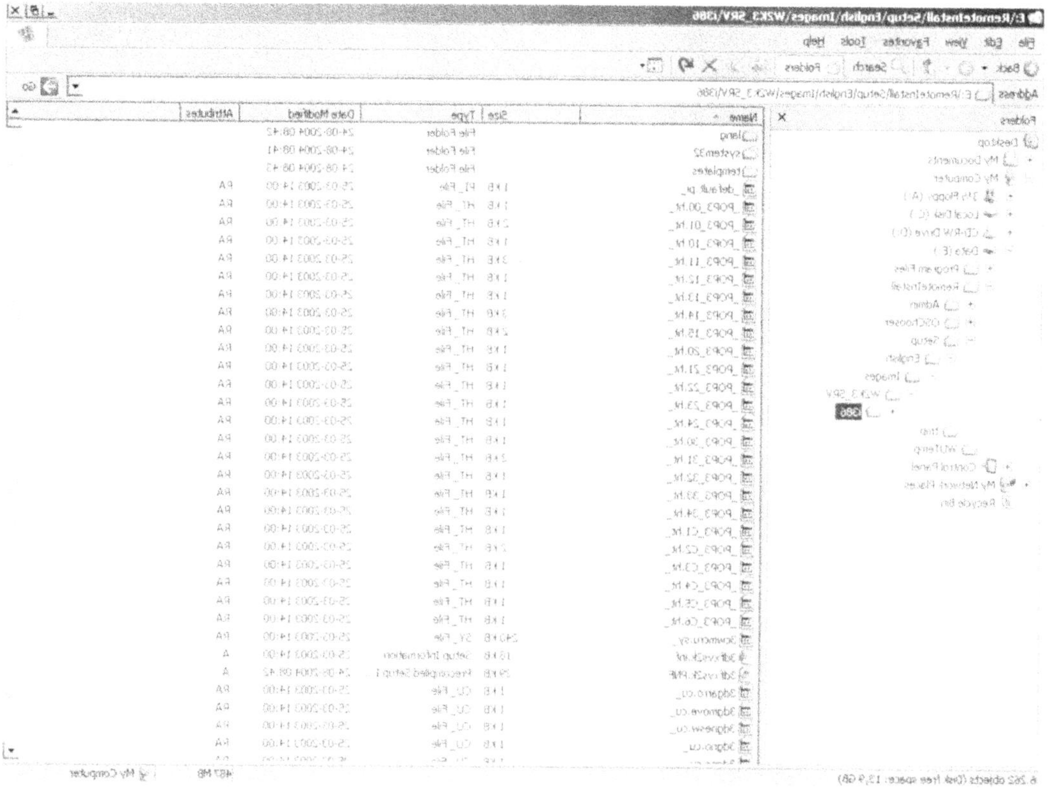

Figure 12.1 *RemoteInstall folder structure.*

The entire folder structure is shown in Figure 12.1.

In order to create support for devices that are not supported by the default drivers, and in order to be able to distribute files and applications, we must extend this folder hierarchy. The first step involves creating the OEM folder. This is often referred to as a *distribution point*. The OEM folder is the root distribution point for a Remote Installation Services client installation. By itself it does not represent a physical folder on the client computer, but rather it should be thought of as a logical server-based point of administration that allows us to distribute content to client installations. A subfolder created below OEM will distribute different content for different purposes to client installation.

This, for example, could be creating a physical folder on the client installation and then copying files to that folder. However, different subfolders of OEM do different things. Some subfolders use a special context. Those subfolder are hard-coded for special use. We will go into detail

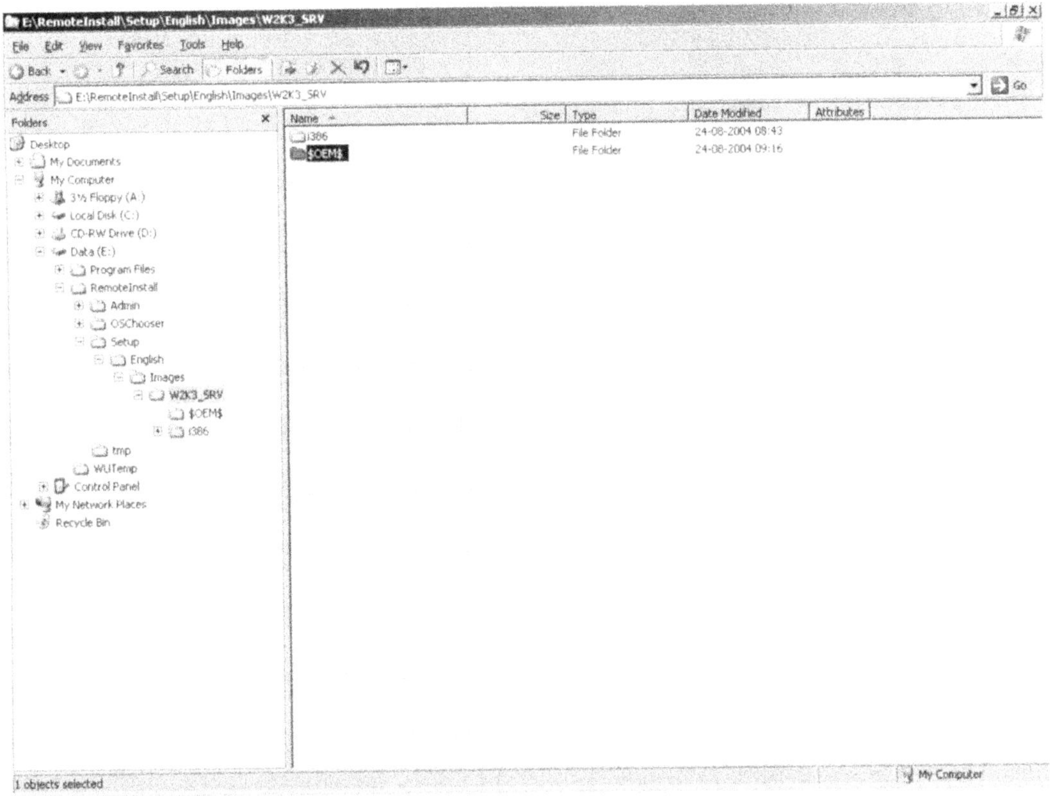

Figure 12.2 *An example of the OEM distribution point.*

about that a little later. Any available image on the Remote Installation Services server can have its own individual OEM folder, and thus its own distribution point. This folder must be located at the same level as the I386 folder level (the I386 folder contains the OS code drop slipstreamed with any Service Pack).

Create the OEM folder at the same level as the \I386 folder of the Remote Installation Services image, as shown in Figure 12.2.

12.1 OEM subfolders and their functionality

Because the OEM folder is really a distribution point, you can add extra files to an installation that might be specific to your software or hardware on your computer—not just driver files, but any sort of files or applications. These are placed below the OEM folder using specific subfolders. There are different behaviors, all depending on the name of the subfolders that are created. Examples in the following sections show the different possibilities.

12.1.1 \OEM\textmode

In this subfolder you can place hardware-specific files for use during the initial Microsoft Windows installation and text mode setup, such as OEM HALs, SCSI drivers, RAID controller files, and such. This is the place where the txtsetup.oem file for a RAID adapter would go. The files placed here are the same as you would include in a manual CD-based installation, using the F6 option to manually include mass storage devices or using the F5 option to manually include another HAL than that included with Windows. All files placed in the OEM\Textmode subfolder (e.g., HALs, drivers, and txtsetup.oem) must be listed in the `[OEMBootFiles]` section of the SIF; otherwise, installation will never initialize the files. This issue is covered in detail in Chapter 13.

12.1.2 \$OEM$\$$

Files in this subfolder are used to replace any core Microsoft Windows system files. They must match the structure of the WinNT structure. For example, to replace files in the winnt\system32 folder, you must create \$OEM$\$$\system32 and then copy the relevant files into the system32 folder.

12.1.3 \$OEM$\$1

Files in this subfolder are copied to the drive where Microsoft Windows is installed (%SystemDrive%), most commonly the C:\ drive. Any subfolder in the $1 directory will be created in the root of the system drive. This is used for placing drivers, but it can also be used for just copying files of any kind (e.g., application files).

12.1.4 \$OEM$\$[drive letter]

This subfolder is almost the same as $1, but it allows you to set a specific drive letter; for example, \$OEM$\$E would copy the contents in it (and its subfolders) to the local E-drive on the client computer. This does not make much sense though, because Remote Installation Services can only partition one drive (the system drive defaulting to C:\). Therefore, this option can really only be used with the System Preparation Tool.

12.1.5 \$OEM$\$$\Help

This subfolder contains OEM Help files to be copied to C:\Winnt\Help during setup.

12.1.6 \$OEM$\$$\System32

This subfolder contains files to be copied to the C:\Winnt\System32 folder during setup. For example, if you wanted to deploy robocopy.exe to all client computers, this would be the place to put the file.

12.1.7 \$OEM$\$1\Sysprep

This subfolder contains the files required to run the Sysprep tool.

Note: Files in these subfolders must use short file names following the 8.3 naming convention unless you also create a $$rename.txt file.

Refer to section 12.4 for more information.

12.2 File and driver distribution example

In this section, we'll try to give you an idea of how to start working with the OEM distribution point, showing you a simple example of how to incorporate folders for distribution of drivers and files. As mentioned in section 12.1, there are various types of folders you can create, so let's start by working with the $1 folder, which, as mentioned, defaults to the %SystemDrive%, the system drive of the client computer.

- Create a $1 folder below the OEM folder.
- Now create a folder called "Drivers" (or anything else for that matter) below the $1 folder.

The $1 folder resolves to %SystemDrive%. During text-mode Setup, the folders and files in this example would be copied to the %SystemDrive%\Drivers folders, which would be C:\Drivers. (See Figure 12.3.)

The "Drivers" folder added beneath the $1 folder in this scenario is the starting point in the Remote Installation Services folder hierarchy to start adding the driver files and software for the devices. You may want to create additional folders in the Drivers subfolder, as shown in Figure 12.3,

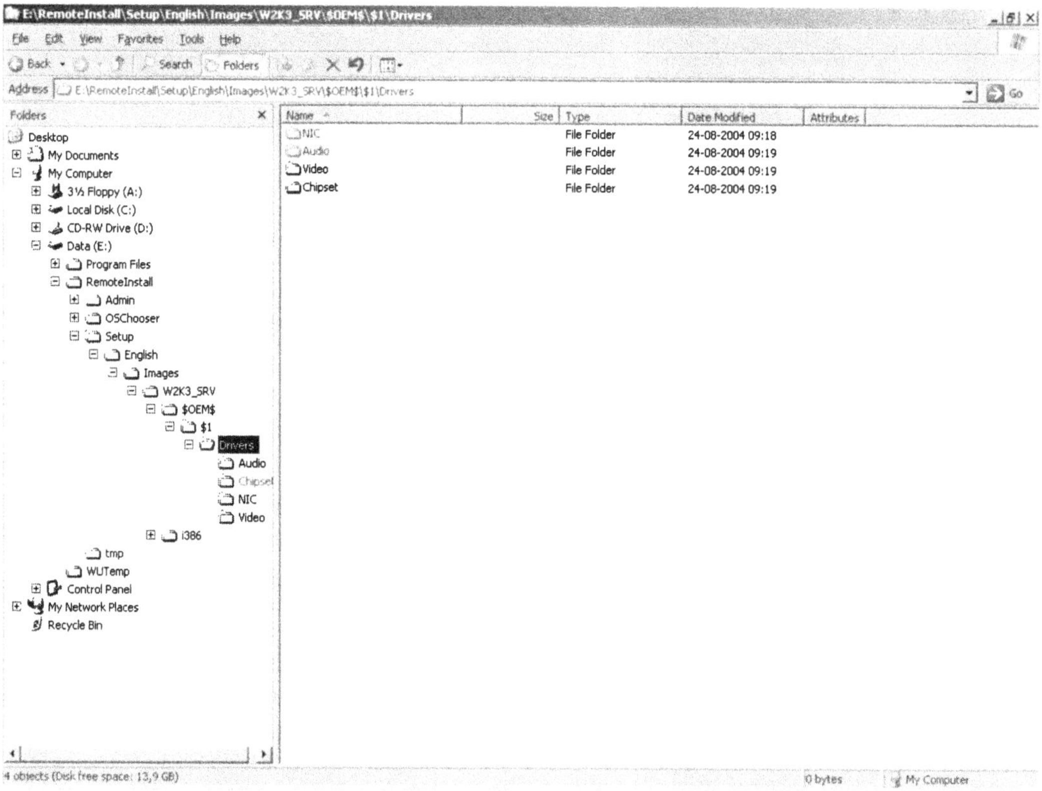

Figure 12.3 *$1 folder structure.*

depending on which files and folders you wish to install (e.g., driver files for network adapters, modems, video drivers).

Copy your driver files into the subfolders created. Remember to maintain the folder and file structure of the original driver software. Note where the .inf and .sys files are placed. The path to these files is used later in the `OEMPnPDriversPath` entry in the answer file.

12.3 Finalizing the distribution point

You have now performed several tasks:

- Created the OEM distribution point
- Added a $1 folder, which defaults to the system drive on the client computer
- Added folders and files below the $1 folder

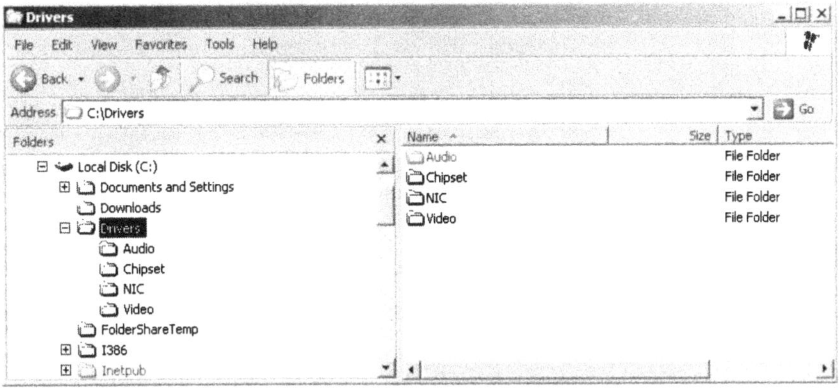

Figure 12.4 *Drivers folder structure.*

In other words, you have extended the functionality of your Windows client installation. In this example, we copied driver files only, but it could be any files (e.g., application files). In Chapter 13 we'll be looking at how to make the Windows client installation aware that new drivers are present. During text-mode Setup, these folders and files are then copied to the %SystemDrive%\Drivers folders. On the client computer, this will result in the "Drivers" folder and all of the subfolders below it being created on C:\, and will appear as shown in Figure 12.4 at initial installation.

12.4 Converting short file names to long file names by using $$Rename.txt

When using Remote Installation Services to perform an unattended installation, your distribution point subfolders (e.g., the $1 folder) can only contain files and folders that have short file names. This is because winnt.exe, the actual installation program that runs during the first text-based mode of installation, only runs in DOS mode, and DOS can only process files and folders that use the 8.3 naming convention. The 8.3 naming convention allows only eight characters to the left of the decimal point and three characters to the right of the decimal point.

Because of this short file name limitation, you might sometimes be forced to shorten the names of files and folders so you can put them into your distribution share. You can convert these short file and folder names back to long file and folder names during setup by using the $$Rename.txt file. $$Rename.txt lists all of the files and folders in a specific folder that need to be renamed. Each folder that contains short file names that need to be renamed must contain a separate version of $$Rename.txt.

To use $$Rename.txt, put the file in a folder that contains files and folders that need to be converted. Installation automatically looks for $$Rename.txt. If a $$Rename.txt file is found, installation will rename the files in that folder. The format for $$Rename.txt is:

```
[section_name_1]
short_name_1 = " long_name_1"
short_name_2 = " long_name_2"
short_name_x = " long_name_x"

[section_name_2]
short_name_1 = " long_name_1"
short_name_2 = " long_name_2"
short_name_x = " long_name_x"
```

Explanation:

- *Section_name* is the path to the folder that contains the files and folders. A section does not need to be named, but it can have a backslash (\) as a name, which indicates that the section contains the names of the files or subfolders that are in the root of the drive.
- *Short_name* is the name of the file or folder within this named folder that needs to be renamed. The name must not be enclosed in quotation marks.
- *Long_name* is the new name of the file or folder. If the name contains spaces or commas, it *must* be enclosed in quotation marks.

An example of a $$rename.txt file is shown in Figure 12.5.

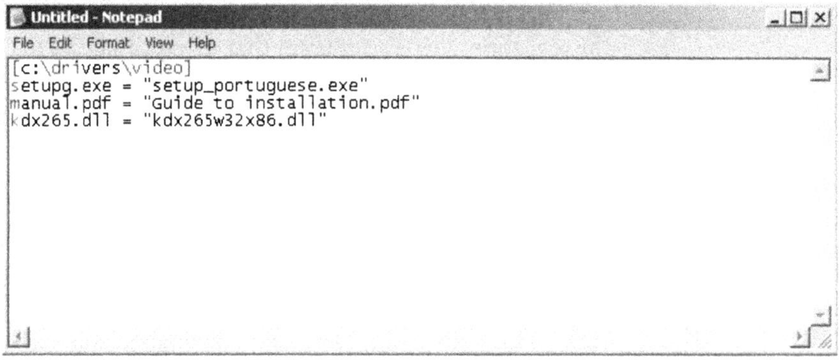

Figure 12.5 *In this example, the section specifies the path to the files.*

12.5 The $1 folder structure best practices

There are different ways of creating a folder hierachy in the $1 folder depending on your logistical requirements. You might want to use your distribution point to deploy a combination of scripts, application program files, and drivers. In this process, it is important to think of the logistics of deploying the file content to the client computer. Using an incorrect logistical approach could end up wasting space and time.

12.5.1 The image logistical approach

We often find that businesses try to maintain the same logistical thoughts when administering Remote Installation Services as they did when they maintained images created with their favorite imaging software. Although this might work fine for many businesses, it is not really the most efficient way of working with Remote Installation Services.

In a typical Remote Installation Services environment, maintaining a per-computer-model-installation-profile means administrative overhead. The reason for this is that you would have to start out creating a unique subfolder in the $1 folder for each computer model in place. Below this level, you would then have to apply yet another different folder for the various types of drivers contained with that specific computer model. Some computer models use the same drivers as other computer models, but some do not.

In the end, remember that every file contained in the $1 folder is deployed to every single client computer. With this in mind, using the image logistical approach, you will end up having copied a lot of driver files onto every single computer. Some of those driver files will reflect the individual computer's devices, but other driver files will not; in other words, there will be too many duplicate files. Businesses using a variety of different computer models will end up having huge amounts of driver files on their client computers. This is what we define as unnecessary data.

Let's illustrate what this means in reality: Using the image logistical approach, your $1 folder structure could possibly end up with a structure similar to the following example:

```
$OEM$
---$1
------Drivers
---------Netvista A20 (computer type 1)
```

```
------------Audio (device class for this computer type)
---------------Turtle (device brand)
---------------SMax (device brand)
------------Video (device class for this computer type)
---------------Nvidia (device brand)
---------------Intel (device brand)
------------Modem (device class for this computer type)
---------------Agere (device brand)
---------Compaq 5500 (computer type 2)
------------Audio (device class for this computer type)
---------------AWE32 (device brand)
---------------SMax (device brand)
------------Video (device class for this computer type)
---------------Nvidia (device brand)
---------------Intel (device brand)
------------Modem (device class for this computer type)
---------------Agere (device brand)
---------------Intel (device brand)
```

As you can see, you would have to define individual device brands and device classes for every computer type. Your `OEMPnpDriversPath` entry in the answer file will be incredibly long. Installation will also take considerably longer given all of the duplicate files that must be copied, but most important, the time used to find the best matching drivers will be extremely long given that duplicate drivers will be checked up to several times. The impact on network traffic will increase because download will take longer.

Even though most new computers today are shipped with huge hard disks, unnecessary data is basically a waste of space and a waste of time (and money). If you choose to use this method, you should consider deleting or hiding driver files at the end of installation.

12.5.2 The "one-image-fits-all" logistical approach

You can create a "one-image-fits-all" structure by creating the $1 folder hierarchy in a smart way. Instead of thinking in terms of machine types, computer models, or images, just think of hardware. What devices do you really need to support? Which driver files are really necessary? The "one-image-fits-all" model is what you need to understand. It is really very simple. Forget all about creating a different folder for each machine type you need to support. Only think of one single folder in the $1 folder, and call it "Drivers". Below this folder, create a subfolder for all devices that are present on your variety of computers (e.g., "NIC", "modem", "audio", "video", "usb", "chipset", "wireless"). Below each device type folder, create another folder referring to the actual device name and include the relevant driver files in it. For example, below the "Audio" subfolder, make a subfolder called "Turtle," referring to Turtle Beach audio cards, and another subfolder called "SMax," referring to SoundMax audio cards.

Using this approach, your OEM\$1\Drivers folder hierarchy will end up using a structure as illustrated in the following example:

```
$OEM$
---$1
------Drivers
---------Audio
------------Turtle
------------SMax
---------Video
------------Nvidia
------------Intel
---------Modem
------------Agere
```

Using this method, there is no need to maintain a computer type referral as with the image logistical approach. In other words, you will have one single image only that works for all computer types in your organization. Of course, using this approach, you will still copy unnecessary data to some client computers, but it will be a lot less than using the image logistical approach. The benefits of using one image only are the following:

- Installation will be faster, because you do not need to copy duplicate files, and time spent for checking the $1 folder for best-match drivers during setup is considerably shorter.
- The whole great idea of using the "one-image-fits-all" method is that it will save you time and money when a new computer type enters your business because you will only need to think in terms of hardware changes.
- First, all you need to do is to identify its drivers and then add the driver files to the respective file locations referring to the device type. There is no need to build a completely new folder hierarchy, which could take hours (or even days).
- Second, if new and better driver files are released from the manufacturer, you only need to update these in one single subfolder.
- Your *OEMPnpDriversPath* entry in the answer file will be considerably shorter than using the image logistical approach.

- Because the process of exchanging old hardware with new hardware is ongoing, removing old driver files and data is just as easy and time saving as adding support for new devices.
- *There is one single point of administration for all client computers.* Administering one image only is time saving and money saving for all the aforementioned reasons, not least of which is that it's a lot easier to deal with.

12.6 Summary

The basis for deploying OEM drivers, files, and applications to a computer is to create a distribution point with the Remote Installation Services file structure. From this point, you can distribute content to the client computer in a variety of ways and make the content available for scripts to be executed. Even long file names can be converted to short file names and then be converted back into long file names. OEM drivers can be deployed in several ways, but the smartest way by far is to structure the files distributed to apply to as many computers as possible to make one Remote Installation Services image fit to all computer types in your organization.

13

Driver Inclusion

Now that we have looked at driver fundamentals, driver characteristics, the OEM folder, and its structure, let's go into how to actually set RIS up so that the OEM drivers work. To do this, you will have to add the driver files and modify the answer file. In this chapter, we will look into how to do this for driver inclusion operation only. In the next chapter, there is a lot more information on the answer file; therefore, the advanced capabilities of the answer file will not be discussed in this chapter.

Highlights:

- Understand how to add OEM drivers
- Understand basic editing of the answer file
- Understand how Windows matches drivers and devices to each other
- Look into details of how different devices behave
- Understand how to add support for SCSI and RAID
- Understand the sequence in which drivers are read

13.1 Adding the driver files

Adding the OEM driver files to the RIS image is a straightforward process. This is naturally the first step in adding driver support for new or unknown devices to your RIS setup. There are some differences in the process for adding support for different device types (e.g., network adapters, HALs, storage), which will be addressed throughout this chapter. Follow these step-by-step instructions to get started (see Figure 13.1):

1. Create the OEM folder at the same level as the I386 folder.
2. Below the OEM folder, create the $1 subfolder.

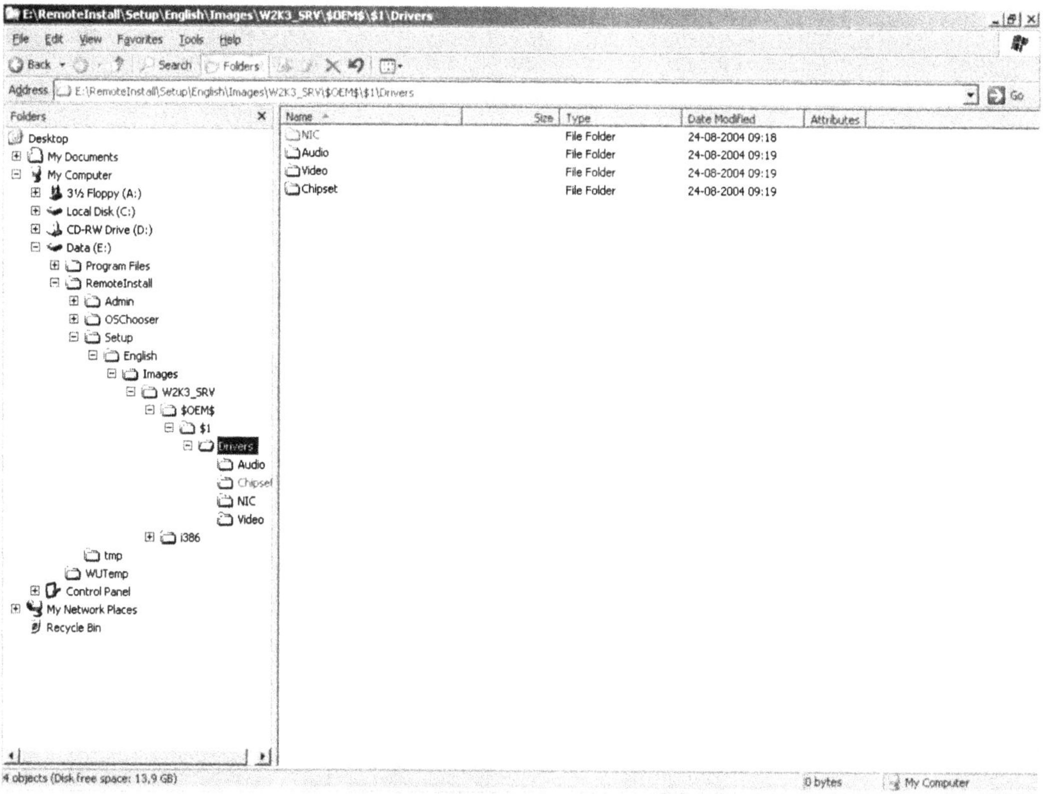

Figure 13.1 *The OEM folder structure.*

3. Below the $1 folder, create a folder with a name of your choice; in this example we'll call it Drivers.

4. Below the OEM\$1\Drivers\ folder, create subfolders reflecting the different devices for which you need to add support. For example, name these subfolders "Audio," "Video," "Modem," "NIC," and so forth. If you have different types of devices belonging to the same device category, create another subfolder for that device below the main device folder.

5. Copy the .inf and .sys files as well as .dll files, .cat files, and all other files and folders belonging to the driver build of files, to the subfolders you just created.

6. *Network adapters only*: Copy *only* the .inf and .sys files of your driver files to the I386 folder from the subfolder(s) you just created in the \$1 folder of the client installation folder structure.

This ensures that the driver matching will be considerably faster. The I386 folder is at the same level as your OEM folder.

Note: If you are copying .inf and .sys files to the I386 folder that are newer than similar source files in the I386 folder, you must overwrite the files in the I386 folder; otherwise, there will be a mismatch of .inf and .sys files in the I386 folder and the actual subfolder containing the real drivers.

After having added drivers, it might sometimes be useful to restart the Remote Installation Services service. From a command prompt, type *net stop binlsvc* and then *net start binlsvc* or simply go to services and restart the Remote Installation Services service.

Tip: The driver search algorithm described previously could possibly become problematic using drivers that are new to the Microsoft Windows driver package when a similar device is supported by the original Microsoft Windows driver. In that case, you must identify the driver's .sys file. You will then have to track down the similar named file in the I386 path of the RIS installation. Rename the file removing the unexpanded file extension defined as an underscore. For example, you would have to rename the file e100bnt5.sy_ to e100bnt5.old. This will force setup to use the newer driver supplied.

13.2 Configuring the answer file to reflect your drivers

Now that we have our driver files in place, you're ready to modify the answer file. Configuring the answer file to reflect our drivers is the process of making RIS aware that it should use other drivers than those included with Microsoft Windows. The first step includes making RIS understand a few things about what we intend to do:

1. We want to ignore Microsoft Windows driver signing. If we do not do this, installation will stop during the best-match drivers process and prompt the user for whether we want to continue installation using the unsigned driver. We don't want that to happen. Ignoring driver signing is not recommended by Microsoft, but it is a supported option.
2. We want to tell RIS where the OEM drivers are located.

To do this, we must make some changes to the answer file by inserting some keys and values. So let's open the answer file (ristndrd.sif) located in the \TEMPLATES folder of the image. You can open it using the incredible Notepad. The section in the .sif to be modified for including OEM driver support is `[Unattended]`.

1. In the `[Unattended]` section, enter this key and value: `OemPreinstall = yes`. This tells RIS that we're using OEM drivers.
2. In the `[Unattended]` section, enter this key and value: `DriverSigningPolicy = Ignore`. This tells RIS that we don't care whether a driver is signed or not. If the driver is not signed, installation continues without any prompting.
3. In the `[Unattended]` section, enter this key and value: `OemPnPDriversPath = ;` The value to enter here should contain the path to your drivers. Read more below.

   The path must be written in parentheses. You can list multiple paths in this key by separating them with a semicolon (`;`).

   For example, if your \$OEM$\$1 driver folder is called "Drivers," and the "Drivers" folder has subfolders named describing different device types, you could enter `OemPnPDriversPath = "Drivers\nic\intel;Drivers\audio\smax;Drivers\video\nvidia"` (this is just an example).

An example of the edited section in the answer file could look like this:

```
[Unattended]
OEMPreinstall = Yes
DriverSigningPolicy = Ignore
OemPnPDriversPath = "Drivers\NIC;Drivers\Modem;Drivers\
Video"
```

The %SystemDrive% environment variable string is automatically inserted before each of the listed search paths in the `OemPnpDriversPath` key; for the same reason, you only need to write the folder name (or names) of the folder(s) below the $1 folder.

During GUI-mode Setup, when the system searches system information files for plug-and-play IDs, it also looks in the paths noted in the `[OemPnPDriversPath]` entry, along with the standard default path of %WinDir%\Inf. The %WinDir%\Inf path is listed first in the search order, but if you have a device that is supported by more than one .inf file (Microsoft Windows may include a driver that offers generic functionality), Setup continues to search all paths specified in the `[OemPnPDriversPath]` entry.

13.3 The driver matching process

To make a best-match driver match, Setup compares the device's hardware IDs and compatible IDs, as reported by the device's parent bus driver, to the hardware IDs and compatible IDs listed in the .inf files on the system. A compatible ID is the vendor-defined identification string that Setup uses to match a device to a system information file. Setup uses compatible IDs if it cannot match the device ID and hardware IDs for a device. Setup then creates a list of possible drivers for the device (i.e., drivers whose INF *Models* section entries contain an ID that matches one of the device's IDs).

If Setup does not find a match in any of the installed .inf files, it would normally start up the *Found New Hardware* wizard, which prompts the user for a driver. Setup also assigns a rank to each possible driver. The rank indicates how well the driver matches the device. The lower the rank number, the better a match the driver is for the device. A rank of zero represents the best match. For Microsoft Windows XP and later, some driver packages are considered to be trusted, whereas others are untrusted. All signed driver packages are trusted, and all unsigned driver packages are untrusted. Now, let's look at more specific issues with different devices.

13.4 Network adapters

Adding support for network adapters (NICs) can at times be a real pain. Nevertheless, it is a very important task to do in the beginning of creating a client or server installation, because the NIC driver is used in the first, text-based portion of a client installation. If the NIC is not supported at this stage, installation of the client will stop. You will then get this error message in the first portion of Setup:

> *The operating system image you selected does not contain the necessary drivers for your network adapter. Try selecting a different operating system image. If the problem persists, contact your administrator. Setup cannot continue. Press any key to exit.*

These days it seems as if every NIC manufacturer has its own idea about how drivers should be handled. Luckily, large corporations such as Intel now support multiple NICs using only a few different sets of driver package builds.

Let's look closer at how to work with NIC drivers. As mentioned earlier, whenever your computer starts, the PCI devices are polled for the following information:

- Vendor ID
- Device ID
- Subsystem ID
- Hardware Revision ID

This information is then stored in the following Microsoft Windows registry location:

```
HKEY_LOCAL_MACHINE\SYSTEM\CurrentControlSet\Enum\PCI\
VEN_<vendorID>&DEV_<deviceID>&SUBSYS_<subsystemID>&REV_
<hardwarerevisionID>
```

The information written to this entry is more commonly known as the PNP Device ID. The system information file of the NIC driver will initially identify the NIC by its PNP Device ID. It will then match the PNP Device ID to the list of device IDs supported in the system information file. If no match is found, the NIC will not be supported. If a match is found, the sys-

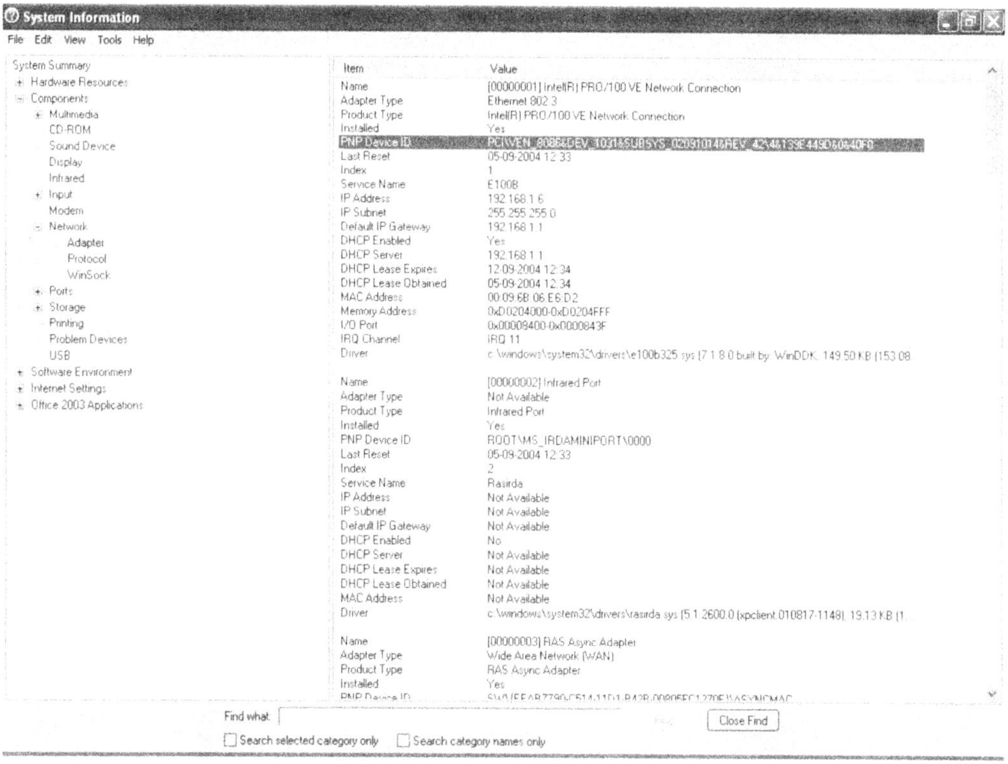

Figure 13.2 *The PNP Device ID.*

tem information file will then initiate the correct driver binary file (the .sys file) and enable NIC functionality.

The PNP Device ID of a NIC can be found by running the *winmsd* command as illustrated in Figure 13.2. It can also be found using a variety of diagnostic tools available to the specific NIC or using the registry as described in Chapter 3.

To ensure that the PNP Device ID is supported, open the system information file and check if the ID has a matching entry in the file. Be careful, though, not to make changes in the system information file. Figure 13.3 shows an open neti557x.inf file, a system information file containing stacks of PNP Device ID entries for different Intel NICs.

If the PNP Device ID of your NIC is listed in its containing system information file, you can be almost completely sure that the system infor-

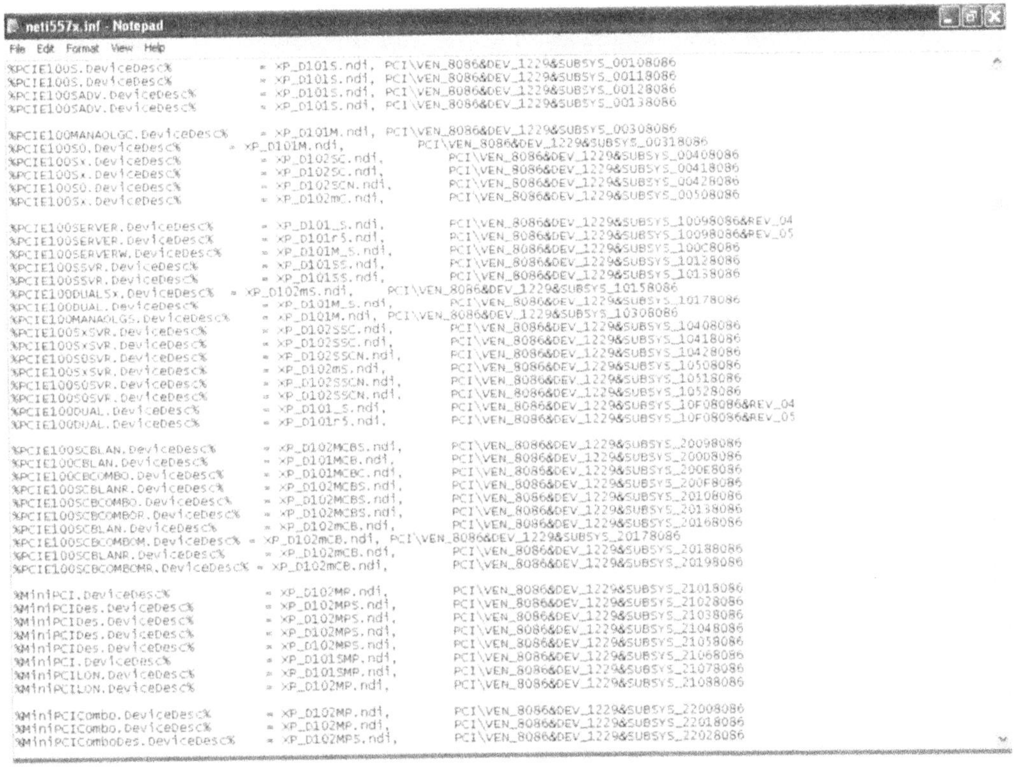


```
%PCIE100S.DeviceDesc%          = XP_D101S.ndi, PCI\VEN_8086&DEV_1229&SUBSYS_00108086
%PCIE100S.DeviceDesc%          = XP_D101S.ndi, PCI\VEN_8086&DEV_1229&SUBSYS_00118086
%PCIE100SADV.DeviceDesc%       = XP_D101S.ndi, PCI\VEN_8086&DEV_1229&SUBSYS_00128086
%PCIE100SADV.DeviceDesc%       = XP_D101S.ndi, PCI\VEN_8086&DEV_1229&SUBSYS_00138086

%PCIE100MANAOLGC.DeviceDesc%   = XP_D101M.ndi, PCI\VEN_8086&DEV_1229&SUBSYS_00308086
%PCIE100S0.DeviceDesc%      = XP_D101M.ndi,       PCI\VEN_8086&DEV_1229&SUBSYS_00318086
%PCIE100Sx.DeviceDesc%         = XP_D102SC.ndi,       PCI\VEN_8086&DEV_1229&SUBSYS_00408086
%PCIE100Sx.DeviceDesc%         = XP_D102SC.ndi,       PCI\VEN_8086&DEV_1229&SUBSYS_00418086
%PCIE100S0.DeviceDesc%         = XP_D102SCN.ndi,      PCI\VEN_8086&DEV_1229&SUBSYS_00428086
%PCIE100Sx.DeviceDesc%         = XP_D102mC.ndi,       PCI\VEN_8086&DEV_1229&SUBSYS_00508086

%PCIE100SERVER.DeviceDesc%     = XP_D101_S.ndi,       PCI\VEN_8086&DEV_1229&SUBSYS_10098086&REV_04
%PCIE100SERVER.DeviceDesc%     = XP_D101r5.ndi,       PCI\VEN_8086&DEV_1229&SUBSYS_10098086&REV_05
%PCIE100SERVERW.DeviceDesc%    = XP_D101M_S.ndi,      PCI\VEN_8086&DEV_1229&SUBSYS_100C8086
%PCIE100SSVR.DeviceDesc%       = XP_D101SS.ndi,       PCI\VEN_8086&DEV_1229&SUBSYS_10128086
%PCIE100SSVR.DeviceDesc%       = XP_D101SS.ndi,       PCI\VEN_8086&DEV_1229&SUBSYS_10138086
%PCIE100DUALSx.DeviceDesc% = XP_D102mS.ndi,    PCI\VEN_8086&DEV_1229&SUBSYS_10158086
%PCIE100DUAL.DeviceDesc%       = XP_D101M_S.ndi,      PCI\VEN_8086&DEV_1229&SUBSYS_10178086
%PCIE100MANAOLGS.DeviceDesc%   = XP_D101M.ndi, PCI\VEN_8086&DEV_1229&SUBSYS_10308086
%PCIE100SxSVR.DeviceDesc%      = XP_D102SSC.ndi,      PCI\VEN_8086&DEV_1229&SUBSYS_10408086
%PCIE100SxSVR.DeviceDesc%      = XP_D102SSC.ndi,      PCI\VEN_8086&DEV_1229&SUBSYS_10418086
%PCIE100S0SVR.DeviceDesc%      = XP_D102SSCN.ndi,     PCI\VEN_8086&DEV_1229&SUBSYS_10428086
%PCIE100SxSVR.DeviceDesc%      = XP_D102mS.ndi,       PCI\VEN_8086&DEV_1229&SUBSYS_10508086
%PCIE100S0SVR.DeviceDesc%      = XP_D102SSCN.ndi,     PCI\VEN_8086&DEV_1229&SUBSYS_10518086
%PCIE100S0SVR.DeviceDesc%      = XP_D102SSCN.ndi,     PCI\VEN_8086&DEV_1229&SUBSYS_10528086
%PCIE100DUAL.DeviceDesc%       = XP_D101_S.ndi,       PCI\VEN_8086&DEV_1229&SUBSYS_10F08086&REV_04
%PCIE100DUAL.DeviceDesc%       = XP_D101r5.ndi,       PCI\VEN_8086&DEV_1229&SUBSYS_10F08086&REV_05

%PCIE100SCBLAN.DeviceDesc%     = XP_D102MCBS.ndi,     PCI\VEN_8086&DEV_1229&SUBSYS_20098086
%PCIE100CBLAN.DeviceDesc%      = XP_D101MCB.ndi,      PCI\VEN_8086&DEV_1229&SUBSYS_200D8086
%PCIE100CBCOMBO.DeviceDesc%    = XP_D101MCBC.ndi,     PCI\VEN_8086&DEV_1229&SUBSYS_200E8086
%PCIE100SCBLANR.DeviceDesc%    = XP_D102MCBS.ndi,     PCI\VEN_8086&DEV_1229&SUBSYS_200F8086
%PCIE100SCBCOMBO.DeviceDesc%   = XP_D102MCBS.ndi,     PCI\VEN_8086&DEV_1229&SUBSYS_20108086
%PCIE100SCBCOMBOR.DeviceDesc%  = XP_D102MCBS.ndi,     PCI\VEN_8086&DEV_1229&SUBSYS_20138086
%PCIE100SCBLAN.DeviceDesc%     = XP_D102mCB.ndi,      PCI\VEN_8086&DEV_1229&SUBSYS_20168086
%PCIE100SCBCOMBOM.DeviceDesc% = XP_D102mCB.ndi, PCI\VEN_8086&DEV_1229&SUBSYS_20178086
%PCIE100SCBLANR.DeviceDesc%    = XP_D102mCB.ndi,      PCI\VEN_8086&DEV_1229&SUBSYS_20188086
%PCIE100SCBCOMBOMR.DeviceDesc% = XP_D102mCB.ndi,      PCI\VEN_8086&DEV_1229&SUBSYS_20198086

%MiniPCI.DeviceDesc%           = XP_D102MP.ndi,       PCI\VEN_8086&DEV_1229&SUBSYS_21018086
%MiniPCIDes.DeviceDesc%        = XP_D102MPS.ndi,      PCI\VEN_8086&DEV_1229&SUBSYS_21028086
%MiniPCIDes.DeviceDesc%        = XP_D102MPS.ndi,      PCI\VEN_8086&DEV_1229&SUBSYS_21038086
%MiniPCIDes.DeviceDesc%        = XP_D102MPS.ndi,      PCI\VEN_8086&DEV_1229&SUBSYS_21048086
%MiniPCIDes.DeviceDesc%        = XP_D102MPS.ndi,      PCI\VEN_8086&DEV_1229&SUBSYS_21058086
%MiniPCI.DeviceDesc%           = XP_D101SMP.ndi,      PCI\VEN_8086&DEV_1229&SUBSYS_21068086
%MiniPCILON.DeviceDesc%        = XP_D101SMP.ndi,      PCI\VEN_8086&DEV_1229&SUBSYS_21078086
%MiniPCILON.DeviceDesc%        = XP_D102MP.ndi,       PCI\VEN_8086&DEV_1229&SUBSYS_21088086

%MiniPCICombo.DeviceDesc%      = XP_D102MP.ndi,       PCI\VEN_8086&DEV_1229&SUBSYS_22008086
%MiniPCICombo.DeviceDesc%      = XP_D102MP.ndi,       PCI\VEN_8086&DEV_1229&SUBSYS_22018086
%MiniPCIComboDes.DeviceDesc%   = XP_D102MPS.ndi,      PCI\VEN_8086&DEV_1229&SUBSYS_22028086
```

Figure 13.3 *If your PNP Device ID is listed in the .inf file, you're using the right driver. If not, get a new set of driver files. As you might imagine, using the search facility in Notepad makes matching the ID a lot easier.*

mation file is correct. In that case, be sure to use the correct driver binary file version to add driver support. However, because the system information file is always bundled with the driver binary, this does not normally present a problem.

Mixing different versions of system information files and driver binary files is definitely something you should avoid, because the system information file then might make wrong references to the driver binary. However, in some cases, it might be necessary to do just that.

The cases where mismatching system information files and driver binaries are being used are the cases where the driver software does not add support for Remote Installation Services. This problem is often described as "difficulties in parsing system information" during the text-based portion of Setup. This has happened a few times for all NIC manufacturers. In the cases we have seen, the driver manufacturers have been quite fast in supplying a new system information file, which then worked with RIS. Sometimes you can cure this problem by using this simple workaround:

- Copy the correct operating system drivers (i.e., those for Microsoft Windows XP) to your \$1\Drivers\[subfolder for the network adapter driver files.
- Instead of copying the same files to the \I386 folder structure, extract the same driver software for an older operating system (e.g., Microsoft Windows 2000).
- Copy these extracted .sys and .inf files to the \I386 folder of the image.
- Restart the Remote Installation Services services and try installing again.

Using this procedure, Setup will use the driver in the \I386 folder during text-based mode of installation. However, it will include the driver from your subfolder during GUI-based mode of installation, thus including the newest and correct driver to the client installation. This is done because the GUI-based portion of setup is 32-bit program operation. Here the best matching of drivers is performed when installation shows that it is the state of "Installing Devices."

The NIC driver support in text-mode is flushed when Setup finds a better driver match in the GUI-based mode of Setup.

This workaround will work in most cases. If it doesn't, there is no other option but to wait for the driver manufacturer to rewrite the driver for RIS (or, alternatively, rewrite it yourself).

13.5 Audio, video, and modem drivers

Adding support for audio, video, and modem devices is a straightforward task to perform and shouldn't normally present any problems. There are exceptions, though, and these are discussed in section 13.11. We have already covered how to add support for devices in general, and working with audio, video, or modem drivers is no different than standard procedure, so just to sum it up, here's the step-by-step method for doing it:

1. Extract the software driver package.
2. Create a subfolder below your \$OEM$\$1\Drivers\ folder. Give it a descriptive name of the device in question.
3. Put the entire extracted software driver package into the subfolder you just created.
4. Identify the location of the system information file(s) and driver binary file(s) within the files you just copied. Note the location.
5. Open the answer file and modify the `[OEMPnpDriversPath]` to reflect the locations of information file(s) and driver binary file(s).
6. Overwrite existing files if prompted for it.

13.6 Chipset drivers and USB devices

For chipsets, chipset driver software will normally consist of several .inf files adding support for numerous types of chipsets. Use different subfolders for Intel and AMD chipsets. It is not necessary to copy the .inf and .sys files to the I386 folder. Of course, you still need to write a valid entry to the `$OEM$\$1\Drivers\[subfolder]` path in the `[OEMPnpDriversPath]` section of the answer file.

We recommend not having unsupported USB devices connected to your computer hardware while performing an RIS client installation, because when RIS setup enters GUI mode, it will try to identify USB devices as well as the devices you included in your OEM\$1\Drivers structure. Two things can happen:

1. If the USB device then requires drivers, and those are not present, the installation will stop at the prompt requiring you to supply the software for it. Setup will not continue.
2. In an environment with low network bandwidth connectivity or a lowly hardware-configured client or server, setup might try for half or whole hours to figure out what to do.

In either situation, installation will stop or seem to continue forever.

13.7 How to use the txtsetup.oem file to integrate SCSI and RAID adapters

In Windows XP Professional and Windows Server 2003, plug-and-play installs most hardware devices that can be loaded later in the setup process. However, mass-storage devices, such as hard disk controllers, must be properly installed for full plug-and-play support to be available during the GUI mode of Setup. For this reason, the installation of mass-storage devices is handled differently from the installation of other hardware devices.

It is possible to add support for Small Computer System Interface (SCSI) and Redundant Array of Independent Disks (RAID) adapters with RIS. This is completely essential if you need to deploy Windows on server hardware, which is often built using a SCSI-based RAID adapter. RAID adapters are normally based on SCSI technology and mostly used only with Microsoft Windows Server installations.

To add support for either a SCSI or RAID controller, you must provide the TXTSETUP.OEM file, which is normally bundled with a RAID adapter driver package along with the belonging .inf and .sys files. Follow these step-by-step instructions to add support for a mass-storage device:

1. Extract the driver files. These files are available from the device vendor and should be extracted before continuing. The required files are specified in the txtsetup.oem file.
2. Create a folder named Textmode below the OEM\$1 folder.
3. Create a subfolder in the OEM\$1\Drivers location (use the same path as specified in the `OemPnPDriversPath` key in the answer file).
4. Give this subfolder a descriptive name (e.g., SCSI or Storage).

5. Copy the following files into the Textmode folder. The name Driver used as follows is only an example and should naturally reflect the name of the real driver:

```
Driver.sys
Driver.dll
Driver.inf
Driver.cat
txtsetup.oem
```

6. Make sure that all of the files listed in txtsetup.oem appear in the textmode folder.
7. Copy the same driver files to the subfolder you created in step 4.
8. In the answer file, create a `[MassStorageDrivers]` section.
9. In the txtsetup.oem file, verify that a section named `[Hardware-Ids.Scsi.yyyyy]` exists. It uses the following context:

```
[HardwareIDs.scsi. yyyyy]
id = "xxxxx" , "yyyyy"
```

10. Copy this text and insert it below the `[MassStorageDrivers]` section.
11. In the answer file, create an `[OEMBootFiles]` section.
12. Below this section, list all of the files in the OEM\Textmode folder.

Your folder structure might now look similar to that shown in Figures 13.4 and 13.5.

13.7.1 Explanation of the answer file sections

General

Driver entries added to the `[MassStorageDrivers]` and `[OEMBoot-Files]` sections should be for bootable mass-storage devices only. Do not include secondary mass-storage devices. Instead, add the drivers for secondary mass-storage devices to the folder specified by the `OemPnPDriversPath` entry in your answer file. Including drivers for nonbootable mass-storage devices in the `[MassStorageDrivers]` or `[OEMBootFiles]` sections causes an error during the setup process.

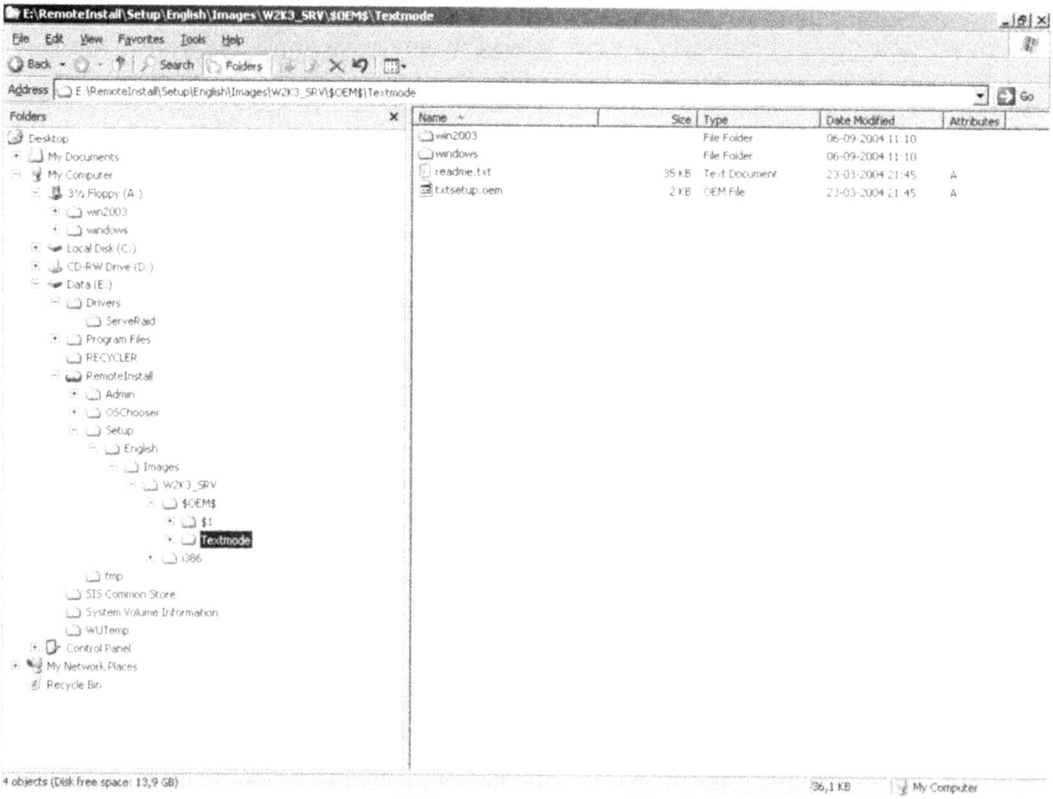

Figure 13.4 *Textmode folder structure.*

The [MassStorageDrivers] section

The `[MassStorageDrivers]` section contains two entries. The first entry identifies whether to use retail or OEM (SCSI) drivers in the Setup Loader during the text-based part of Setup. The is the context:

```
mass_storage_driver_description = "Retail" / "OEM"
```

The *mass_storage_driver_description* must match one of the strings defined in the right side of the `[SCSI]` section of txtsetup.sif for a retail driver or txtsetup.oem for an OEM driver. You can specify multiple instances of *mass_storage_driver_description*. If you choose to use the Retail value, it will indicate that the driver is part of the retail Microsoft Windows product. If you choose to use the OEM value, it will indicate that the driver is OEM-supplied. If the value is OEM, it is also required that you list the driver in the `[OEMBootFiles]` section of the answer file. If this section is

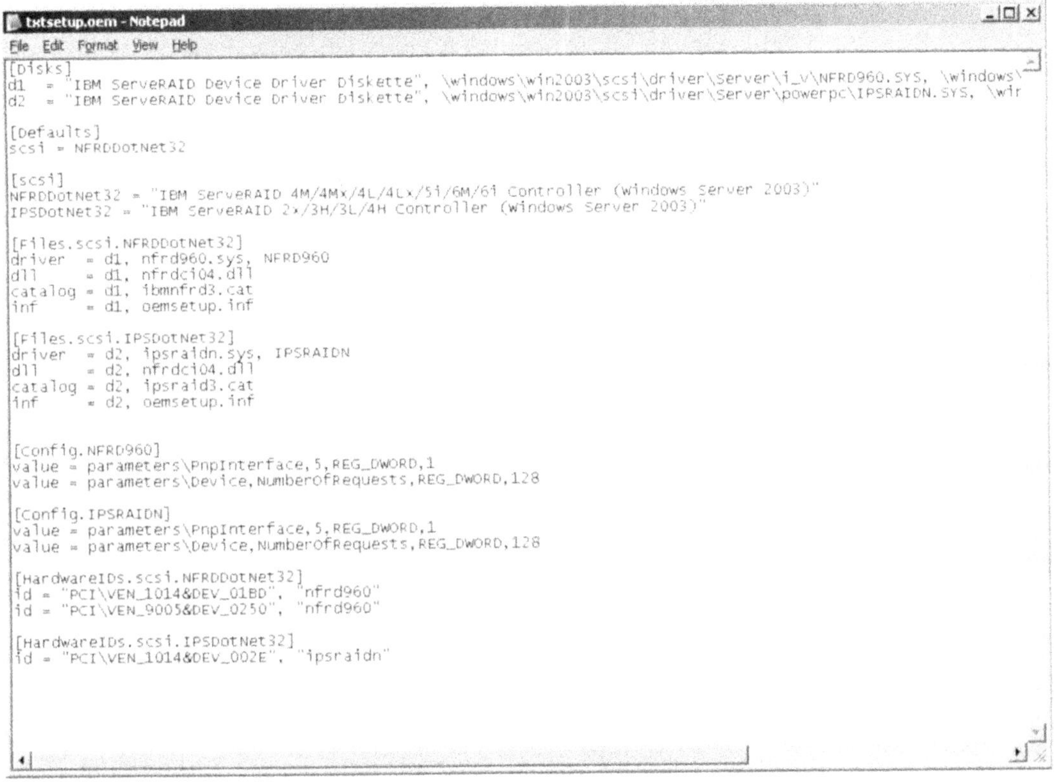

```
[Disks]
d1  = "IBM ServeRAID Device Driver Diskette", \windows\win2003\scsi\driver\Server\i_v\NFRD960.SYS, \windows\
d2  = "IBM ServeRAID Device Driver Diskette", \windows\win2003\scsi\driver\Server\powerpc\IPSRAIDN.SYS, \wir

[Defaults]
scsi = NFRDDotNet32

[scsi]
NFRDDotNet32 = "IBM ServeRAID 4M/4Mx/4L/4Lx/5i/6M/6i Controller (Windows Server 2003)"
IPSDotNet32 = "IBM ServeRAID 2x/3H/3L/4H Controller (Windows Server 2003)"

[Files.scsi.NFRDDotNet32]
driver  = d1, nfrd960.sys, NFRD960
dll     = d1, nfrdci04.dll
catalog = d1, ibmnfrd3.cat
inf     = d1, oemsetup.inf

[Files.scsi.IPSDotNet32]
driver  = d2, ipsraidn.sys, IPSRAIDN
dll     = d2, nfrdci04.dll
catalog = d2, ipsraid3.cat
inf     = d2, oemsetup.inf


[Config.NFRD960]
value = parameters\PnpInterface,5,REG_DWORD,1
value = parameters\Device,NumberOfRequests,REG_DWORD,128

[Config.IPSRAIDN]
value = parameters\PnpInterface,5,REG_DWORD,1
value = parameters\Device,NumberOfRequests,REG_DWORD,128

[HardwareIDs.scsi.NFRDDotNet32]
id = "PCI\VEN_1014&DEV_01BD", "nfrd960"
id = "PCI\VEN_9005&DEV_0250", "nfrd960"

[HardwareIDs.scsi.IPSDotNet32]
id = "PCI\VEN_1014&DEV_002E", "ipsraidn"
```

Figure 13.5 *txtsetup.oem contents.*

missing or empty, Setup will attempt to detect the SCSI devices on the computer and install the corresponding retail drivers.

The other entry is a hardware description of the device in question. This entry can be copied directly from the txtsetup.oem file, and you should copy the entire `[HardwareIDs.scsi.yyyyy]` section with all its subsequent values. If this section does not exist in the Txtsetup.oem, you can create it by using the following format:

```
[HardwareIDs.scsi.ID]
id = "deviceID","service"
```

To understand which values to enter, follow these rules:

- The *`ID`* value must be equal to the *`ID`* entry in the `[HwComponent]` section of your txtsetup.oem file.
- The *`DeviceID`* value specifies the plug-and-play device ID for the mass-storage device.

- The `service` value specifies the service to be installed for the device. The service is specified by the filename of its executable file excluding the .sys extension.

For a Symc810 driver, which has a device ID of PCI\VEN_1000&DEV_0001, you can create the section shown in the following example:

```
[HardwareIDs.scsi.symc810]
id = "PCI\VEN_1000&DEV_0001" , "symc810"
```

This entry must be written to and saved in the txtsetup.oem file as well as being written into the `[MassStorageDrivers]` section. To sum up this section, an example of the entire `[MassStorageDrivers]` section could potentially look like this:

```
[MassStorageDrivers]
"IBM ServeRAID 4M/4Mx/4L/4Lx/5i/6M/6i Controller
(Windows Server 2003)" = "OEM"
[HardwareIDs.scsi.IPSDotNet32]
id = "PCI\VEN_1014&DEV_002E", "ipsraidn"
```

The [OEMBootFiles] section

The `[OEMBootFiles]` section contains entries that list the OEM-supplied boot files. Below the section entry, you must create a list of the files contained in the OEM\Textmode directory. Write one file entry per line. Here's an example. The name Driver used as follows is only an example and should naturally reflect the name of the real driver:

```
[OEMBootFiles]
Driver.sys
Driver.dll
Driver.inf
txtsetup.oem
```

This section will only work if you also use the entry `OemPreinstall = Yes` in the `[Unattended]` section and you list the files here that are placed in the \OEM\Textmode folder. This section is required if you use the ComputerType entry in either the `[Unattended]` or `[MassStorageDrivers]` sections of the answer file.

13.7.2 Configuring the RAID

Completely installing a server with SCSI/RAID drivers using RIS will avoid going through the process of manually installing the operating system, using the F6 option, where again, you'd manually have to add the mass-storage device driver software from a diskette. However, deploying a server unattended, with RIS all set up with your mass-storage device drivers, wouldn't make sense if your RAID configuration wasn't in place first.

If the RAID configuration isn't already defined in the BIOS of the actual RAID controller, RIS will not be able to identify any disks at all, even if the SCSI/RAID driver works. So, is there any way to include the SCSI/RAID driver *and* define the RAID configuration before continuing installation of the operating? Theoretically, it *is* possible; however, there are no tools available with RIS that makes the operation possible just like that. To do this, you'd have to do one of the following things:

- Use a third-party product, such as RISme™ from Argon Technology.
- Create a PXE code drop, which initializes a RAM Drive during negotiation with the client computer. Using the RAM Drive, execute commands from the network to configure the RAID. Most RAID controller manufacturers have command-line utilities available that can configure RAID.

Other deployment applications might be able to perform the tasks.

13.8 Adding an OEM Hardware Abstraction Layer

You can specify an OEM Hardware Abstraction Layer (HAL) for installation if this is required for your hardware to function correctly with the Windows operating system. To do this, you must provide a txtsetup.oem file and the HAL driver files that are provided by the vendor, just as when adding a SCSI mass-storage device. Also, you need to use the same txtsetup.oem as the one for your mass-storage devices file if you are installing mass-storage device drivers as well. Only one txtsetup.oem file can be used.

If you have to install HALs and mass-storage device drivers, all of the entries should be combined in one single txtsetup.oem file by adding the information of the specific txtsetup.oem file to an already existing txtsetup.oem file.

13.9 Installing the HAL

Follow these step-by-step instructions to add support for an OEM HAL for your operating system:

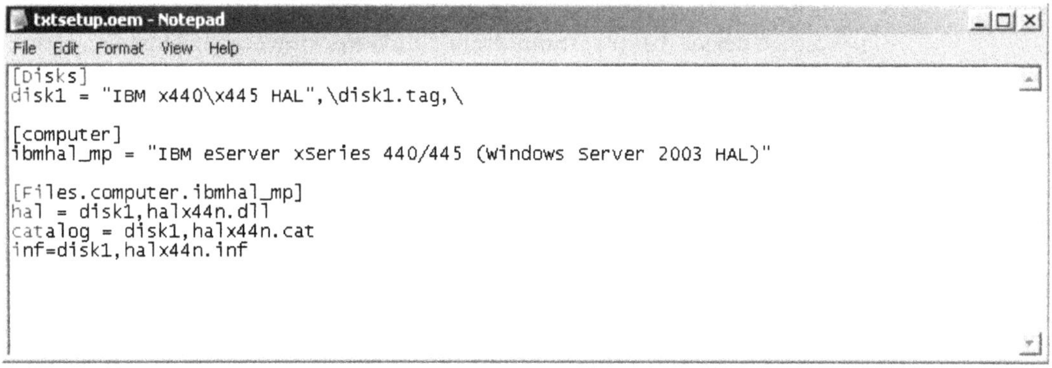

txtsetup.oem - Notepad
File Edit Format View Help
[Disks]
disk1 = "IBM x440\x445 HAL",\disk1.tag,\
[computer]
ibmhal_mp = "IBM eServer xSeries 440/445 (Windows Server 2003 HAL)"
[Files.computer.ibmhal_mp]
hal = disk1,halx44n.dll
catalog = disk1,halx44n.cat
inf=disk1,halx44n.inf

Figure 13.6 *An example of the txtsetup.oem file. All necessary files are listed in the [Files....] section.*

1. *Extract the driver files.* These files are available from the device vendor and should be extracted before continuing. The required files are specified in the txtsetup.oem file (Figure 13.6).
2. *Create a folder named Textmode below the OEM folder.* Below the section entry, you must create a list of the files contained in the OEM\Textmode directory. Write one file entry per line.
3. *Copy the following files into the Textmode folder.* The name Hal used as follows is only an example and should naturally reflect the name of the real files:

```
hal.dll
hal.inf
hal.cat
txtsetup.oem
```

4. *Make sure that all of the files listed in txtsetup.oem appear in the textmode folder.* There might be more files than the ones shown in the example.
5. *In the answer file, edit the* `[Unattended]` *section for the HAL, and add any drivers that you want to install.* The standard value entry for the ComputerType key uses this format:

```
[Unattended]
ComputerType = "HALDescription", OEM
```

Note: You can copy the `HALDescription` value from the `[Computer]` section of the txtsetup.oem file, which is provided by the hardware manufacturer. (See Figure 13.7.)

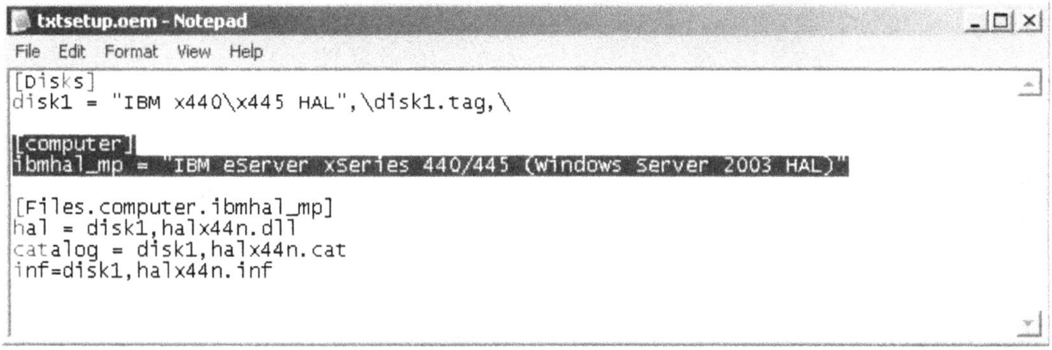

Figure 13.7 *The HALDescription entry in the [Computer] section.*

Given the information in the previous example, your `[Unattended]` would look like this:

```
[Unattended]
ComputerType = "IBM eServer xSeries 440/445
(Windows Server 2003 HAL)", OEM
```

6. *In the answer file, create an `[OEMBootFiles]` section.* Below the section entry, you must create a list of the files contained in the OEM\Textmode directory. Write one file entry per line, for example:

```
[OEMBootFiles]
halx440n.dll
halx44n.inf
halx44n.cat
txtsetup.oem
```

13.10 Multiple mass-storage devices and/or HALs

Please note, again, that there can only be one txtsetup.oem file present in both the \$OEM\Textsetup folder and in the `[OEMBootFiles]` section. If you're using a combination of mass-storage device drivers, HALs, or multiple numbers of both, you need to append the content of each individual txtsetup.oem into the single txtsetup.oem file you're using.

In Figure 13.8, we appended the content of a HAL driver to an existing txtsetup.oem file for a RAID controller. If you're using an OEM HAL, the HAL txtsetup.oem file information should be in the beginning of the txtsetup.oem file.

txtsetup.oem - Notepad

File Edit Format View Help

```
[Disks]
disk1 = "IBM x440\x445 HAL",\disk1.tag,\

[computer]
ibmhal_mp = "IBM eServer xSeries 440/445 (Windows Server 2003 HAL)"

[Files.computer.ibmhal_mp]
hal = disk1,halx44n.dll
catalog = disk1,halx44n.cat
inf=disk1,halx44n.inf

[Disks]
d1  = "IBM ServeRAID Device Driver Diskette",
\windows\win2003\scsi\driver\Server\i_v\NFRD960.SYS, \windows\win2003\scsi\driver\Server\i_v
d2  = "IBM ServeRAID Device Driver Diskette",
\windows\win2003\scsi\driver\Server\powerpc\IPSRAIDN.SYS,
\windows\win2003\scsi\driver\Server\powerpc

[Defaults]
scsi = NFRDDotNet32

[scsi]
NFRDDotNet32 = "IBM ServeRAID 4M/4Mx/4L/4Lx/5i/6M/6i Controller (Windows Server 2003)"
IPSDotNet32 = "IBM ServeRAID 2x/3H/3L/4H Controller (Windows Server 2003)"

[Files.scsi.NFRDDotNet32]
driver   = d1, nfrd960.sys, NFRD960
dll      = d1, nfrdci04.dll
catalog  = d1, ibmnfrd3.cat
inf      = d1, oemsetup.inf

[Files.scsi.IPSDotNet32]
driver   = d2, ipsraidn.sys, IPSRAIDN
dll      = d2, nfrdci04.dll
catalog  = d2, ipsraid3.cat
inf      = d2, oemsetup.inf


[Config.NFRD960]
value = parameters\PnpInterface,5,REG_DWORD,1
value = parameters\Device,NumberOfRequests,REG_DWORD,128

[Config.IPSRAIDN]
```

Figure 13.8 *Example of a txtsetup.oem file containing both a HAL and a RAID controller merged together into the same file..*

13.11 Driver placement sequence

On certain hardware systems, it is necessary to install the chipset driver before audio, video, or modem drivers. The reason for this is that the audio, video, USB, or modem device in question might be integrated on the motherboard, thus requiring chipset functionality to work before installing other devices controlled by the motherboard controller circuits.

The way to control this order is to simply enter the path to the chipset driver *before* the path to the other drivers in the `OemPnpDriversPath` entry in the answer file and renaming the subfolder in which the chipset drivers are located to another name starting with a letter with a lower alphabetical value than the name of the subfolder containing the other drivers.

Likewise, if you do not wish to rename the subfolder containing the chipset driver, you could rename the subfolders containing the other drivers to a name starting with a letter that has a higher alphabetical value. RIS reads folders in a sequence from A to Z. Using the following folder structure, the "Audio" drivers would be matched before the "Chipset" drivers, because "Audio" starts with an A, which is a lower alphabetical value than C.

```
$OEM$
... ... $1
... ... ... Drivers
... ... ... ... Audio
... ... ... ... Chipset
```

Now, having renamed the "Audio" folder to "Soundcards," in the following example, the chipset drivers would be matched before the "Soundcards" drivers, because "Chipset" starts with a C, which is a lower alphabetical value than S.

```
$OEM$
... ... $1
... ... ... Drivers
... ... ... ... Chipset
... ... ... ... Soundcard
```

13.12 Summary

In this chapter, we've covered some detailed aspects of including support for different types of devices, from audio cards to mass-storage devices and HALs. Using the different techniques described, you can make any device work with Remote Installation Services and perform streamlined, silent installation on any type of Intel-based computer, be it a PC or a server or even a point-of-sale system. As long as a Windows driver exists for the exact Windows operating system version in question, it will work with Remote Installation Services.

14

Deploying Files and Software

Remote Installation Services was designed to not only have the ability to deploy an operating system, but also to deploy applications, scripts, files, and commands. Using these abilities can help you perform powerful deployments in distributing files, applications, making registry changes, and executing scripts in the same process as deploying a client or server installation. The result is a client computer deployment where installations will become almost 100% complete and ready to use and where all the characteristics and applications belonging to your organization or environment are available to your users immediately after installation.

Highlights:

- Understand the terminology of silent installations
- Understand how to deploy files, applications, and software with RIS
- Get familiar with cmdlines.txt and GUIRunOnce
- See samples of popular scripts and registry keys
- Understand how to deploy printers

14.1 General

As you read in Chapter 12, using a distribution point, the OEM folder structure, allows you to distribute files to a computer. We've looked at how we could distribute drivers, but essentially any files can be distributed. This includes registry files, scripts, and application files. Once files are on the local computer, it is possible to do with them whatever you want, including the following:

- Run scripts that perform various tasks
- Execute registry changes

- Install applications
- Create directories and work with files
- Install printers

The files or folders can be hidden or not; it makes no difference in the installation process. Another possibility is to execute applications, scripts, registry changes, and so on from a network share. There are two tools for doing all this:

- cmdlines.txt
- GUIRunOnce parameters

In this chapter we'll be delving into how to use these tools for various purposes, such as application installation, registry tweaking, and printer deployment.

14.2 Silent installations

Many applications have a built-in ability to be installed silently. The term *silent* indicates that the installation is carried out with no need for user intervention. It removes the need for clicking *Next* or prompting the user for file locations, and so on. Not all applications have this ability, though. Executing an installation silently is often just a question of running the setup program with parameters specifying that the installation should be performed silently.

To find the correct parameter, go to a command prompt and type "setup /?" as illustrated in Figure 14.1. Of course, if the setup program has a different name, "Install.exe," for example, use that name in the command prompt.

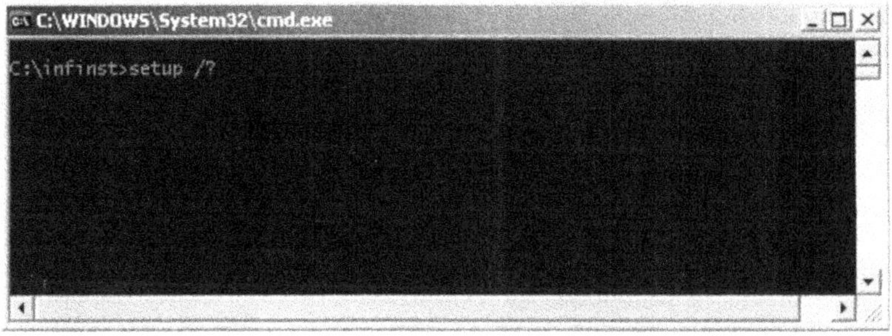

Figure 14.1 *setup /? at a command prompt.*

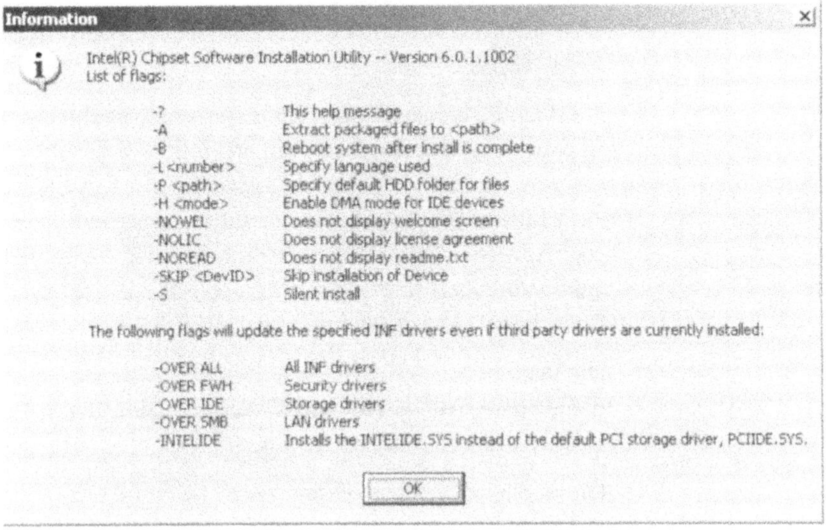

Figure 14.2 *Setup.exe command parameters.*

Having executed this command, this information appears. It informs you of all the different parameters that can be used with the setup program.

As clearly indicated in Figure 14.2, installing this program silently would require using the –S parameter. You would then run "setup –S" from the command prompt to make a silent installation. Running an installation this way is a great way to make silent installations through scripts (login scripts or startup/shutdown scripts).

14.3 Using cmdlines

Using cmdlines.txt is a wonderful way to make a client computer run commands during RIS installation. The cmdlines.txt file contain commands that GUI mode setup runs when installing optional components, and it can be made manually or using Setup Manager. This could be applications that must be available immediately when Windows starts up for the first time. It could also be scripts, registry changes, or anything else that can be executed for that matter.

At the point where cmdlines.txt commands are run, no user is logged onto the computer yet and there is no network connectivity. This means that any command that runs must execute from the local machine using data resident on the local machine. Also, when cmdlines.txt commands are run, setup writes user-specific information to the default portion of the registry, thus making the all users profile receive that information. As a result, all subsequently created users receive whatever information commands in cmdlines.txt has written.

The Windows Installer service is not available during this part of setup. If you plan to use cmdlines.txt, the file itself and its associated batch files (if any) should be placed at the same level in the RIS folder hierarchy as the OEM folder. The actual content to be executed must be placed in folders or files below the \$OEM$\$1 folder, otherwise the content will not be distributed to the local hard disk. Other useful information about using cmdlines.txt includes the following:

- The `OemPreinstall = Yes` key/value in the `[Unattended]` section of the answer file is required if you are using the \OEM folder to add any more files to the system.
- The application that you are installing must not configure itself for multiple users.
- The application must be designed to be installed by one user.
- Cmdlines.txt requires that you place the files that you have to run for an application or tool in directories that you can access during the setup process. This means that the files must be on the hard disk. In other words, they must be copied from the $1 folder structure.
- Files copied from the $1 folder are not automatically deleted at the end of the installation process. You can optionally include a command in cmdlines.txt to delete the files and folders if you wish to do so.

Let's look at how to integrate a cmdlines.txt file:

1. First create the OEM folder and a $1 folder structure (see Chapter 4 for information on how to do this).
2. Now create subfolders in the $1 folder. Copy your data, applications, scripts, or registry changes in the appropriate subfolders. Give the folders descriptive names. Your folder structure might then look like this. It is only an example:

```
$OEM$
... ... $1
... ... ... Drivers (contains driver files)
... ... ... IE6 (contains Internet Explorer 6
                installation files)
... ... ... Adobe (contains Adobe Acrobat Reader
                  installation files)
... ... ... Regkeys (contains commands of any
                    registry keys/tweeks)
```

```
... ... ... Scripts (contains any scripts you
                    might want to execute)
```

3. Now, at the same level as the OEM folder, create a blank text file and name it cmdlines.txt.

The cmdlines.txt is a simple text file, which you can edit using the incredible Notepad. The syntax is as follows:

```
[Commands]
"[command string 1]"
"[command string 2]"
"[command string n]"
```

The `[command string]` entry does not necessarily have to be the actual command; it can also just call a batch file, which then executes a given command in different ways. You cannot use a parameter surrounded by quotes in cmdlines.txt. If you need quotes, use a batch file, which you call from cmdlines.txt. The top of the file must contain the `[Commands]` entry. Place the batch files directly at the same level as cmdlines.txt. You can install any executable program from here, but make sure that no user input is needed. In other words, the installation must be silent. Figure 14.3 is an example of a cmdlines.txt file.

The ".\" reference indicates that the batch file, which is referenced as a command, is present in the executing directory, which is the same directory as where cmdlines.txt is placed, the root of the OEM folder.

In the file example in Figure 14.3, the first command is `".\localadmin.cmd"`, which points to the localadmin.cmd file. The command executed in this batch file makes the Domain Users security group member of the local Administrators group on the local machine. (See Figure 14.4.)

Figure 14.3 *Commands in a cmdlines.txt file.*

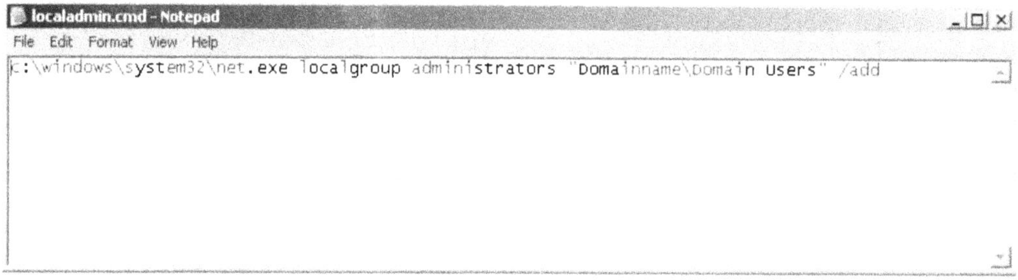
localadmin.cmd - Notepad
File Edit Format View Help
c:\windows\system32\net.exe localgroup administrators "Domainname\Domain Users" /add

Figure 14.4 *The .\localadmin.cmd batch file. Running this command will add the Domain Users Group to the Administrators group on the local client computer.*

The `".\ie.cmd"` command calls the ie.cmd batch file (shown in Figure 14.5), which contains a simple command that installs a branded version of Internet Explorer 6.1 SP1. The Internet Explorer program files are located in c:\drv\ie, and they were distributed to this location because we initially made the drv\ie subfolder containing the program files in the \$OEM$\$1 folder. The /R:N parameter prevents the computer from restarting after installation.

This last example is `".\logon.cmd"`, which calls the logon.cmd file illustrated in Figure 14.6. This batch file calls a registry tweak, ld.reg. The –s parameter used after regedit.exe loads the registry change silently. If the parameter wasn't there, the registry editor would prompt the user to accept the registry change being loaded.

Figure 14.7 shows the actual registry change. It sets a default logon Domain Name and a text string in the User Name field of the login screen of Windows. This is a useful little registry tweak because the default Domain Name is set to the local computer name after an RIS client installation.

As you can see from the previous examples, there are lots of possibilities when using cmdlines.txt and batch files. As long as the files have been distributed to the hard drive of the client computer (from \$OEM$\$1 and its

ie.cmd - Notepad
File Edit Format View Help
cd\
c:\drv\ie\ie6setup.exe /R:N

Figure 14.5 *A CMD file that installs Internet Explorer without rebooting the computer.*

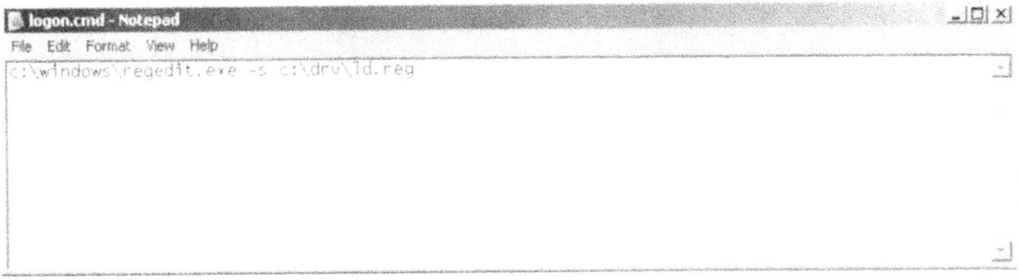
logon.cmd - Notepad
File Edit Format View Help
c:\windows\regedit.exe -s c:\drv\ld.reg

Figure 14.6 *A CMD file which executes a registry change silently*

subfolder), cmdlines.txt together with your commands and batch files will perform whatever task you want them to. It's up to you to fill in the correct commands and data.

Note: Commands in cmdlines.txt are performed in the same sequence as they are listed in the file. However, a command does not wait for the previous command stream of processes to finish before executing itself. When a cmdlines.txt command is processed, the next command will start as soon as the previous command has been executed, unaware of what that command really does. This can lead to two or more installations running simultaneously, and because more than one instance of an installation mechanism is running, starting a second installation might fail. A workaround to this issue is to use the start/wait command directly from cmdlines.txt. Start/wait starts a command or application and then waits for it to terminate before a new start command can execute. An example of the format is:

```
Start/wait C:\drv\ie\ie6setup.exe /R:N
```

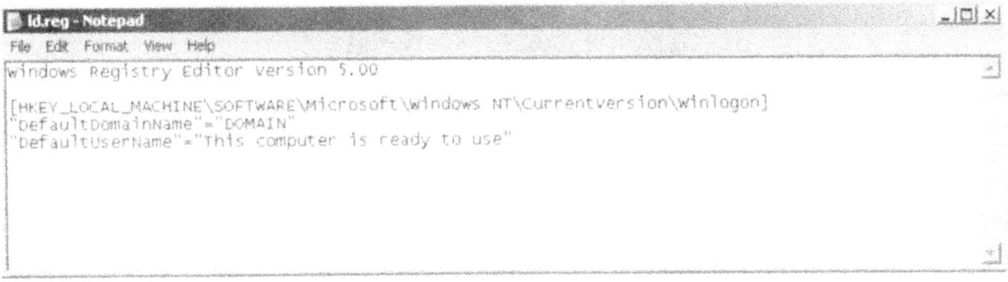
ld.reg - Notepad
File Edit Format View Help
Windows Registry Editor Version 5.00
[HKEY_LOCAL_MACHINE\SOFTWARE\Microsoft\Windows NT\CurrentVersion\Winlogon]
"DefaultDomainName"="DOMAIN"
"DefaultUserName"="This computer is ready to use"

Figure 14.7 *The .reg file containing a registry change. This registry entry will preset text in the User Name dialog box as well as preset the computer to log in to the Domain Name of your choice.*

14.4 Using GuiRunOnce

The [GuiRunOnce] section of your unattend.txt or .sif file can contain a list of commands that run the first time a user logs onto the computer after final installation is complete. Commands called in the [GuiRunOnce] section process synchronously. Each application runs in the order listed in this section, and each command must finish before the next command can run. Each line specifies a command that is run by the following registry entry:

```
HKEY_CURRENT_USER\Software\Microsoft\Windows\
CurrentVersion\Runonce
```

It is slightly similar to cmdlines.txt, but GuiRunOnce parameters are executed after installation has finished, whereas cmdlines.txt commands are executed the first time setup enters GUI mode. This is important to understand, especially when you want an application installed that only writes information to the current user. This is because commands running using the [GuiRunOnce] section are run in the context of the currently logged-in user. If the user does not have the permissions necessary to run the command in question, then the installation fails.

Because GuiRunOnce commands run in the context of a logged-in user instead of as a service, the registry entries that the application creates are created for the current user instead of for the default user. Setup will propagate default user registry settings to new users. If you want any settings and updates to appear only for the specifically logged-in user, then this might be appropriate. Otherwise, using cmdlines.txt is a better approach to running commands and installing applications, because it runs as a system service. GuiRunOnce setup commands can be set up manually or using Setup Manager. The format of the [GuiRunOnce] section is as follows:

```
[GuiRunOnce]

Command0 = [command string 0]
Command1 = [command string 1]
Commandn = [command string n]
```

Command strings referring to a UNC path must be written within quotation marks. Command strings referring to a local folder or file can be written without quotations unless a space character is part of the folder or file name. Figure 14.8 is a real-world example of the GuiRunOnce section in the answer file.

If you plan to use the [GuiRunOnce] section to initiate installations, there are some additional issues to take into consideration:

- If an application requires a Windows Explorer shell to install, the `[GuiRunOnce]` section will not work because the shell is not loaded when the Run and RunOnce commands are processed.
- If this is the case, you will have to repackage the application as a Windows Installer package (a .msi file).
- If the application requires a restart, determine whether there is a way to suppress the restart. This is important because any time the system restarts, all of the following entries in the `[GuiRunOnce]` section are lost and are not processed.
- You will have to either check the help menu or review your software documentation to identify the suppress reboot command.
- Software vendors use different switches or parameters for silent installations. See the previous section about silent installations to read more.

If there is no way within the application to suppress a restart, you can try to repackage the application to a Windows Installer package to form a .msi file of the software. A tool that can help you do exactly that is WinInstall LE 2003, which is freely available from OnDemand Software (*www.ondemandsoftware.com*). While the free version of WinInstall LE 2003 can repackage many software products, it cannot repackage all of them.

If you want to deal with advanced repackaging that can do it all, we suggest you look at the products available from Wise Solutions (*www.wise.com*) or InstallShield (*www.installshield.com*). Still, if you cannot stop the program

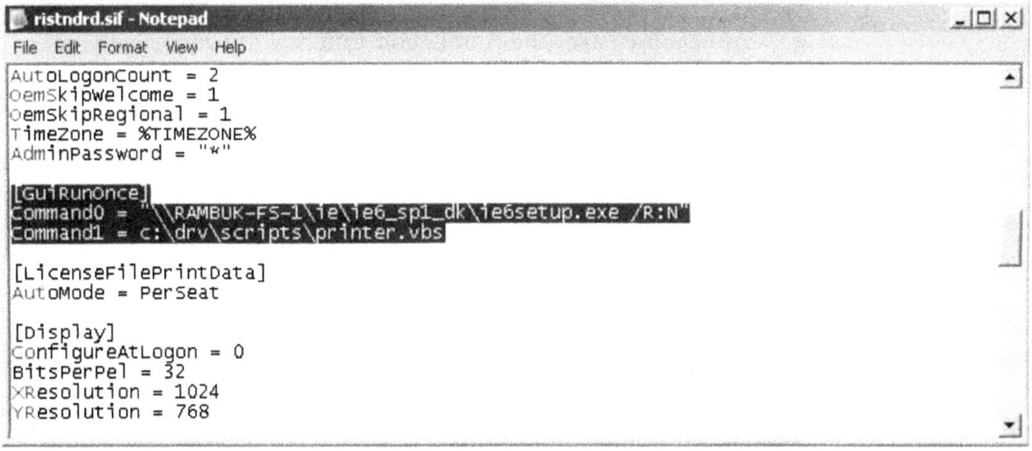
ristndrd.sif - Notepad
File Edit Format View Help

```
AutoLogonCount = 2
OemSkipWelcome = 1
OemSkipRegional = 1
TimeZone = %TIMEZONE%
AdminPassword = "*"

[GuiRunOnce]
Command0 = "\\RAMBUK-FS-1\ie\ie6_sp1_dk\ie6setup.exe /R:N"
Command1 = c:\drv\scripts\printer.vbs

[LicenseFilePrintData]
AutoMode = PerSeat

[Display]
ConfigureAtLogon = 0
BitsPerPel = 32
XResolution = 1024
YResolution = 768
```

Figure 14.8 *Example of cheerful commands in the GuiRunOnce section in the answer file.*

from restarting the computer, and the Windows Installer package is out of your reach, there is an option to continue processing GuiRunOnce commands and then install the application in question the next time a user logs onto the computer. It's not beautiful, but it works.

Start by creating a registry file, as in the following example:

```
Windows Registry Editor Version 5.00

[HKEY_LOCAL_MACHINE\SOFTWARE\Microsoft\Windows\
CurrentVersion\RunOnce]
"Application"="[Path to installation file]"
```

- Save the registry file in \$OEM$\$1 in a place of your choice to make sure it gets distributed to the local computer.
- Create a command string entry in the `[GuiRunOnce]` using the with this command: `regedit -s [path to registry file]`.

This workaround will simply add the installation command to the RunOnce key in registry, telling the computer to run your installation the next time the computer reboots. This restart can be done automatically, though.

In connection with GuiRunOnce command strings, there are some more keys of interest in the answer file. These are located in the `[GuiUnattended]` section:

- `AutoLogon`, which can be a value of YES or NO
- `AutoLogonCount`, the value is a number that specifies a number of automatic logons
- `AutoLogon` enables the AutoLogon feature when the value is set to yes.

This function allows you to perform various tasks of an installation a number of times; the specific number of times is the value defined in the `AutoLogonCount` key. Setting these values might be useful if you're deploying scripts, settings, or applications that require restarting the computer. Each time the computer is restarted and the administrator is automatically logged on, the AutoLogonCount value is decremented by one until the count reaches zero. The automatic logon occurs only when the computer is rebooted, not when the user logs off. Once the AutoLogonCount value reaches zero, the AutoAdminLogon value is set to 0 (disabled), and the AutoLogonCount value in the Winlogon key is removed.

As mentioned earlier, command strings in the `[GuiRunOnce]` section are executed only the first time a user logs onto a computer, and when the computer is restarted after this, remaining entries in the `[GuiRunOnce]` section that are not processed will not be processed. In this case, using the `AutoLogon` feature might be useful, if you're also using the registry file example mentioned earlier, because it will force restarting automatically rather than manually by the user.

Note: For the automatic administrator logon to work, the Administrator account must have a password. A blank password is allowed only one time before the AutoAdminLogon value is set to 0 (disabled). The password is set using the AdminPassword key from the SIF.

14.5 Deploying and executing scripts

Executing scripts is simple. Just call the script using cmdlines.txt or GuiRunOnce. Using cmdlines.txt you must put your script into a .bat or .cmd file and refer to it as a `[commandstring]` in the cmdlines.txt file. Remember, though, that if the script is somewhat classified, you need to be sure to include a deletion command in the end of cmdlines.txt to remove the script from the local computer. The same procedure is valid for calling the script from the `[GuiRunOnce]` section of the answer file, only with GuiRunOnce, the script does not have to be located on the local computer.

14.6 Deploying and using registry keys

Deploying registry changes during setup is as easy as compiling the script using cmdlines.txt or GuiRunOnce. An irritating thing about registry files (.reg) is that when you double-click to execute them, Windows asks if you want to write the information into the registry.

To force a registry change to execute silently, you must use this command string:

```
Regedit -s [full path to *.reg file]
```

The following example sets up the installation source path of a Windows installation media. It is a great little tweak that will make Windows search for the original Windows installation files in a file/share location of your choice rather than on the RIS server or prompt you for inserting the original CD:

```
Windows Registry Editor Version 5.00

[HKEY_LOCAL_MACHINE\SOFTWARE\Microsoft\Windows\
CurrentVersion\Setup]
"SourcePath"="\\\\server\\share$\\w2k\\"
"ServicePackSourcePath"="\\\\server\\share$\\
servicepacks\\w2ksp4us\\"

[HKEY_LOCAL_MACHINE\SOFTWARE\Microsoft\Windows NT\
CurrentVersion]
"SourcePath"="\\\\server\\share$\\w2k\\I386"
```

14.7 Adding printers

This chapter also explores the possibilities of including printers in a client computer deployment scenario. In a given situation of deploying hundreds or even thousands of computers, it might make good sense to deploy printer settings simultaneously, making client computers readily available with printer settings and connections immediately after installation. You can deploy printers using Setup Manager or scripts. This can be accomplished using some rather simple scripting techniques, based on either VB Script or (even simpler) using rundll32 commands.

These are the possibilities of deploying printer settings:

- Adding network printer connections
- Adding local printer connections
- Adding driver support for printers not supported by Windows
- Sharing a printer
- Setting up printer characteristics

Depending on the printer infrastructure, it is possible to set up printers based on usernames, group names, or computer names, or to simply apply printer settings equally on all client installations.

Whether using a VBScript or rundll32 commands, the printer settings could be executed using cmdlines.txt or GuiRunOnce. You can also use either method to include the commands or scripts in a login script or a startup/shutdown script.

14.7.1 Using rundll32

Using rundll32 it is possible to write a simple cmd file including the various rundll32 commands you need. The rundll32 could also be integrated into a login script or a startup/shutdown script. Use the command `rundll32 printui.dll,PrintUIEntry [options] [@commandfile]`.

Note: All `rundll32 printui.dll,PrintUIEntry` commands are case-sensitive.

To take a look at all rundll32 command parameters, go to a command prompt and type the following:

rundll32 printui.dll,PrintUIEntry /? (case-sensitive)

The screen shown in Figure 14.9 will then pop up.

As you can see, there are a lot of parameters, and we'll show the use of the most important of them as follows. Different parameters are used in Windows 2000 and Windows XP. For the same reason, it is important that your cmd file with rundll32 commands reflects the supported parameters of the client operating system in question. Let's look at some of the most commonly used parameters and commands. The following command will add a printer connection to the network printer "marketing" on the server "printserver":

```
rundll32 printui.dll,PrintUIEntry /in
/n\\printserver\marketing
```

The "/in" parameter translates to "add network printer connection."

The "/n" parameter translates to "printer name."

The following command will add a printer connection to the network printer "marketing" on the server "printserver" and then set it as the default printer:

```
rundll32 printui.dll,PrintUIEntry /y /in
/n\\printserver\marketing
```

The "/y" parameter translates to "set printer as the default."

The following command will delete the printer connection to the network printer "marketing" on the server "printserver":

```
rundll32 printui.dll,PrintUIEntry /dn
/n\\printserver\marketing
```

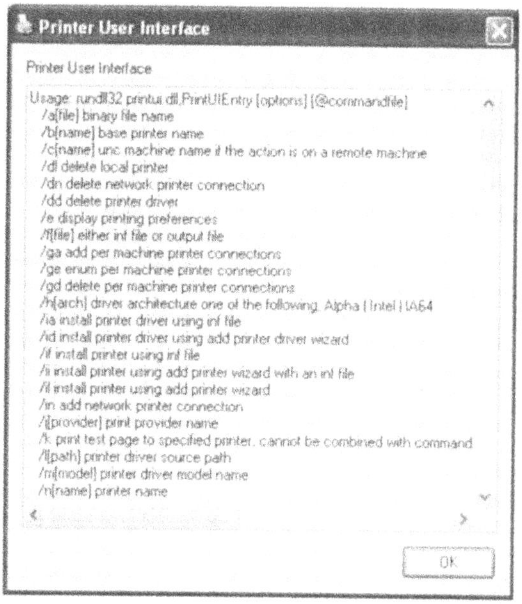

Figure 14.9 *The Printer User Interface screen. There's a whopping amount of possibilities.*

The "/dn" parameter translates to "delete network printer connection."

In this case you might also want to use the "/q" parameter, which will suppress the warning message if you happen to delete the last default printer connection.

If the printer name contains blanks, use parentheses before and after the entire UNC path of the printer. As you might have guessed, using rundll32 commands to connect to a shared network printer wouldn't make much sense to include in a cmdlines.txt file, because there is no network connectivity when commands in cmdlines.txt are executed.

If connecting to shared network printers, use GuiRunOnce instead or execute the command in logon scripts or startup/shutdown scripts. Including rundll32 commands in cmdlines.txt is only useful if you wish to make a local printer connection. Given that the printer driver is not included with Windows, you will first have to copy the extracted printer driver files using a \$OEM\$1 subfolder to a location on the local hard drive on the client computer. You can see the command in Figure 14.10.

If you use rundll32, you'll notice that it does not actually make a connection to the printer unless the printer is connected to the computer at the time of execution. It adds support for the printer, and then whenever the printer is connected, the plug-and-play subsystem will recognize the printer and then make the actual connection.

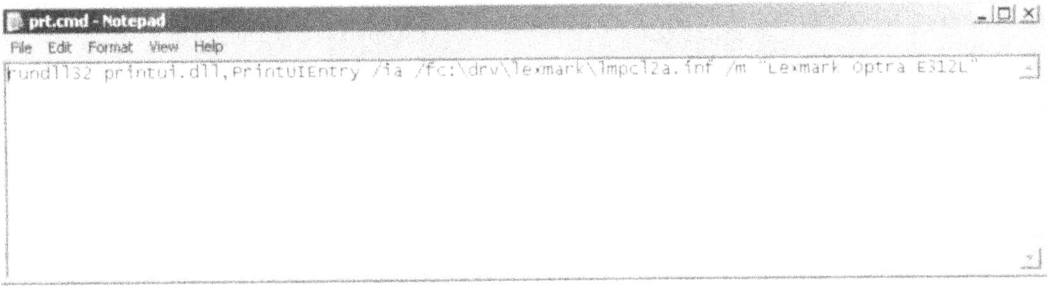
prt.cmd - Notepad
File Edit Format View Help
rundll32 printui.dll,PrintUIEntry /ia /fc:\drv\lexmark\lmpcl2a.inf /m "Lexmark Optra E312L"

Figure 14.10 *Adding support for a locally attached printer unknown to Windows.*

The entire command is:

```
rundll32 printui.dll,PrintUIEntry /ia /fc:\drv\lexmark\
lmpcl2a.inf /m "Lexmark Optra E312L"
```

The "/ia" parameter translates to "install printer driver using .inf file."

The "/f" parameter translates to "either .inf file or output file," and the full path to the location of the .inf file must be written.

The "/m" translates to "printer driver model name."

Note: When using the "/m" parameter, the name entered must be exactly the same as the name stated in the system information file in question.

14.7.2 Using VBScript and WMI

This isn't a book about Visual Basic and WMI scripting, so in this section we'll show some examples of using VBScript and WMI to create, delete, and modify printer connections. These scripts can be integrated into cmdlines.txt, as GuiRunOnce commands, or they can be used more logically in login/logoff/startup/shutdown scripts in connection Active Directory group policy objects.

Microsoft has a great deal of resources available online and in the Windows Server 2003 and Windows XP Resource Kits that are being finished, downloadable scripts as well as a great deal of well-written documentation that covers every aspect of VBScript and printing. A great place to start looking for more advanced options of printer deployment with VBScript is the Microsoft Technet Scripting Center. A prerequisite for being able to execute VBScripts and WMI scripts is that the computer supports WMI and that it has Windows Scripting Host installed.

The following examples will help you perform simple printer management using VBScript. These scripts will only work for Windows XP and Windows Server 2003.

- *Example 1, using VBScript:* This script will add a network printer connection to your computer and set the printer as the default. If you don't want to set the printer as the default printer, just leave out the last line:

```
Set objNetwork = CreateObject ("Wscript.Network")
objNetwork.AddWindowsPrinterConnection "\\PrintServer\
PrinterName"
objNetwork.SetDefaultPrinter \\PrintServer\Printername
```

- *Example 2, using VBScript:* This script will delete a given network printer connection:

```
Set objNetwork = WScript.CreateObject("WScript.Network")
objNetwork.RemovePrinterConnection "\\PrintServer\
PrinterName"
```

- *Example 3, using WMI:* This script will assign a default printer on a computer:

```
strComputer = "."
Set objWMIService = GetObject("winmgmts:" _
    & "{impersonationLevel=impersonate}!\\" & strComputer
& "\root\cimv2")
Set colInstalledPrinters =  objWMIService.ExecQuery _
    ("Select * from Win32_Printer Where Name = 'Printer
name'")
For Each objPrinter in colInstalledPrinters
    objPrinter.SetDefaultPrinter()
Next
```

- *Example 4, using WMI:* This script will delete a printer:

```
strComputer = "."
Set objWMIService = GetObject("winmgmts:" _
    & "{impersonationLevel=impersonate}!\\" & strComputer
& "\root\cimv2")
Set colInstalledPrinters =  objWMIService.ExecQuery _
    ("Select * from Win32_Printer where DeviceID =
'Printer name'")
For Each objPrinter in colInstalledPrinters
    objPrinte
r.Delete_
Next
```

- *Sample script resources:* prnmngr.vbs, prncnfg.vbs, prnjobs.vbs, prndrvr.vbs, prnport.vbs, and prnqctl.vbs are all powerful scripts available from the Windows Server 2003 Resource Kit. These scripts allow for advanced printer management functionality using VBScript.

14.8 Summary

Deploying files, application files, scripts, printers, and so forth is as easy as creating a distribution point, creating some batch files, and then gluing it all together using cmdlines.txt and/or GuiRunOnce to execute what you need. Even if one of the drawbacks of cmdlines.txt is that it will not provide connectivity between the computer and the Active Directory, there are still so many powerful tasks it can perform that ignoring the use of it would be silly. Planning is essential, and you should always consider what you want cmdlines.txt or GuiRunOnce to do and when you want Active Directory Group Policy Objects to take over.

15

Working with OSC files

This chapter gives an overview of how the RIS process uses OSC files, the way they work, and how they can be modified to add more functionality to the RIS server. This chapter covers the steps needed to create additional OSC files and provides an overview of the possibility in OSC files. In this chapter, all reserved variables and the standard tags are also described. Last in this chapter is an overview of all error OSC files that exist on the RIS server.

Highlights:

- Overview
- Standard OSC file process
- Custom OSC files
- Supported OSCML tags
- Reserve OSC variables
- Common OSC errors files

15.1 Overview

When starting an RIS installation, the client begins by pressing F12. That starts the PXE boot process, and at the end of that process, the RIS server transfers the first CIW screen to the client computer. That screen is called welcome.osc and is a standard screen installed at the RIS server installation. All OSC files are located on the RIS server in the folder called: *RemoteInstall\OSChooser\language*, where *language* is used if the OSC files are in multiple languages. Each language must exist in a language folder beneath the OSChooser folder. In a standard RIS installation, only the English language is installed.

After the Welcome screen, some standard screens follow. These screens are specified in the standard OSC section. If an RIS installation fails, then an error OSC file is displayed. The error OSC files are described in section 15.6. It's possible to customize the standard OSC files to, for example, change the help text to include contact information for the support department.

Figure 15.1
OSC file process.

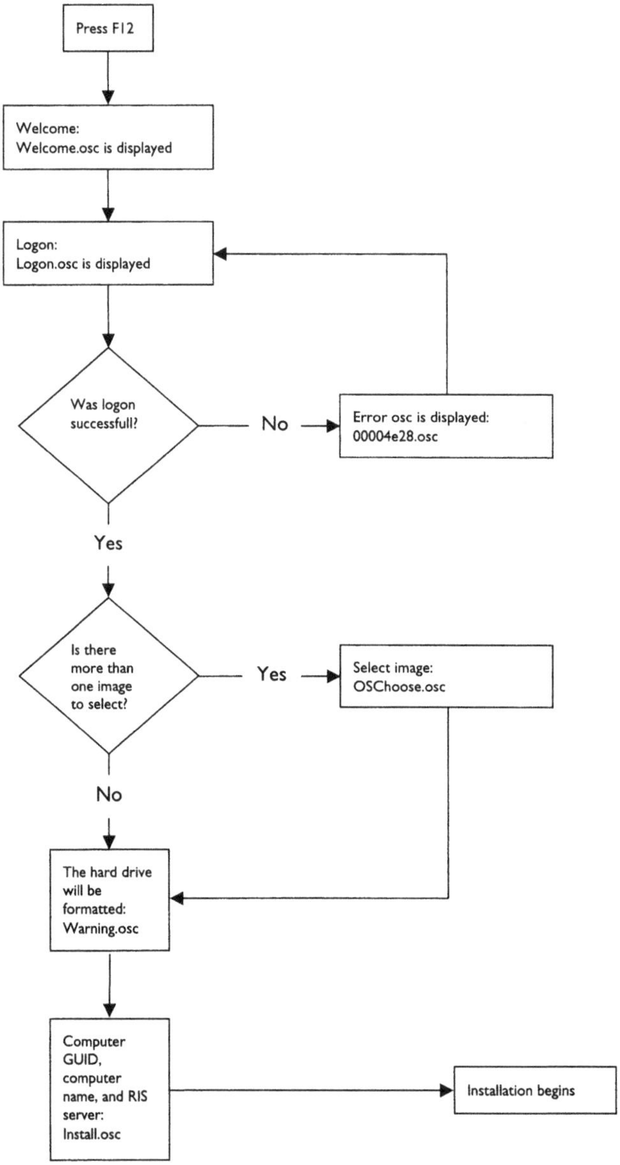

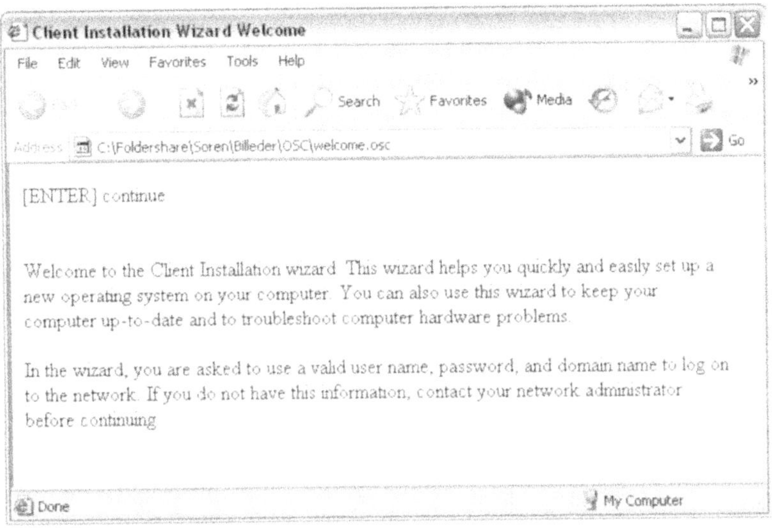

Figure 15.2 *The Welcome.osc file in Internet Explorer.*

OSC files are created by a simple language called OSChooser Markup Language (OSCML), which is formed like HTML version 2. The files have the extension OSC and can be modified in Notepad and displayed with Internet Explorer. Unlike HTML, which start with the tag <HTML> and end with </HTML>, the OSC files use <OSCLM> and </OSCLM> to start and end the formatting of the OSC file. All supported tags are described in section 15.4. Let's look closer at the process and the OSC files involved and when they are applied. The whole process is described in Figure 15.1.

When looking at the standard process of the RIS installation and the OSC files involved, and knowing that the OSC files are written in a standard OSCLM format, this gives the possibility to change the standard behavior in the process and to add more functionality to the process. Let's look at the first screen: welcome.osc in Internet Explorer (Figure 15.2).

At the top there is an Action key, meaning when you press *Enter*, the screen will continue to the next screen. On this figure there is no option to see which screen comes next. All of the standard text can be changed by using Notepad. Let's look at the code behind the text. The text in bold is a description of the OSCLM tag.

```
<OSCML>    Start tag for OSC files
<META KEY=ENTER HREF="LOGIN">
           If the user hits Enter, then go to Logon.osc file
<META KEY=F3 ACTION="REBOOT">
           Press F3 to reboot computer
```

```
<META KEY=ESC HREF="LOGIN">
          If the user hits ESC, then go to Logon.osc file
<META KEY=F1 HREF="LOGIN">
          If the user hits F1, then go to Logon.osc file
<TITLE> Client Installation Wizard Welcome </TITLE>
          Text at top of screen
<FOOTER>  [ENTER] continue </FOOTER>
          Text at bottom of screen
<BODY left=5 right=75>
          Where to place the body text
<BR>      Line breaks. Standard text follows
<BR>
<BR>
Welcome to the Client Installation wizard. This wizard
helps you quickly and easily set up a new operating system
on your computer. You can also use this wizard to keep your
computer up-to-date and to troubleshoot computer hardware
problems.
<BR>
<BR>
In the wizard, you are asked to use a valid user name,
password, and domain name to log on to the network. If you
do not have this information, contact your network
administrator before continuing.
</BODY>   End of body
</OSCML>  End of OSCLM file
```

It's simple to change or localize the standard text so it reflects the information the user needs at this point in the installation. The welcome.osc is only in English and has no knowledge of different languages. To change this, the welcome.osc must be renamed. Change the name to welcome.osc.bak and rename multilng.osc to welcome.osc. By doing this, the welcome.osc includes multiple languages. Let's look at the file in Internet Explorer (Figure 15.3).

Again, the user can press Enter to continue the RIS process, but now there is an option to choose a language to fit the OSC files. Remember that the RIS server only installs the English language. If there is a need for other or multiple languages, a language folder must exist beneath the OSChooser library on the RIS server, and all OSC files must be translated to the languages that are needed. Also, if the regional settings on the RIS server aren't in English, then the multilng.osc must be renamed. Let's look inside the code:

```
<OSCML>
<META KEY=ENTER HREF="LOGIN">
<META KEY=F3 ACTION="REBOOT">
```

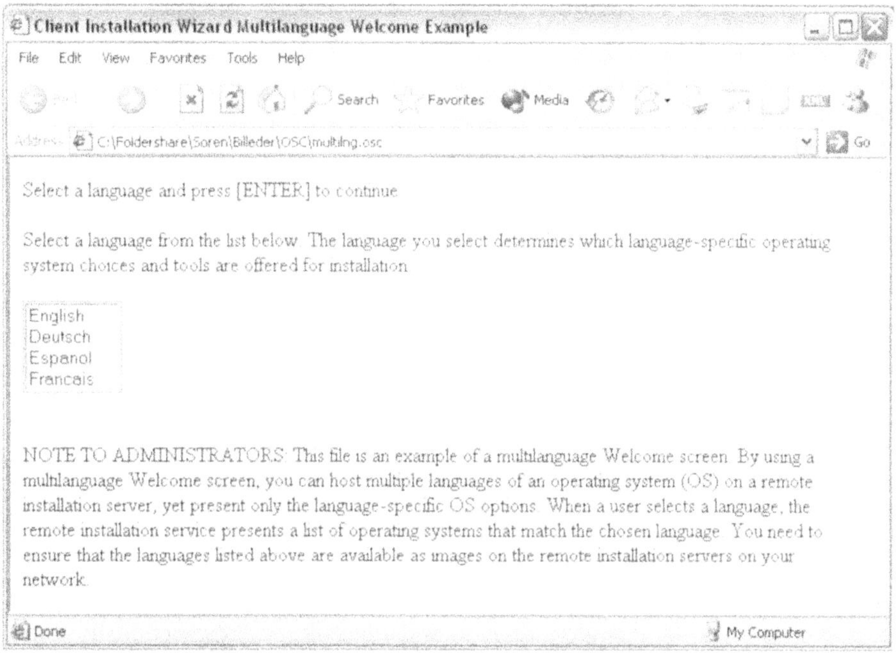

Figure 15.3 *The multilng.osc file in Internet Explorer.*

```
<TITLE> Client Installation Wizard Multilanguage Welcome
Example </TITLE>
<FOOTER> Select a language and press [ENTER] to continue </
FOOTER>
<BODY left=5 right=75>
<BR>
<BR>
Select a language from the list below.  The language you
select determines which language-specific operating system
choices and tools are offered for installation.
<BR>
<FORM ACTION="WELCOME">
            Start a form to capture the user's choice
<SELECT NAME="LANGUAGE" SIZE=4>
            Start the Select tag
<OPTION VALUE="ENGLISH"> English
            Options the user can choose from. These
            values can be modified to support the languages
            needed or more languages can be added.
<OPTION VALUE="GERMAN"> Deutsch
<OPTION VALUE="SPANISH"> Espanol
<OPTION VALUE="FRENCH"> Francais
</SELECT>    End Select
```

```
</FORM>        End Form
<BR>
NOTE TO ADMINISTRATORS: This file is an example of a
Multilanguage Welcome screen. By using a Multilanguage
Welcome screen, you can host multiple languages of an
operating system (OS) on a remote installation server, yet
present only the language-specific OS options. When a user
selects a language, the remote installation service
presents a list of operating systems that match the chosen
language. You need to ensure that the languages listed above
are available as images on the remote installation servers
on your network.
</BODY>
</OSCML>
```

Now that the standard tags and the formatting of OSC files are understood, let's continue to customize the OSC files.

15.2 Custom OSC files

When customizing the OSC files, more functionality can be added and the standard text can be customized to reflect the company's needs. The simplest approach is to change the text in standard OSC files to reflect the contact information on error screens and give additional information to the user. This can be done in Notepad and is a fairly simple process. There are more options to change the standard process by changing the default flow in the OSC files process (e.g., there could be an extra screen, where the user can apply more information before the RIS installation begins).

Another example is to let the user choose which components must be installed in the basic RIS deployment (e.g., IIS could either be part of the installation or not, or the user could choose the display settings before the installation begins). To create more OSC files and let then add functionality to the RIS server, an understanding of the symbioses between OSC files and SIF must be understood.

Every value in the SIF is used when the RIS installation begins. The RIS server creates a copy of the SIF and places it in the *TMP* folder on the RIS server. So to future customize the SIF through OSC files, there is a need to use some simple variables in the OSC file and merge it into the SIF. To create the flow, the following three steps are needed:

1. *Create the new OSC file.* This example shows entries in a new file called Display.osc:

```
<OSCML>
<FORM ACTION="WARNING">      Go to Warning.osc
<META KEY=F3 ACTION="REBOOT">
<META KEY=ESC HREF="CHOICE">Go
<TITLE> Display Setting Choice </TITLE>
                             New title on the screen
<FOOTER> [ENTER] continue [ESC] go back [F1] help [F3]
restart computer</FOOTER>
<BODY left=5 right=75>
<BR>
<BR>
Please enter your desired Display settings or accept the
defaults below.
<BR>                         Custom text on the screen
<BR>
<FORM ACTION="WARNING">      Form begins. Three variables are
                             used: X-Res, Y-Res, and Refresh
X resolution: <INPUT NAME="X-res" VALUE="640" SIZE=4
MAXLENGTH=4><BR>
Y resolution: <INPUT NAME="Y-res" VALUE="480" SIZE=4
MAXLENGTH=4><BR>
Refresh rate: <INPUT NAME="Refresh" VALUE="60" SIZE=3
MAXLENGTH=3><BR>
<BR>
</FORM>
<BR>
<BOLD>Examples:</BOLD><BR> Help text
X resolution: 1024<BR>
Y resolution: 768<BR>
Refresh rate: 70<BR>
</BODY>
</OSCML>
```

2. *Post the file in the right place in the OSC process.* In this example, the OSChoice.osc will be changed from going to Warning.osc when hitting Enter to go to the new page called Display.osc. There is only one variable that must be changed in the standard OSChoice.osc file. Let's look at the standard OSChoice.osc file and the change that must exist:

```
<OSCML>
<META KEY=F3 ACTION="REBOOT">
<META KEY=ESC HREF="CHOICE">
<META SERVER ACTION="ENUM IMAGES">
<TITLE>Client Installation Wizard OS Choices</TITLE>
<FOOTER>[ENTER] continue          [ESC] go back
[F3] restart computer</FOOTER>
<BODY left=5 right=75>
<BR>
```

```
<BR>
Use the arrow keys to select one of the following operating
systems:
<P left=8>
<FORM ACTION="WARNING">          Change <FORM ACTION="WARNING">
                                 to <FORM ACTION="Display">, This
                                 will redirect the OSC file to
                                 Display.osc.
<SELECT NAME="SIF" SIZE=12>
%OPTIONS%
</SELECT>
</FORM>
</P>
<BOLD>Description:</BOLD>  
<TIPAREA>
</BODY>
</OSCML>
```

3. *Use the three new variables in the SIF.* By merging the variables into the SIF, the RIS installation can be fully automated and customized. Let's look at the Display section in the SIF:

```
[Display]
XResolution = %X-Res%        Variable 1 from Display.osc
YResoultion = %Y-Res%        Variable 2 from Display.osc
VRefresh = %Refresh%         Variable 3 from Display.osc
```

Using these simple steps to create highly customized OSC files and the added functionality to the standard RIS installations can be done fast. Remember that changing OSC files is immediately noticeable to the users, so modifying must be done in a test environment and be carefully tested before it's implemented in the production environment.

Some reserved variables are used by the RIS server internally. These variables can't be used externally in OSC files. They are all described in the reserved OSC variables section.

Note: If you customize Login.osc, be careful not to modify any of the values within the following OSML tags:

```
<INPUT NAME="NTLMV2Enabled" VALUE=%NTLMV2Enabled%
MAXLENGTH=255 type=VARIABLE>

<INPUT NAME="ServerUTCFileTime"
VALUE=%ServerUTCFileTime% MAXLENGTH=255 type=VARIABLE>
```

Changing any of these values causes you to lose NTLM v2 support.

15.3 Standard OSC files

Table 15.1 describes the standard OSC files used by the RIS server.

Table 15.1 *Standard OSC Files*

Screen	Filename	Description
Welcome screen	Welcome.osc	The first screen displayed to the user
Logon screen	Login.osc	Requires a user to log on. The user logs on to the network using their existing user account, password, and domain. After the user successfully logs on, RIS uses the credentials entered by the user to determine which installation options should be displayed to the user on the Setup Options screen, based on the RIS Group Policy settings that apply to the user. If the process is not successful, and the logon account, password, or domain is not recognized, the user is prompted to log on again.
Setup Options screen	Choice.osc	Displays setup options to the user: Automatic, Custom, Restart, Maintenance, and Troubleshooting. The degree to which this screen and its options are displayed is controlled through RIS Group Policy settings.
	OSAuto.osc	This screen is not displayed to users. Performs a check to see if a computer account object already exists in Active Directory with the same GUID as the computer running the Client Installation Wizard. If a duplicate GUID is found, DupAuto.osc is displayed. If no duplicate GUID is found, OSChoice.osc is displayed.
Error screen	DupAuto.osc	If a duplicate GUID is found in Active Directory, the user is presented with this screen, which instructs the user to contact the network administrator.
Operating system choice screen	OSChoice.osc	Displays the list of operating system images on the RIS server that are available to the logged-on user. If there is only one possible image for the user to install, then that image is selected and the user does not see this screen. (When RIS is initially installed, the user has only one choice on the screen.) When an operating system image choice is added to an RIS server, it is available for all users who receive service from that server.
Caution screen	Warning.osc	The caution screen displays a warning message that the hard disk will be formatted. The user is cautioned that an operating system is about to be installed on this computer, which requires the local hard disk to be repartitioned and formatted, thus erasing all data that currently resides on the disk.
Summary screen	Install.osc	The summary screen displays information about the computer including computer name, computer GUID, and the RIS server to be used for downloading the image. Pressing any key begins the installation process. At this point, the RIS server has created a computer account object in Active Directory for this computer. The RIS server is now able to look up this computer and associate the computer name and other settings if this computer is reinstalled.

15.4 Supported OSCML tags

All tags that are supported in the OSCLM file are described in Table 15.2.

Table 15.2 *Supported OSCML Tags*

Tag	Description
`<OSCML> </OSCML> (!HTML2.0)`	Indicates that the file is an OSCML file. The `<OSCML>` tag must be the first tag that is found; otherwise, OSChooser ignores all other header tags (i.e., `<META>`, `<TITLE>`, and `<FOOTER>`). The `</OSCML>` tag must be at the end of the file. An item or text that is entered after the `</OSCML>` end tag is not displayed. (The space after `</OSCML>` is where you can place administrative comments and notes.)
`<META SERVER ACTION="`*`server side action`*`">`	Instructs the Remote Installation service to perform a particular action. `<META>` tags are supported by HTML 2.0, but the specifics of the metadata vary from server to server. The following tags conform to HTML 2.0 and are specific to the OSChooser-Remote Installation (binl.svc) conversation. Currently defined actions include the following: ■ ENUM *directory* Enumerates the Setup Information File (SIF) under the `X:\RemoteInstall\Setup %LANGUAGE%\images\"directory"` name. The path under which an SIF is searched for is the following: `\images\"directory name"\`. OSC stores the results of its search in the %OPTIONS% variable. ■ `WARNING` Indicates that using `WARNING` represents the repartition warning screen. If `"Repartition=No"` is in the selected SIF, this screen is skipped; the server searches for the `<META KEY=ENTER .....>` line and goes to that screen. ■ `DNRESET` Resets all variables to their initial state (as logged on again). ■ `FILTER` *name* Instructs Remote Installation to check the Group Policy object of the domain to determine what choices can be displayed to the user. ■ `CHECKGUID` Checks Active Directory to determine whether this globally unique identifier (GUID) duplicates an existing GUID.
`<META KEY= F1 | F3 | ENTER | ESC HREF="`*`screen name`*`">`	Goes to the screen name that is specified when the user presses the function key that is specified within the tag. (The .osc file name extension is appended by the server.) F1, F3, ENTER, and ESC are the only keys that are supported for use within this tag.

Table 15.2 *Supported OSCML Tags (continued)*

<table>
<tr><th>Tag</th><th>Description</th></tr>
<tr><td><META ACTION="<i>LOGIN</i>"></td><td>Instructs OSChooser to authenticate the user with the credentials that OSChooser has stored after the user has pressed ENTER. If authentication is not successful, OSChooser goes to Loginerr.osc. If authentication is successful, OSChooser goes to the screen in <META KEY=ENTER.....>. The variables that are sent from the .osc screen are encrypted; all screens sent after this screen are encrypted as well.</td></tr>
<tr><td><TITLE> Title </TITLE></td><td>Indicates a title line. The title is written at the top of the screen in blue text on a white background.</td></tr>
<tr><td><FOOTER>(!HTML2.0)Footer </FOOTER> (!HTML2.0)</td><td>Indicates a footer line. The footer is written at the bottom of the screen in blue text on a white background.</td></tr>
<tr><td><BODY [LEFT="<i>left margin</i>" (!HTML2.0)] [RIGHT="<i>right margin</i>" (!HTML2.0)]></td><td>Indicates the end of the header tags and the beginning of the text that are to be shown to the user, both the left margin and the right margin (in characters).</td></tr>
<tr><td><PRE [LEFT="<i>left margin</i>" (!HTML2.0)] [RIGHT="<i>right margin</i>" (!HTML2.0)]> </PRE></td><td>Indicates that the text that follows the tag is preformatted with no text wrapping. OSChooser truncates any lines that are longer than the current margin settings, with the option, however, of specifying the left and right margins (in characters).</td></tr>
<tr><td><FORM ACTION="<i>screen name</i>"> </FORM></td><td>Indicates that there are input controls on this page. It also specifies what screen is to be retrieved next. If no name is provided and the controls on the page within the file don't have "NAME=" tags in them, the resulting value for the control is the next screen that is retrieved. There can be only one <FORM.....> tag per page.</td></tr>
<tr><td><INPUT [NAME="<i>osc var name</i>"] [TYPE="<i>TEXT | PASSWORD</i>"] [VALUE="<i>starting value</i>"] [SIZE="<i>display size</i>"] [MAXLENGTH="<i>max length</i>"]></td><td>Creates an edit control on the page. The edit control in OSCML works the same as an edit control in HTML 2.0. The following are descriptions of the parameters for this tag:
■ NAME="osc var name"
Indicates what OSC variable is sent back when a value is entered in the edit box by the user.
■ TYPE="TEXT | PASSWORD"
Defaults to TEXT. Specify the password type PASSWORD to make all text that has been entered appear as asterisks. The password type HIDDEN is not supported by OSChooser.
■ VALUE="starting value"
Allows a default value to be added by the user to the edit box.
■ SIZE="display size"
Specifies the number of characters that the user can enter in the edit box.</td></tr>
</table>

Table 15.2 *Supported OSCML Tags (continued)*

Tag	Description
(cont'd.)	■ MAXLENGTH="*max length*" Indicates the maximum length of the string that can be entered in the edit box. If the value of the SIZE parameter is greater than the number of characters that remain on the line, the INPUT tag defaults to the automatic size. The *automatic size* is calculated by subtracting the number of characters that have been entered from the number of characters for the default length of the edit box. REMAINING is the number of character spaces from the end of the string to the right margin minus four character spaces for the pair of brackets and two extra end spaces.
<SELECT [MULTIPLE] [NOAUTO (!HTML2.0) [NAME="*oscvarname*"] [SIZE="*height*"]> [<OPTION.....><OPTION.....>] </SELECT>	Creates a list from which users can use arrow keys to select an option. An example is <SELECT SIZE=10>. The following <OPTION> tags specify what the option list contains: ■ <OPTION VALUE="OSAUTO" TIP="....."> is the Automatic Setup option. Use this option to install an operating system on the computer. It's the easiest way to install an operating system on the computer because most installation options are already configured by the network administrator. ■ <OPTION VALUE="CUSTOM"> is the Custom Setup option. Use this option to define a unique name for the computer that is being set up and specify where the computer account is to be located in Active Directory. ■ <OPTION VALUE="RESTART"> is the Restart a Previous Setup Attempt option. Use this option to restart a computer on which a previous remote installation attempt has been detected. ■ <OPTION VALUE="TOOLS"> is the Maintenance and Troubleshooting option. Use this option to gain access to tools that can be use to keep the computer up-to-date and to troubleshoot problems.
<OPTION [SELECTED] [TIP="*help text*" (!HTML2.0)] [VALUE="*return value*"]> *Item description*	Indicates what items are going to be shown in a list and is used in conjunction with the <SELECT> tag. The text that follows the <OPTION> tag is displayed in the list. The <VALUE> tag indicates what string is sent back to the server. The <TIP> tag is a way to display Help text in the <TIPAREA>. The <SELECTED> tag indicates what items must be selected first. If more than one <OPTION> tag is designated, the last option is used.

Table 15.2 *Supported OSCML Tags (continued)*

Tag	Description
`<SELECT> </SELECT>`	`<SELECT>` indicates the beginning of a list. The visible size of the list defaults to 1 and can be overridden by the `SIZE` field. There is no user interface to indicate extra items in the list (such as scroll bars), so make sure that the list is large enough to show all of your items. This tag is often used with the `%OPTIONS%` variable after a `<META SERVER ACTION="ENUM .....>` tag has been used to list the SIFs available under a particular directory. If the `<SELECT>` tag has only one `<OPTION>` tag, `OSChooser` automatically selects that option and continues. The `<NOAUTO>` tag prevents `OSChooser` from automatically selecting an option. `</SELECT>` indicates the end of a list
` `	Indicates a new line break.
`<P [LEFT="`*`left margin`*`" (!HTML2.0)] [RIGHT="`*`right margin`*`" (!HTML2.0)] > </P>`	Indicates a new paragraph. In OSCML, this tag acts like the ` ` tag to conserve space, except that it has options that allow you to change the margins.
`<BOLD>` *`text`* `</BOLD>`	Displays the word "text" in white type.
`<FLASH>` *`text`* `</FLASH>`	Flashes the word "text" on the screen.
`<TIPAREA [LEFT="`*`left margin`*`"] [RIGHT="`*`right margin`*`"] SIZE="`*`height`*`"]> (!HTML2.0)`	Indicates where any tips can be displayed. All tips are wrapped to the margins. The default height of the tip area is the amount of screen area that remains, unless the amount of screen area is overridden by the SIZE parameter.
`<OPTION VALUE="OSAUTO"TIP= ".....">`	Indicates automatic installation of the operating system. This is the easiest way to install an operating system on a computer. When this tag is used, the user sees the option `AUTOMATIC SETUP` in the list; when that option is selected, the text that is noted by the `TIP="....."` is displayed in the area noted by `<TIPAREA>` in the .osc file.

15.5 Reserved OSC variables

Some OSC variables are reserved internally by the RIS server and cannot be used externally in OSC files. All reserved variables are described in Table 15.3.

Table 15.3 *Reserved OSC Variables*

Variable	Description
`Language`	The only OSC variable that can be set before the user successfully logs on. This variable controls which folders are used to obtain Client Installation Wizard screens, to generate the list of available operating system images, and when performing any ENUM actions. The default value of this variable matches the default language of the server.
`SubError`	The server sets this variable internally for any errors it encounters. This can be added to an error screen to help administrators diagnose internal server failures.
`MachineOU`	Indicates to the server where the new computer account is to be generated. If this variable is not set before installation, the setting specified in the properties of the RIS server is used.
`MachineName`	Indicates to the server the name of the new computer. If this variable is not set before installation, a name is generated based on the computer naming policy specified in the properties of the RIS server. By default, this variable is used to set the ComputerName value in the answer file.
`ServerName`	Set to the name of the server to which the Client Installation Wizard is connected. By default, this variable is used to set the OriSrc value in the answer file.
`Language`	The only OSC variable that can be set before the user successfully logs on. This variable controls which folders are used to obtain Client Installation Wizard screens, to generate the list of available operating system images, and when performing any ENUM actions. The default value of this variable matches the default language of the server.
`ServerDomain`	Set to the domain name of the server to which the Client Installation Wizard is connected.
`BootFile`	Set when a tool is about to be opened.
`NetBiosName`	The generated NetBIOS name of the new computer.
`Siffile`	The path of the answer file (.sif) for the operating system image that the user selects, in the form of X:\RemoteInstall\Setup\English\Images\Win2000.pro\i386\Templates\Ristndrd.sif.
`Options`	This variable is filled with the results of an ENUM action performed by the RIS server. It contains OSCML and is typically placed between a `<SELECT>` tag and a `</SELECT>` tag. (See Tools.osc for an example.)
`CheckDomain`	Used internally. Set to 1 or 0 to indicate verification that the user domain has been processed.

Table 15.3 *Reserved OSC Variables (continued)*

Variable	Description
`MachineDomain`	The domain that the new computer attempts to join during setup. By default, this variable is used to set the JoinDomain value in the answer file.
`SysPrepPath`	Used for RIPrep images to indicate the path to the image source files. Example: Setup\English\Images\Win2000.prep\i386
`InstallPath`	The TFTP relative path to the installation image. Example: Setup\English\Images\win2000.pro. By default, this value is used to set the OriSrc, SetupSourceDevice, LaunchFile, and InstallFilesPath values in the answer file.
`SysPrepDrivers`	The path used to find plug-and-play drivers, determined by the RIS server as the best fit for a RIPrep image. If the RIS server cannot make a determination, it is set to blank.
`MAC`	Sent by the Client Installation Wizard to indicate the media access control (MAC) address of the client. This is sent right after the user logs on and before the next screen is viewed.
`GUID`	Sent by the Client Installation Wizard to indicate the GUID address of the client. This is sent right after the user logs on and before the next screen is viewed.
`MachineType`	Sent by the Client Installation Wizard to indicate the type of hardware on which OSChooser is running. This is sent right after the user logs on and before the next screen is viewed. By default, this variable is used to set the OriSrc, LaunchFile, and InstallFilesPath values in the answer file.
`UserName, Password, UserDomain`	The values entered by the user in Login.osc. These values are used by the RIS server when performing functions specific to the logged-on user, such as determining Group Policy settings and available operating system images. Password is not available to OSC or SIFs.
`UserFullName`	Name generated by the BINL service that is the user's first name followed by the user's last name. By default, this variable is used to set the FullName value in the answer file.
`UserFirstName`	The first name of the user who has entered their credentials.
`UserLastName`	The last name of the user who has entered their credentials.
`TimeZone`	Set by the server to the server's time zone setting. By default, this variable is used to set the Timezone value in the answer file.
`OrgName`	Defaults to the organization name set on the RIS server. By default, this variable is used to set the OrgName value in the answer file.

15.6 Common OSC error files

The common error OSC files are all described in Table 15.4.

Table 15.4 *Common OSC Error Files*

Filename	Description
00004e22.osc	The specified computer name exists in Active Directory.
00004e23.osc	The specified computer name contains invalid characters.
00004e24.osc	The specified Directory Service Container cannot be found.
00004e25.osc	The specified Directory Service Container cannot be found. A unique computer name could not be generated for the computer installation.
00004e26.osc	A temporary unattended setup answer file could not be created.
00004e28.osc	The specified username, password, or domain name could not be validated.
00004e29.osc	An account is missing batch logon rights. The logon was validated but a specified and necessary right has not been granted.
00004e2a.osc	Timeout error: The RIS Server dropped the connection because of a lack of activity.
00004e2f.osc	The RIS Server received invalid information from the PXE Client.
00004e30.osc	An invalid or corrupted computer account object was detected.
00004e43.osc	Unable to contact Directory Services.
00004e45.osc	A requested action cannot be performed because of missing or invalid information. One of the Client Installation Wizard screens may be missing a key variable.
00004e47.osc	The RIS Server cannot convert information. The folder/object may not exist in the Active Directory.
00004e48.osc	The Globally Unique Identifier (GUID) provided by the client computer is not valid.
00004e4b.osc	The DNS path cannot be converted to a Fully Qualified Domain Name.
00004e4c.osc	The computer account object could not be updated in the Active Directory.
00004e4e.osc	The PXE client computer state could not be initialized.
00004e4f.osc	The currently logged-in user does not have the appropriate rights to create or modify a computer account in Active Directory.
00004e50.osc	The RIS Server cannot create temporary client files.
00004e51.osc	Setup cannot restart because the answer file is missing.

Table 15.4 *Common OSC Error Files (continued)*

Filename	Description
00004e52.osc	Setup cannot restart because the answer file is either missing or corrupted.
00004e53.osc	The message from an RIS Server was too long and could not be displayed in the Client Installation Wizard screen.
Choice.osc	Presents the user with the available types of installation options: Automatic, Custom, Restart Setup, Tools.
Choichlp.osc	Help screen describing the options for choice.osc.
Custhelp.osc	Help screen for custom installation option.
Custom.osc	Presents the user with fields to customize the installation: set the computer name and DS Path.
Dupauto.osc	Screen that is displayed when duplicate GUIDs exist in the Active Directory.
Dupcust.osc	Screen that is displayed when duplicate GUIDs are detected. This screen allows setup to continue.
Install.osc	Computer settings that will be applied during the installation: computer account, GUID, servicing RIS Server.
Login.osc	Initial logon screen.
Loginhlp.osc	Help screen for login.osc.
Multilng.osc	Lists available multilanguage installation flats/images.
Nochoice.osc	The RIS Server is not able to present any installation selection options.
Nooses.osc	The RIS Server is not able to display any operating system choices.
Oschoice.osc	This screen presents available operating systems to install.
Rstrterr.osc	The option to restart setup has failed on the client.
Tools.osc	Allows the user to choose which tools option to launch.
Toolshlp.osc	Help screen for tools.osc.
Warning.osc	Warning screen indicating that the hard drive will be formatted as part of the installation.
Welcome.osc	Welcome to the Client Installation Wizard screen.

15.7 Summary

By changing the standard OSC files, the functionality and user interface can be taken to a user-friendly level. There must be a connection between the variables used in the OSC files and the SIF. Last in this chapter, overviews of standard and error OSC files and a list of reserved variables and tags supported by the OSCLM standard were presented.

A

Components

The `[Components]` section contains entries for installing the components of Windows XP or Windows Server 2003 family.

Entry	Description
`AccessOpt`	Specifies whether to install the Accessibility wizard.
`appsrv_console`	Specifies whether to install the Application Server Console.
`aspnet`	Specifies whether to install the ASP.NET Web development platform.
`BitsServerExtensionsISAPI`	Specifies whether to install Internet Server Application Programming Interface (ISAPI) for Background Intelligent Transfer Service (BITS) server extensions on client computers.
`BitsServerExtensionsManager`	Specifies whether to install the Microsoft Management Console (MMC) snap-in, administrative Application Programming Interfaces (APIs), and Active Directory® Service Interfaces (ADSI) extensions for Background Intelligent Transfer Service (BITS) server extensions.
`Calc`	Specifies whether to install the Calculator feature.
`certsrv`	Specifies whether to install the Certificate Services components.
`certsrv_client`	Specifies whether to install the Web client components of Certificate Services.
`certsrv_server`	Specifies whether to install the server components of the Certificate Services feature for the Windows Server 2003 family only.

Entry	Description
charmap	Specifies whether to install the Character Map feature that inserts symbols and characters into documents.
chat	Specifies whether to install the Chat feature.
clipbook	Specifies whether to install the clipboard viewer.
cluster	Specifies whether to install the Cluster service.
complusnetwork	Specifies whether to enable network COM+ access.
deskpaper	Specifies whether to install a desktop background on the computer desktop.
dialer	Specifies whether to install the Phone Dialer feature.
dtcnetwork	Specifies whether to enable Microsoft Distributed Transaction Coordinator (DTC) network access.
fax	Specifies whether to install the Fax feature.
fp_extensions	Specifies whether to install Microsoft FrontPage® server extensions.
fp_vdir_deploy	Specifies whether to install Visual InterDev® RAD Remote Deployment Support.
freecell	Specifies whether to install the Freecell game.
hearts	Specifies whether to install the Hearts game.
hypertrm	Specifies whether to install the HyperTerminal feature.
IEAccess	Specifies whether to install visible entry points to Internet Explorer.
IEHardenAdmin	Applies the Enhanced Security Configuration to members of the Administrators and Power Users groups.
IEHardenUser	Applies the Enhanced Security Configuration to members of the Restricted Users and Guests groups.
iis_asp	Specifies whether to install Active Server Pages for Internet Information Services (IIS).

Entry	Description
iis_common	Specifies whether to install the common set of files required by IIS.
iis_ftp	Specifies whether to install the File Transfer Protocol (FTP) service.
iis_inetmgr	Specifies whether to install the Microsoft Management Console (MMC)-based administration tools for IIS.
iis_internetdataconnector	Specifies whether to install the Internet Data Connector.
iis_nntp	Specifies whether to install the Network News Transfer Protocol (NNTP) service for the Windows Server 2003 family.
iis_serversideincludes	Specifies whether to install Server-Side Includes.
iis_smtp	Specifies whether to install the Simple Mail Transfer Protocol (SMTP) service for the Windows Server 2003 family.
iis_webdav	Specifies whether to install WebDAV Publishing.
iis_www	Specifies whether to install the World Wide Web (WWW) service.
indexsrv_system	Specifies whether to install the Indexing Service files.
inetprint	Specifies whether to install Internet Printing.
licenseserver	Specifies whether to turn Terminal Services licensing on.
media_clips	Specifies whether to install sample sound clips on the computer.
media_utopia	Specifies whether to install the Utopia Sound Scheme on the computer.
minesweeper	Specifies whether to install the Minesweeper game on the computer.
mousepoint	Specifies whether to install all the available mouse pointers distributed with Windows XP or Windows Server 2003 family.
msmq_ADIntegrated	Specifies whether to integrate Message Queuing (also known as MSMQ) with Active Directory if the computer belongs to a domain.

Entry	Description
msmq_Core	Specifies whether to set up the Message Queuing components and provide functionality for any dependent clients.
msmq_HTTPSupport	Specifies whether to enable the sending and receiving of messages using the HTTP protocol.
msmq_LocalStorage	Specifies whether to store messages locally, so the computer can send and receive messages even when not connected to a network.
msmq_MQDSService	Specifies whether to provide access to Active Directory and site recognition for downstream clients.
msmq_RoutingSupport	Specifies whether to provide efficient routing.
msmq_TriggersService	Specifies whether to associate the arrival of incoming messages at a queue with functionality in a Component Object Model (COM) component or a stand-alone executable program.
msnexplr	Specifies whether to install MSN Explorer.
mswordpad	Specifies whether to install the WordPad feature on the computer.
netcis	Specifies whether to install Microsoft Component Object Model (COM) Internet Services.
netoc	Specifies whether to install additional optional networking components.
objectpkg	Specifies whether to install the Object Packager feature (packager.exe) on the computer.
OEAccess	Specifies whether to install visible entry points to Outlook Express.
paint	Specifies whether to install the Microsoft Paint feature on the computer.
pinball	Specifies whether to install the Pinball game on the computer.
Pop3Admin	Specifies whether to install the optional Web UI for the Remote Administration Tools on the computer.
Pop3Service	Specifies whether to install the main POP3 service on the computer.

Entry	Description
Pop3Srv	Specifies whether to install the root POP3 component on the computer.
rec	Specifies whether to install the Sound Recorder feature on the computer.
reminst	Specifies whether to install Remote Installation Services, which enables you to install an operating system remotely onto a computer with either a new PXE-based remote boot read-only memory (ROM) or a network card supported by the remote installation boot floppy disk.
rootautoupdate	Specifies whether to turn on the Optional Components Manager (OCM) Update Root Certificates.
rstorage	Specifies whether to install the Remote Storage feature that enables the use of tape libraries as extensions of NTFS file system volumes.
sakit_web	Specifies whether to install the Remote Administration Tools (formerly known as the Server Administration Kit).
solitaire	Specifies whether to install the Solitaire game on the computer.
spider	Specifies whether to install the Spider Solitaire game on the computer.
templates	Specifies whether to install Document Templates on the computer.
TerminalServer	Specifies whether to install Terminal Server (Terminal Services for multiple users) on the computer.
TSWebClient	Specifies whether to install the ActiveX® control and sample pages for hosting Terminal Services client connections over the Web.
vol	Specifies whether to install the Volume Control feature on the computer.
WbemCrrl	Specifies whether to install the Windows Management Instrumentation (WMI) event correlation component.

Entry	Description
WbemFwrd	Specifies whether to install the Windows Management Instrumentation (WMI) event forwarding components.
WbemMSI	Specifies whether to install the Windows Management Instrumentation (WMI) Windows installer provider.
WMAccess	Specifies whether to install visible entry points to Windows Messenger.
WMPOCM	Specifies whether to install visible entry points to Windows Media Player.
wms	Specifies whether to install the core Windows Media Server components.
wms_admin_asp	Specifies whether to install the Windows Media Services Web-based administrative components.
wms_admin_mmc	Specifies whether to install the Windows Media Services Microsoft Management Console (MMC)-based administrative components.
wms_isapi	Specifies whether to install the Windows Media Services Multicast and Advertisement Logging Agent components.
wms_server	Specifies whether to install the Windows Media Services server components.
zonegames	Specifies whether to install the Microsoft Gaming Zone Internet games on the computer.

Sample

This sample demonstrates one use of the `[Components]` section of Unattend.txt.

```
[Components]
AccessOpt = On
Appsrv_console = Off
Aspnet = Off
BitsServerExtensionsISAPI = On
BitsServerExtensionsManager = On
Calc = On
Certsrv = On
Certsrv_client = On
Certsrv_server = On
```

```
Charmap = On
Chat = Off
Clipbook = On
Cluster = On
Complusnetwork = Off
Deskpaper = On
Dialer = On
Dtcnetwork = Off
Fax = On
Fp_extensions = On
Fp_vdir_deploy = On
Freecell = On
Hearts = On
Hypertrm = On
IEAccess = On
IEHardenAdmin = On
IEHardenUser = On
Iis_asp = Off
Iis_common = On
Iis_ftp = On
Iis_inetmgr = On
Iis_internetdataconnector = Off
Iis_nntp = On
Iis_serversideincludes = Off
Iis_smtp = On
Iis_webdav = Off
Iis_www = On
Indexsrv_system = On
Inetprint = On
Licenseserver = On
Media_clips = On
Media_utopia = On
Minesweeper = On
Mousepoint = On
Msmq_ADIntegrated = On
Msmq_Core = On
Msmq_HTTPSupport = On
Msmq_LocalStorage = On
Msmq_MQDSService = On
Msmq_RoutingSupport = On
Msmq_TriggersService = On
Msnexplr = On
Mswordpad = On
Netcis = On
Netoc = On
Objectpkg = On
OEAccess = On
Paint = On
Pinball = On
```

```
Pop3Admin = On
Pop3Service = On
Pop3Srv = On
Rec = On
Reminst = On
Rootautoupdate = On
Rstorage = On
Sakit_web = Off
Solitaire = On
Spider = On
Templates = On
TerminalServer = On
TSWebClient = On
Vol = On
WbemCrrl = On
WbemFwrd = On
WbemMSI = On
WMAccess = On
WMPOCM = On
Wms = On
Wms_admin_asp = On
Wms_admin_mmc = On
Wms_isapi = On
Wms_server = On
Zonegames = On
```

AccessOpt

Specifies whether to install the Accessibility wizard.

Syntax `AccessOpt = On | Off`

Values

`On`

Installs the Accessibility wizard.

`Off`

Does not install the Accessibility wizard.

Default Value `On`

Example AccessOpt = On

Registry Subkey
```
HKEY_LOCAL_MACHINE\Software\Microsoft\Windows\
    CurrentVersion\Setup\OC Manager\
    Subcomponents\accessopt
```

appsrv_console

Specifies whether to install the Application Server Console.

Syntax	**appsrv_console = On | Off**
Values	**On** Installs the Application Server Console. **Off** Does not install the Application Server Console.
Default Value	**Off**
Example	appsrv_console = On
Registry Subkey	`HKEY_LOCAL_MACHINE\Software\Microsoft\Windows\CurrentVersion\Setup\OC Manager\Subcomponents\appsrv_console`

aspnet

Specifies whether to install the ASP.NET Web development platform.

Syntax	**aspnet = On | Off**
Values	**On** Installs the ASP.NET Web development platform. **Off** Does not install the ASP.NET Web development platform.
Default Value	**Off**
Example	`aspnet = Off`
Registry Subkey	`HKEY_LOCAL_MACHINE\Software\Microsoft\Windows\CurrentVersion\Setup\OC Manager\Subcomponents\aspnet`

AutoUpdate

See the `AutomaticUpdates` entry in the `[Data]` section of Unattend.txt.

BitsServerExtensionsISAPI

Specifies whether to install Internet Server Application Programming Interface (ISAPI) for Background Intelligent Transfer Service (BITS) server extensions on client computers.

BITS provides two very useful features to the client:

- Automatically adjusts the amount of network bandwidth used to make sure all other foreground applications use up all the bandwidth they need, then BITS uses up the rest.
- Automatically continues a file transfer if the download (or upload) was interrupted by a computer restart or an unplugged network cable.

Syntax `BitsServerExtensionsISAPI = On | Off`

Values

`On`

Installs ISAPI for BITS server extensions on client computers.

`Off`

Does not install ISAPI for BITS server extensions on client computers.

Default Value `Off`

Dependencies Requires `BITSServerExtensionsManager` and `iis_www`.

Example `BitsServerExtensionsISAPI = On`

Registry Subkey

```
HKEY_LOCAL_MACHINE\Software\Microsoft\Windows\
    CurrentVersion\Setup\OC Manager\
    Subcomponents\bitsserverextensionsisapi
```

BitsServerExtensionsManager

Specifies whether to install the Microsoft Management Console (MMC) snap-in, administrative Application Programming Interfaces (APIs), and Active Directory Service Interfaces (ADSI) extensions for Background Intelligent Transfer Service (BITS) server extensions.

Syntax `BitsServerExtensionsManager = On | Off`

Values

`On`

Installs the MMC snap-in, administrative APIs, and ADSI extensions for BITS server extensions.

`Off`

Does not install the MMC snap-in, administrative APIs, and ADSI extensions for BITS server extensions.

Default Value `Off`

Dependencies Requires `iis_inetmgr`.

Example `BitsServerExtensionsManager = On`

Registry Subkey
```
HKEY_LOCAL_MACHINE\Software\Microsoft\Windows\
    CurrentVersion\Setup\OC Manager\
    Subcomponents\bitsserverextensionsmanager
```

Calc

Specifies whether to install the Calculator feature.

Syntax **`Calc = On | Off`**

Values

`On`

Installs the Calculator feature.

`Off`

Does not install the Calculator feature.

Default Value **`On`**

Example `Calc = On`

Registry Subkey
```
HKEY_LOCAL_MACHINE\Software\Microsoft\Windows\
    CurrentVersion\Setup\OC Manager\
    Subcomponents\calc
```

certsrv

Specifies whether to install the Certificate Services components.

Syntax **`certsrv = On | Off`**

Values

`On`

Installs the Certificate Services components.

`Off`

Does not install the Certificate Services components.

Default Value **`Off`**

Example `Certsrv = On`

Registry Subkey
```
HKEY_LOCAL_MACHINE\Software\Microsoft\Windows\
    CurrentVersion\Setup\OC Manager\
    Subcomponents\certsrv
```

certsrv_client

Specifies whether to install the Web client components of Certificate Services.

Syntax	**certsrv_client = On | Off**
Values	**On** Installs the Web client components of Certificate Services. **Off** Does not install the Web client components of Certificate Services.
Default Value	**Off**
Example	`Certsrv_client = On`
Registry Subkey	`HKEY_LOCAL_MACHINE\Software\Microsoft\Windows\ CurrentVersion\Setup\OC Manager\ Subcomponents\certsrv_client`
Comments	These components enable you to publish Web pages on your server for submitting and requesting certificates from a Certification Authority (CA). You must specify options for the Web client services in the `[certsrv_client]` section in Unattend.txt.

certsrv_server

Specifies whether to install the server components of the Certificate Services feature for the Windows Server 2003 family only.

Syntax	**certsrv_server = On | Off**
Values	**On** Installs the server components of the Certificate Services feature for the Windows Server 2003 family only. **Off** Does not install the server components of the Certificate Services feature for the Windows Server 2003 family only.
Default Value	**Off**
Example	`certsrv_server = On`
Registry Subkey	`HKEY_LOCAL_MACHINE\Software\Microsoft\Windows\ CurrentVersion\Setup\OC Manager\ Subcomponents\certsrv_server`

Comments These components enable you to create a Certification Authority (CA) on your server for issuing digital certificates. When `certsrv_server` is set to `On`, the `certsrv_client` entry must also be set to `On`. You must specify options for the server services in the `[Certsrv_Server]` section in Unattend.txt.

charmap

Specifies whether to install the Character Map feature that inserts symbols and characters into documents.

Syntax **`charmap = On | Off`**

Values

`On`

Installs the Character Map feature.

`Off`

Does not install the Character Map feature.

Default Value **`On`**

Example `Charmap = On`

Registry Subkey

```
HKEY_LOCAL_MACHINE\Software\Microsoft\Windows\
    CurrentVersion\Setup\OC Manager\
    Subcomponents\charmap
```

chat

Specifies whether to install the Chat feature.

Syntax **`chat = On | Off`**

Values

`On`

Installs the Chat feature.

`Off`

Does not install the Chat feature.

Default Value **`Off`**

Example `Chat = On`

Registry Subkey

```
HKEY_LOCAL_MACHINE\Software\Microsoft\Windows\
    CurrentVersion\Setup\OC Manager\
    Subcomponents\chat
```

clipbook

Specifies whether to install the clipboard viewer.

Syntax `clipbook = On | Off`

Values

`On`

Installs the clipboard viewer.

`Off`

Does not install the clipboard viewer.

Default Value `On`

Example `Clipbook = On`

Registry Subkey

```
HKEY_LOCAL_MACHINE\Software\Microsoft\Windows\
    CurrentVersion\Setup\OC Manager\
    Subcomponents\clipbook
```

cluster

Specifies whether to install the Cluster service.

Syntax `cluster = On | Off`

Values

`On`

Installs the Cluster service.

`Off`

Does not install the Cluster service.

Default Value `Off` (for the Windows 2000 Server family)

Example `cluster = On`

Registry Subkey

```
HKEY_LOCAL_MACHINE\Software\Microsoft\Windows\
    CurrentVersion\Setup\OC Manager\
    Subcomponents\cluster
```

Comments This is supported only by the Windows 2000 Server family. For the Windows Server 2003 family, the Cluster service is automatically installed.

complusnetwork

Specifies whether to enable network COM+ access.

Syntax `complusnetwork = On | Off`

Values

`On`

Enable network COM+ access.

`Off`

Does not enable network COM+ access.

Default Value `Off`

Example `complusnetwork = On`

Registry Subkey

```
HKEY_LOCAL_MACHINE\Software\Microsoft\Windows\
    CurrentVersion\Setup\OC Manager\
    Subcomponents\complusnetwork
```

deskpaper

Specifies whether to install a desktop background on the computer desktop.

Syntax `deskpaper = On | Off`

Values

`On`

Installs a desktop background on the computer desktop.

`Off`

Does not install a desktop background on the computer desktop.

Default Value `On`

Example `deskpaper = On`

Registry Subkey

```
HKEY_LOCAL_MACHINE\Software\Microsoft\Windows\
    CurrentVersion\Setup\OC Manager\
    Subcomponents\deskpaper
```

Comments If `deskpaper = Off`, only the standard Windows XP or Windows Server 2003 family background bitmaps are not installed. Background files for the Active Desktop® interface are not affected and are still installed.

dialer

Specifies whether to install the Phone Dialer feature.

Syntax	**`dialer = On	Off`**
Values	**`On`** Installs the Phone Dialer feature only if modem is detected. **`Off`** Does not install the Phone Dialer feature.
Default Value	**`On`**
Example	`dialer = On`
Registry Subkey	`HKEY_LOCAL_MACHINE\Software\Microsoft\Windows\CurrentVersion\Setup\OC Manager\Subcomponents\dialer`
Comments	If `dialer = on` and a modem is not present, the Phone Dialer feature is not installed.

dtcnetwork

Specifies whether to enable Microsoft Distributed Transaction Coordinator (DTC) network access.

Syntax	**`dtcnetwork = On	Off`**
Values	**`On`** Enables Microsoft Distributed Transaction Coordinator (DTC) network access. **`Off`** Does not enable Microsoft Distributed Transaction Coordinator (DTC) network access.
Default Value	**`Off`**
Example	`dtcnetwork = On`
Registry Subkey	`HKEY_LOCAL_MACHINE\Software\Microsoft\Windows\CurrentVersion\Setup\OC Manager\Subcomponents\dtcnetwork`

fax

Specifies whether to install the Fax feature.

Syntax `fax = On | Off`

Values

`On`

Installs the Fax feature.

`Off`

Does not install the Fax feature.

Default Value `Off`

Dependencies Requires that you also include the parameters for the `[Fax]` section in Unattend.txt in this installation.

Example `fax = On`

Registry Subkey

```
HKEY_LOCAL_MACHINE\Software\Microsoft\Windows\
    CurrentVersion\Setup\OC Manager\
    Subcomponents\fax
```

fp_extensions

Specifies whether to install Microsoft FrontPage server extensions.

Syntax `fp_extensions = On | Off`

Values

`On`

Installs Microsoft FrontPage server extensions.

`Off`

Does not install Microsoft FrontPage server extensions.

Default Value `Off`

Dependencies Requires `iis_common`, `iis_inetmgr`, and `iis_www`.

Example `fp_extensions = On`

Registry Subkey

```
HKEY_LOCAL_MACHINE\Software\Microsoft\Windows\
    CurrentVersion\Setup\OC Manager\
    Subcomponents\fp_extensions
```

fp_vdir_deploy

Specifies whether to install Visual InterDev RAD Remote Deployment Support.

Syntax	**`fp_vdir_deploy = On	Off`**
Values	**`On`** Installs Visual InterDev RAD Remote Deployment Support. **`Off`** Does not install Visual InterDev RAD Remote Deployment Support.
Default Value	**`Off`**
Dependencies	Requires `fp_extensions`.
Example	`Fp_vdir_deploy = On`

freecell

Specifies whether to install the Freecell game.

Syntax	**`freecell = On	Off`**
Values	**`On`** Installs the Freecell game. **`Off`** Does not install the Freecell game.
Default Value	**`On`** (not available in the Windows Server 2003 family)
Example	`freecell = On`
Registry Subkey	`HKEY_LOCAL_MACHINE\Software\Microsoft\Windows\ CurrentVersion\Setup\OC Manager\ Subcomponents\freecell`

hearts

Specifies whether to install the Hearts game.

Syntax	**`hearts = On	Off`**
Values	**`On`** Installs the Hearts game. **`Off`** Does not install the Hearts game.
Default Value	**`On`** (not available in the Windows Server 2003 family)

Example `hearts = On`

Registry Subkey
```
HKEY_LOCAL_MACHINE\Software\Microsoft\Windows\
    CurrentVersion\Setup\OC Manager\
    Subcomponents\hearts
```

hypertrm

Specifies whether to install the HyperTerminal feature.

Syntax **`hypertrm = On | Off`**

Values

`On`

Installs the HyperTerminal feature.

`Off`

Does not install the HyperTerminal feature.

Default Value **`On`** (Windows XP)
`Off` (Windows Server 2003 family)

Example `hypertrm = On`

Registry Subkey
```
HKEY_LOCAL_MACHINE\Software\Microsoft\Windows\
    CurrentVersion\Setup\OC Manager\
    Subcomponents\hypertrm
```

IEAccess

Specifies whether to install visible entry points to Internet Explorer.

Syntax **`IEAccess = On | Off`**

Values

`On`

Installs visible entry points to Internet Explorer.

`Off`

Does not install visible entry points to Internet Explorer.

Default Value **`On`**

Example `IEAccess = On`

Comments

Not supported by the Windows Server 2003 family. A shortcut link on the Start menu is an example of a visible entry point. This entry does not remove any Windows code, including any Internet Explorer code, other than these visible entry points. Various Windows components and third-party applications rely upon Internet Explorer code.

`IEAccess` has no effect on Internet Explorer branding or the configuration of Internet settings.

Comments *(cont'd.)*

Note: You must set `IEAccess` to `Off` and then install a different Internet Explorer installation package on the computer, so the user will see the Internet Explorer visible entry points. Other forms of subsequent Internet Explorer configuration (such as autoconfiguration of Internet setttings) do not affect whether the Internet Explorer visible entry points are visible on the Windows desktop.

IEHardenAdmin

Applies the Enhanced Security Configuration to members of the Administrators and Power Users groups.

Syntax `IEHardenAdmin = On | Off`

Values

`On`

Applies the Enhanced Security Configuration to members of the Administrators and Power Users groups. Changes the Internet Explorer home page to IEHardenAdmin.htm.

`Off`

Does not apply the Enhanced Security Configuration to members of the Administrators and Power Users groups.

Default Value `On`

Example `IEHardenAdmin = On`

IEHardenUser

Applies the Enhanced Security Configuration to members of the Restricted Users and Guests groups.

Syntax `IEHardenUser = On | Off`

Values

`On`

Applies the Enhanced Security Configuration to members of the Restricted Users and Guests groups. Changes the Internet Explorer home page to IEHardenAdmin.htm.

`Off`

Does not apply the Enhanced Security Configuration to members of the Restricted Users and Guests groups.

Default Value `On`

Example `IEHardenUser = On`

iis_asp

Specifies whether to install Active Server Pages for IIS.

Syntax `iis_asp = On | Off`

Values

On

Installs Active Server Pages.

Off

Does not install Active Server Pages.

Default Value `Off`

Example `iis_asp = On`

Registry Subkey

```
HKEY_LOCAL_MACHINE\Software\Microsoft\Windows\
    CurrentVersion\Setup\OC Manager\
    Subcomponents\iis_asp
```

iis_common

Specifies whether to install the common set of files required by IIS.

Syntax `iis_common = On | Off`

Values

On

Installs the common set of files required by IIS.

Off

Does not install the common set of files required by IIS.

Default Value

`On` (Windows Server 2003, Web Edition, and Microsoft Small Business Server)

`Off` (Windows XP and the Windows Server 2003 family)

Dependencies

The following components require `iis_common`:

- All of the IIS components (`iis_ftp`, `iis_inetmgr`, `iis_nntp`, `iis_smtp`, and `iis_www`.)
- FrontPage Extensions (`fp_extensions`)
- Indexing Service (`indexsrv_system`)
- MSMQ (`msmq_Core`)
- Windows Media Server Web-based administration tools (`wms_admin_asp`)
- Microsoft® Exchange Server
- Microsoft® BackOffice® Server

Any component that requires the `iis_common` entry will install it even if `iis_common = Off`.

Example `iis_common = On`

Registry Subkey
```
HKEY_LOCAL_MACHINE\Software\Microsoft\Windows\
    CurrentVersion\Setup\OC Manager\
    Subcomponents\iis_common
```

Comments **Important:** Windows XP Professional and Windows XP 64-Bit Edition contain Internet Information Services 5.1. All members of the Windows Server 2003 family contain Internet Information Services 6.0.

Windows XP Home Edition does not contain any Web server software components.

iis_ftp

Specifies whether to install the FTP service.

Syntax **`iis_ftp = On | Off`**

Values

`On`

Installs the FTP service.

`Off`

Does not install the FTP service.

Default Value **`Off`**

Dependencies Requires `iis_common` and `iis_inetmgr`.

Example `iis_ftp = On`

Registry Subkey
```
HKEY_LOCAL_MACHINE\Software\Microsoft\Windows\
    CurrentVersion\Setup\OC Manager\
    Subcomponents\iis_ftp
```

Comments Use `PathFTPRoot` in the `[InternetServer]` section of Unattend.txt to change the default installation path for the FTP root.

iis_inetmgr

Specifies whether to install the Microsoft Management Console (MMC)-based administration tools for IIS.

Syntax **`iis_inetmgr = On | Off`**

Values

`On`

`Installs the MMC-based administration tools for IIS.`

`Off`

Does not install the MMC-based administration tools for IIS.

Default Value	**On** (Windows Server 2003, Web Edition, and Microsoft Small Business Server) **Off** (Windows XP and the Windows Server 2003 family)
Dependencies	Requires `iis_common`.
Example	`iis_inetmgr = On`
Registry Subkey	`HKEY_LOCAL_MACHINE\Software\Microsoft\Windows\CurrentVersion\Setup\OC Manager\Subcomponents\iis_inetmgr`

iis_internetdataconnector

Specifies whether to install the Internet Data Connector.

Syntax	**`iis_internetdataconnector = On	Off`**
Values	**On** Installs the Internet Data Connector. **Off** Does not install the Internet Data Connector.
Default Value	**Off**
Example	`iis_internetdataconnector = On`
Registry Subkey	`HKEY_LOCAL_MACHINE\Software\Microsoft\Windows\CurrentVersion\Setup\OC Manager\Subcomponents\iis_internetdataconnector`

iis_nntp

Specifies whether to install the Network News Transfer Protocol (NNTP) service for the Windows Server 2003 family.

Syntax	**`iis_nntp = On	Off`**
Values	**On** Installs the NNTP service for the Windows Server 2003 family. **Off** Does not install the NNTP service for the Windows Server 2003 family.
Default Value	**Off**
Dependencies	Requires `iis_common`, `iis_inetmgr`, and `iis_www`.
Example	`iis_nntp = On`

Registry Subkey `HKEY_LOCAL_MACHINE\Software\Microsoft\Windows\CurrentVersion\Setup\OC Manager\Subcomponents\iis_nntp`

iis_serversideincludes

Specifies whether to install the Server-Side Includes.

Syntax **`iis_serversideincludes = On | Off`**

Values

`On`

Installs the Server-Side Includes.

`Off`

Does not install the Server-Side Includes.

Default Value **`Off`**

Example `iis_serversideincludes = On`

Registry Subkey `HKEY_LOCAL_MACHINE\Software\Microsoft\Windows\CurrentVersion\Setup\OC Manager\Subcomponents\iis_serversideincludes`

iis_smtp

Specifies whether to install the Simple Mail Transfer Protocol (SMTP) service for the Windows Server 2003 family.

Syntax **`iis_smtp = On | Off`**

Values

`On`

Installs the SMTP service for the Windows Server 2003 family.

`Off`

Does not install the SMTP service for the Windows Server 2003 family.

Default Value **`On`** (Windows Server 2003, Web Edition, and Microsoft Small Business Server)

`Off` (Windows XP and the Windows Server 2003 family)

Dependencies Requires `iis_common`, `iis_inetmgr`, and `iis_www`.

Example `iis_smtp = On`

Registry Subkey `HKEY_LOCAL_MACHINE\Software\Microsoft\Windows\CurrentVersion\Setup\OC Manager\Subcomponents\iis_smtp`

iis_webdav

Specifies whether to install WebDAV Publishing.

Syntax	**`iis_webdav = On | Off`**
Values	**`On`** Installs WebDAV Publishing. **`Off`** Does not install WebDAV Publishing.
Default Value	**`Off`**
Example	`iis_webdav = On`

Registry Subkey	`HKEY_LOCAL_MACHINE\Software\Microsoft\Windows\`
	`CurrentVersion\Setup\OC Manager\`
	`Subcomponents\iis_webdav`

iis_www

Specifies whether to install the World Wide Web (WWW) service.

Syntax	**`iis_www = On | Off`**
Values	**`On`** Installs the WWW service. **`Off`** Does not install the WWW service.
Default Value	**`On`** (Windows Server 2003, Web Edition, and Microsoft Small Business Server) **`Off`** (Windows XP and the Windows Server 2003 family)
Dependencies	Requires `iis_common` and `iis_inetmgr`. Use `PathWWWRoot` in the `[InternetServer]` section in Unattend.txt to change the default installation path for the WWW root.
Example	`Iis_www = On`

Registry Subkey	`HKEY_LOCAL_MACHINE\Software\Microsoft\Windows\`
	`CurrentVersion\Setup\OC Manager\`
	`Subcomponents\iis_www`

indexsrv_system

Specifies whether to install the Indexing Service files.

Syntax **indexsrv_system** = **On** | **Off**

Values **On**

Installs the Indexing Service files.

Off

Does not install the Indexing Service files.

Default Value **On** (the Windows Server 2003 family);

Off (Windows XP Professional)

Dependencies Requires iis_common, iis_inetmgr, and iis_www.

Example `indexsrv_system = On`

Registry Subkey
```
HKEY_LOCAL_MACHINE\Software\Microsoft\Windows\
    CurrentVersion\Setup\OC Manager\
    Subcomponents\indexsrv_system
```

inetprint

Specifies whether to install Internet Printing.

Syntax **inetprint** = **On** | **Off**

Values **On**

Installs Internet Printing.

Off

Does not install Internet Printing.

Default Value **Off**

Dependencies Requires iis_common, iis_inetmgr, and iis_www.

Example `inetprint = On`

Registry Subkey
```
HKEY_LOCAL_MACHINE\Software\Microsoft\Windows\
    CurrentVersion\Setup\OC Manager\
    Subcomponents\inetprint
```

licenseserver

Specifies whether to turn Terminal Services licensing on.

Syntax `licenseserver = On | Off`

Values

`On`

Turns Terminal Services licensing on.

`Off`

Does not turn Terminal Services licensing on.

Example `licenseserver = On`

Registry Subkey

```
HKEY_LOCAL_MACHINE\Software\Microsoft\Windows\
    CurrentVersion\Setup\OC Manager\
    Subcomponents\LicenseServer
```

Comments You can run Terminal Services licensing on a domain controller or on a member server. For more information, see "Terminal Services Licensing" in Windows Server 2003 Help.

media_clips

Specifies whether to install sample sound clips on the computer.

Syntax `media_clips = On | Off`

Values

`On`

Installs sample sound clips on the computer.

`Off`

Does not install sample sound clips on the computer.

Default Value

`On` (Windows XP)

`Off` (Windows Server 2003 family)

Example `media_clips = On`

Registry Subkey

```
HKEY_LOCAL_MACHINE\Software\Microsoft\Windows\
    CurrentVersion\Setup\OC Manager\
    Subcomponents\media_clips
```

media_utopia

Specifies whether to install the Utopia Sound Scheme on the computer.

Syntax	**media_utopia = On | Off**
Values	**On** Installs the Utopia Sound Scheme on the computer. **Off** Does not install the Utopia Sound Scheme on the computer.
Default Value	**Off**
Example	`media_utopia = On`
Registry Subkey	`HKEY_LOCAL_MACHINE\Software\Microsoft\Windows\CurrentVersion\Setup\OC Manager\Subcomponents\media_utopia`

minesweeper

Specifies whether to install the Minesweeper game on the computer.

Syntax	**minesweeper = On | Off**
Values	**On** Installs the Minesweeper game on the computer. **Off** Does not install the Minesweeper game on the computer.
Default Value	**On** (not available in the Windows Server 2003 family)
Example	`minesweeper = On`
Registry Subkey	`HKEY_LOCAL_MACHINE\Software\Microsoft\Windows\CurrentVersion\Setup\OC Manager\Subcomponents\minesweeper`

mousepoint

Specifies whether to install all the available mouse pointers distributed with Windows XP or Windows Server 2003 family.

Syntax `mousepoint = On | Off`

Values

`On`

Installs all the available mouse pointers distributed with Windows XP or Windows Server 2003 family.

`Off`

Does not install all the available mouse pointers distributed with Windows XP or the Windows Server 2003 family.

Default Value `On`

Example `mousepoint = On`

Registry Subkey

```
HKEY_LOCAL_MACHINE\Software\Microsoft\Windows\
    CurrentVersion\Setup\OC Manager\
    Subcomponents\mousepoint
```

msmq_ADIntegrated

Specifies whether to integrate Message Queuing (also known as MSMQ) with Active Directory if the computer belongs to a domain.

Syntax `msmq_ADIntegrated = On | Off`

Values

`On`

Integrates MSMQ with Active Directory if the computer belongs to a domain.

`Off`

Does not integrate MSMQ with Active Directory if the computer belongs to a domain.

Default Value `Off`

Dependencies Requires `msmq_LocalStorage`.

Example `msmq_ADIntegrated = On`

Registry Subkey

```
HKEY_LOCAL_MACHINE\Software\Microsoft\Windows\
    CurrentVersion\Setup\OC Manager\
    Subcomponents\msmq_ADIntegrated
```

Comments Recommended for a minimal Message Queuing installation. Only for use in unattended installations of members of the Windows Server 2003 family.

msmq_Core

Specifies whether to set up the Message Queuing components and provide functionality for any dependent clients.

Syntax	**`msmq_Core = On	Off`**
Values	**`On`** Sets up the Message Queuing components. **`Off`** Does not set up the Message Queuing components.
Default Value	**`Off`**
Example	`msmq_Core = On`
Registry Subkey	`HKEY_LOCAL_MACHINE\Software\Microsoft\Windows\ CurrentVersion\Setup\OC Manager\ Subcomponents\msmq_Core`
Comments	Required for a minimal Message Queuing installation. Only for use in unattended installations of members of the Windows Server 2003 family.

msmq_HTTPSupport

Specifies whether to enable the sending and receiving of messages using the HTTP protocol.

Syntax	**`msmq_HTTPSupport = On	Off`**
Values	**`On`** Enables the sending and receiving of messages using the HTTP protocol. **`Off`** Does not enable the sending and receiving of messages using the HTTP protocol.
Default Value	**`Off`**
Dependencies	Requires `msmq_LocalStorage` and `iis_www`.
Example	`msmq_HTTPSupport = On`
Registry Subkey	`HKEY_LOCAL_MACHINE\Software\Microsoft\Windows\ CurrentVersion\Setup\OC Manager\ Subcomponents\msmq_HTTPSupport`
Comments	Only for use in unattended installations of members of the Windows Server 2003 family.

msmq_LocalStorage

Specifies whether to store messages locally, so the computer can send and receive messages even when not connected to a network.

Syntax **`msmq_LocalStorage = On | Off`**

Values

`On`

Stores messages locally.

`Off`

Does not store messages locally.

Default Value **`Off`**

Dependencies Requires `msmq_Core`.

Example `msmq_LocalStorage = On`

Registry Subkey

```
HKEY_LOCAL_MACHINE\Software\Microsoft\Windows\
    CurrentVersion\Setup\OC Manager\
    Subcomponents\msmq_LocalStorage
```

Comments Required for a minimal Message Queuing installation. Only for use in unattended installations of members of the Windows Server 2003 family.

msmq_MQDSService

Specifies whether to provide access to Active Directory and site recognition for downstream clients.

Syntax **`msmq_MQDSService = On | Off`**

Values

`On`

Provides access to Active Directory and site recognition for downstream clients.

`Off`

Does not provide access to Active Directory and site recognition for downstream clients.

Default Value **`Off`**

Dependencies Requires `msmq_ADIntegrated`.

Example `msmq_MQDSService = On`

Registry Subkey

```
HKEY_LOCAL_MACHINE\Software\Microsoft\Windows\
    CurrentVersion\Setup\OC Manager\
    Subcomponents\msmq_MQDSService
```

Comments `msmq_MQDSService` is an advanced Message Queuing component that you can install only on the Windows Server 2003 family.

msmq_RoutingSupport

Specifies whether to provide efficient routing.

Syntax `msmq_RoutingSupport = On | Off`

Values

`On`

Provides efficient routing.

`Off`

Does not provide efficient routing.

Default Value `Off`

Dependencies Requires `msmq_ADIntegrated`.

Example `msmq_RoutingSupport = On`

Registry Subkey

```
HKEY_LOCAL_MACHINE\Software\Microsoft\Windows\
    CurrentVersion\Setup\OC Manager\
    Subcomponents\msmq_RoutingSupport
```

Comments `msmq_RoutingSupport` is an advanced Message Queuing component that you can install only on the Windows Server 2003 family.

msmq_TriggersService

Specifies whether to associate the arrival of incoming messages at a queue with functionality in a Component Object Model (COM) component or a stand-alone executable program.

Syntax `msmq_TriggersService = On | Off`

Values

`On`

Associates the arrival of incoming messages at a queue with functionality in a Component Object Model (COM) component or a stand-alone executable program.

`Off`

Does not associate the arrival of incoming messages at a queue with functionality in a Component Object Model (COM) component or a stand-alone executable program.

Default Value `Off`

Dependencies Requires `msmq_LocalStorage`.

Example `msmq_TriggersService = On`

Registry Subkey

```
HKEY_LOCAL_MACHINE\Software\Microsoft\Windows\
    CurrentVersion\Setup\OC Manager\
    Subcomponents\msmq_TriggersService
```

Comments Only for use in unattended installations of members of the Windows Server 2003 family.

msnexplr

Specifies whether to install MSN Explorer.

Syntax `msnexplr = On | Off`

Values

On

Installs MSN Explorer.

Off

Does not install MSN Explorer.

Default Value **On**

Example `msnexplr = On`

Registry Subkey

```
HKEY_LOCAL_MACHINE\Software\Microsoft\Windows\
    CurrentVersion\Setup\OC Manager\
    Subcomponents\msnexplr
```

Comments Not supported by the Windows Server 2003 family. If MSN Internet Access is available in Windows Welcome, you must install MSN Explorer.

To replace the MSN shortcut with an MSN Internet Access shortcut, use the following entries in winbom.ini:

- `IEAccess` entry in the `[Components]` section
- `MSNExplorer` entry in the `[Shell]` section

Do not set `msnexplr = No` in the `[Components]` section of Winbom.ini or Unattend.txt.

mswordpad

Specifies whether to install the WordPad feature on the computer.

Syntax `mswordpad = On | Off`

Values

On

Installs the WordPad feature on the computer.

Off

Does not install the WordPad feature on the computer.

Default Value **On**

Example `mswordpad = On`

Registry Subkey `HKEY_LOCAL_MACHINE\Software\Microsoft\Windows\CurrentVersion\Setup\OC Manager\Subcomponents\mswordpad`

netcis

Specifies whether to install Microsoft Component Object Model (COM) Internet Services.

Syntax **`netcis = On | Off`**

Values

`On`

Installs Microsoft COM Internet Services.

`Off`

Does not install Microsoft COM Internet Services.

Default Value **`Off`**

Dependencies Requires `iis_common = On`, `iis_inetmgr = On`, and `iis_www = On`.

Example `netcis = On`

Registry Subkey `HKEY_LOCAL_MACHINE\Software\Microsoft\Windows\CurrentVersion\Setup\OC Manager\Subcomponents\netcis`

netoc

Specifies whether to install additional optional networking components.

Syntax **`netoc = On | Off`**

Values

`On`

Installs additional optional networking components.

`Off`

Does not install additional optional networking components.

Default Value **`On`**

Example `netoc = On`

Registry Subkey `HKEY_LOCAL_MACHINE\Software\Microsoft\Windows\CurrentVersion\Setup\OC Manager\Subcomponents\netoc`

Comments To modify the default components installed, use the `[NetOptionalComponents]` section of Unattend.txt or Sysprep.inf. If you set the value of `netoc` to `Off`, the `[NetOptionalComponents]` section is not processed.

objectpkg

Specifies whether to install the Object Packager feature (packager.exe) on the computer.

Syntax	**`objectpkg = On	Off`**
Values	**`On`** Installs the Object Packager feature on the computer. **`Off`** Does not install the Object Packager feature on the computer.
Default Value	**`On`**
Example	`objectpkg = On`

OEAccess

Specifies whether to install visible entry points to Outlook Express.

Syntax	**`OEAccess = On	Off`**
Values	**`On`** Installs visible entry points to Outlook Express. **`Off`** Does not install visible entry points to Outlook Express.
Default Value	**`On`**
Example	`OEAccess = On`
Comments	Not supported in the Windows Server 2003 family. A shortcut link on the Start menu is an example of a visible entry point. This entry does not remove any Windows code, including any Outlook Express code, other than these visible entry points.

paint

Specifies whether to install the Microsoft Paint feature on the computer.

Syntax	**`paint = On	Off`**
Values	**`On`** Installs the Microsoft Paint feature on the computer. **`Off`** Does not install the Microsoft Paint feature on the computer.
Default Value	**`On`**

Example `paint = On`

Registry Subkey
```
HKEY_LOCAL_MACHINE\Software\Microsoft\Windows\
    CurrentVersion\Setup\OC Manager\
    Subcomponents\paint
```

pinball

Specifies whether to install the Pinball game on the computer.

Syntax **`pinball = On | Off`**

Values

`On`

Installs the Pinball game on the computer.

`Off`

Does not install the Pinball game on the computer.

Default Value **`On`** (not available in the Windows Server 2003 family)

Example `pinball = On`

Registry Subkey
```
HKEY_LOCAL_MACHINE\Software\Microsoft\Windows\
    CurrentVersion\Setup\OC Manager\
    Subcomponents\pinball
```

Pop3Admin

Specifies whether to install the optional Web UI for the Remote Administration Tools on the computer.

Syntax **`Pop3Admin = On | Off`**

Values

`On`

Installs the optional Web UI for the Remote Administration Tools on the computer.

`Off`

Does not install the optional Web UI for the Remote Administration Tools on the computer.

Default Value **`Off`**

Dependencies Requires `sakit_web`.

Example `Pop3Admin = On`

Pop3Service

Specifies whether to install the main POP3 service on the computer.

Syntax	**`Pop3Service = On	Off`**
Values	**`On`** Installs the main POP3 service on the computer. **`Off`** Does not install the main POP3 service on the computer.
Default Value	**`On`**
Dependencies	Requires `iis_smtp`.
Example	`Pop3Service = On`

Pop3Srv

Specifies whether to install the root POP3 component on the computer.

Syntax	**`Pop3Srv = On	Off`**
Values	**`On`** Installs the root POP3 component on the computer. **`Off`** Does not install the root POP3 component on the computer.
Default Value	**`On`**
Example	`Pop3Srv = On`

rec

Specifies whether to install the Sound Recorder feature on the computer.

Syntax	**`rec = On	Off`**
Values	**`On`** Installs the Sound Recorder feature on the computer. **`Off`** Does not install the Sound Recorder feature on the computer.
Default Value	**`On`**
Example	`rec = On`
Registry Subkey	`HKEY_LOCAL_MACHINE\Software\Microsoft\Windows\CurrentVersion\Setup\OC Manager\Subcomponents\rec`

reminst

Specifies whether to install Remote Installation Services, which enables you to install an operating system remotely onto a computer with either a new PXE-based remote boot read-only memory (ROM) or a network card supported by the remote installation boot floppy disk.

Syntax `reminst = On | Off`

Values

`On`

Installs Remote Installation Services.

`Off`

Does not install Remote Installation Services.

Default Value `Off`

Example `reminst = On`

Registry Subkey

```
HKEY_LOCAL_MACHINE\Software\Microsoft\Windows\
    CurrentVersion\Setup\OC Manager\
    Subcomponents\reminst
```

rootautoupdate

Specifies whether to turn on the Optional Components Manager (OCM) Update Root Certificates.

Syntax `rootautoupdate = On | Off`

Values

`On`

Turns on the OCM Update Root Certificates.

`Off`

Does not turn on the OCM Update Root Certificates.

Default Value `On`

Example `rootautoupdate = On`

Registry Subkey

```
HKEY_LOCAL_MACHINE\Software\Microsoft\Windows\
    CurrentVersion\Setup\OC Manager\
    Subcomponents\rootautoupdate
```

rstorage

Specifies whether to install the Remote Storage feature that enables the use of tape libraries as extensions of NTFS file system volumes.

Syntax `rstorage = On | Off`

Values

`On`

Installs the Remote Storage feature.

`Off`

Does not install the Remote Storage feature.

Default Value `Off`

Example `rstorage = On`

Registry Subkey

```
HKEY_LOCAL_MACHINE\Software\Microsoft\Windows\
    CurrentVersion\Setup\OC Manager\
    Subcomponents\rstorage
```

sakit_web

Specifies whether to install the Remote Administration Tools (formerly known as the Server Administration Kit).

Syntax `Sakit_web = On | Off`

Values

`On`

Installs the Remote Administration Tools.

`Off`

Does not install the Remote Administration Tools.

Default Value `Off`

Dependencies

`Sakit_web = On` also installs `iis_common`, `iis_inetmgr`, and `iis_www`.

Use `%WINDIR%\System32\ServerAppliance` to install the Remote Administration Tools.

Example `sakit_web = Off`

Registry Subkey

```
HKEY_LOCAL_MACHINE\Software\Microsoft\Windows\
    CurrentVersion\Setup\OC Manager\
    Subcomponents\sakit_web
```

solitaire

Specifies whether to install the Solitaire game on the computer.

Syntax `solitaire = On | Off`

Values

`On`

Installs the Solitaire game on the computer.

`Off`

Does not install the Solitaire game on the computer.

Default Value `On` (not available in the Windows Server 2003 family)

Example `solitaire = On`

Registry Subkey

```
HKEY_LOCAL_MACHINE\Software\Microsoft\Windows\
    CurrentVersion\Setup\OC Manager\
    Subcomponents\solitaire
```

spider

Specifies whether to install the Spider Solitaire game on the computer.

Syntax `spider = On | Off`

Values

`On`

Installs the Spider Solitaire game on the computer.

`Off`

Does not install the Spider Solitaire game on the computer.

Default Value `On` (not available in the Windows Server 2003 family)

Example `spider = On`

Registry Subkey

```
HKEY_LOCAL_MACHINE\Software\Microsoft\Windows\
    CurrentVersion\Setup\OC Manager\
    Subcomponents\spider
```

templates

Specifies whether to install Document Templates on the computer.

Syntax `templates = On | Off`

Values

`On`

Installs Document Templates on the computer.

`Off`

Does not install Document Templates on the computer.

Default Value	**On**
Example	`templates = On`
Registry Subkey	`HKEY_LOCAL_MACHINE\Software\Microsoft\Windows\ CurrentVersion\Setup\OC Manager\ Subcomponents\templates`

TerminalServer

Specifies whether to install Terminal Server (Terminal Services for multiple users) on the computer.

Syntax **TerminalServer** = **On** | **Off**

Values

On

Installs Terminal Server (Terminal Services for multiple users) on the computer.

Off

Does not install Terminal Server (Terminal Services for multiple users) on the computer.

Default Value **Off**

Example `TerminalServer = On`

Comments

If `TerminalServer = On`, Setup installs Terminal Server and configures the computer to run in multi-user mode. If `TerminalServer = Off`, Setup does not install Terminal Server. The value of this entry does not affect your ability to establish a remote connection to the computer using Terminal Services Remote Desktop.

`TerminalServer` applies only to Windows Advanced Server, Limited Edition; Windows Server 2003, Datacenter Edition; and the 64-bit version of Windows Server 2003, Datacenter Edition.

To specify important security settings for a server with Terminal Server enabled, use the `PermissionsSetting` entry in the `[TerminalServices]` section.

To specify the type of licensing you are using for Terminal Server, use the `LicensingMode` entry in the `[TerminalServices]` section of Unattend.txt.

TSWebClient

Specifies whether to install the ActiveX control and sample pages for hosting Terminal Services client connections over the Web.

Syntax `TSWebClient = On | Off`

Values

`On`

Installs the ActiveX control and sample pages for hosting Terminal Services client connections over the Web.

`Off`

Does not install the ActiveX control and sample pages for hosting Terminal Services client connections over the Web.

Default Value `Off`

Dependencies Requires `iis_common`, `iis_inetmgr`, and `iis_www`.

Example `TSWebClient = On`

vol

Specifies whether to install the Volume Control feature on the computer.

Syntax `vol = On | Off`

Values

`On`

Installs the Volume Control feature on the computer.

`Off`

Does not install the Volume Control feature on the computer.

Default Value `On`

Example `vol = On`

Registry Subkey

```
HKEY_LOCAL_MACHINE\Software\Microsoft\Windows\
    CurrentVersion\Setup\OC Manager\
    Subcomponents\vol
```

WbemCrrl

Specifies whether to install the Windows Management Instrumentation (WMI) event correlation component.

Syntax `WbemCrrl = On | Off`

Values **`On`**

Installs the WMI event correlation component.

`Off`

Does not install the WMI event correlation component.

Default Value **`On`**

Example `WbemCrrl = On`

WbemFwrd

Specifies whether to install the Windows Management Instrumentation (WMI) event forwarding components.

Syntax `WbemFwrd = On | Off`

Values **`On`**

Installs the WMI event forwarding components.

`Off`

Does not install the WMI event forwarding components.

Default Value **`On`**

Example `WbemFwrd = On`

WbemMSI

Specifies whether to install the Windows Management Instrumentation (WMI) Windows installer provider.

Syntax `WbemMSI = On | Off`

Values **`On`**

Installs the WMI Windows installer provider.

`Off`

Does not install the WMI Windows installer provider.

Default Value **`On`**

Example `WbemMSI = On`

WMAccess

Specifies whether to install visible entry points to Windows Messenger.

Syntax `WMAccess = On | Off`

Values

`On`

Installs visible entry points to Windows Messenger.

`Off`

Does not install visible entry points to Windows Messenger.

Default Value `On`

Example `WMAccess = On`

Comments Not supported in the Windows Server 2003 family. A shortcut link on the Start menu is an example of a visible entry point. This entry does not remove any Windows code, including any Windows Messenger code, other than these visible entry points.

WMPOCM

Specifies whether to install visible entry points to Windows Media Player.

Syntax `WMPOCM = On | Off`

Values

`On`

Installs visible entry points to Windows Media Player.

`Off`

Removes visible entry points to Windows Media Player, if the visible entry points are installed.

Default Value `On`

Example `WMPOCM = On`

Comments Not supported by the Windows Server 2003 family. A shortcut link on the Start menu is an example of a visible entry point. This entry does not remove any Windows code, including any Windows Media Player code.

wms

Specifies whether to install the core Windows Media Server components.

Syntax **`wms = On | Off`**

Values

`On`

Installs the core Windows Media Server components.

`Off`

Does not install the core Windows Media Server components.

Default Value **`Off`**

Dependencies Requires `wms_admin_asp`, `wms_admin_mmc`, or `wms_server`.

Valid only for the Windows Server 2003 family.

Example `wms = On`

Registry Subkey

```
HKEY_LOCAL_MACHINE\Software\Microsoft\Windows\
    CurrentVersion\Setup\OC Manager\
    Subcomponents\wms
```

wms_admin_asp

Specifies whether to install the Windows Media Services Web-based administrative components.

Syntax **`wms_admin_asp = On | Off`**

Values

`On`

Installs Windows Media Services Web-based administrative components.

`Off`

Does not install Windows Media Services Web-based administrative components.

Default Value **`Off`**

Dependencies Requires `wms`, `iis_common`, `iis_inetmgr`, and `iis_www`.

Valid only for the Windows Server 2003 family.

Example `wms_admin_asp = On`

Registry Subkey

```
HKEY_LOCAL_MACHINE\Software\Microsoft\Windows\
    CurrentVersion\Setup\OC Manager\
    Subcomponents\wms_admin_asp
```

wms_admin_mmc

Specifies whether to install the Windows Media Services Microsoft Management Console (MMC)-based administrative components.

Syntax	**wms_admin_mmc = On | Off**
Values	**On** Installs the Windows Media Services MMC-based administrative components. **Off** Does not install the Windows Media Services MMC-based administrative components.
Default Value	**Off**
Dependencies	Requires `wms`. Valid only for the Windows Server 2003 family.
Example	`wms_admin_mmc = On`
Registry Subkey	`HKEY_LOCAL_MACHINE\Software\Microsoft\Windows\ CurrentVersion\Setup\OC Manager\ Subcomponents\wms_admin_mmc`

wms_isapi

Specifies whether to install the Windows Media Services Multicast and Advertisement Logging Agent components.

Syntax	**wms_isapi = On | Off**
Values	**On** Installs Windows Media Services Multicast and Advertisement Logging Agent components. **Off** Does not install Windows Media Services Multicast and Advertisement Logging Agent components.
Default Value	**Off**
Dependencies	Requires `iis_common`, `iis_inetmgr`, and `iis_www`. Valid only for the Windows Server 2003 family.
Example	`wms_isapi = On`
Registry Subkey	`HKEY_LOCAL_MACHINE\Software\Microsoft\Windows\ CurrentVersion\Setup\OC Manager\ Subcomponents\wms_isapi`

wms_server

Specifies whether to install the Windows Media Services server components.

Syntax	**wms_server = On | Off**
Values	**On** Installs the Windows Media Services server components. **Off** Does not install the Windows Media Services server components.
Default Value	**Off**
Dependencies	Requires `wms` and `wms_server`.
Example	`wms_server = On`
Registry Subkey	`HKEY_LOCAL_MACHINE\Software\Microsoft\Windows\ CurrentVersion\Setup\OC Manager\ Subcomponents\wms_server`
Comments	Valid only for the Windows Server 2003 family.

zonegames

Specifies whether to install the Microsoft Gaming Zone Internet games on the computer.

Syntax	**zonegames = On | Off**
Value	**On** Installs the Microsoft Gaming Zone Internet games on the computer. **Off** Does not install the Microsoft Gaming Zone Internet games on the computer.
Default Value	**On** (not available in the Windows Server 2003 family)
Example	`zonegames = On`
Registry subkey	`HKEY_LOCAL_MACHINE\Software\Microsoft\Windows\ CurrentVersion\Setup\OC Manager\ Subcomponents\zonegames`

B

GuiUnattended

The `[GuiUnattended]` section contains entries for preparing the graphical user interface (GUI) for unattended Setup.

Entry	Description
`AdminPassword`	Sets the Administrator account password.
`Arguments`	Indicates that arguments or entries accompany the custom program that runs concurrently with the Setup program.
`AutoLogon`	Configures the computer to log on once with the Administrator account.
`AutoLogonCount`	Specifies the number of times that the computer automatically logs on with the specified Administrator account and password.
`DetachedProgram`	Indicates the path of the custom program that runs concurrently with the Setup program.
`EMSBlankPassword`	Enables the use of a blank administrator password in unattended installations to EMS servers.
`EMSSkipUnattendProcessing`	Prevents Windows Setup from processing Unattend.txt or sysprep.inf during an unattended installation to an EMS server.
`EncryptedAdminPassword`	Enables Setup to install encrypted passwords for the Administrator account.
`OEMSkipRegional`	Enables unattended Setup to skip the Regional and language options page in gui-mode setup and mini-setup.
`OEMSkipWelcome`	Enables unattended Setup to skip the Welcome page in GUI-mode Setup and Mini-Setup.

Entry	Description
ProfilesDir	Specifies the location of Microsoft® Windows® XP or Windows Server 2003 family profiles.
ServerWelcome	Specifies whether to install the Web UI for Remote Administration at first logon on a member of the Windows Server 2003 family.
TimeZone	Specifies the time zone of the computer.

Sample

This sample demonstrates one use of the `[GuiUnattended]` section of unattend.txt.

```
[GuiUnattended]
AdminPassword = "YhJ##3"
Arguments = /n/s
AutoLogon = Yes
AutoLogonCount = 5
DetachedProgram = "%SYSTEMDRIVE%\extras\install.exe"
EMSBlankPassword = Yes
EMSSkipUnattendProcessing = 1
EncryptedAdminPassword = Yes
OEMSkipRegional = 0
OEMSkipWelcome = 0
OEMPreinstall = Yes
ProfilesDir = "%SYSTEMROOT%\Profiles"
ServerWelcome = Yes
TimeZone = 030
```

AdminPassword

Sets the Administrator account password.

Syntax **AdminPassword** = "*password*" | *

Values *password*

The password may contain as many as 127 characters. Passwords are case-sensitive and must be enclosed in quotation marks. End users cannot change or specify their own passwords in `Mini-Setup`. You can enter a new password in the appropriate dialog box, but the password does not change.

*

The administrator password is blank (null).

Example `AdminPassword = "YhJ##3"`

Registry subkey HKEY_LOCAL_MACHINE\Software\Microsoft\Windows\CurrentVersion\WinLogon\DefaultPassword

Dependencies If AdminPassword is set to blank, null, or not set, the registry subkey HKEY_LOCAL_MACHINE\Software\Microsoft\Windows NT\CurrentVersion\WinLogon\AutoAdminLogon (controlled by the `AutoLogon` entry) is set to 0 (false), which disables the automatic Administrator account logon feature.

Comments If you specify a `password` in the `Administrator` account, you cannot use the `AdminPassword` entry in the sysprep.inf file to change it; the administrator password remains the same. However, if the administrator password was initially blank (either manually or through unattended Setup), you can use `AdminPassword` to change it to a non-blank password.

Important:

- Security breaches can occur if you use a common, non-blank administrator password for all computers provided to end users. We recommend that you use an automation process to set the administrator password to blank before you run `Sysprep`. End users can then specify their own passwords after receiving the computers.
- In an unattended installation, Windows Setup will force any password string that begins with an asterisk to null.

Arguments

Indicates that arguments or entries accompany the custom program that runs concurrently with the Setup program.

Syntax **`Arguments`** `=` *`string`*

Value *`string`*

Example `Arguments = /n/s`

Comments This entry is required if you are using `DetachedProgram`.

AutoLogon

Configures the computer to log on once with the Administrator account.

Syntax	**`AutoLogon = Yes	No`**
Values	**`Yes`** Configures the computer to log on once with the Administrator account. **`No`** Does not automatically log on to the computer.
Default Value	**`No`**
Example	`AutoLogon = Yes`
Registry subkey	HKEY_LOCAL_MACHINE\Software\Microsoft\Windows NT\CurrentVersion\WinLogon\AutoAdminLogon
Dependencies	If `AdminPassword` is set to blank, null, or not set, the registry subkey HKEY_LOCAL_MACHINE\Software\Microsoft\Windows NT\CurrentVersion\WinLogon\AutoAdminLogon (controlled by `AutoLogon`) is set to 0 (false) which disables the automatic Administrator account logon feature.
Comments	The entry is not valid on upgrades. When you set `AutoLogon` to `Yes`, you cannot log off. If you try to log off, you will be logged back on automatically. The only way to log off is to reboot, which decrements the value of `AutoLogonCount`. If you specify a password in the `AdminPassword` entry, Setup uses that password when you log on automatically to the computer. After the installation finishes, Setup deletes the password from the copy of the `answer file` left on the computer. **Important:** ■ Encrypting the Administrator password in the `EncryptedAdminPassword` entry disables `AutoLogon`. ■ To skip Windows Welcome, set `UnattendSwitch` to **Yes** in the `[Unattended]` section of unattend.txt. ■ If you wish to log on automatically after running Sysprep in Factory mode, set `AuditAdminAutoLogon` to `Yes` in the `[ComputerSettings]` section of winbom.ini.

AutoLogonCount

Specifies the number of times that the computer automatically logs on with the specified Administrator account and password.

Syntax `AutoLogonCount = integer`

Value *integer*

Example `AutoLogonCount = 5`

Registry subkey `HKEY_LOCAL_MACHINE\Software\Microsoft\Windows\CurrentVersion\WinLogon\AutoLogonCount`

Comments The value decrements after each logon, and WinLogon disables the feature after the specified number of logon attempts.

Requires `AutoLogon = Yes` and `AdminPassword = password` in Unattend.txt. If `AutoLogon = Yes`, WinLogon checks the value of `AutoLogonCount`. If the number for `AutoLogonCount` is greater than 0, WinLogon decrements the count and then checks `AdminPassword`. If `AdminPassword = password`, WinLogon uses this password to log on automatically. If `AdminPassword = *`, the user must enter a password.

If `AutoLogonCount = 0`, then WinLogon deletes `AutoAdminLogon`, `AutoLogonCount`, and `DefaultPassword` from the registry. During the next reboot, the user must log on manually.

Important:

- The function of this entry has changed slightly between Windows 2000 and Windows XP. Please review this entry carefully before using it in your answer file.
- Make sure that the password for the `master installation` (that you plan to duplicate onto one or more destination computers) is blank.
- You must `reboot` the computer to decrement the value of `AutoLogonCount`.

DetachedProgram

Indicates the path of the custom program that runs concurrently with the Setup program.

Syntax `DetachedProgram = detached_program_string`

Value *detached_program_string*

Example `DetachedProgram = "%SYSTEMDRIVE%\extras\install.exe"`

Comments If the program requires any arguments, you must specify them in the `Arguments` entry.

EMSBlankPassword

Enables the use of a blank administrator password in unattended installations to EMS servers.

Syntax	**`EMSBlankPassword = Yes	No`**
Values	**`Yes`** Enables the use of "*" with `AdminPassword` when preinstalling to EMS servers. **`No`** Disables the use of "*" with `AdminPassword` when preinstalling to EMS servers.
Default Value	**`No`**
Example	`EMSBlankPassword = Yes`
Comments	Applies only to the Windows Server 2003 family. By default, blank administrator passwords (`AdminPassword = "*"`) are not allowed in unattended installations of any member of the Windows Server 2003 family to EMS servers.

EMSSkipUnattendProcessing

Prevents Windows Setup from processing unattend.txt or sysprep.inf during an unattended installation to an EMS server.

Syntax	**`EMSSkipUnattendProcessing = 0	1`**
Values	**`0`** Does not prevent Windows Setup from processing unattend.txt or sysprep.inf during an unattended installation to an EMS server. **`1`** Prevents Windows Setup from processing unattend.txt or sysprep.inf during an unattended installation to an EMS server.
Default Value	**`0`**
Example	`EMSSkipUnattendProcessing = 0`
Comments	Applies only to the Windows Server 2003 family.

EncryptedAdminPassword

Enables Setup to install encrypted passwords for the Administrator account.

Syntax `EncryptedAdminPassword = Yes | No`

Values

`Yes`

Instructs Setup to install the encrypted Administrator account password.

`No`

Instructs Setup to keep the Administrator account password as clean text.

Default Value **`No`**

Example `EncryptedAdminPassword = Yes`

Comments To encrypt your Administrator passwords, use Setup Manager on the Windows OPK CD (in Tools) and in deploy.cab.

Important: If you use this key to install an encrypted Administrator password during an unattended installation, Setup disables `Autologon`.

OEMSkipRegional

Enables unattended Setup to skip the Regional and Language Options page in `GUI-mode Setup` and `Mini-Setup`.

Syntax `OEMSkipRegional = 0 | 1`

Values

`0`

Displays the Regional and Language Options page in GUI-mode Setup and Mini-Setup.

`1`

Skips the Regional and Language Options page in GUI-mode Setup and Mini-Setup.

Example `OEMSkipRegional = 0`

Dependency `OEMPreinstall = Yes`

Comments If, in the `[Unattended]` section, you set `OemPreinstall` to `Yes` and provide values for the `[RegionalSettings]` section, set the value of the `OEMSkipRegional` entry equal to `1` to ensure that Setup completes without prompting the end user for regional information.

OEMSkipWelcome

Enables unattended Setup to skip the Welcome page in GUI-mode Setup and Mini-Setup.

Syntax `OEMSkipWelcome = 0 | 1`

Values

`0`

Displays the Welcome page in GUI-mode Setup and Mini-Setup.

`1`

Skips the Welcome page in GUI-mode Setup and Mini-Setup.

Example `OEMSkipWelcome = 0`

Dependency `OEMPreinstall = Yes`

Comments **Important:** If `OemPreinstall` in the `[Unattended]` section of unattend.txt is set to `Yes`, `unattended Setup` automatically stops on the Welcome page. To avoid this pause in your factory or testing environment, set `OEMSkipWelcome = 1`. *Do not* ship any computer with `OEMSkipWelcome = 1`. Instead, change `OEMSkipWelcome` in the `[GuiUnattended]` section of sysprep.inf to `0` before delivering the computer to the customer.

ProfilesDir

Specifies the location of Windows XP or Windows Server 2003 family profiles.

Syntax `ProfilesDir = path_to_profile_folder`

Value *`path_to_profile_folder`*

Default Value `"%SYSTEMDRIVE%\Documents and Settings"`

Example `ProfilesDir = "%SYSTEMROOT%\Profiles"`

Comments This entry is useful if you require new installations to use the same profile folder as Windows NT 4.0 or Windows 2000. This entry is valid only on clean installations of Windows XP or Windows Server 2003 family. Setup ignores this entry during upgrades.

The specified directory can contain an environment variable such as %SYSTEMDRIVE% or %SYSTEMROOT%. Enclose *path_to_profile_folder* in quotation marks if it is a `long file name` or if it contains an environment variable.

ServerWelcome

Specifies whether to install the Web UI for Remote Administration at first logon on a member of the Windows Server 2003 family.

Syntax	**`ServerWelcome = Yes	No`**
Value	**`Yes	No`**
Default Value	**`Yes`**
Example	`ServerWelcome = Yes`
Comments	On the Windows Server 2003, Web Edition, if this entry is set to `Yes`, then on first logon, sasetup.msi will be run from the hard drive, the Web UI for Web server administration will be added to the Startup program group for the Administrator account, and the Web UI will be launched. On Windows Server 2003, Standard Edition, Windows Server 2003, Enterprise Edition, Microsoft Small Business Server, and Windows Server 2003, Datacenter Edition, if this entry is set to `Yes`, then the Configure Your Server Wizard will be run on first user logon. If this parameter is set to `No`, then the Configure Your Server Wizard will not be run. This parameter will not be utilized during a Sysprep (sysprep.inf) installation.

TimeZone

Specifies the time zone of the computer.

Syntax TimeZone = *index*

Value *index*

This table lists the numeric values corresponding to the time zones.

Index	Time Zone	Display
000	Dateline Standard Time	(GMT-12:00) International Date Line West
001	Samoa Standard Time	(GMT-11:00) Midway Island, Samoa
002	Hawaiian Standard Time	(GMT-10:00) Hawaii
003	Alaskan Standard Time	(GMT-09:00) Alaska
004	Pacific Standard Time	(GMT-08:00) Pacific Time (US and Canada); Tijuana

Value	Index	Time Zone	Display
(cont'd.)	010	Mountain Standard Time	(GMT-07:00) Mountain Time (US and Canada)
	013	Mexico Standard Time 2	(GMT-07:00) Chihuahua, La Paz, Mazatlan
	015	U.S. Mountain Standard Time	(GMT-07:00) Arizona
	020	Central Standard Time	(GMT-06:00) Central Time (US and Canada)
	025	Canada Central Standard Time	(GMT-06:00) Saskatchewan
	030	Mexico Standard Time	(GMT-06:00) Guadalajara, Mexico City, Monterrey
	033	Central America Standard Time	(GMT-06:00) Central America
	035	Eastern Standard Time	(GMT-05:00) Eastern Time (US and Canada)
	040	U.S. Eastern Standard Time	(GMT-05:00) Indiana (East)
	045	S.A. Pacific Standard Time	(GMT-05:00) Bogota, Lima, Quito
	050	Atlantic Standard Time	(GMT-04:00) Atlantic Time (Canada)
	055	S.A. Western Standard Time	(GMT-04:00) Caracas, La Paz
	056	Pacific S.A. Standard Time	(GMT-04:00) Santiago
	060	Newfoundland and Labrador Standard Time	(GMT-03:30) Newfoundland and Labrador
	065	E. South America Standard Time	(GMT-03:00) Brasilia
	070	S.A. Eastern Standard Time	(GMT-03:00) Buenos Aires, Georgetown
	073	Greenland Standard Time	(GMT-03:00) Greenland
	075	Mid-Atlantic Standard Time	(GMT-02:00) Mid-Atlantic
	080	Azores Standard Time	(GMT-01:00) Azores
	083	Cape Verde Standard Time	(GMT-01:00) Cape Verde Islands
	085	GMT Standard Time	(GMT) Greenwich Mean Time: Dublin, Edinburgh, Lisbon, London
	090	Greenwich Standard Time	(GMT) Casablanca, Monrovia
	095	Central Europe Standard Time	(GMT+01:00) Belgrade, Bratislava, Budapest, Ljubljana, Prague
	100	Central European Standard Time	(GMT+01:00) Sarajevo, Skopje, Warsaw, Zagreb
	105	Romance Standard Time	(GMT+01:00) Brussels, Copenhagen, Madrid, Paris

Value	Index	Time Zone	Display
(cont'd.)	110	W. Europe Standard Time	(GMT+01:00) Amsterdam, Berlin, Bern, Rome, Stockholm, Vienna
	113	W. Central Africa Standard Time	(GMT+01:00) West Central Africa
	115	E. Europe Standard Time	(GMT+02:00) Bucharest
	120	Egypt Standard Time	(GMT+02:00) Cairo
	125	FLE Standard Time	(GMT+02:00) Helsinki, Kyiv, Riga, Sofia, Tallinn, Vilnius
	130	GTB Standard Time	(GMT+02:00) Athens, Istanbul, Minsk
	135	Israel Standard Time	(GMT+02:00) Jerusalem
	140	South Africa Standard Time	(GMT+02:00) Harare, Pretoria
	145	Russian Standard Time	(GMT+03:00) Moscow, St. Petersburg, Volgograd
	150	Arab Standard Time	(GMT+03:00) Kuwait, Riyadh
	155	E. Africa Standard Time	(GMT+03:00) Nairobi
	158	Arabic Standard Time	(GMT+03:00) Baghdad
	160	Iran Standard Time	(GMT+03:30) Tehran
	165	Arabian Standard Time	(GMT+04:00) Abu Dhabi, Muscat
	170	Caucasus Standard Time	(GMT+04:00) Baku, Tbilisi, Yerevan
	175	Transitional Islamic State of Afghanistan Standard Time	(GMT+04:30) Kabul
	180	Ekaterinburg Standard Time	(GMT+05:00) Ekaterinburg
	185	West Asia Standard Time	(GMT+05:00) Islamabad, Karachi, Tashkent
	190	India Standard Time	(GMT+05:30) Chennai, Kolkata, Mumbai, New Delhi
	193	Nepal Standard Time	(GMT+05:45) Kathmandu
	195	Central Asia Standard Time	(GMT+06:00) Astana, Dhaka
	200	Sri Lanka Standard Time	(GMT+06:00) Sri Jayawardenepura
	201	N. Central Asia Standard Time	(GMT+06:00) Almaty, Novosibirsk
	203	Myanmar Standard Time	(GMT+06:30) Yangon (Rangoon)
	205	S.E. Asia Standard Time	(GMT+07:00) Bangkok, Hanoi, Jakarta

Value *(cont'd.)*

Index	Time Zone	Display
207	North Asia Standard Time	(GMT+07:00) Krasnoyarsk
210	China Standard Time	(GMT+08:00) Beijing, Chongqing, Hong Kong SAR, Urumqi
215	Singapore Standard Time	(GMT+08:00) Kuala Lumpur, Singapore
220	Taipei Standard Time	(GMT+08:00) Taipei
225	W. Australia Standard Time	(GMT+08:00) Perth
227	North Asia East Standard Time	(GMT+08:00) Irkutsk, Ulan Bator
230	Korea Standard Time	(GMT+09:00) Seoul
235	Tokyo Standard Time	(GMT+09:00) Osaka, Sapporo, Tokyo
240	Yakutsk Standard Time	(GMT+09:00) Yakutsk
245	A.U.S. Central Standard Time	(GMT+09:30) Darwin
250	Cen. Australia Standard Time	(GMT+09:30) Adelaide
255	A.U.S. Eastern Standard Time	(GMT+10:00) Canberra, Melbourne, Sydney
260	E. Australia Standard Time	(GMT+10:00) Brisbane
265	Tasmania Standard Time	(GMT+10:00) Hobart
270	Vladivostok Standard Time	(GMT+10:00) Vladivostok
275	West Pacific Standard Time	(GMT+10:00) Guam, Port Moresby
280	Central Pacific Standard Time	(GMT+11:00) Magadan, Solomon Islands, New Caledonia
285	Fiji Islands Standard Time	(GMT+12:00) Fiji Islands, Kamchatka, Marshall Islands
290	New Zealand Standard Time	(GMT+12:00) Auckland, Wellington
300	Tonga Standard Time	(GMT+13:00) Nuku'alofa

Example TimeZone = 030

Registry subkey `HKEY_LOCAL_MACHINE\SYSTEM\CurrentControlSet\Control\TimeZoneInformation\DaylightName`

Comments If the entry is not present, the end user must select a time zone.

Note: If you do not configure a specific time zone setting, the default time zone depends on the language version of Windows that is installed. For example, in the Japanese version, the default time zone is `"GMT+9 (Osaka, Sapporo, Tokyo)"`.

C

Unattended

The [Unattended] section contains entries for running Setup.

Entry	Description
ActivateProxy	Specifies the proxy settings to use when connecting to the Internet to activate this installation of Windows XP, if you set AutoActivate to Yes.
AutoActivate	Specifies whether Setup attempts to activate this installation of Windows XP automatically through an existing Internet connection.
ComputerType	Specifies the type of custom hardware abstraction layer (HAL) that Setup Loader loads and installs by text-mode Setup.
CrashDumpSetting	Specifies the creation and type of the dump file.
DisableVirtualOemDevices	Specifies whether to load virtual original equipment manufacturer (OEM) devices during Setup.
DUDisable	Specifies whether to connect to the Windows Update site to download updates during Setup.
DUShare	Specifies the location for downloaded Dynamic Update .cab files.
DUStopOnError	Specifies whether to stop the Windows Update process when an error is detected.
DriverSigningPolicy	Specifies how to process unsigned drivers during unattended Setup.
ExtendOemPartition	Specifies whether to extend the partition on which you install Windows.
FactoryMode	Specifies whether %SYSTEMDRIVE%\Sysprep\Factory.exe runs on first boot.

Entry	Description
FileSystem	Specifies whether to convert the primary partition to NTFS or to leave it alone.
ForceHALDetection	Specifies whether text-mode Setup examines the operating system and determines the most appropriate hardware abstraction layer (HAL) to install during an upgrade.
Hibernation	Specifies whether to enable the hibernation option in the Power Options control panel.
KeyboardLayout	Specifies the type of keyboard layout to install during text-mode Setup.
NTUpgrade	Specifies whether Setup upgrades a previous version of Windows NT 3.51, Windows NT 4.0, Windows 2000, Windows XP, or the Windows Server 2003 family.
OemFilesPath	Specifies the path to the \OEM folder (containing OEM files) if it does not exist under the i386 folder of the distribution share point.
OemPnPDriversPath	Specifies the path to one or more folders that contain plug-and-play drivers not distributed in drivers.cab on the Windows product CD.
OemPreinstall	Specifies whether Setup installs its files from distribution folders.
OemSkipEula	Specifies whether the end user must accept the End-User License Agreement (EULA) included with Windows.
OverwriteOemFilesOnUpgrade	Specifies whether to overwrite OEM-supplied files that have the same name as Windows XP or Windows Server 2003 operating system files during an unattended upgrade.
Repartition	Specifies whether to delete all partitions on the first drive of the client computer and to reformat the drive with the NTFS file system.
TargetPath	Determines the installation folder in which you install Windows.
UnattendMode	Defines the unattended mode to use during GUI-mode Setup.

Entry	Description
UnattendSwitch	Specifies whether Setup skips Windows Welcome or Mini-Setup when preinstalling Windows XP Home Edition or Windows XP Professional using the CD boot method.
WaitForReboot	Specifies whether the computer waits 15 seconds after GUI-mode Setup finishes.
Win9xUpgrade	Specifies whether Setup upgrades previous installations of Windows 98, Windows 98 Second Edition, or Windows Millennium Edition to either Windows XP Home Edition or Windows XP Professional, as specified in the [Win9xUpg] section.

Sample

This sample demonstrates one use of the [Unattended] section of unattend.txt.

```
[Unattended]
ActivateProxy = Proxy
AutoActivate = Yes
ComputerType = "OEM HAL", OEM
CrashDumpSetting = 0
DisableVirtualOemDevices = Yes
DUDisable = No
DUShare = "%SYSTEMDRIVE%\DU_Cabs"
DUStopOnError = Yes
DriverSigningPolicy = Block
ExtendOemPartition = 1000
FactoryMode = Yes
FileSystem = ConvertNTFS
ForceHALDetection = Yes
Hibernation = Yes
KeyboardLayout = Us
NTUpgrade = Yes
OemFilesPath = "%SYSTEMDRIVE%\OEM_Files"
OemPnPDriversPath = MyFolder1;MyFolder2
OemPreinstall = Yes
OemSkipEula = No
OverwriteOemFilesOnUpgrade = Yes
Repartition = Yes
TargetPath = *
UnattendMode = FullUnattended
UnattendSwitch = Yes
WaitForReboot = Yes
Win9xUpgrade = Yes
```

ActivateProxy

Specifies the proxy settings to use when connecting to the Internet to activate this installation of Windows XP, if you set `AutoActivate` to `Yes`.

Syntax	**`ActivateProxy`** `=` *`section_name`* | **`Proxy`**
Values	*`section_name`* **`Proxy`**
Example	`ActivateProxy = Proxy`
Comments	If *section_name* is `Proxy`, Windows Product Activation (WPA) uses the proxy settings specified in the `[Proxy]` section. If *section_name* is anything else, WPA uses the proxy settings specified in `[`*`section_name`*`]` in the unattend.txt file. The entries in `[`*`section_name`*`]` must match the syntax specified in the `[Proxy]` section. **Note:** If your network uses Web Proxy Auto-Discovery (WPAD), you may not need to set the proxy explicitly.

AutoActivate

Specifies whether Setup attempts to activate this installation of Windows XP automatically through an existing Internet connection.

Syntax	**`AutoActivate`** `=` **`Yes`** | **`No`**
Values	**`Yes`** Attempts to activate this installation of Windows XP during unattended Setup through an existing Internet connection on the computer. **`No`** Requires the end user to activate Windows XP either through an Internet connection or by telephone.
Default Value	No
Example	`AutoActivate = Yes`

Comments

You must specify a valid Product Key in the `ProductKey` entry of the `[UserData]` section. If the Internet connection is through a firewall, you may need to specify the relevant proxy settings in the `ActivateProxy` entry.

Important:

- Always requires a Product Key.
- The Product Key that you use to activate this installation using Windows Product Activation (WPA) must match the number on the Certificate of Authenticity (COA). The original equipment manufacturer (OEM) packages the COA with the retail product or affixes it to the computer case.
- Standard licensing agreements specify that you can use a given Product Key to activate only one installation of Windows XP on one computer. WPA enforces this requirement.
- If you use winnt.exe to install Windows, you must set `UnattendSwitch` to `Yes`.
- Setting `AutoActivate` to `Yes` does not guarantee successful activation of this installation of Windows XP. For example, the activation attempt will fail if the computer cannot successfully connect to the Internet.

ComputerType

Specifies the type of custom hardware abstraction layer (HAL) that Setup Loader loads and installs by text-mode Setup.

Syntax

ComputerType = *HAL_description* [, **Retail** | **OEM**]

Values

HAL_description [, **Retail** | **OEM**]

Retail

Informs Setup that the HAL to install is part of Windows XP or Windows Server 2003 family.

OEM

Indicates that the HAL to load is OEM-supplied. If this is the case, you must also list the driver name in the `[OEMBootFiles]` section of the unattend.txt file.

Examples

```
ComputerType = "OEM HAL", OEM
ComputerType = "Advanced Configuration and Power
Interface (ACPI) PC", Retail
```

Comments

This entry is valid only when the value of `OemPreinstall` is `Yes`. If the `ComputerType` entry is not present, Setup attempts to detect the type of computer and install the appropriate retail HAL.

The *HAL_description* string identifies the Hardware Abstraction Layer (HAL) to install. It must match one of the strings in the `[Computer]` section of txtsetup.sif (for a retail HAL) or txt-setup.oem (for an OEM HAL).

CrashDumpSetting

Specifies the creation and type of the dump file.

Syntax

`CrashDumpSetting = 0 | 1 | 2 | 3`

Values

`0`

Does not create a dump file.

`1`

Complete Memory Dump: Records the entire contents of system memory to *%SYSTEMROOTt%*\Memory.dmp when the system stops unexpectedly. If you choose this option, you must have a paging file on the boot volume large enough to hold all of the physical random access memory (RAM) plus 1 megabyte (MB).

`2`

Kernel Memory Dump: Records only kernel memory to *%SYSTEMROOTt%*\Memory.dmp when the system stops unexpectedly. This speeds up the process of recording information in a log. Depending on the amount of RAM in your computer, you must have 50 MB to 800 MB available for the paging file on the boot volume.

`3`

Small Memory Dump (64K): Records the smallest set of useful information that can help identify the problem to *%SYSTEMROOTt%*\Mini.dmp. This option requires a paging file of at least 2 MB on the boot volume of your computer and specifies that Setup creates a new file each time the system stops unexpectedly.

Default Value

Windows XP Home Edition and Windows XP Professional: **3**
Windows Server 2003 family: **`1`**

Example

`CrashDumpSetting = 0`

Comments

When the system fails, you can create a dump file that contains information useful for debugging. Dump file types vary by size. The system checks for available space on the boot volume and writes the largest possible dump file.

DisableVirtualOemDevices

Specifies whether to load virtual OEM devices during Setup.

Syntax	**`DisableVirtualOemDevices = Yes	No`**
Values	**`Yes`** Disables loading virtual OEM devices during Setup. **`No`** Does not disable loading virtual OEM devices during Setup.
Default Value	**`Yes`** for preinstallation; **`No`** otherwise
Example	`DisableVirtualOemDevices = Yes`
Comments	An example of a virtual OEM device is a RAM disk that has mass-storage drivers, related .inf files, and so on. During attended Setup, you can disable loading of virtual OEM devices by pressing F4 at the prompt to press the F6 key.

DUDisable

Specifies whether to connect to the Windows Update site to download updates during Setup.

Syntax	DUDisable = Yes | No
Values	**`Yes`** Instructs Setup not to connect to the Windows Update site. **`No`** Instructs Setup to connect to the Windows Update site to download any available Windows XP Setup updates. Setup also downloads any necessary drivers that are not on the Windows XP CD-ROM.
Default Value	**`Yes`**
Example	`DUDisable = No`
Comments	Specifies whether Setup connects to the Windows Update site to download any available Windows Setup updates or necessary drivers that are not on the Windows CD-ROM. `DUDisable` is equivalent to the command: **`winnt32 /unattend /dudisable`** Setup disables dynamic updates by default so corporate administrators can more easily standardize on a known set of Windows system components.

DUShare

Specifies the location for downloaded Dynamic Update .cab files.

Syntax	**DUShare** = *path_to_downloaded_cabs*
Values	*path_to_downloaded_cabs* Specifies the location for all downloaded Dynamic Update .cab files.
Example	`DUShare = "%SYSTEMDRIVE%\DU_Cabs"`
Requires	You must run winnt32 /DUPrepare:*path_to_downloaded_cabs* before using this entry.
Comments	When a path is specified, the Dynamic Update wizard page is not shown and Setup does not try to connect to Windows Update. Instead, Setup uses the Dynamic Update .cab files from this share.

DUStopOnError

Specifies whether to stop the Windows Update process when an error is detected.

Syntax	**DUStopOnError** = **Yes** | **No**
Values	**Yes** Stops the Windows Update process when an error is detected. **No** Does not stop the Windows Update process when an error is detected.
Example	`DUStopOnError = Yes`
Comments	Windows Update errors include any failure to process Windows Update files, or the inability to connect to Windows Update. By default, the Windows Update process stops when an error is detected.

DriverSigningPolicy

Specifies how to process unsigned drivers during unattended Setup.

Syntax **`DriverSigningPolicy = Block | Warn | Ignore`**

Values

`Block`

Setup does not install the unsigned device driver.

`Warn`

Setup stops the installation and prompts the end user for input before accepting the unsigned device driver.

`Ignore`

Setup continues despite the unsigned driver.

Default Value **`Warn`**

Example `DriverSigningPolicy = Block`

Comments

Signed drivers have gone through the Microsoft driver testing and signing process to ensure they are compatible with Windows XP and the Windows Server 2003 family.

Important:

- Microsoft strongly advises against using `DriverSigningPolicy = Ignore` unless you have fully tested the device driver in your environment and are sure that it works properly. Using unsigned drivers increases the risk of device driver problems that can affect the performance or stability of the computer.
- If you are using `DriverSigningPolicy = Ignore` and you attempt to install a newer, unsigned copy of a driver that distributed with Windows XP or the Windows Server 2003 family, Setup installs the signed Windows XP driver instead of the unsigned drivers, in accordance with the ranking process used by the operating system.
- A catalog certificate (.cat) file authenticates a driver signature. Microsoft can only use the given certificate to sign drivers for a finite length of time, generally six months. However, as long as you have a digitally signed driver, the subsequent expiration date of the certificate does not affect the status of the driver. A driver signature does not expire, even after the certificate used to sign the driver has expired.

For more information, see:

- Windows Hardware and Driver Central Web site (*www.microsoft.com/whdc/*)
- Driver Signing for Windows (*www.microsoft.com/whdc/hwdev/driver/digitsign.mspx*)

For more information about driver ranking and how Setup chooses the correct driver, see the Microsoft Device Development Kit (*www.microsoft.com/ddk/*).

ExtendOemPartition

Specifies whether to extend the partition on which you install Windows.

Syntax `ExtendOemPartition = 0 | 1 | extra_size_in_MB`

Values

0

Setup does not extend the partition.

1

Setup extends the partition to fill out the hard disk.

extra_size_in_MB

Setup increases the current partition size by this amount. This is useful if you want to configure more than one partition on the hard disk.

Example `ExtendOemPartition = 1000`

Comments

This entry causes Setup to extend this destination partition into any available unpartitioned space that physically follows it on the disk.

`ExtendOemPartition` automatically leaves the last cylinder on the hard disk free to allow dynamic disk support.

Important:

- You can extend only NTFS file system partitions.
- When you use `ExtendOEMPartition` in sysprep.inf for imaged computers, the destination computer's hard disk must be the same size or larger than the hard disk of the original master installation.
- The partition that you want to extend must have unpartitioned space available following the partition.

If your manufacturing process requires FAT32, use the `Oformat` command-line tool included in the OEM Preinstallation Kit to format the hard disk so that you configure it for NTFS. Use the `Convert` command-line tool to convert the file system.

You can also convert the partition during text-mode Setup by setting the `FileSystem` entry in the `[Unattended]` section of unattend.txt to `ConvertNTFS`. `FileSystem` is not a valid entry in sysprep.inf. However, the hard drive performs better if you use `Convert` with `Oformat` and/or `Cvtarea` instead of the `FileSystem` entry. For more information, see the *Legacy Methods* section of NTFS Preinstallation and Windows XP.

You can also use the `ExtendPartition` entry in the `[ComputerSettings]` section of winbom.ini to extend the partition using the Factory tool.

FactoryMode

Specifies whether %SYSTEMDRIVE%\Sysprep\Factory.exe runs on first boot.

Syntax	**FactoryMode = Yes | No**
Value	**Yes** %SYSTEMDRIVE%\Sysprep\Factory.exe runs on first boot. **No** %SYSTEMDRIVE%\Sysprep\Factory.exe does not run on first boot. (Default)
Default Value	**Yes**
Example	`FactoryMode = Yes`
Comments	Use this entry when performing a clean install of the operating system as the first step in building a master installation, which you then plan to duplicate onto multiple destination computers. `FactoryMode = Yes` will start the computer into Factory mode, where system configuration can be done before imaging. You must place the OPK tools in the %SYSTEMDRIVE%\Sysprep folder.

FileSystem

Specifies whether to convert the primary partition to NTFS or to leave it alone.

Syntax	**FileSystem = ConvertNTFS LeaveAlone**
Values	**ConvertNTFS** Converts the primary partition to NTFS. **LeaveAlone** Does not change the primary partition file system.
Example	`FileSystem = ConvertNTFS`

Comments

This entry is provided for backward compatibility with the Windows 2000 unattended Setup.

For the Windows XP and Windows Server 2003 family of operating systems, if your manufacturing processes require that you format the hard disk as FAT32, use the `Oformat` tool to create a FAT32 volume with clusters aligned in an optimal way for later conversion to the NTFS file system. Then use the `Convert` command-line tool to convert the file system to NTFS.

You can also convert the partition during text-mode Setup by setting the `FileSystem` entry equal to `ConvertNTFS`. However, the hard drive performs better if you use `Convert` with `Oformat` and/or `Cvtarea` instead of using the `FileSystem` entry. For more information, see the *Legacy Methods* section of NTFS Preinstallation and Windows XP.

Note:

- If you plan to use `ExtendOemPartition` during Setup, the file system must be NTFS.
- `FileSystem` is not a valid entry in sysprep.inf.

ForceHALDetection

Specifies whether text-mode Setup examines the operating system and determines the most appropriate Hardware Abstraction Layer (HAL) to install during an upgrade.

Syntax

`ForceHALDetection = Yes | No`

Values

`Yes`

Installs the most appropriate HAL for the new operating system.

`No`

Keeps the HAL from the previous operating system.

Default Value

`No`

Example

```
ForceHALDetection = Yes
```

Comments

Important:

- If `ForceHALDetection=Yes` during an upgrade, Setup may lose some user-specified hardware settings.
- If `ForceHALDetection=No` during an upgrade, Setup preserves user-specified hardware settings.

Hibernation

Specifies whether to enable the hibernation option in the Power Options control panel.

Syntax	**`Hibernation = Yes	No`**
Values	**`Yes`** Enables hibernation. **`No`** Disables hibernation.
Default Value	**`Yes`**
Example	`Hibernation = Yes`
Comments	Not supported on the 64-bit versions of the Windows Server 2003 family. This setting adds `Hibernate` to the Shutdown menu and creates the hiberfil.sys file.

Notes:

- To keep the size of your image file as small as possible, you may delete the hibernation file (hiberfil.sys) (if it exists) from your image file.
- The hiberfil.sys file created during hibernation mode is as large as the available random access memory (RAM) on the computer. Before beginning hibernation mode, verify that the amount of free disk space on your computer hard drive is greater than or equal to the amount of RAM in the computer.
- Setup does not support hibernation if any driver or video card does not support plug-and-play.
- For Windows Server 2003, Enterprise Edition, Windows Server 2003, Datacenter Edition, you cannot use hibernation if the computer uses Terminal Server or if the Physical Address Extension (PAE) Kernel supports 3 GB or more of memory.

For more information on the PAE Kernel, see the *Microsoft Driver Development Kit* (DDK), which you can order from the Microsoft DDK Web site (*www.microsoft.com/ddk/*). You can also read the DDK documentation in the MSDN Library (*http://msdn.microsoft.com/library/*): Select Windows Development, then Driver Development Kit.

KeyboardLayout

Specifies the type of keyboard layout to install during text-mode Setup.

Syntax	**KeyboardLayout** = *layout_description*
Value	`layout_description`
Example	`KeyboardLayout = Us`
Comments	If this entry does not exist, Setup detects and installs a keyboard layout. This entry must match one of the right-hand strings (in quotation marks) in the `[Keyboard Layout]` section of txtsetup.sif.

NTUpgrade

Specifies whether Setup upgrades a previous version of Windows NT 3.51, Windows NT 4.0, Windows 2000, Windows XP, or the Windows Server 2003 family.

Syntax	**NTUpgrade = Yes | No**
Values	**Yes** Upgrades a previous version of Windows. Only these additional unattend.txt entries are processed: `ProductKey`, `AutoActivate`, `DUDisable`, `DUShare`, and `DUStopOnError` **No** Does not upgrade a previous version of Windows.
Example	`NTUpgrade = Yes`
Comments	This entry is valid only for winnt32.exe. **Note:** To upgrade from Windows 98 or Windows Millennium Edition, use the `Win9xUpgrade` entry. Set `NTUpgrade = Yes` to upgrade the previous Windows installation. If `OemPreinstall` is `Yes`, do not set `NTUpgrade` equal to `Yes`. This entry upgrades your previous version of Windows XP, Windows Server 2003 family, Windows 2000, Windows NT 4.0, or Windows NT 3.51. Setup takes all user settings from the previous installation, and does not require end-user intervention. The following table provides a comprehensive list of valid upgrade scenarios.

Upgrade from	Upgrade to		
	Windows Server 2003, Standard Edition	Windows Server 2003, Enterprise Edition	Windows Server 2003, Datacenter Edition
Windows NT 3.51 Server	No	No	No
Windows NT 4.0 Server (with Service Pack 5)	Yes	Yes	No
Windows NT 4.0 Terminal Server	Yes*	Yes*	No
Windows NT 4.0 Enterprise Edition (with Service Pack 5)	No	Yes	No
Microsoft Back-Office® Small Business Server 4.0/4.5	No	No	No
Windows 2000 Server	Yes	Yes	No
Microsoft Small Business Server 2000	No	No	No
Windows 2000 Advanced Server	No	Yes	No
Windows 2000 Datacenter Server	No	No	Yes
Windows Server 2003, Standard Edition	Yes	Yes	No
Windows Server 2003, Standard Edition	Yes	Yes	No
Windows Server 2003, Datacenter Edition	No	No	Yes

* You can upgrade from Windows NT 4.0 Terminal Server Edition or Windows 2000 Application Server mode to Windows Server 2003 family, but Setup will warn you that it does not support Terminal Service Application mode.

OemFilesPath

Specifies the path to the \OEM folder (containing OEM files) if it does not exist under the i386 folder of the distribution share point.

Syntax	**`OemFilesPath`** `=`*`path_to_$OEM$_folder`*
Value	`path_to_$OEM$_folder`
Example	`OemFilesPath = "%SYSTEMDRIVE%\OEM_Files"`
Comments	The path can be a UNC name. Enclose *path_to_OEM_folder* in quotation marks if it is a long file name. For more information about the \OEM folder, if you are a computer manufacturer, see the *Microsoft Windows XP OEM Preinstallation Kit (OPK) User Guide*. Otherwise, see the *Microsoft Windows 2000 Server Deployment Guide.*

OemPnPDriversPath

Specifies the path to one or more folders that contain plug-and-play drivers not distributed in Drivers.cab on the Windows product CD.

Syntax	**`OemPnPDriversPath`** `=` *`folder_1_on_system_drive[;folder_2_on_system_drive]...`*
Values	*`folder_1_on_system_drive[;folder_2_on_system_drive]...`*
Example	`OemPnPDriversPath = MyFolder1;MyFolder2`
Dependency	`OEMPreinstall = Yes`
Registry subkey	`HKEY_LOCAL_MACHINE\Software\Microsoft\Windows\CurrentVersion\DevicePath`
Comments	The folders must contain all the files necessary to install the particular devices: catalog files, .inf files, and drivers. For example, if you have a folder called \Drivers with subfolders called \Audio and \Net, specify `OemPnPDriversPath = drivers\audio;drivers\net` in the unattend.txt file. Setup adds: ■ %SYSTEMDRIVE% to each of the folder names ■ the path for each subfolder to the Plug-and-play device search path.

Comments *(cont'd.)*

Important:

- The length of the `OemPnPDriversPath` entry in unattend.txt must not exceed 4096 characters.
- You cannot use environment variables to specify the location of a folder.
- Always use signed drivers. Signed drivers make the operating system more stable and significantly reduce requests for product support.

When using `OemPnPDriversPath` in unattend.txt, be sure that the folders are available during GUI-mode Setup or the end user first-run experience. The easiest way to do this is to place the plug-and-play drivers in the \$OEM$\$1 folder. To prevent end users from inadvertently deleting driver folders located at the root of the drive, you can place drivers under the \$OEM$\$$ folder (for example: OEM\$$\PnP\Audio).

If the drivers are not in the drivers.cab file on the computer's hard disk or in the location specified by `OemPnPDriversPath`, Setup prompts the end user for the location of the drivers during the first boot of the machine, before Windows Welcome or Mini-Setup.

You can also use the `[PnPDrivers]` section in winbom.ini to update drivers on a previously-created image of the installed operating system.

OemPreinstall

Specifies whether Setup installs its files from distribution folders.

Syntax

`OemPreinstall = Yes | No`

Values

`Yes`

Setup copies the subfolders and files contained in the *platform*\\oem folder.

`No`

Setup does not copy these files.

Example

```
OemPreinstall = Yes
```

Comments

Note:

- If `OemPreinstall = Yes`, do not set `NTUpgrade` to `Yes`.
- If `OemPreinstall = Yes`, unattended Setup automatically stops at the Welcome page. To avoid this pause in your factory environment, set `OEMSkipWelcome` to `1`. Do not distribute any computer with `OEMSkipWelcome = 1`. Instead, set `OEMSkip-Welcome` to `0` in the sysprep.inf file you use before delivering the computer to the customer.

OemSkipEula

Specifies whether the end user must accept the End-User License Agreement (EULA) included with Windows.

Syntax	**`OemSkipEula = Yes	No`**
Values	**`Yes`** Implies that the person performing the installation has read and agreed to the contents of the license agreement included with the product. It also implies that the end user on whose behalf you install Windows has agreed to the license agreement. **`No`** Implies that the person performing the installation and the end user have not read and agreed to the license agreement.
Example	`OemSkipEula = No`
Comments	**Important:** You must not use this entry to remove the Microsoft® End-User License Agreement screen because end users must see and accept it. Use `Sysprep` to ensure that end users see the EULA when the computer starts for the first time.

OverwriteOemFilesOnUpgrade

Specifies whether to overwrite OEM-supplied files that have the same name as Windows XP or Windows Server 2003 family of operating system files during an unattended upgrade.

Syntax	**`OverwriteOemFilesOnUpgrade =`**
Values	**`Yes`** Overwrites the files if found. **`No`** Does not overwrite the files if found.
Default Value	**`Yes`**
Example	`OverwriteOemFilesOnUpgrade = Yes`
Comments	This entry is provided for backward compatibility with Windows 2000 unattended Setup.

Repartition

Specifies whether to delete all partitions on the first drive of the client computer and to reformat the drive with the NTFS file system.

Syntax `Repartition = Yes | No`

Values

Yes

Deletes all partitions on the first drive and reformats the drive with NTFS.

No

Does not delete partitions or reformat the drive.

Example `Repartition = Yes`

Comments **Important:** Repartition is valid only when performing an unattended Setup by starting the computer from the Windows product CD.

TargetPath

Determines the installation folder in which you install Windows.

Syntax `TargetPath = * | target_path`

Values

*****

Setup generates a unique folder name for the installation.

target_path

Setup installs to the specified folder.

Example `TargetPath = *`

Comments * indicates that Setup generates a unique folder name for the installation. The folder name given is usually Windows, unless that folder already exists. In that case, Setup installs into Windows.*x* (where *x* is 0, 1, . . . , 999) if these folders do not already exist.

The path must use 8.3 file names. Do not include the drive letter in *target_path*. If you want to specify the target drive, you must use the `/tempdrive` command-line switch when you run winnt32.exe.

UnattendMode

Defines the unattended mode to use during GUI-mode Setup.

Syntax

`UnattendMode = DefaultHide | FullUnattended | GuiAttended | ProvideDefault | ReadOnly`

Values

`DefaultHide`

Specifies that answers in the answer file are defaults. Unlike `UnattendMode = ProvideDefault`, Setup does not display the user interface to end users if you specify in the answer file all the answers relating to a particular Setup page. If you specify only subsets of the answers on a page, the page appears with the provided answers. The end user can modify any of the answers on the displayed page.

Use `UnattendMode = DefaultHide` in deployment scenarios where an administrator might want only end users to provide the administrator password on the computer. This behavior is the default if you do not specify unattended mode.

`FullUnattended`

Specifies a fully unattended GUI-mode Setup. If you do not specify a required Setup answer in the answer file, Setup generates an error.

During an attended Setup, improperly signed hardware drivers generate a warning dialog box. If `UnattendMode = FullUnattended`, then Setup does not install hardware drivers unless they are properly signed.

Use `UnattendMode = FullUnattended` in deployment scenarios where you require a complete unattended installation.

`GuiAttended`

Specifies an attended GUI-mode section of Setup. When specified, the end user must answer all questions in the GUI-mode portion of Setup before Setup finishes.

Use `UnattendMode = GuiAttended` in preinstallation scenarios when you want to automate only text-mode Setup.

`ProvideDefault`

Specifies default answers in the answer file. In this case, Setup displays these default answers to the end user, who can change them if they are not appropriate.

Use `UnattendMode = ProvideDefault` in preinstallation scenarios where the OEM or administrator wants to give the person setting up the computer the option to change the predefined default answers (especially network options).

Values *(cont'd.)*

ReadOnly

Specifies read-only answers in the answer file if the Windows Setup pages containing these answers appear to the end user. Like `UnattendMode = ProvideDefault`, no user interface appears if the answer file contains all the answers on a page. Unlike `UnattendMode = DefaultHide`, however, the end user can specify only new answers on a displayed page.

Use `UnattendMode = ReadOnly` in scenarios where an administrator wants to force specific answers on one page but not others.

Default Value `DefaultHide`

Example `UnattendMode = FullUnattended`

Comments The default value is `DefaultHide` when you do not specify the entry. When you specify this entry, it fully automates text-mode Setup with or without the necessary answers.

UnattendSwitch

Specifies whether Setup skips Windows Welcome or Mini-Setup when preinstalling Windows XP Home Edition or Windows XP Professional using the CD boot method.

Syntax **`UnattendSwitch = Yes | No`**

Values

Yes

Instructs Setup to skip Windows Welcome.

No

Instructs Setup not to skip Windows Welcome.

Default Value **No**

Example `UnattendSwitch = Yes`

Comments Use `UnattendSwitch` only when you perform an unattended Setup with winnt.exe, winnt.sif, and the CD boot method. This entry is not necessary if you use winnt32.exe to run Setup.

Note: `UnattendSwitch` is not the same as the `UnattendedInstall` entry in the `[Data]` section of the answer file. `UnattendSwitch` controls Windows Welcome; `UnattendedInstall` does not.

WaitForReboot

Specifies whether the computer waits 15 seconds after GUI-mode Setup finishes.

Syntax	**`WaitForReboot = Yes	No`**
Values	**`Yes`** Delays the reboot for 15 seconds after GUI-mode Setup finishes. **`No`** Restarts immediately after GUI-mode Setup finishes.
Default Value	**`Yes`**
Example	`WaitForReboot = Yes`

Win9xUpgrade

Specifies whether Setup upgrades previous installations of Windows 98, Windows 98 Second Edition, or Windows Millennium Edition to either Windows XP Home Edition or Windows XP Professional, as specified in the `[Win9xUpg]` section.

Syntax	**`Win9xUpgrade = Yes	No`**
Values	**`Yes`** Instructs Setup to upgrade the Windows installation, if found. **`No`** Instructs Setup not to upgrade the Windows installation, if found.
Default Value	**`No`**
Example	`Win9xUpgrade = Yes`
Comments	This entry is necessary only when using an answer file to upgrade an existing Windows 98 or Windows Millennium Edition computer to Windows XP Home Edition or Windows XP Professional. This entry is valid only for winnt32.exe. For more information, see `[Uninstall]`.

D

UserData

The [UserData] section contains entries for specifying user settings during Setup.

Entry	Description
ComputerName	Specifies the computer name.
FullName	Specifies the end user's full name.
OrgName	Specifies an organization's name.
ProductKey	Specifies the Product Key for each unique installation of Microsoft® Windows®.

Sample

This sample demonstrates one use of the [UserData] section of unattend.txt.

```
[UserData]
ComputerName = MYCOMPUTER
FullName = "Pat Coleman"
OrgName = "Woodgrove Bank"
ProductKey = "12345-ABCDE-12345-ABCDE-12345"
```

ComputerName

Specifies the computer name.

Syntax	**ComputerName** = *computer_name*
Value	computer_name
Registry subkey	HKEY_LOCAL_MACHINE\SYSTEM\CurrentControlSet\Control\ComputerName\ComputerName

Example `ComputerName = MYCOMPUTER`

Comments If the `ComputerName` entry is empty or missing, the end user must enter a computer name. If the value is `*`, Setup generates a random computer name based on the organization name specified.

If *computer_name* is longer than 63 characters, the string truncates to 63 characters.

FullName

Specifies the end user's full name.

Syntax **`FullName`** `=` *`string`*

Value `string`

Registry key `HKEY_LOCAL_MACHINE\SOFTWARE\Microsoft\Windows NT\CurrentVersion\RegisteredOwner`

Example `FullName = "Pat Coleman"`

Comments If the entry is empty or missing, the end user must enter a name, so that Setup can finish unattended.

OrgName

Specifies an organization's name.

Syntax **`OrgName`** `=` *`string`*

Value `string`

Registry subkey `HKEY_LOCAL_MACHINE\SOFTWARE\Microsoft\Windows NT\CurrentVersion\RegisteredOrganization`

Example `OrgName = "Woodgrove Bank"`

ProductKey

Specifies the Product Key for each unique installation of Windows.

Syntax **`ProductKey`** `= "`*`xxxxx-xxxxx-xxxxx-xxxxx-xxxxx`*`"`

Value `"`*`xxxxx-xxxxx-xxxxx-xxxxx-xxxxx`*`"`

Example `ProductKey = "12345-ABCDE-12345-ABCDE-12345"`

Comments

Each *x* is either an alphabetic character or a number. Requires the quotation marks and the hyphens.

Important:

- You must always specify a value for the `ProductKey` entry.
- The Product Key that you use to activate the installation must match the number on the Certificate of Authenticity (COA) sticker that accompanies the retail product or that is physically attached to the computer case by the original equipment manufacturer (OEM).
- Standard licensing agreements specify that you can use a given Product Key only to activate one installation of Windows XP on one computer. Windows Product Activation (WPA) enforces this requirement.
- If you preinstall Windows XP or Windows Server 2003 family under a volume license agreement, consult your specific license agreement to determine the number of installations allowed per Product Key.
- When using the unattend.txt file, this entry assigns the same Product Key to all computers on which you install Windows XP or a member of the Windows Server 2003 family.
- When using the unattend.txt file, enter the `ProductKey` in both the unattend.txt file and the sysprep.inf file. Sysprep deletes the `ProductKey` entry in the unattend.txt file and replaces it with the entry specified in sysprep.inf.

Index

www.ingramcontent.com/pod-product-compliance
Lightning Source LLC
Chambersburg PA
CBHW080716220326
41598CB00033B/5439
* 9 7 8 1 5 5 5 5 8 3 3 7 8 *